Community (komiu·niti). ME [from the Latin communitatem]
A body of people organized into a political, municipal, or social
unity
example: The Jewish c. 1888

Polity (po·liti). 1538 [from the Latin politia and the Greek πολιτεια]
a. A particular form of political organization 1597. b. An
organized society . . . 1650.
example: Nor is it possible that any form of politie, much less
politie ecclesiasticall should be good, unless God himselfe
bee the authour of it—Hooker

—from the *Oxford English Dictionary*

Community

The Organizational

Daniel J. Elazar

and Polity
Dynamics of American Jewry

Philadelphia 5740 / 1980

The Jewish Publication Society of America

This book is a volume in the series
JEWISH COMMUNAL AND PUBLIC AFFAIRS
in cooperation with the
Center for Jewish Community Studies
Jerusalem / Philadelphia

Dedicated to the loving memory
of my aunt, Rose Barzon Goldman,
and my uncle, Samuel Goldman,
who in their lives were each a special kind
of pillar of a very special community
and who are sorely missed
by the many whose lives they touched

Contents

Illustrations

Preface to the Paperback Edition

Since the appearance of the hardcover edition of *Community and Polity* in 1976, the American Jewish community has crossed the watershed from the post-World War II generation to a new generation whose dimensions will become apparent in the coming decade. The crossing of this watershed is manifest in various ways.

There are signs that the United States as a whole is moving on to a fourth frontier stage, a "citybelt-cybernetic-frontier," whose principal manifestations will occur in the sunbelt regions of the country to which Jews are now flocking. This is apparent in the shifting of Jews toward smaller communities, a movement which is reflected in Table 9. Organizing these Jews into effective communities has emerged as a major item on the agenda of the new generation.

The excitement over ethnicity that animated the 1960s has diminished substantially except in certain limited circles—perhaps mostly Jewish. On the other hand, the assimilation of Jews into American society has reached critical proportions, as described in this volume. At the same time, however, Jewish immigration has become a publicly recognized issue once again as Jews from the USSR, Israel, Iran, South Africa, and Latin America appear on American shores in substantial numbers and draw upon Jewish communal resources. American Jews have now discovered the sixth wave (see p. 38).

Between 1977 and 1979, the Council of Jewish Federations and Welfare Funds underwent a reorganization, symbolically manifested in the shortening of its name to the Council of Jewish Federations. This is a sign of the recognition by its leadership of the new role of the federation movement within American Jewish life, a role that is amply described and analyzed herein. Although this reorganization was designed to strengthen the federation movement countrywide, it comes—somewhat ironically—at a time when one of the major sources of the Federations' power, their fund raising for Israel, has had to compete with another role. This new responsibility is mobilizing political support for Israel in Congress, or, at the very least, securing massive United States aid for the Jewish State that goes far beyond the capabilities of voluntary fund raising. It is a task for which the federation movement is not particularly suited and which has focused some attention on other institutions in Jewish life that, however, can only remain secondary to the Federations in the overall scheme of the Jewish polity.

This, in itself, reflects a change in Jewish influence in the political sphere. Israel has taken its first steps toward peace and American public opinion with regard to the Israel-Arab conflict has shifted to a more "even-handed" stance. There has even been a concomitant diminution of the intensity of American Jewish concern for Israel, in part because there is no "crisis" and in part because American Jews are confronting Israel's blemishes for the first time.

The combination of inflation, assimilation, and "peace" seems to have reduced the fund-raising capabilities of the Federations at a time when the costs of providing even existing local services are growing at a very rapid rate, thus leading not only to an immediate dollar squeeze in the Jewish communal budget, but also to a conservatism with regard to new departures. The aggressive, advancing Jewish community of the late 1960s and early 1970s has given way to a far more quiescent one. The colleges are quiet and Jewish students are busy pursuing their individual careers rather than seeking to reform Jewish life. The enhanced individualism of American society generally works against organizational initiatives.

Moreover, American Jewry has entered a period of transition, as one generation of leaders begins to give way to another. In their early stages such periods are necessarily marked by a certain quiescence until new figures emerge with new issues and causes to advance. In sum, as for every new generation, this is a "time of new troubles" and as such requires a rethinking of communal concerns.

This edition of *Community and Polity* is essentially a reprinting of the original edition and does not explore these issues any further. However, it does include minor revisions and corrections and updated population data where appropriate. The exploration of the new agenda and its impact will have to await another occasion.

D.J.E.

Jerusalem and Philadelphia

Tishri 5740—October 1979

Preface

This book is designed to serve two purposes: to provide a basic survey of the structure and functions of the American Jewish community and to suggest how the community should be understood as body politic, a polity that is not a state but is no less real from a political perspective. The organized life of American Jewry is of interest in its own right. All those concerned with the present and future state of the Jewish people cannot help but seek to learn as much as possible about the largest Jewish collectivity in the world, perhaps of all time. For the student of politics the American Jewish community has the additional interest of being an example of a voluntary political order that functions authoritatively for those who acknowledge their connection with it, but does not seek a monopoly on the loyalties of its members. Federal in its own internal character, it may well be the ultimate federal arrangement, in that it assumes that the world is based upon shared citizenship and is the better for it.

One result of my experiences has been a growing appreciation of the American Jewish polity as one that deserves close attention by everyone concerned with the future of humanity in the postmodern era, for it offers an opportunity to examine the possibilities of governing without sovereignty and the mobilization of collective energy with an absolute minimum of coercion.

This book is a product of over two decades of study of the American Jewish community. First conceived in more conventional sociological terms as a result of my experiences teaching in Hebrew schools and adult Jewish education programs in various parts of the United States, it took its present form as a result of a growing realization that a recognition of the importance of the structural and institutional aspects of American Jewish life was sorely lacking. While the commitment of individual Jews and Jewish families to Jewish life is obviously a prerequisite to the life of a Jewish community, the character of Jewish life is ultimately shaped by the institutions that Jews create collectively. This realization led me to redirect the thrust of this book toward an understanding of communal phenomena in Jewish life. In this I was aided in 1968 by being given the responsibility for directing a worldwide study of contemporary Jewish community organization, initially cosponsored by the Institute of Jewish Affairs of the World Jewish Congress and the Center for the Study of Federalism of Temple University and subsequently by the latter body and the Center for Jewish Community Studies. This volume is the overview of the American Jewish community prepared as part of that study. A portion of the material was developed in connection with my work as a member of the Task Force on the Future of the American Jewish Community of the American Jewish Committee, for which I prepared a paper, "Decision-making in the American Jewish Community." Another part originally appeared, in slightly different form, in *Midstream* (June–July 1971) as "The Institutional Life of American Jewry." In 1974 the Institute of Jewish Policy Planning and Research of the Synagogue Council of America invited me to undertake a study of the synagogue in the American Jewish community, an appropriate next step in the Center for Jewish Community Studies' research program into the dynamics of the American Jewish polity. While the results of that study will be published separately, elements of what I have learned from it of necessity have been incorporated in the final version of this volume and deserve acknowledgment.

I am indebted to many people who have assisted in my education in the ways of the American Jewish community. I wish it were possible to acknowledge all of them here. My parents provided me with my formative experiences in observing communal affairs, in Saint Paul, Chicago, Denver, and Detroit. My aunt and uncle, to whom this book is dedicated, ably seconded them in Minneapolis. Subsequently I learned about community affairs as an active participant as well as observer in Detroit, Chicago, Champaign-Urbana, Illinois, Minneapolis, and most recently

Philadelphia, not to mention various involvements in communal affairs on the national scene, all of which have contributed to the shaping of the perspective presented in the following pages. Aside from the systematic research done for this study, I have benefitted greatly from myriad conversations with the leading figures of the American Jewish civil service and rabbinate, under a wide variety of conditions and in many different locales. Those dedicated men and women are the architects of the American Jewish polity as we know it. I am particularly grateful to the leaders of the Jewish community of Philadelphia in whose company I have worked for a decade. Ezekiel Pearlman of the Federation of Jewish Agencies was particularly helpful in developing estimates of the expenditures of the Philadelphia Jewish community.

In its present form, this book is very much the product of the Center for Jewish Community Studies. Elaine Stewart, of the Center's Philadelphia office, was particularly helpful in the final stages of the book's production. I owe a particular debt to Mary Duffy, Deborah Hess, and Maureen Wallace of the staff of the Center for the Study of Federalism, who handled the mechanics of preparing the manuscript and the tables within it. As always, my wife, Harriet, was indispensable to the writing of this book in every way. Finally, very special appreciation is due Maier Deshell and Kay Powell of the Jewish Publication Society, who performed editorial tasks above and beyond the call of duty to bring this book into print during the Bicentennial of American independence. They have my deepest gratitude.

D.J.E.
Jerusalem and Philadelphia
Tishri 5736–September 1975

Community and Polity

Abbreviations

AAJE American Association for Jewish Education
CJF Council of Jewish Federations
COJO Conference of World Jewish Organizations
COLPA National Commission on Law and Public Affairs
HIAS Hebrew Sheltering and Immigrant Aid Society
JDC American Jewish Joint Distribution Committee
JPS Jewish Publication Society of America
JTA Jewish Telegraphic Agency
JTS Jewish Theological Seminary
LCBC Large City Budgeting Conference
NJCRAC National Jewish Community Relations Advisory Council
ORT Organization for Rehabilitation and Training
UAHC Union of American Hebrew Congregations
UJA United Jewish Appeal
UOJC Union of Orthodox Jewish Congregations

Introduction

I

In 1976 the people of the United States of America celebrate the Bicentennial of American independence. In so doing, they will also be bringing to a close the postwar generation, with its special concerns and special responses to those concerns. For American Jewry the postwar generation has been a decisive one, witnessing as it did the almost total integration of American Jews into American society, the establishment of the state of Israel and its emergence as a prime focus for Jewish identity and concern, the transformation of Jewish religious life so as to conform with American modes, and the revival of the sense of Jewish ethnic identity. In the two hundred years since 1776 American Jewry has been transformed from a group of perhaps twenty-five hundred persons, linked with each other through a scattering of congregations, into a highly organized—some would say overorganized—body of six million persons, encompassing half the Diaspora, with a congeries of institutions and programs for all Jewish needs and purposes.

The coincidence of the culmination of two hundred years of American independence and the closing of a critical generation in American and American Jewish history make an analysis of the organized life of American Jewry doubly important. At this moment of commemoration neither the American people nor the Jews among them stand secure in their feelings about the immediate future. There are those who argue that the bloom has faded from the "American century" and that American Jews will be among the first to feel the consequences of the changes that are imminent.

Whatever the future may bring—and I am not as pessimistic as other observers—it is clear that the metropolitan-technological frontier, which has occupied the attention of Americans for the last thirty years and provided opportunities for both material enrichment and social change on an immense scale, has become stabilized. America is between frontiers, as it were, and, as in every similar situation in the past, has to confront serious problems, many of them frontier-generated, without being able to bury or outflank them within the framework of continuous development. Since American Jews were among major beneficiaries of both aspects of the metropolitan frontier, their position may be particularly precarious. At the same time, the results of a generation of institutional transformation have left the community organizationally stronger than ever before. If the problems are many, the institutional means for dealing with them have never been better.

The theme of this book is developed around the two key words in the title: *community* and *polity*. It is customary to think of American Jewry as a community. That relatively neutral term has been accepted by one and all as appropriately descriptive of the corporate dimensions of American Jewish life, embracing within it both the strictly religious and the not so clearly religious dimensions of Jewish existence, the ethnic ties of individual Jews, and the political strivings of Jews as a group. By and large it is a useful term, affording Jews and non-Jews alike a sense of the Jewish affiliation, without at the same time binding Jews in any particularly rigid fashion to any one form of linkage.

The *Oxford English Dictionary* records that the first use of the phrase "the Jewish Community" occurred in 1888. Whether that date is precise or not, it is clear that the term entered common usage at that time, when Jews were seeking some neutral means to describe their continued corporate existence during the height of the era of emancipation. It was the time when certain Jews developed the awkward word "coreligionists" to describe their relationship to fellow Jews because they were only willing to acknowledge themselves as bound by religious ties, for fear of jeopardizing their newfound status as civic equals in the countries of the West, but nevertheless did perceive that they were connected to other Jews even across national boundaries. It was also a time when the Western world was most sharply committed to separating states, governments, and politics generally from society as a whole, a period in which laissez-faire ideas dominated half the Western world and various conceptions of utopian socialism the other half. Laissez-faire liberals and socialists alike agreed on one ultimate point: in the good society, government would barely exist, if at all, and politics would be replaced by some vague form of neutral administration.

In the real world it was an era in which it was generally agreed that nations and states had to be coterminous and that all permanent residents of a particular territory should share a common citizenship. Thus it was no wonder that Jews were stimulated to abjure anything smacking of political self-definition, not only for fear of jeopardizing their newly won rights as citizens in their respective countries, but also because of a common understanding that politics could take place only within the realm of the nation-state without being subversive. This view had replaced an older one that not only saw politics as an inevitable part of the very marrow of human existence, indeed as one of the distinguishing characteristics of humanity, but understood that polities could come in various forms and need not all be states. As the *Oxford English Dictionary* reminds us, every church conceived itself to be a polity until the nineteenth century, and most accorded the Jews the same status by tradition.

The twentieth century witnessed the rediscovery of politics as a necessary ingredient of human existence, albeit reluctantly in some quarters. Since World War II at least, sensible people have concluded that the task of humanity is to humanize politics, not to eliminate it. In the course of that effort we have come to discover that no community can interact without politics. Moreover, Western contact with African and Asian cultures as well as the surviving tribal cultures of the Americas has brought a renewed cognizance of the existence of polities that are not states. In the wake of two world wars the nation-state itself has come under severe criticism in the West, and while we have not yet moved beyond it as some have suggested and the world has yet to become a global village, there is a recrudescence of transnational and subnational attachment on the part of religious, ethnic, and sociological communities that promises to be of great import as the physical boundaries established during the modern era become less significant.

The United States stands on the frontier of this new experience. Indeed, Americans have been among its foremost pioneers. The United States came into existence two hundred years ago through an abjuration of statism in the modern sense, rejecting the cornerstone of modern statism: the principle of state sovereignty. From the first, Americans have held that only the people are sovereign, that a government possesses only delegated powers, and that the state does not exist as a reified entity apart from its citizens, but is only a convenient designation for those institutions devised by its citizens to undertake common tasks authoritatively. The American tradition is one of *public* rather than *state* institutions, with all that the semantic distinction implies. Thus the United States has had little difficulty in reconciling itself to the existence of many publics knit together in partnership for certain purposes, while preserving their separate identities for others. American federalism is based upon the constitutionalization of that premise territorially, and American pluralists have sought to extend some portion of that constitutional legitimacy to nonterritorially based groups.

There is little doubt that American society's openness to the Jews is in no small measure due to this aspect of the American character. At the same time the Jews themselves brought with them a tradition quite compatible with the evolving American culture and even convergent with it in certain significant ways. Jewish conceptions of polity never recognized state sovereignty either, holding that all sovereignty was vested in the Sovereign of the universe and that earthly polities—at least good ones, such as the Jewish polity—were essentially partnerships of their members, who delegated powers to necessary institutions only insofar as necessary, a view whose practical implications were close to those sought by the founders of the United States, most of whom drew their inspiration from the same biblical sources.

As the experience of the two civilizations converged, the first response of the Jews who came to the United States in the nineteenth century was to abandon in the name of modernity those elements of polity that had previously been considered an indivisible aspect of Jewishness and Judaism. But this was not to be. It is the way of communities to develop a political dimension if they are to survive, and since Jews chose to survive as a community, they slowly began to forge a polity appropriate to American conditions: voluntaristic, limited by the reality of Jewish integration into American life, and far from exclusivist in its goals, but no less genuine for all that. The forging of that polity and its relationship to the community it serves are the subjects of this book.

II

The American Jewish community, the first fully emancipated Jewish community, is entirely a product of the modern era. As such it is in most respects a model of what Jewish life has become or is becoming for all but a handful of Jews: the voluntary commitment of individuals to be Jewish in a variety of ways. Once that initial commitment is made the Jewish community comes into being, animated by the voluntary commitment of a small number of Jews to serve as its movers and shakers and shaped by the institutions they create to embrace everyone who wishes to be Jewish. Except in the case of Israel it is a community held together by the strength and magnetism of its core, rather than by clear boundaries at its peripheries, and even in Israel being Jewish except in the most casual sense is becoming more and more a matter of personal choice.

The magnetism of the core makes its real impact felt through the institutions of the community—the organized patterns of life and the bodies that maintain them—to make the whole more than the sum of its parts; hence to know American Jewry as a force and a factor in Jewish life or Jewish history is only peripherally a matter, say, of intermarriage statistics or demographic trends. More carefully, it is a matter of how those Jews who choose to be Jews act collectively to achieve Jewish goals. How the American Jewish community has overcome the problems of a postemancipation existence to define Jewish goals for itself and build institutions to achieve those goals will be explored in these pages.

Organizationally, the American Jewish community is best understood as a mosaic, a multidimensional matrix of institutions and organizations that interact with each other in their attempts to cover the range of communal concerns while preserving their respective integrities. These institutions and organizations are bound by shared patterns of culture, have somewhat overlapping memberships, and are governed by more or less the same leadership cadres.

The institutions and organizations of the American Jewish community serve local, countrywide, overseas (including Israel), and occasionally regional constituencies. They group themselves, de facto, around five major functions or spheres of public activity: (1) religious-congregational, (2) educational-cultural, (3) community relations, (4) communal-welfare, and (5) Israel-overseas. The activities of the American Jewish community are organized along the lines inherent in this matrix. Rather than functioning through neat structures of authority and responsibility, as would be the case in a more hierarchical system, the mosaic of institutions and organizations depends upon a network of formal federative arrangements enlivened by an informal communications network among their leaders.

The character of the matrix and its communications network varies from local community to community within the countrywide system. In some cases the network is connected through a common center that serves as the major (but rarely if ever the exclusive) channel for communication. In others the network forms a matrix without any real center, with the lines of communication crisscrossing in all directions. In all cases the boundaries of the community are revealed only when the pattern of the network is uncovered. The pattern itself stands revealed only when both its components are, namely, its institutions and organizations, with their respective roles and the way in which communications pass among them.

The casual observer of the American Jewish scene cannot help but be impressed by the extraordinary variety of forms of Jewish association. Any organized interconnections within the maze of institutions and organizations of American Jewry have had to be created in the face of many obstacles, including the lack of any inherent legitimacy attaching to any coordinating institutions, the penchant for individualism inherent in the American Jewish community (derived from both American and Jewish sources), and the difficulty of enforcing any kind of coordinating effort within the context of an American society that treats all Jewish activities as private and voluntary.

Thus the pattern of relationships within American Jewish life must be a dynamic one. There is rarely a fixed division of authority and influence with American Jewry, but rather one that varies from time to time and usually from issue to issue, with different elements taking on different "loads" at different times and in relation to different issues. Moreover, since the community is a voluntary one, persuasion rather than compulsion, influence rather than power are the tools available for making decisions and implementing policies. All this works to strengthen the character, quality, and relevance of what is communicated, and how it is communicated frequently determines the extent of the authority and influence of the parties to the communication.

The American Jewish community, like the United States generally, is an exceedingly complex organism. It is not a highly integrated structure but a loosely knit "system" of institutions, organizations, groups, families, and individuals whose roles and areas of concern are relatively specialized, often overlapping, and not infrequently shifting. Within each of the five major public-purpose spheres there is considerable overlap among the aforementioned elements; across those arenas they overlap only to a limited degree.

At least five factors shape the American Jewish polity. First, there are factors stemming from the environment (internal and external) in which the community functions—the general American context, the context of American Jewish life, the environment of the Jewish world as a whole, including the persistent patterns of Jewish political culture, and the impact of modernism and technological change. Second, there are the preeminence of local institutions in American Jewish life and the emphasis on local control that they both represent and reinforce. Third, there are the above-mentioned functional groupings that have emerged in the community. Fourth, there are the basic divisions that both separate and link institutions, people, and leaders within the community—principally the division between "religious" and "secular" activities and the division between "cosmopolitans" and "locals." Fifth, there are the character and interests of persons who are active in the community and become the actual or potential leaders within it.

III

The focus of this study is political-historical. It concerns itself with the American Jewish community as something more than a kinship group or a collection of individuals sharing a common ancestry and seeking a common identity. It sees American Jewry as a body politic (albeit one of a very special kind), a community formed through the consent of its members with a collective sense of purpose, capable of forming associations and acting to pursue and achieve its own goals. Moreover, it seeks to understand that body politic by looking at its development over a period of time.

While the particular demands placed upon Jewish life by the American environment have caused American Jews to adopt the protective coloring of religion as their point of departure as a community, it is in fact as a body politic that American Jewry has functioned best. It is no accident that "philanthropy"—the accepted American pseudonym used for this kind of political existence—is a greater point of Jewish identification than worship, despite the various religious "revivals" in American Jewish history. Rightly or wrongly, secretly or openly, Jews function as Jews in response to their needs as a collectivity first and foremost—in other words, as a polity, truncated as it may be under any given circumstances.

What follows is a discussion—incomplete, to be sure—of how the American Jewish community has responded to the problems of transforming the passive bonds of kinship into active associational ties based on the bonds of consent; how the community's responses have been stimulated by the "sixth sense" that makes Jews aware of their common interests; and how the responses themselves relate to traditional patterns of Jewish organization. The thrust of the discussion is generally optimistic, perhaps overly so. Contrary to the conventional wisdom on the subject, it suggests that organizationally American Jewry has made great strides in the past forty years, and progress on that front seems to be continuing.

Yet the emphasis on successful polity-building should not obscure the crisis of Jewish survival presently besetting the American Jewish community. On one plane the gap between the organizational life of the community and the majority of the Jews within it seems to be growing to unmanageable proportions, so that even as the community's institutional capability increases, the danger of losing millions of Jews through assimilation grows apace. On another, American Jewry may well have passed the peak of its influence in the general community and may find its interests increasingly at odds with those of the non-Jewish majority, a prospect that promises to test American Jews as never before. The following discussion is presented with the knowledge that organization alone cannot solve those problems.

Assimilation and Authenticity
The Problem
of the American Jewish Community

The Jewish community as a whole is a unique blend of kinship and consent. This amalgam is apparent as early as the biblical account of the Jewish people's origins: a family of tribes becomes a nation by consenting to the Covenant. It is reflected in subsequent biblical narratives, and postbiblical Jewish history gave the blend new meaning. The fact that Jews are born Jewish places them in a special position to begin with, one that more often than not has forced them together for self-protection. Yet conversion, assimilation, or simple apathy toward Jewish life has almost always been available as options. In the modern era these opportunities to break away from Judaism have expanded considerably in every respect. Today they stand at what is probably an all-time high, although counterpressures have begun to emerge once more.

Consequently, the preservation of Jewish life can be understood to be a matter of familial solidarity, but it must also be seen as the product of the active will of many Jews to function as a community. The Jewish community in the largest sense is defined as all those people who were born Jews or who, though born outside the Jewish fold, consciously and formally embraced Judaism. At the same time Jews can be fully understood only when they are recognized to be members of a covenantal community who are linked by a shared destiny and a common pattern of communications, a people whose essential community of interest and purpose is reflected in a very wide range of organizations. In traditional terms Judaism itself is essentially a theopolitical phenomenon, a means of seeking salvation by constructing God's polity, the proverbial "city upon a hill," through which the covenantal community takes on meaning and fulfills its purpose in the divine scheme of things. While American civilization has influenced Jews to the extent that "being Jewish" is no longer an all-embracing way of life for most members of the Jewish community, nevertheless the concept of "being Jewish" and the behavior that it involves remain far broader in scope than the concepts and behavior involved in "being Catholic" or "being Protestant."*

The American Jewish community is built upon an associational base to a far greater extent than any other in Jewish history. In other words, not only is there no external or internal compulsion to affiliate with organized Jewry, but there is no automatic way to become a member of the Jewish community. Nor is there even a clear way to affiliate with the community as a whole. To participate in any organized Jewish life in America one must make a voluntary association with some particular organization or institution, whether in the form of synagogue membership, contribution to the local Jewish Welfare Fund (which is generally considered to be an act of joining as well as contributing), or affiliation with a B'nai B'rith lodge or Hadassah chapter.[1]

Because of its particular nature, the Jewish people have always relied upon associational activities to a greater or lesser degree, but at no point in Jewish history have they become as important as they are today. In the past such activities have always been fitted into the framework of an organic community, one linked to the tradition of the fathers as understood by their descendants, who felt bound—by that tradition and by their kinship to one another—to stand together apart from and even against the rest of the world. In the process of modernization these organic ties disappeared for Jews, as they have for other peoples who have gone through the same process, to be replaced by associational ties, at least for people who wished to maintain the ties at all. It is no accident that organized activity—often philanthropic in character—has come to be the most common manifestation of Judaism, replacing prayer, study, and the normal private intercourse of kin as a means of being Jewish.

*Even the phrase, which is common enough in modern Jewish discourse, is rarely found in Christian discourse. There are distinct ways in which different people are Catholic or Protestant, but they have to do with the denominational and, more important, the ethnocultural factors that shape the various Catholic and Protestant subcommunities. Traditional discussions of these matters in America have tended to ignore worldly diversities and to assume that a certain universalism inheres in Catholicism or Protestantism that is, ipso facto, absent from Judaism.

The associational approach is typically American, a reflection of a social order that is based on chosen affiliation rather than heritage. Because Americans do not like to think of themselves as bound to anything by birth, they seek to transform all organic ties into associational ones. Even the family frequently takes on an associational character in American Jewish life—for example, the development and spread of the "family club," which is a formal association of relatives.

Indeed, like their fellow Americans, affiliated Jews usually have memberships in different kinds of organizations, which reinforce one another and create a network of Jewish ties that binds any individual who chooses to become enmeshed in them more firmly to the community. Without that associational base there would be no organized Jewish community at all; with it, the Jewish community attains the social status —and even a certain legal status—that enable it to fit well into the larger society of which it is a part.

While associational activity provides the impetus for the maintenance and continuation of Jewish life, the organic ties persist and tend to be strengthened when the survival of the community seems to be at stake. We have spoken of the fact that Jews—even very marginal ones—tend to have that "sixth sense" about threats to their security and survival as Jews. Since the Holocaust, when the Jewish people lost one-third of their total number, this sense has been sharpened considerably. American Jewry's response to the Yom Kippur War of 1973 and subsequent developments reflects a heightened concern with security and survival, almost to the point of completely reversing the sense of Jewish well-being in America that had flourished since the 1950s. A new sense of unease has come to pervade the community as a result of the Arab oil embargo, world readiness to legitimize the Arab terrorists, actions by leading members of the world community interpreted to be anti-Semitic, the spreading Arab boycott, and, most recently, the infamous attacks on Zionism at the United Nations. All this has undoubtedly made many Jews, even peripheral ones, perceive their common fate as Jews. Nevertheless, their response is only visible, as perforce it must be, through their institutions.

The American Jewish community is not only the largest Diaspora community but is rapidly becoming the contemporary paradigm for Jewish communal organization by voluntary association and "religious" identification, a pattern that has spread to virtually every part of the world since World War II. An inquiry into the American Jewish experience, then, offers an important starting point for the study of contemporary Diaspora Jewry.

Viewed from the perspective of Jewish history and the Jewish people as a whole, some central questions about American Jewish life present themselves at the very outset of our inquiry.

1. How do American Jews live their lives within the framework of the general community? What must they do to conform to its mores and demands? What can they do to be different? How must American Jewry adjust to American life? In what ways can it maintain its own institutions?

2. What is happening to American Jews as a result of their integration into American society, particularly in respect to traditional Jewish values? What have they gained? What have they lost? What is happening to the American Jewish community?

3. What patterns and techniques have American Jews developed to maintain Jewish life under American conditions? To what extent are they unique? To what extent do they provide for the continuity of traditional principles of Jewish community organization?

AMERICAN JEWISH UNIQUENESS

To answer these questions one must begin by recognizing the uniqueness of the American Jewish community in the annals of Jewish history. This singularity is often proclaimed but rarely explained. Five factors were crucial in creating American uniqueness. U. S. Jewry is entirely a product of the modern era, an era dominated by capitalism, science, popular government, secularism, and technological change. The modern era may be said to have begun in the middle of the seventeenth century; 1648 is a convenient year to mark its beginning. In that year the English civil war was concluded, the Treaty of Westphalia ended continental Europe's wars of religion, and East European society was shaken to its roots by the great Ukrainian cossack uprising of Bogdan Chmielnicki.[2]

The events of that era, born out of the seventeenth-century revolution in science, technology, politics, and religion, brought radical changes for world Jewry. First and foremost, the Jewish community was transformed from a semiautonomous ghettoized corporation, a "nation within a nation" holding substantial power over its own members, into a voluntary association of emancipated Jews who as individuals had been granted full citizenship in the larger societies of which they were a part.[3]

The modern era also brought a crisis for Judaism, arising from the general de-emphasis of the religious aspect of life in the Western world as a whole and the thrusting of secular science and politics into the forefront of human concern. With the breakdown of the corporate structure of Jewish life, which had sustained Jewish law for over two thousand years, and with the concomitant destruction of the foundations of religious faith that had made the corporate structure reasonable, most Jews ceased to observe the Law, study it, or try to understand its meaning as a vehicle for human fulfillment.

Jews as individuals now had access to the wider opportunities of the modern world, and, utilizing skills developed during centuries of struggle for sheer survival, they rapidly rose to preeminent positions in secular society. Subsequently, however, European society rejected the Jews, turning the welcome of emancipation into anti-Semitism and, in the twentieth century, genocide. As early as the nineteenth century Jews began to abandon Europe in search of a better life, initially a voluntary process but later made necessary by the events of two world wars.

World War II and the Holocaust brought the modern era to an abrupt and terrible end. However, during the final two generations of the modern era the Jewish people acted to restore their self-conscious existence as a body politic, resettling their ancient land and establishing the state of Israel, while at the same time creating a great new Jewish community in the New World. In the process, increasing numbers of Jews sought to make peace with their Jewish heritage and revive it as a way of life.

The first American Jewish community was founded in 1654, with the arrival in New Amsterdam of twenty-three refugees from the Dutch colony in Brazil, where they had been integrated into the local civil community before they were forced to leave. Despite some early difficulties in gaining acceptance—all of which were trivial in comparison with the problems of securing equal rights in Europe, even on paper—the twenty-three fugitives and those who came to British North America after them in the seventeenth and eighteenth centuries were soon accepted as individuals and potential citizens. Even the difficulties they did encounter were caused less by the fact of their Jewishness than by the principles of religious exclusiveness that animated many of the colonies and were applied indiscriminately to Protestants and Catholics as well.[4]

Thus the American Jewish community is a fully postemancipation community—the first and foremost, by far. Its community structure was built by Jews already emancipated as individuals who did not have to struggle for their civil rights and who formed their association as Jews voluntarily.

U.S. Jewry, moreover, has a special destiny. Since it is the largest Jewish community in the world and the major Diaspora community, there are no Diaspora communities that it can draw upon for strength or that compete with it for influence. Achieving this status during a period when American power generally is at its peak, in the "American century," it has become the world's most powerful Jewry in the world's most powerful nation. It achieved this status at just that moment in history when it was needed most as a fount of material and political power to assist in creating and maintaining the state of Israel, and as a source of spiritual and intellectual power needed to replace the destroyed European reservoirs of the Jewish people. In the past generation it has served well in both capacities—in the first as expected and rather unexpectedly in the second.

U. S. Jewry—the first Diaspora community to function in a fully voluntary milieu that offers its members almost complete freedom of choice "to be or not to be" Jews—has had to adjust to this climate of freedom in which individual Jews may or may not choose to identify with Jewish life, or may even choose to drop their Jewish ties altogether and completely assimilate. These choices must be made in a "host" civilization that is not only attractive, but also has basic ideals more like traditional Judaism's than those of any other host civilization that Jews have ever encountered—ideals that have been embraced with passion by modern Jews.[5] (Even the basic problems of American society are reminiscent of the classic failings of the Jewish people.)

In fact, the struggle for Jewish self-acceptance that has been common during the modern era is largely a thing of the past. Most American Jews of the generation that has emerged since 1950 accept their Jewish birth as a matter of course. Though they accept their Jewish position they do not much care about their Jewishness. No longer negative toward Judaism, the reaction of many is best characterized as apathetic.

In this respect most of the new Jews are as secularist as the most secular elements in American society. Unlike the secularists of a generation or two ago, though, they are not militant in their opposition to organized religion. Indeed, many of today's Jews are nominally affiliated with the synagogue, but they are like their American counterparts among urban upper-middle-class college graduates in the professions and the big organizations, in that religion is tangential to their lives and relatively insignificant as an influence in most of their affairs. Even their Jewish concerns, where they exist, tend to be "tribal" in character, not motivated by any hope for the redemption, individual or collective, traditionally associated with the Jews' covenant with God, but by the comforts derived from the association of like with like, or, with renewed importance, fears for survival.

The new generation is as assimilated into American society as possible. The rise of the new religious pluralism—in which Jews identifying with the Jewish faith have the same status as Catholics identifying with Catholicism or Protestants identifying with recognized Protestant denominations—has made it possible for American Jews to assimilate even socially. So even when Jews segregate themselves, the standards they embrace are not significantly different from the standards of non-Jews of the same socioeconomic class.

Because of the particular character of the United States as a modern society, with no history of segregating Jews in the literal sense, no Jewish communal organization of the traditional kind has even been able to develop. Hence there are few barriers between Jews and non-Jews—this is the natural consequence of an open society. Furthermore, there are few differences in values between Jews and non-Jews, the natural consquence of there being few barriers, plus two other factors: the character of American society, which makes assimilation easy for Jews, and the general secularization of everyone today, including Jews.

It is not an exaggeration to say that American Jewry has been called to a great, even a noble, purpose: that of creating a viable and creative Jewish life within a modern setting, one which involves the preservation of Jewish individual and corporate existence while enabling Jews to participate fully in the fulfillment of the American idea. This is easier said than done, but that in no way diminishes the greatness of the task.

JEWS AND RELIGION IN A NONMYTHIC SOCIETY

Because America is a demythologized society, it is easier for Jews to assimilate its values. The monotheistic revolution wrought by the Jews at the very beginning of their history as a people initiated a decisive break with the mythic world view that had animated all human societies until then. The mythic world view saw the universe as animate in all its parts —or at least made no distinction between the animate and inanimate— investing all natural phenomena with divinity. In the life cycles of the various elements in the universe it saw a cyclical pattern of events that was repeated continually without end, as the gods that inhabited or dominated the universe continued their own internal struggles for power and favor as part of the very nature of things. Although humans were merely tools of the gods in the struggle, they could occasionally manipulate their masters by appropriate magic. Since history was conceived to be cyclical, humanity had no goal other than to try to survive in the face of the malevolent forces arrayed against it; hence fertility was a central preoccupation.

The monotheistic revolution introduced more than the notion of one God. It originated the idea of progress in history, of linear development from a beginning toward an end, and the idea of a transcendent Deity who could not be manipulated by magic but required men to lead certain kinds of lives and to create a certain kind of social order in order to fulfill His wishes. As Yehezkel Kaufmann has pointed out, the Jews were so transformed by the monotheistic revolution that the mythic view of the world ceased to have any real meaning for them as a people.[6]

When the rest of the Western world accepted "Jewish" monotheism it did so through Christianity, which represented a compromise with the mythic world view. In those parts of the world that originally converted to Catholicism and have remained Catholic, the mythic world view has remained particularly strong within the framework of Christianity. In those regions of Europe that later became Protestant as a result of the Reformation, the second transformation moved the adherents of the new movement away from the mythic outlook. This was especially true among followers of John Calvin and his compatriots.

The crucial factor in determining if a particular population group would break away from its mythic base or not was whether the group migrated from its original home during the time the transformation took place. In this respect the biblical account of God's instruction to Abraham to leave his family's home and move to a new land and the subsequent Israelite exodus from Egypt to return to that land are paradigms of the effects of migration on the demythologization of a people.

When they converted to Christianity, the communities of southern Europe, who did not migrate, simply adapted their mythic world view to the terminology and basic demands of Catholicism. They continued to endow the same local features and shrines with divinity, transforming them into points of association with saints. But any mythic basis that survived among northern and West Europeans until the beginning of the modern era was lost by those among them who migrated across the Atlantic to the United States. When they entered this new land that had no mythic associations for them, they became as effectively demythologized as the Jews. One way this can be seen is in local place-names and the meanings attached to them. Like the ancient Israelites, the Americans borrowed place-names from the original inhabitants of the land; but while those names had explicitly mythological meanings to the Canaanites and the Indians respectively, they had no such meanings to the Israelites and the Americans who borrowed them.

Thus even Christianity was substantially demythologized in the United States. (This process was intensified by the fact that most of the early settlers of America were Calvinists; at the time of the Revolutionary War over half the population were connected with Calvinist churches of one kind or another.) Today the "Christmas problem" reflects this very well. Because Christmas in the United States is a holiday of goodwill more than a celebration of the birth of the Christian messiah, it is more difficult for Jews to resist the pressures to participate in the events surrounding the holiday.

Precisely because religion in America is not a means for perpetuating a mythic understanding of the world, it has served as an engine for social change and has been considered in many quarters as a vehicle for the construction of the American "city upon a hill." This has given religion a crucial position in the fabric of American civilization. Moreover, America's Protestant roots made an individual's religion a matter of his or her personal choice or "calling," thus reaffirming the associational character of the United States as a new society. Alexis de Tocqueville wrote:

Anglo-American civilization . . . is the product . . . of two perfectly distinct elements which elsewhere have often been at war with one another but which in America it was somehow possible to incorporate into each other, forming a marvelous combination. I mean the *spirit of religion* and the *spirit of freedom.* . . .

Far from harming each other, these two apparently opposed tendencies work in harmony and seem to lend mutual support.

Religion regards civil liberty as a noble exercise of men's faculties, the world of politics being a sphere intended by the Creator for the free play of intelligence. Religion, being free and powerful within its own sphere and content with the position reserved for it, realizes that its sway is all the better established because it relies only on its own powers and rules men's hearts without external support.

Freedom sees religion as the companion of its struggles and triumphs, the cradle of its infancy, and the divine source of its rights. Religion is considered as the guardian of mores, and mores are regarded as the guarantee of the laws and pledge for the maintenance of freedom itself.[7]

Thus American aspirations for social justice have been religiously motivated to a substantial degree, though at times somewhat indirectly. The positive role of religion in American social progress must be appreciated in order to understand American civilization. Religious motivations have been incorporated into the American way of life, even while being disavowed from time to time by many American intellectuals. It is true that specific reforms have often been originated by persons who repudiated religion (or at least its organized forms) and later adopted by people of overt religious inclination, and that many churches have been so conservative during periods of social reform that even the religiously-motivated reformers have had to operate outside of their framework. Despite these qualifications, the religious impulse that has continued to exist among Americans within and outside of the churches has been a powerful factor in every movement for social progress, from the Revolutionary War and the abolition of slavery to the reform of the industrial system and the protest against American intervention in Southeast Asia.

This "Jewish" conception of the role of religion has contributed its share to making Jews feel so completely at home in the United States. Individual Jews, including rabbis, have been involved in reform movements with their Christian colleagues from the first, and Jewish religious movements have participated in such efforts at least since the turn of the century.

What is the situation today? On the surface, at least, the picture is confusing. Articulate spokesmen among the intellectual community do not refer to the religious impulse except in passing, but political leaders do. As for organized religion, it takes its prophetic role seriously. Since they are no longer at the center of American institutional life, even the "establishment" churches no longer feel the need to defend the status quo and are prepared to compete for public attention by being reformist. The major reform movements of the 1950s and 1960s drew much of their impetus from the religious tradition and the churches, so much so that many exceeded the tolerance of their congregants for rapid change in their willingness to support new reformist causes. Consequently we are presently witnessing a pulling back from the most extreme positions of the sixties, a clipping of the wings of the social activists, and a reemphasis on the personal aspects of religion. It would be a mistake, however, to assume that this reflects any fundamental change in the social role religion plays in America; it is, rather, a normal cyclical adjustment.

A POSTEMANCIPATION COMMUNITY

As Ben Halpern has pointed out, no ideologies of emancipation, or in response to emancipation, developed in the United States.[8] Those that immigrants brought here from abroad continued to exist as transient elements only, and only as long as an immigrant generation dominated American Jewish life. The fate of the leading European Jewish ideologies induced by emancipation is a case in point.

1. Socialism as a solution to the "Jewish problem" was a temporary phenomenon on the American Jewish scene, sponsored and supported by immigrant socialists for barely a generation.

2. Assimilationism never developed as a full-blown ideology—as it did in Europe, where there were even assimilationist Jewish political parties—though it was periodically advocated by individuals. Its closest counterpart was the notion, embraced by radical reformers at the turn of the century, that American Christians and Jews should merge into a higher religion of science and the Social Gospel, a notion that was never widespread enough to take on ideological proportions, except among the persons who founded the Ethical Culture Society.

3. Diaspora nationalism never developed in the United States because American Jews never sought autonomous communal rights.

4. Zionism, though at one time powerful organizationally, never took hold as an ideology in the United States, or even as a serious doctrine, as it had in Europe. It was early transformed from a striving for personal self-realization, or at the very least national fulfillment, into a "support the Jews in Israel (or Palestine)" program. Hence the pointlessness and failure of the American Council for Judaism, a small group that vociferously defends emancipation against bogeymen of its own invention—as if most American Jews could possibly be persuaded to seek lives outside of American society.

To understand the failure of these European ideologies to take root here, it is necessary to understand the dissimilar forms that anti-Semitism, emancipation, and nationalism took in Europe and the United States. In Europe emancipation was connected with the revolutionary crises and the new liberalism of the late eighteenth and the nineteenth centuries. (Conventional historical wisdom links Jewish emancipation with the French Revolution as a matter of course.) The counterrevolutionaries ("conservatives" or "reactionaries") were normally anti-Semitic, since they associated Jewish emancipation with the hated revolution and viewed it as a symbol of an unpleasant new order. Since the counterrevolutionaries represented a mainstream movement with considerable political power, their anti-Jewish attitudes were crystallized as anti-Semitism, which became a respectable doctrine that carried great weight, particularly, but not exclusively, among those who longed for the ancien regime. Anti-Semitic ideas also came to play a role among those revolutionaries who sought a new homogenization of society and for whom the Jews seemed unhomogenizable.

In the United States there was no organized movement for Jewish emancipation. American ways were very different from European ones, and the changes that gave Jews full civil and political rights took place as part of a normal liberalization of American life that was extended to individuals from all sorts of minority groups. (Contrast this with Negro emancipation in the United States, which had to be extended to a group explicitly and only came about through a wrenching crisis—the Civil War—and then only in the formal sense.)

In Europe nationalism was based on certain myths about uniform ethnic origins (or "race," in the terminology of the age). Since the Jews were of a different "race," by definition they were excluded from full participation in the new nationalism unless they ceased to be Jews (and in some cases not even then). This was true even when the Jews argued otherwise. In the United States nationalism was based on the acceptance of the national vocation to build a new society by any individual who chose to cast his lot with the United States. Since Americans were all immigrants originally and stemmed from a wide variety of ethnic and racial groups, there could be no single ethnic (or even racial) basis for an American ethic of nationalism. What bound Americans together were shared values—the "American way of life"—which anyone could embrace. Indeed, consenting to those values as the basis of citizenship is a fundamental tenet of American political thought. These shared values, this mystique, became the ethnically neutral basis for American nationalism which Jews could easily share and accept.[9]

These characteristics of American Jewry are not necessarily shared by other New World Jewries, which are also nominally postemancipation communities, as Moshe Davis has pointed out.[10] Contrast Canadian and Latin American Jewries with Jews in the United States and this becomes apparent. In Canada the Jews are a cultural minority in an ethnically diverse society whose stated aim is cultural pluralism. They are "governed" through a communal structure that organizes the entire Canadian Jewish establishment into one overall system. In Latin America the Jews are an ethnic minority in countries whose nationalism is also based on ethnic origins. They are seen as having their own *madre patria* (mother country) in Israel in addition to their local loyalties. Jews in the United States are a socioreligious community with a religious institutional orientation, set in a society where religious pluralism is considered desirable but cultural or ethnic separation is frowned on. An individual's religious preference is voluntarily assumed in the United States, which means that it is a legitimate way to maintain differences when organic ways are suspect.

This remains true despite the recent upsurge of interest in ethnicity and ethnic identity. With the exception of certain reactive movements among the black and Hispanic minorities, the "ethnics" are not seeking separate institutions within American society, not even cultural pluralism in the accepted sense. Rather, they are seeking recognition of the worth of their heritage and legitimation of their rights to struggle as a bloc to protect their individual members in the larger society. In this respect they are reminiscent of the descendants of the Scots, Welsh, Dutch, and some Germans in the late nineteenth century, whose similar efforts represented the last gasp of overt ethnicity among those groups before their full acceptance into the American establishment.

THE AMERICAN EXPERIENCE AND THE JEWS: SIMILARITIES AND DIFFERENCES

The similarities that link the Jewish and American world views have been delineated often. Both civilizations are classically based upon the effort to build the good commonwealth. Both look to their tasks with a sense of chosenness and vocation based on the Bible-rootedness of their founders and subsequent generations. And both have had to adjust their vocation and its demands to the demands of a frontier experience with its dislodgments. Even their corruptions have a similarity born out of their initial vocational perceptions.

At the same time, there are essential differences between American and traditional Jewish ideals. In the first place, American society is basically liberal and individualistic. While liberalism and individualism have certain Jewish roots, since the eighteenth century they have been carried far beyond these roots by Americans—with some decisive consequences. In its classic form Jewish society is based on transcendent principles that are not always supportive of liberalism and is far more communitarian in its orientation.[11]

Second, despite the continued influence of classic Jewish and American principles, the great characteristic of the modern era, during which the United States was founded, settled, and developed, has been the general secularization of society. First there was a massive transference of attention from the otherworld to this world, though Americans were still pious; then this-worldly piety became straightforward worldliness. This shift in forms has affected Jews and Christians alike. In essence, we are all living within the framework of degenerated tradition, and, especially since the social upheavals of the 1960s (the "Age of Aquarius" syndrome), it is almost as difficult to remain an authentic Christian in American society as it is to remain an authentic Jew.

When Jews first started analyzing their position in the United States, around the turn of the century, their leading intellectual spokesmen formulated the idea of cultural pluralism to describe the kind of society that they envisioned in the New World: each immigrant group would retain some of its cultural identity while its members became fully part of the American scene as individuals.[12] But the kind of cultural pluralism envisioned then never developed in the United States. Instead, traditional American religious pluralism was given a broader base to allow late-migrating Catholics and Jews (or their children) full access to the benefits of American society.[13]

New Americans chose religious affiliation as a vehicle for the preservation of what they wished to preserve of their heritage because they quickly perceived that America was a religiously attuned civilization and had been so from the beginning. Consequently, religion became the easiest way to identify with American life as a whole while preserving certain differences in life-style, and to retain an attachment to one's ancestral connections and way of life in a socially acceptable manner.

As the price of entry into American life new immigrants had to give up all their overt native habits except those identified with their religions. Because their religions, being within the Judeo-Christian tradition, fit legitimately within the American schema, they could be retained. Religion became the link with the "other way of life," and everything that was to be preserved from that way of life had to be fitted into a religious context.

Ethnic groups that wished to preserve something of their identities adapted to this situation by making their national churches the basis for subcommunal organization within the framework of American religious pluralism. Obvious examples are the Jews, the Greeks, the Ukrainians, and the various Scandinavian ethnic groups, but this was also done by such groups as the Yankees of New England and the southern whites. One consequence of this has been the development of religious communities that include both formal religious associations and less formal interpersonal relationships, which tie people who are not formally affiliated to a particular denomination or congregation-centered group. While the formal membership in the congregation represents the heart of the community, every denomination embraces people who are not formal members but have grown up within the framework of that denomination. Because of family membership ties they ultimately live out much of their lives as part of the community which the congregation has fostered.[14]

Thus every religious association becomes the heart of a larger religious community and takes on certain characteristics that have not been considered the province of religion in traditional Protestantism. Gradually this has led to a broader definition of religion. American Protestantism, with its strong Puritan and Calvinistic influences, has always tended to see the role of religion as something more than churchgoing, as something like a way of life, and has periodically emphasized its role in promoting social justice. American Jews as a community stand to gain from this broadened definition, because it comes closer to the Jewish conception of a religious community.

Jews far more than Christians use their synagogues and religious institutions as social rather than as religious centers in the usual sense of the word.[15] The available evidence uniformly reveals that by and large Jews are far less observant than Christians when it comes to participation in worship.[16] At the same time it is clear that synagogues and other institutions with a religious aura are doing relatively well within the Jewish community. As Marshall Sklare has pointed out, they are doing well precisely because they serve social far more than religious purposes. Even the religious activities that go on within them—primarily those revolving around the rites of passage that Jewish families have maintained whatever their level of observance—tend to be more social than religious in character, offering families the opportunity to come together to extend their hospitality to friends and business associates. The rites of passage do not generally include whole congregations, and the ceremonies themselves are not generally meaningful in a personal sense to any substantial number of the members. Rather, the synagogues function as service centers for member families and their friends.

In emphasizing the more obvious social aspects of synagogue life in the United States today, people often overlook the fact that it also embraces social behavior that is essentially political in character. To the extent that congregations function as congregations, they are often fulfilling what are in reality political purposes, such as maintaining their organized activities (and by extension the organized life of the Jewish community), educating their young so as to perpetuate that community, supporting Israel, and making other similar responses to problems of the Jewish people as an entity—all this in a society that severely limits overt corporate political activity by any of its communities. Handling the necessary and persistent tasks of political life in this way is both effective and socially acceptable.

THE UNITED STATES AS A PLURALISTIC SOCIETY: PROBLEMS, IRONIES, AND CONTRADICTIONS

When Judaism became a fully legitimate American religion, one of the three major faiths that are the mainstays of the American way of life, it incurred responsibilities as well as benefits. The Jews themselves fostered much of this new climate by their own organized efforts to escape from the segregationist limitations that had been placed upon them as individuals and as a community in the past. Since Judaism was one of the three religious pillars of American society, American demands were placed upon Jews as Jews, many of which gave them added opportunities to participate in American life while preserving their own special interests and identity. However, some of the demands could only weaken traditional aspects of the Jewish way of life.

As full-fledged Americans, Jews were expected to mix with other Americans without reservation, often to the detriment of the observance of the Sabbath and religious festivals and almost certainly, kashruth. Increasingly, Jews were expected to open up their own activities to non-Jews and to expose their internal life to the same scrutiny as any other institution in American society. Moreover, since Americans like to keep tabs on their institutions, a great deal of public, particularly journalistic, attention came to be devoted to probing aspects of Jewish communal life that Jews had never before been interested in sharing with non-Jews.

American society had, in effect, created preserves in the social and economic spheres allocated to one group or another. It is true that the choicest preserves were essentially reserved for the descendants of the original settlers of the United States or those who had migrated to this country before the Civil War. The Jews had their preserves, too, but they were lower in the hierarchy of social and economic influence. Through their "defense" organizations the Jews successfully conducted a massive assault against what they considered to be barriers to their progress toward full equality in American society, but success had its price. As Jews were admitted to executive suites they were expected to emulate the other occupants of those exalted quarters, that is, to become less obviously Jewish.

Despite all the benefits of the open American society, two immediate consequences of the legitimation accorded Jews and Judaism have not been favorable to the Jewish people as a corporate entity. The increased propinquity of Jews and non-Jews in college and after, and the diminution of differences in their life-styles and thought patterns have led to a great increase in the rate of intermarriage.[17] Moreover, there is now far greater social assimilation even among those Jews who remain, in their own eyes, fully within the Jewish fold. For example, the differences in divorce rates, drinking and drug-taking habits, and juvenile delinquency that used to prevail between Jews and the general non-Jewish population are rapidly disappearing.[18]

Then, too, in the 1960s many Americans began to lose interest in their churches and in organized religion generally—this despite record church efforts to come to grips with social and political problems. It was not that Americans were necessarily becoming less religious, but rather that many of them were looking to other quarters for substitutes for the faith of their fathers. This was particularly true among the young, but it had its repercussions among their elders as well. Interest in Eastern religions, mysticism, and even such phenomena as the belief in spirits and satanism flourished in what seemed to be, on one hand, a breaking away from traditional religion in favor of presumably more modern trends and, on the other, an outbreak of the kind of mythic thinking that has occurred in all monotheistic religions, including Judaism, from time to time.

As the membership rolls of Christian churches declined, so too did those of the synagogues. As religion became less important as a point of identification for the younger generation of American Jews, their ties to the Jewish people, which had been presented to them in their earlier years as being primarily religious in character, were correspondingly weakened. Unequipped to deal with anything like the full range of Jewish civilization, youth, once they began to lose interest in the ritual practices of the synagogue, had nothing left to tie them to the Jewish community.

The impact of this trend would have been much worse had there not been a parallel revival of interest in ethnicity at the same time. Young Jews whose parents had embraced the religious dimension of Jewish life in order to survive as Jews in the 1950s, regardless of how secular they may have felt at heart, now became interested in Jewish ethnicity as their means for securing Jewish survival. Jews were not the originators of this trend, but they soon were to be found among its leading proponents, finding in it a fortuitous means for self-perpetuation.

At the present moment the situation regarding the future is still unclear. Neither a religious nor an ethnic definition of Jewishness, it would seem, is sufficient in and of itself, and the external pressures for assimilation continue to grow. What seems to persist, however, no matter what form it takes, is the drive for associational links to Jewish life to replace those organic links lost in the process of modernization.

The somewhat ambiguous position of American Jewry is nowhere better illustrated than in the legal status of the American Jewish community and its institutions. Strictly speaking, American Jews have no separate legal status in the United States. American law is based on the premise that all citizens stand before it equally as individuals and are not recognized, a priori, as members of any ethnic, religious, or racial group. Nevertheless, such groups do exist, and people are born into them and must bear the sociological consequences that result from their particular heritage.

When it comes to correcting disabilities that may result from an individual's background, the law can be used as a neutral device to outlaw them. However, people born into these groups frequently choose to actively maintain their identification with them and even develop institutions through which to do so. These acquire legal status as a matter of course, since legally everybody has to be somewhere. Thus over a period of time there has developed a de facto recognition of group identity in American law, generally based upon a clear affirmation of every American's right to choose to adhere to a particular group or not. Jewish organizations and institutions, for example, are incorporated under the appropriate provisions of state law, and their members can attempt to force them to live up to their legal responsibilities through civil courts. These responsibilities may include maintenance of specific Jewish ritual practices (for instance, a synagogue that was established as an Orthodox institution, and has written into its charter or bylaws that it is to maintain Jewish tradition according to the *Shulhan Arukh,* may be forced by a state court to do so).

In the process, American courts may even be in a position of enforcing Jewish religious law as they interpret it. Some nineteen states have enacted legislation to assure consumers that food labeled kosher truly is. In defining what is kosher they explicitly rely upon Jewish law. In New York both the state and city governments maintain elaborate offices to assure compliance with the particular legislation. Challenged in the name of separation of church and state, the courts have ruled that the states are perfectly within their rights to enact and enforce such laws to maintain fair-marketing practices and that the matter has nothing whatsoever to do with religion per se.

American courts enforce Jewish law in areas other than kashruth. For instance, a Jewish family in Michigan was compelled by a court to pay a pledge it had made for the construction of a synagogue, on the ground that Jewish religious law required the fulfillment of obligations. Many more such cases could be cited.

In at least one instance, American law literally defines a person's status. The adoption law in most states requires that children born of parents of a specific faith and put out for adoption or foster care must be placed with families of the same faith, whether or not the natural parents wish it. Thus in at least that respect the law does recognize an organic Jewish tie.

All these seeming contradictions and ambiguities are quite tolerable in American society, where all Americans live under dual legal systems, state and federal, every day of their lives. In a case-law system, it is possible to make accommodations on the basis of specifics without laying down broad principles beforehand. While it is unlikely that American law will ever explicitly endow the Jews with a clear legal status as Jews, unless the country's constitutional system is radically transformed, their legal status as Jews is becoming increasingly institutionalized simply by virtue of their presence in American society.

THE PROBLEM OF PEOPLEHOOD: THE UNANTICIPATED POLITY

It is clear that American Jewry is left with a substantial problem: how to maintain itself as a people with a civilization of its own now that it has been reduced to the status of a "religion" or the possessor of an "ethnic heritage" in the public mind and in the minds of so many Jews. Emancipation rendered the national status of world Jewry equivocal, with some Jews abandoning Judaism entirely, others ignoring the problem, and still others seeking national revival as the only proper way to achieve true emancipation. Jewish thinkers in the United States who understood that Jews could not take the first route and abandon all aspects of Judaism other than those associated with formal worship, and who certainly did not want to take the latter course (that is, to define themselves out of the American body politic and into a segregated existence), developed the notion of peoplehood. By advocating peoplehood they argued that Jews (and other ethnic groups) did not need to seek the full expression of autonomy implicit in the modern conception of nationalism to maintain their character as something more than a church.

Mordecai M. Kaplan, the great exponent of the concept of peoplehood in America, defined Judaism as the "evolving religious civilization of the Jewish people," stressing not only its religious character but its civilizational aspects.[19] Since his definition emphasized the religious character of Judaism, it was fully consonant with American thought on the subject of religious pluralism; nor did the emphasis on Judaism's civilizational aspects necessarily go counter to American views.

Although Kaplan emphasized the necessity for Jews to live in two civilizations simultaneously, in practice most Jews did not want to do so. They were quite happy to be part of a religious group within American civilization and did not want to develop the civilizational aspects of

Judaism in the United States. Thus the peoplehood of American Jewry became truncated, as Jews acculturated rapidly and began to confine the Jewish aspects of their lives to the same niches as did their Christian compatriots.

Jewish peoplehood was truncated but not eliminated, simply because the world around them did not let American Jews forget that they were connected to their fellow Jews in other parts of the world in ways that have relatively little to do with what Americans define as religion. First the tragedy of East European Jewry during World War I, then the Holocaust, and finally the rise of the state of Israel and its successive crises have awakened and activated feelings of Jewishness that greatly transcend the narrow definition of Judaism as a religion, thereby leaving American Jewry with a tremendous ambivalence as to the nature of Jewishness and their own relationship to it. The fact that young Jews today seem vitally concerned with Israel—and some even suggest that they would be willing to defend its existence—yet at the same time many of them declare that they would not hesitate to marry outside the Jewish community, is only an extreme manifestation of this ambivalence.

Thus almost without knowing it, and certainly without consciously planning it, the American Jewish community has organized itself politically to handle the tasks of survival and participation in the life of the world Jewish community. It has done so in ways that are unprecedented in Jewish history, utilizing devices that they themselves do not recognize for what they are. In the process American Jews have created an unanticipated polity fully within the framework of American society, as Jewish in its commitments as any Jewish community in the past, yet as American as any other segment of the mosaic that is present-day America.

Jewish Adaptations to American Life

WHO CAME TO AMERICA?

As a general rule, the Jews who came to the United States were ordinary people—potential merchants and traders, not scholars. They were the more cosmopolitan and worldly, not people whose primary concern was Jewish life. In other words, they were the Jews most predisposed to departing from the path of traditional Judaism.[1]

This was true from 1654 to the end of the mass migration in the 1920s. For a while, however, during the 1930s and 1940s, the Nazi persecutions in Europe drove to these shores Jews who would otherwise never have entertained the notion of emigration to America, including great scholars in the traditional mold, leading academics and intellectuals, and Hasidim and others with extreme Orthodox commitments, who have had a profound effect on American Orthodoxy, if not on the Jewish community as a whole. By and large, the situation has reverted to the former pattern, and today the small but steady stream of Jewish emigrants from Europe, Israel, and Latin America come mainly to seek their fortunes in the United States and have minimal Jewish commitments.

Obviously, the character of the immigration has had important effects on Jewish life in America. In the first place, all but a handful of the immigrants actively sought to become Americanized. They quickly shed much of their traditional Jewish "baggage"—including most of their religious patterns and habits—and certainly made no effort to transmit them to the next generation. Most immigrants assumed that their children would be Americans no longer holding to old-country traditions and life-styles. Thus not only did the children seek to become Americanized, but their parents actively encouraged them.

Moreover, the lack of a Jewishly educated public from the beginning meant that even people who wished to maintain their Jewish heritage and transmit it to their children were handicapped in doing so. There was little transmission of the meaning of Jewish life to new generations because most people did what they did or lived the way they lived out of habit, rather than understanding, and were unable to communicate any sense of tradition.

Even those who wished to maintain certain traditional patterns were sufficiently Americanized to seek to fit those traditional practices into the prevailing American religious style, into the Protestant mold. This led to the emphasis on decorum, family pews, and the use of English; the services were transformed into orchestrated performances by Americanized rabbis, who now assumed ministerial—and later, pastoral—functions and abandoned the traditional rabbinical role (partly, at least, for lack of a concerned constituency). "Protestantization" of Jewish life became the American norm.

WHAT DID THEY DO WHEN THEY ARRIVED?[2]

From the beginning Jews engaged in commerce or, to a lesser extent, belonged to the professions. Merchants set the tone for the Jewish community, the first Jewish professionals were doctors; so from the beginning the Jews were both visible and influential out of proportion to their small numbers.

The reasons for this are significant in understanding the important roles Jews have come to play in the United States. The United States is built on the principles of commerce (broadly defined as the exchange of goods, services, and ideas)—in the terminology of *The Federalist* it is a commercial republic in which commerce is the basis of stability as well as of prosperity and is the motivating force for human achievement. The Jews were better equipped for such a society than any other non-British immigrant group that came to these shores. The merging of the Jews' talent for commerce with the demands and opportunities of a commercial republic does much to explain the Jews' success on the American scene, their disproportionate affluence and influence.

The Jews entered those middle-class occupations that were open—that is, that had not been preempted by earlier settlers—and immediately began to make contributions to American life comparable to those made by groups who began by doing manual labor (see Table 1). Among the occupations that Jews took up were:

1. Medicine, which they practiced from the earliest days (Jacob Lumbrozo was known as the "Jew doctor" of Maryland in 1634,

TABLE 1   AMERICAN JEWISH OCCUPATIONAL PATTERNS

Period	Principal Occupations	Elite Occupations
Colonial and Revolution- ary (1654–1789)	retail sales (hardware, dry goods, liquors) artisans (tailors, soapmakers, distillers, tobacconists, saddlers, bakers, silversmiths)	commission and export-import merchants (including slave trade and army purveyors) fur trade and land speculation planters (rare)
Early national (1789–1816)	retail sales wholesale merchants professions (law, medicine, education, engineering, journalism)	planters land speculators banking insurance, stock exchange
Western expansion (1816–1876)	peddling retail sales skilled crafts	wholesale merchants professions banking and finance
Great migration (1877–1917)	petty trade and peddling retail sales garment workers skilled crafts	law and politics banking and finance department stores publishing, literature, and science medicine clothing industry
"Second generation" (1917–1947)	retail sales small business white-collar employment professions (law, medicine, dentistry, pharmacy) public-school teaching	department stores publishing and literature clothing industry entertainment and media finance, stock exchange
Metropolitan frontier	liberal and scientific professions (25%) proprietors and managers (30%) clerical and sales (25%) crafts, skilled and semiskilled labor (15%) unskilled labor and agriculture (5%)	academicians manufacturers real estate and construction mass media stock brokerage Jewish professions

twenty years before the first group settlement of Jews in North America)

2. Peddling, anywhere that the Yankees did not go (the South, the central Midwest, the Southwest, and New England after the Yankee peddlers moved westward); they were not seen much in the Northwest, which was preempted by the Yankees, except among the lumberjacks and the miners in the wilder regions

3. Merchandising, which was an outgrowth of peddling

4. Industries that were either considered to be undesirable or were new (and therefore open to anyone who had the talent and energy to enter them):

    a. Manufacturing ready-to-wear clothes (an industry that was relatively new when Jews came in the post-Civil War era)

    b. Mass communications—the young industries of motion pictures, radio, and television; newspapers in cities where Jews arrived early enough (Ochs in Chattanooga, Adler in Davenport)

5. The new sciences, especially the ones that have developed since World War II.

Two trends can be observed from Table 1. As a general rule, one generation's "breakthrough" occupations—those open only to the elite —became commonplace in the next, unless they were otherwise rendered obsolete. The major break in this pattern occurred between the 1870s and the 1940s, when anti-Semitism (one of the principal manifestations of a general racism in the Western world in those years) led to the exclusion of even Jewish elites from occupations formerly open to Jews, particularly in banking, finance, and the professions. In every generation Jews followed the frontier and the opportunities it provided, seeking to enter even the most pioneering ventures, usually in a commercial way. The importance of this phenomenon to the economic success of American Jewry cannot be overestimated.

In a very real sense their history for thousands of years had prepared the Jews for living in the United States—not only by virtue of their commercial skills, which apparently date back to the earliest days, but also because of their instinct for being at the center of every communications network in which they have found themselves.[3] This instinct, a recurring phenomenon in Jewish history, has given the Jews their disproportionate influence in human affairs and at the same time has disproportionately exposed them to various hazards. Even the Jewish homeland shares that characteristic, for Israel is located at the crossroads of the

Middle East, which is in the heart of the geographic communications network of the continents of Europe, Asia, and Africa.

The Jews' heavy involvement in the communications industry and the mass media (radio, television, motion pictures) in the United States reflects this. Now that the university has become one of the main communications centers in American society, we find Jews disproportionally represented and influential in the universities.[4] (The communication of ideas is, as Alfred North Whitehead has pointed out, simply an extension of commerce in another direction.) The Jews arrived in the United States in great numbers just when the country was becoming urbanized and hence when its communications systems were undergoing changes. Thus even the Jews' urban inclination fitted in perfectly with the new directions American society was taking.

As a result, today the Jews are basically an upper-middle-class group. In this respect they most resemble the predominantly upper-middle-class Protestant denominations such as the Episcopalian, Presbyterian, and Congregational, the churches with the highest status in the country. The latter two, in particular, also happen to be the churches most influenced by Jewish ideals and the Bible. The Jews share the virtues and achievements—as well as the vices and problems—of that social stratum, and in fact those virtues and vices are accentuated among them. Moreover, the Jews as a group are not particularly leavened by other social strata, since there are not many Jews in the working class or among the upper classes. Even the Jewish poor are essentially middle-class people without sufficient money.[5]

THE JEWS AND THE AMERICAN FRONTIER

The most important factor in the development of the United States has been America's continuing frontier and the American population's response to that phenomenon.[6]

Since the first settlements on these shores, American society has been a frontier society, geared to the progressive extension of man's control over his environment and the utilization of the social and economic benefits gained from widening that control, i.e., pushing the frontier line back. The very dynamism of American society is a product of this commitment to the conquest of the ever-advancing frontier, a commitment that is virtually self-generating since, like a chain reaction, the conquest of one frontier has led to the opening of another.

Since the first settlers arrived in 1607, the American frontier has passed through three stages. First came the *rural-land* frontier—the classic American frontier described by the historians—lasting roughly from the seventeenth through the nineteenth centuries. It was characterized by the westward movement of a basically rural population interested in settling and exploiting the land and by development of a socioeconomic system based on agriculture and extractive pursuits in both its urban and rural components.

Early in the nineteenth century, the rural-land frontier gave birth to the *urban-industrial* frontier, which began in the Northeast and spread westward, in the course of which it transformed the nation into an industrial society settled in cities and dedicated to the spread of new technology as the primary source of the nation's economic and social forms. The dominant characteristic of this frontier was the transformation of cities from service centers or workshops for the rural areas into independent centers of opportunity, producers of new wealth, and social innovators possessing internally generated reasons for existence and growth. At first overlapping the rural-land frontier, the urban-industrial frontier became dominant by the last third of the century.

By the mid-twentieth century, it had given birth, in turn, to the *metropolitan-technological* frontier, which is characterized by the radical reordering of an industrial society through rapidly changing technologies and a settlement pattern that encourages the diffusion of an urbanized population within large metropolitan regions. These radically new technologies, ranging from atomic energy and automation to synthetics and cybernetics, and the accompanying suburbanization of the population influenced further changes in the nation's social and economic forms in accord with their new demands. Like the first two frontier stages, the metropolitan-technological frontier has also moved from east to west since the 1920s, becoming nationally dominant after World War II.

Each successive frontier stage has opened new vistas and new avenues of opportunity for the American people by developing new economic activities, creating new settlement patterns, and mastering new social problems growing out of the collision of old patterns and new demands. Consequently, each frontier has generated new political concerns revolving around the accommodation of the challenges and opportunities within the civil society.

Jews continued to arrive in the United States during every stage of the frontier process, and their position in American society is connected with the ways in which they adjusted to the predominant frontier at the time of their arrival (Table 2 shows the waves of Jewish immigration to the United States). No adequate exploration of the frontier's impact on the Jews of America has ever been undertaken; here we can only set forth the outlines that need to be filled in.

The first wave of Jews engaged in foreign and western commerce, two of the major frontier outlets of the seventeenth and eighteenth centuries. The second and third waves took to the rural-land frontier on the western and northern fringes of colonial settlement and moved with it throughout the nineteenth century, usually as peddlers or merchants.

TABLE 2   WAVES OF JEWISH IMMIGRATION TO U. S.

Wave	Dates	Primary Source of Migrants	Principal Areas of Settlement	Estimated Jewish Population*	
I	1654–1790	Sephardic Diaspora, followed by mixed Ashkenazic	New York, Newport, eastern Pennsylvania, Charleston, Savannah	1654 1776	30 1,000
II	1790–1830	England, Western Europe	East Coast, Ohio, Louisiana	1790 1818 1826	1,200 3,000 6,000
III	1830–1880	Germany, Hungary, Bohemia	East Coast, Middle West, California, western mining areas	1840 1848 1880	15,000 50,000 230,000
IV	1880–1924	Poland, Russia, Eastern Europe	cities across the country, particularly on East Coast	1888 1897 1900 1917	400,000 938,000 1,058,000 3,389,000
V	1933–1950	Germany, Central and Eastern Europe	major cities across the country	1927 1937 1950	4,228,000 4,771,000 5,000,000
VI	1950–present	Israel, Latin America, Hungary, Middle East, U.S.S.R.	major cities on East and West coasts	1960 1972 1978	5,531,000 6,000,000 5,781,000

*Population estimates are taken from Sidney Goldstein, "American Jewry, 1970: A Demographic Profile," *American Jewish Year Book* (1971) except for the 1972 estimate, which is from the *National Jewish Population Study* (New York: Council of Jewish Federations and Welfare Funds, 1974). The 1978 figure is from the *American Jewish Year Book* (1979).

The fourth wave of Jews arrived in the United States at the time when the rural-land frontier had given way to the urban-industrial frontier. Consequently, the overwhelming majority settled in the cities, where the urban-industrial frontier had created the greatest opportunities. Finally, the most recent waves of Jewish immigrants have become associated with the metropolitan-technological frontier, the latest stage in America's continuing frontier of development. They have been involved particularly in the technological aspects of the metropolitan-technological frontier, but they have also availed themselves of the settlement patterns associated with another frontier: the movement to the suburbs.

Their varying adaptations to the successive frontier stages dictated the settlement patterns of the Jewish immigrants and the subsequent settlement patterns of the Jewish community. The first wave of immigrants tended to concentrate in the major commercial cities along the East Coast or at the edge of the western frontier. While by and large they established congregations wherever there was a sufficient number of Jews to do so, only the settlers in the major coastal cities became the cores of permanent communities. As for the others, they moved on with the advance of the frontier, either proceeding farther west or transferring their bases of operations to the large commercial centers that were increasingly coming to dominate the hinterland. Their small numbers assured that, economically and socially, they would be highly integrated into the general community. In places like Connecticut, where there was a convergence of Jewish and general values and cultures, every Jew who remained in the colony intermarried and the descendants were lost to Judaism.

As well as settling on the East Coast, the second and third waves of Jewish immigrants, arriving at the height of the westward movement, pushed on into the interior in pursuit of the economic opportunities prevalent in that era of rapid expansion westward across the continent. They were better distributed around the United States than any other wave, reaching into small towns and mining camps as well as the emerging cities of the West. Even today, much of small-town Jewry in the South, the Mississippi valley, and the Far West traces its ancestry back to the original settlers from the second and third waves. Thus the most even dispersal of Jews across the United States was probably achieved by the time of the Civil War, after which many of those in the small towns or mining centers also followed the flow of commercial power to the cities. They were integrated into the local rather than the regional or national economies and society. They integrated less well into the general population than their colonial predecessors had, except on the far frontiers, where conditions paralleled those of the coastal societies at an earlier stage. Thus they began to adapt to America *as Jews,* developing their own institutions in the spirit of the nineteenth century.

The fourth and fifth waves of immigrants concentrated heavily in the major cities. They did so because this was where the greatest economic opportunity now lay, the result of the opening up of the urban-industrial frontier. To be sure, settlement in the urban centers was attractive for yet another reason: the fact of Jews living in close proximity provided comfort and made it easier to maintain Jewish customs and practices. However, it was the economic opportunity that counted first and foremost, as indicated by the fact that those Jews who did not find proper or suitable opportunities in the big cities moved elsewhere. Those Jews who had settled first in smaller towns or rural areas but found no opportunity there, resettled in the big cities. For the most part immigrant Jews in urbanized America were economically and socially segregated from their fellow Americans of longer standing and even from the other immigrant groups, concentrating in a few "Jewish" industries or businesses, living in their own neighborhoods, and mixing only with one another. Ironically, the urban-industrial frontier, which for the first time brought a majority of Americans into proximity with one another in the densely populated cities, also generated the most segregated social and economic patterns to be found in postcolonial American history.

Only in a few cases was the criterion of opportunity secondary for the Jewish immigrants. Some Jews who found opportunity in out-of-the-way places, became concerned with the Jewish education of their children and moved to cities with larger Jewish communities when their children reached school age, seeking the critical mass of Jews necessary for Jewish living. The Jewish "oases" in central and southern sections of the country often reflect this movement: Minneapolis and Saint Paul are good examples. Not only did the Twin Cities attract worthy Jewish settlers directly, and so become significant on the Jewish map beyond their numbers—Minneapolis today has about twenty-two thousand Jews and Saint Paul, ten thousand—but they also proved to be a magnet for Jewish families who had settled and prospered in isolated communities in the Northwest, but were in search of an active Jewish life for themselves and a better Jewish education for their children. As a result, Minneapolis and Saint Paul came to boast a pool of truly devoted people who worked hard to build Jewish communities of exceptional quality.

In Denver, Colorado, another example of this phenomenon, the Orthodox Jewish community got its start when attempts at agricultural colonization in Colorado and Kansas collapsed and the colonists sought a greater concentration of Jews of the kind only to be found in an urban environment. Until the end of World War II the Jewish community of Denver's West Side actually maintained a shtetllike pattern of living, raising livestock and chickens in their backyards while remaining within walking distance of synagogues and schools. Other Jews established ranches or acquired mining interests and then repaired to Denver to become synagogue presidents and pioneers of western Zionism.

Today the metropolitan-technological frontier continues to shape the pattern of Jewish settlement. The children and the grandchildren of immigrants to the cities in the days of the urban-industrial frontier were among the first to move out along what Samuel Lubell has called the "old tenement trail" to become pioneers of suburbia; so that although the Jewish population today is heavily concentrated in metropolitan areas, it is, perhaps for the first time in American history, essentially a small-town and small-city population, one which has abandoned the big central cities for suburbia and even exurbia. On the East Coast, for example, it is almost impossible to find a city of any size within a hundred miles of a metropolis that does not have its own Jewish community. The same is true in southern California. This pattern is spreading to other sections of the country as well, conditioned only by the total number of Jews in the area. Cleveland, Detroit, and Saint Louis are almost without Jewish residents; Boston, Baltimore, and Washington are rapidly moving in that direction. These major Jewish communities are now really congeries of suburban and exurban Jewish nuclei that are having difficulty holding together an increasingly scattered Jewish population.

In the process the Jews have achieved social and economic integration on an unprecedented scale. Their choice of occupations has brought them into the mainstream of the American economy, which in turn has broken down many, if not most, of the social barriers separating them from the gentiles. Moreover, small-town living, even in suburbs, has intensified their general political and civic involvement as well as "backyard" social connections.

While Jews were migrating to the frontiers of development of the larger society, they were also adapting to that society on a generational basis. In each of the five generations from 1820 to the present, a number

TABLE 3 ACCULTURATION-ASSIMILATION STAGES SINCE 1820

Generation	Character of Population	Communal Organization	Role in General Society
First–Sixth (1654–1848)	adventurers in varying stages of assimilation	cemeteries and benevolent societies, perhaps a traditional synagogue	high participation in all phases of social and political life
Seventh (1848–1878)	sons of adventurers usually actively acculturating	synagogue becomes central institution, usually undergoing religious reform	beginnings of forced withdrawal from certain sectors of society
Eighth (1878–1917)	more broadly based population, larger numbers	rudimentary communal organizations appear alongside synagogues	maximum exclusion from society
Ninth (1917–1948)	americanizing generation dominant	federations emerge as dominant actors; leadership cadres diversified; emergence of indigenous intellectual life	beginnings of reintegration into general society
Tenth (1948–1977)	native American generation dominant	entrenchment and linkage of community organizations	reintegration far advanced; Judaism becomes an "American religion"

of significant changes in the character of Jewish life took place, as shown in Table 3. First, the character of the Jewish population shifted from adventurers, many of whom immigrated to the United States out of a desire to abandon their Jewish ties, to a native American Jewish community that seeks to maintain its Jewishness. It is also possible to follow the development of Jewish communal organizations from the first cemeteries and benevolent societies designed to provide those minimal services that even nominal Jews seemed to require, to a consolidation of community organizations within some kind of rationalized network and a shift of concern from welfare to education. Finally, the Jews' role in general society can be seen as shifting from high participation to substantial exclusion and back again to open participation.

THE LOCATION OF AMERICAN JEWS[7]

The settlement of Jews in the United States—and the resultant impact of the American frontier on their integration into American society—varies considerably from section to section. For our purposes the United States can be divided into eight sections: (1) New England—Maine, New Hampshire, Vermont, Massachusetts, Rhode Island, and Connecticut; (2) the Middle Atlantic states—New York, New Jersey, Pennsylvania, Delaware, and Maryland, and the District of Columbia; (3) the upper South—Virginia, West Virginia, North Carolina, Tennessee, and Kentucky; (4) the lower South—South Carolina, Georgia, Alabama, Mississippi, Louisiana, and Florida; (5) the western South—Arkansas, Missouri, Oklahoma, and Texas; (6) the Great Lakes states—Ohio, Indiana, Illinois, Michigan, and Wisconsin; (7) the Northwest—Minnesota, Iowa, the Dakotas, Nebraska, Kansas, Montana, Wyoming, and Colorado; and (8) the Far West—California, Oregon, Washington, Arizona, Nevada, Utah, Idaho, Hawaii, and Alaska. In each of these sections Jews came to settle at different periods, often from different countries or regions of origin in the Old World. In each they were required to mix with non-Jewish settlers of a variety of backgrounds, and to fit into the general environment that was in itself a reflection of sectional patterns.

American Jewry is the largest aggregation of Jews ever located under a single government, with the possible exception of czarist Russia on the eve of the mass migration. Its major *local* communities are larger than all but a handful of *countrywide* communities in the past. Unlike czarist Russia with its Pale of Settlement, in the United States the Jewish population has spread into every corner of the country.

The spread of Jews from coast to coast and from the northern border to the Deep South, despite its unevenness, has led to the creation of organized Jewish communities in every state, with major concentrations in every section. California now has more Jews than any country in the world other than the United States itself, the Soviet Union, and Israel. Los Angeles, the second largest local Jewish community in the world, has as many Jews as all of France, which is ranked as the country with the fourth largest Jewish population in the world. Greater Miami's Jewish community—the sixth largest in the United States—exceeds that of Brazil.

One of the crucial factors shaping Jewish adaptations to American life is where the Jews have located themselves throughout the country.

TABLE 4 JEWISH POPULATION BY STATE, 1877–1978

Size	1877	1918	1960	1978
Over 2 million			New York	New York
Over 1 million		New York		
500,000– 1 million			California	California
250,000– 499,999		Pennsylvania	Illinois New Jersey Pennsylvania	Florida Illinois Massachusetts New Jersey Pennsylvania
100,000– 249,999		Illinois Massachusetts New Jersey Ohio	Connecticut Florida Maryland Massachusetts Michigan Ohio	Maryland Ohio
50,000– 99,999	New York	California Connecticut Maryland Michigan Missouri	Missouri Texas	Connecticut Michigan Missouri Texas Virginia

25,000– 49,999		Indiana
		Minnesota
		Texas
		Wisconsin
			District of
			   Columbia
			Minnesota
			Virginia
			Wisconsin
				Arizona
				Colorado
				District of
				   Columbia
				Georgia
				Minnesota
				Wisconsin

15,000– 24,999	California Pennsylvania	Georgia Iowa Rhode Island Virginia	Colorado Georgia Indiana Louisiana Rhode Island Tennessee	Indiana Louisiana Rhode Island Tennessee Washington
10,000– 14,999	Illinois Maryland Ohio	Alabama Colorado District of Columbia Kentucky Louisiana Nebraska Tennessee	Alabama Arizona Kentucky North Carolina Washington	Kansas Kentucky Nevada North Carolina Oregon

TABLE 4 (*continued*)

Size	1877	1918	1960	1978
5,000–9,999	Louisiana Massachusetts Missouri New Jersey	Arkansas Florida Kansas Maine Oklahoma Oregon Washington West Virginia	Delaware Iowa Maine Nebraska New Hampshire Oklahoma Oregon South Carolina West Virginia	Alabama Delaware Iowa Maine Nebraska New Mexico Oklahoma South Carolina
1,000–4,999	Alabama Arkansas Connecticut District of Columbia Georgia Iowa Mississippi Rhode Island South Carolina Tennessee Virginia Wisconsin	Arizona Delaware Idaho Mississippi Montana New Hampshire North Carolina North Dakota South Carolina Utah Vermont	Arkansas Kansas Mississippi Nevada New Mexico North Dakota Utah Vermont	Arkansas Hawaii Mississippi New Hampshire North Dakota Utah Vermont West Virginia
500–999	Delaware Florida Kansas Maine Nevada North Carolina Oregon West Virginia	Alaska Nevada New Mexico South Dakota	Hawaii Idaho Montana South Dakota	Alaska Idaho South Dakota
Less than 500	Alabama Colorado Idaho Minnesota Montana Nebraska New Hampshire New Mexico North Dakota South Dakota Utah Vermont Washington Wyoming	Hawaii Wyoming	Alaska Wyoming	Montana Wyoming

Looking at the Jewish population of the fifty states, certain important patterns immediately become clear. *The National Jewish Population Study,* completed in 1973, estimates the Jewish population of the United States at 6 million. Nearly half this number live in the states of New York and New Jersey: 2.3 million in New York City and adjacent Long Island and Westchester County, another 400,000 in nearby areas in New Jersey, and another 150,000 in the hinterlands of those states. The state of New York alone has at least as many Jews as the Soviet Union. In fact, three-fifths (some 3.7 million) of all American Jews live in the great northeastern megalopolis that stretches six hundred miles from Maine to northern Virginia between the Atlantic and the mountains. That concentration of Jews is itself greater than that in any single country in the world, including Israel. The megalopolis, with more than a quarter of the general population of the country, is the country's "Main Street," containing its political (Washington), commercial and artistic (New York), and intellectual (Boston) capitals. The influence of American Jews remains disproportionate at least partly because of their concentration in the megalopolis.

The other two-fifths of American Jewry, some 2.3 million strong, are scattered unevenly from coast to coast. Some 600,000—10 percent—live in the Great Lakes states, over half in the arc that stretches for 130 miles from Milwaukee through Chicago into northern Indiana. While substantially less than the eastern concentration, even that figure exceeds the number of Jews in all but three countries. Another 10 percent live in the greater South (from Virginia through Texas), nearly half of them in Florida. While the South is the least Jewishly populated of the major sections of the country, it has more Jews than France. Over 1 million Jews live west of the Mississippi (including 180,000 in the western South), or almost as many as in all of western Europe. California alone has 700,000, or more than in all of Latin America. The other 2.5 million square miles of the greater West contain 300,000 Jews concentrated in a few oases in a region characterized by an oasis culture.

Table 4 outlines the distribution of Jewish population by state over the past century. Two points are notable. The relative rankings of the states with the major Jewish centers have remained much the same over that period, even as their populations have grown tremendously. Where population shifts have occurred, the larger states have grown larger and the smaller have decreased.

While the New York metropolitan area and the Northeast contain the largest concentrations of Jews in the U.S., the proportion of Jews in both is declining, either absolutely or relative to the rest of the country. A decade ago New York State alone was estimated to contain more than half America's Jews. The Jewish population of the Northeast as a whole has increased absolutely while losing somewhat relatively. Still, the center of Jewish population in the United States is probably somewhere in New Jersey, in contrast to the center of population for the country as a whole, which is approaching the Mississippi River in southern Illinois.

Perhaps equally important in considering the regional differences in the distribution of Jewish population is the percentage of Jews in the total population of the various regions. Jews now constitute approximately 2.8 percent of the total population of the United States. Excluding the states of northern New England, the only northeastern states with a lower percentage of Jews are Rhode Island with 2.3 percent and Delaware with 1.6 percent. In fact, the other states range from 3.5 percent to 13.8 percent. By the same token, the only state outside that region which matches or exceeds the national average is California with 3.5 percent. Among the other regions, in only one of the five Great Lakes states (Indiana) do Jews make up significantly less than 1 percent of the total population. With the exceptions of Florida and Missouri, two states that depart from the overall pattern for very explicit reasons, percentages in the southern states all range from 0.2 to 0.8. The range would be further narrowed (0.2 to 0.6) if the Washington spillover were eliminated from Virginia.

While the pattern in the aforementioned regions shows an even intraregional spread, that of the remainder of the West reveals small oases of Jews amidst a Jewishly empty land. Arizona, Colorado, and Minnesota have Jewish concentrations that range slightly above 1 percent of their total population. Five others (Nebraska, Oregon, Nevada, Washington, and New Mexico) have approximately 0.5 percent, and the remaining ten range from less than 0.19 to 0.3 percent.

Table 5 summarizes the situation for 1960 and 1973. It clearly reveals the relative drop in percentage of Jews across the country. The exceptions are to be found in some of those states that have benefited from massive in-migration of Jews. The regional pattern of distribution is also clearly visible.

TABLE 5 JEWISH POPULATION AS PERCENTAGE OF STATE
POPULATION, 1960, 1978

Percentage	1960	1978
10+	New York	New York
5–9.9	District of Columbia, New Jersey	District of Columbia, New Jersey
3.5–4.9	Connecticut, Maryland, Massachusetts, Pennsylvania	Florida, Maryland, Pennsylvania
2.5–3.4	California, Illinois, Rhode Island	California, Connecticut, Massachusetts
1.5–2.4	Delaware, Florida, Missouri, Ohio	Delaware, Illinois, Missouri, Nevada, Ohio, Rhode Island
1–1.4	Arizona, Colorado, Michigan, Minnesota	Arizona, Colorado, Michigan, Virginia
0.5–0.9	Georgia, Indiana, Maine, Nebraska, Nevada, New Hampshire, Oregon, Texas, Vermont, Virginia, Wisconsin	Georgia, Indiana, Maine, Minnesota, Nebraska, New Hampshire, Oregon, Texas, Vermont, Wisconsin
0.25–0.49	Alabama, Iowa, Kentucky, Louisiana, New Mexico, Oklahoma, South Carolina, Tennessee, Washington, West Virginia	Alabama, Kentucky, Louisiana, New Mexico, South Carolina, Tennessee, Washington
0.15–0.24	Arkansas, Kansas, Mississippi, North Carolina, North Dakota, Utah, Wyoming	Alaska, Arkansas, Hawaii, Iowa, Kansas, Mississippi, North Carolina, North Dakota, Oklahoma, Utah, West Virginia
Less than 0.14	Alaska, Hawaii, Idaho, Montana, South Dakota	Idaho, Montana, South Dakota, Wyoming

SECTIONALISM AND JEWISH SETTLEMENT[8]

The limitations placed on nonconformists in New England clearly influenced the course of Jewish settlement in that section. Still it was not without its individual Jews and even its organized Jewish communities in the years of New England Puritanism. The first Jews to settle in New England were Spanish and Portuguese ex-Marranos. They began to arrive in Connecticut, Massachusetts, and Rhode Island in the middle of the seventeenth century, after the initial Puritan settlement of those states. They came as individuals and individual families, seeking refuge or opportunity in what was from their perspective an already settled land with an established and remarkably aggressive civilization, within which they had to find their niche. Small Jewish communities or quasi-communities developed in all three colonies in the eighteenth century and continued to exist for two or three generations despite the pressures against pluralism in the Puritan colonies. The famed Jewish community of Newport, Rhode Island, for example, flourished in the eighteenth century and essentially disappeared at the century's end. But lasting organized communities were not founded in any of the three until the mid-nineteenth-century German Jewish immigration.

A corresponding pattern can be seen in northern New England in Jewish settlement in Maine, New Hampshire, and Vermont. The histories of all three states reveal traces of individual Jewish settlers, mainly Sephardic, who settled as individuals in the late eighteenth century but left no Jewish institutions behind them. Economic opportunities in these three states being limited, Jews were not attracted to them. Permanent Jewish communities were not organized until the 1880s, either primarily or substantially by East European Jews. Bangor, Maine, is a case in point. Here a German Jewish community was founded in the 1840s but it proved to be temporary, passing out of existence in the 1850s when the boom that brought the immigrants to Maine ended. Most of the members of this community moved to Boston, where it is possible to trace their descendants to this day.

The patterns of Jewish settlement in the Middle Atlantic states were colored by the general pluralism which has always characterized that part of the country. In those states Jews were accepted, if not welcomed, as part of the multitude of sects and ethnic groups that settled there. As is well known, New York was the site of the first Jewish community in North America. Its old, established community, founded originally by ex-Marranos and populated at first by Sephardic Jews, soon developed a hispanicized non-Sephardic majority. German and Polish Jews who came to New York were assimilated into the Sephardic community almost as a matter of course until the nineteenth century.

Pennsylvania presented a modified version of this pattern. Here the first Jewish settlers arrived later than in New York. Though Sephardic Jews were strong enough to set the community's basic pattern, the relatively heavy in-migration of Ashkenazic Jews led to a Jewish counterpart of the uniquely pluralistic Pennsylvania society. The territories now part of the states of New Jersey and Delaware were penetrated by Jews from New York and Philadelphia throughout the colonial period, as were portions of upstate New York and western Pennsylvania. Only in the latter state were permanent Jewish settlements west of Philadelphia established before 1830. The two smaller states and the greater part of the two larger ones remained outside the frontier of Jewish settlement until the arrival of German Jews in large numbers. As in New England, a dynamic process of internal development within the section and its divisions is evident. The central communities were settled first; the settlement of the subsidiary communities in the hinterland by entirely different population groups came considerably later.

Jewish settlement in the Middle Atlantic states has been continuous since 1654. Every wave of Jewish migration whose principal area of settlement was the Middle Atlantic states has had a major impact there. Since the section was mixed and pluralistic from the first, there was room for Jews to find a place for themselves; in fact, the Jews were among the pioneers in developing a tolerance for pluralism in New York and to some extent in the other states of the section as well. One of Governor Peter Stuyvesant's reasons for wishing to refuse to allow the original twenty-three Jews to remain in New Amsterdam was that if Jews were to be tolerated, then Lutherans and papists (Catholics) would have to be as well—and so it turned out. At the same time, the multiplicity of groups meant that Jews had fewer opportunities to rise as individuals, and since the overwhelming majority of Jews arrived at least two centuries after the initial settlement of the Middle Atlantic states, as latecomers they were at a decided disadvantage in the allocation of social position and even economic access.

Pluralism in the Middle Atlantic states, as in the Northeast generally, remains a pluralism of permanent intergenerational groups, ethnic or racial in character. By and large people are born into a group and, regardless of whether they wish to or not, remain somehow identified with it all the days of their lives, tacitly accepting this fact and being accepted in that spirit by others. Since the Northeast is America's "Main Street" in the ways we have mentioned, its definition of pluralism has become the dominant one in the United States; but, as we shall see, this is not the only one by any means.

In the end Jews passed through all three frontier stages in the Middle Atlantic states. The first Jews fit into the new society as individuals simply because they were small enough in number to do so. Even today the surviving Sephardic elite based on New York's Congregation Shearith Israel seems to have a different relationship to the United States than do the Jews whose forebears arrived at a much later date. The latter, unlike the early Sephardic arrivals, experienced all the immigrant struggles in their severest form, with the Lower East Side of New York emerging as the classic immigrant neighborhood that symbolizes all such urban districts in the United States. Because of the large concentration of Jews to be found in these immigrant neighborhoods, Jewish life here could remain more organic than anywhere else, and people could maintain their Jewishness simply by living in Jewish neighborhoods. However denatured this Jewishness might be, it did not lead to a lack of Jewish consciousness.

The associational basis of Jewish life developed more slowly in the Middle Atlantic states and in the Northeast generally than in any part of the country. While this is now changing as the immigrant generation fades into history, it is still true that Jews in the Middle Atlantic states are less likely to affiliate with Jewish groups than Jews in any other part of the country. Moreover, when they do affiliate the chances are that they will do so on a very personalistic basis. Thus Jewish life is more fragmented in the Middle Atlantic states than anywhere else, with New York City and its surrounding area a byword for fragmentation in Jewish life.

Permanent Jewish settlement in the new states west of the Appalachian Mountains and north of the Ohio River took place in the second and third decades of the nineteenth century, even before Jewish settlement in the hinterlands of the Middle Atlantic states. Ohio and Indiana were the first states west of the Alleghenies to be settled by Jews. As in the Northeast (and unlike the situation in the South and the West), Jews did not arrive until after the territories had been initially settled (in Ohio the first permanent Jewish settlers did not arrive until almost a decade and a half after statehood had been achieved). While a handful of individual Jews may have reached Indiana before it achieved statehood, in both states organized Jewish communities did not develop until at least two decades after statehood. In both states the first Jewish settlers came from England or from English Jewish stock. Indeed, all five states of the Old Northwest were first settled by English Jews, who, by virtue of their previous assimilation into "Anglo-Saxon" civilization, may have had a peculiar talent for pioneering this first major inland frontier.

Unlike the territory that became Ohio and Indiana, the territory north and west of the Great Lakes that was to become Illinois, Michigan, and Wisconsin was first subjected to European influence through the French, while the English were still struggling to establish colonies on the eastern

seaboard. The few individual Jews who found their way into this territory during the French occupation did not remain permanently, but
when the British took possession of the Great Lakes region after 1761
a number of Jews moved in to replace the French entrepreneurs of the
fur trade. Though individual Jews (mostly from England by way of
Canada) arrived in these three states-to-be before the American occupation (1796), organized Jewish communities in all three were products of
the German immigration some two generations or more later. Of the
three, Illinois corresponds most closely to the pattern set by Ohio and
Indiana, since an organized Jewish community did not come into existence until well after statehood. In Michigan and Wisconsin, statehood
and Jewish communal organization came about almost simultaneously.

The Jews who settled in the Great Lakes region before the Civil War
were caught up as individuals in the westward movement of the land
frontier. They were among the pioneers of that frontier, rarely in any
agrarian or agricultural business capacity, but rather as peddlers and
merchandisers, introducing the benefits of more settled areas to the
newly won West. As a result, they were key factors in the transition from
the rural-land to the urban-industrial frontier, serving as the middlemen
in bringing the fruits of the new industrial revolution to the countryside
and thus providing the urban-industrial frontier with its commercial
outlets.

A century later the descendants of many of these Jews were to be
found in the pioneering mainstream of the metropolitan frontier, not
only taking an active role in promoting the new technologies of that
frontier, but also involved in commercial ventures related to the settlement of suburban areas. Jewish real-estate operations, the great shopping
centers in which Jews had such a prominent hand, the very suburbanization of Jewish communities in the early stages of the suburban movement
were all crucial factors in the advance of the metropolitan frontier. In
the latter stages of the urban-industrial and metropolitan-technological
frontiers, of course, the Central and West European Jews were joined by
those from Eastern Europe, who became the majority and (at least in the
twentieth century) followed the same pioneering patterns.

While the Great Lakes region also had a pluralistic mix in its general
population, it followed a somewhat different pattern from that of the
Northeast. In the first place the original settlers of the section were native
Americans, who had come out of already-developed American subcul-
tures that had rooted themselves on the East Coast in the five or six

generations between its original settlement and the crossing of the Appalachians. This original migration has been consistently reinforced by other native migrants. While immigrants from the Old World followed relatively rapidly on the heels of those first settlers, it was only in parts of Michigan, Wisconsin, and Illinois that they shared in the very founding of new settlements on the land frontier to become part of the original population, with all that this entailed in the way of social status and privilege.

By and large the northern part of the Great Lakes states was settled by Yankees from New England, the middle part by settlers coming out of the Middle Atlantic states, particularly Pennsylvania, and the southern part by southerners who came down the Ohio River and then spread northward until they reached the settlement areas staked out by other population groups. The Irish, Germans, and Scandinavians were the first to arrive directly from Europe in large numbers. The Irish and Germans found the regions settled by Americans from the Middle Atlantic states most congenial, with some of the Germans also moving into regions settled originally by southerners. Scandinavians found themselves most at home in areas settled by the Yankees. Thus, for the most part the various groups were able to fit into regions where they soon felt at home and were accepted without major culture conflicts between oldtimers and new arrivals. This was less true after the opening of the urban-industrial frontier, when East Europeans poured into the whole area almost indiscriminately (although fewer into the southern third, where there was less industrialization). While not a particular threat to the by then well-established original settlers, these latest arrivals were of a different cultural background and thus more easily excluded from the mainstream of society.

The Jews managed to fit in reasonably well from the first, achieving their greatest successes where the migrants from the middle states had settled in and where they had neither to compete with the Yankees nor to combat the relatively self-contained society of the southerners. The Great Lakes region was the first "American" environment that the Jewish immigrants encountered, and they tended to become americanized with far greater rapidity there than in the Northeast. Classical Reform Judaism reached its American apogee in the Great Lakes states, becoming more like American Protestantism there than in any other section.

In general, associational ties rapidly replaced organic ones in all but the core neighborhoods of the biggest cities during the height of the East European migration. This was in line with the character of pluralism in the Great Lakes region. Ethnic, religious, and cultural groups preserved their identity in that section by created associational frameworks through which to express themselves, usually churches and other religious institutions or organizations. Indeed, this area became a stronghold for an associational pluralism that went even beyond such primary associational links. Thus the impact of the frontier was such that people were less tied to the groups into which they were born than on the East Coast. However, since these states were characterized by stable societies, it was expected that people would choose some kind of permanent link to which they would remain faithful throughout their lives, unless there was a good reason to change. Usually the group into which one was born determined what these ties would be, but it could be otherwise, and in time almost any association could form the basis of one's lifelong attachments—not only church, but a political party, the Masons, or even a fraternal lodge or veterans' organization.

The Jews fitted into this scheme by building their own associations: congregations at first, and later charitable institutions, which were ultimately combined into Jewish welfare federations. Thus fourteen out of the twenty-two federations formed before World War I were established either in the Great Lakes states or in that part of the Mississippi valley immediately adjacent, where the same pattern prevailed.

All the states west of the Mississippi River shared a new and unique characteristic on the American Jewish scene: in every one of them, organized or quasi-organized Jewish communities existed prior to statehood. With four exceptions (Nebraska, the two Dakotas, and Oregon), individual Jews had settled within their territorial limits even before the areas in question were individually organized as territories, and in two of the four exceptions Jews arrived within a year of their achieving territorial status. West of the Mississippi the Jews were not only among the American pioneers as individuals, but were also pioneers as Jews, bringing Jewish life with them from the first. The only significant differentiation in Jewish settlement west of the Mississippi River is in respect to those five states in which Jewish communities were organized within three years after the first Jewish settlement. With the exception of Kansas (whose settlement in general was unusual), these states were all mining states (Colorado, Idaho, Montana, and Nevada). Settled in a rush, their Jewish communities sprang up, flourished, and often disappeared within a relatively short time. All the trans-Mississippi states were settled and the communities organized by German Jews, who were very soon reinforced by the arrival of East European Jews. Few Sephardic Jews were involved in the settlement of the trans-Mississippi West, although those that were often played roles of disproportionate importance.

Despite the boom-and-bust character of so many settlements in the trans-Mississippi West, permanent Jewish communities were established throughout its several sections and were able to sink roots as those sections developed. Thus San Francisco Jewry dates its organized existence back to 1848–49, the year that the city became an American settlement; the Jews in Los Angeles organized themselves in 1854, while the first synagogue in Minnesota (founded at the same time) made the Jews the fifth religious group to organize within what was still Minnesota Territory. Nevertheless, the massive settlement of Jews in the Far West came only after World War II, a result of the metropolitan-technological frontier, which brought second- and third-generation Jews westward, primarily from the Great Lakes states but also from the Northeast, seeking new opportunities. In this respect the Jews were following a general American pattern, the so-called tilt westward of the American population, a phenomenon that has been part of the American experience since the first settlement of the continent and continues virtually unabated today. This has made the trans-Mississippi West simultaneously the most homogeneous and the most integrated of all the sections in America.

In the Northwest, particularly where the Yankees were the first to settle, ethnic groups have a certain visibility, principally because the Scandinavians and Germans, attracted to familiar climes as they were in Michigan and Wisconsin, also sought to preserve a certain ethnic consciousness. Where the middle-states group settled, the mixing was more pronounced and the pressure for group maintenance much reduced, while in areas settled by southerners there was little challenge to homogeneity for a long time, until the metropolitan frontier began to make its mark.

In general, pluralism in the farther reaches of the trans-Mississippi West has become a pluralism of individuals, with virtually no emphasis placed on the maintenance of group ties or even permanent associational ones. Individuals are free to choose what they want to be, whom they want to be with, and for how long. On the West Coast there is an almost total lack of social pressure even to maintain the marriage bond. This, of course, has made it considerably more difficult for Jews to maintain group cohesion, even through associational ties, since the environment runs directly contrary to the Jewish commitment to permanent "tribal" links, however manifested. People in the Far West are more likely to be "into" Judaism for a time and then move on to something else than in any other part of the country. Individualistic pluralism, as a manifestation of the contemporary temper, is now spreading to other sections of the country as well, but it remains most pronounced in the Far West.

As individuals, Jews related to the trans-Mississippi environment by rapidly acquiring substantial positions in the general community as individuals. As in the Great Lakes states, Jews rapidly became americanized and their entrepreneurial skills were put to good use in building new communities from scratch. Moreover, Jews were accepted in the trans-Mississippi West from the first. They were even valued as people who were likely to help bring stability to a wild region and were usually to be found in the forefront of the solid citizenry struggling to tame the cow towns and mining camps of the land frontier. As a result, Jews attained elective office in significant numbers for the first time in the trans-Mississippi West, where they achieved their positions as a result of their attractiveness as individuals, not because of bloc voting (which was nonexistent). Jewish mayors began to appear in communities across the entire area, and the first several Jewish governors were elected in western mining and lumbering states (Idaho, Utah, Washington), a clear reflection of their success as solid citizens and as pioneers in those states.

Although Jewish associations emerged throughout the trans-Mississippi West even in the prestate period, these were rarely transformed into communities except in a few exceptional places. Partly because of the openness of western society and partly because relatively few Jews settled in the West, Jews in these places joined together for limited purposes only, while they otherwise sought their community in the larger society that welcomed them. The San Francisco pattern is an extreme example of this. While the Jews founded several synagogues in the early years of their settlement there, they also became leading citizens in the new city from the first, and in time their first families were numbered among the pillars of San Francisco society. Even the wave of anti-Semitism that spread across the United States (as it did the entire Western world), in the late nineteenth century, did not lead to the exclusion of Jews from San Francisco society, and to this day Jews play a far more prominent role in the Bay City's elite than in any other comparable community in the United States. At the same time, while these Jews may have retained nominal attachments to their Reform temples, they were not interested in fostering an active Jewish community life. They stayed with classic Reform longer than almost any other part of the United States, relying upon the temple to serve as a surrogate church, no more and no less important to them than churches were for their Christian peers. They certainly did not seek to build communal institutions beyond the most rudimentary welfare societies. It is only in the last ten years that a different element has emerged in San Francisco, one which is now struggling with the old guard to make the community more Jewish.

The contrasting impact of open and closed environments can be seen at its starkest in Minnesota. The Jews came to Saint Paul at the same time that they did to San Francisco and rapidly integrated in the same way, becoming figures in local society. However, Minnesota was an ethnically divided state, in which Old World groups came to settle even before the American-born settlers arrived, and so were able to preserve their ethnic traditions far more fully than their counterparts in other regions of the country. This was particularly true in the post–Civil War period, when Minneapolis began to grow and a Jewish community was formed there. From the first, Minneapolis was settled by East European rather than German Jews. They settled into a more ethnically crystallized context, so that they too acquired a more separatist character. While the anti-Semitism of the late nineteenth century managed to affect all of Minnesota, leading to the partial exclusion of Jews from Saint Paul's society, it hit Minneapolis much harder, developing into the most thoroughly institutionalized anti-Semitic atmosphere of any comparable community in the United States. In the 1930s Jews were even barred from membership in the Automobile Club.

One consequence of ethnic separatism in Minneapolis, and to a lesser extent in Saint Paul, was to lead to the development of highly articulated Jewish communities with a wide range of Jewish institutions, especially impressive considering the small size of their Jewish populations. Moreover, these were Jewish communities that preserved Jewish culture and attempted to pass it on to their children through their Talmud Torah systems, which have ranked among the best Jewish educational institutions in the country since the turn of the century.

Even in the Twin Cities the trans-Mississippi environment ultimately prevailed. When anti-Semitism collapsed after World War II, Jews rapidly moved into positions of civic and political prominence, particularly in Minneapolis. The past evaporated so thoroughly that at one point in the mid-1950s the city's mayor, the president of the Chamber of Commerce, and the president of the Community Welfare Council were all identified Jews.

Jewish settlement in the South began in Georgia, South Carolina, and Virginia. Individual Sephardic Jews settled in Virginia in the mid-seventeenth century, but an organized community did not arise until the Revolutionary War, by which time the Jewish population was already mixed (though Sephardic practice was adopted in the Richmond community). Jewish settlement in the lower South began later than in the upper South, but developed into organized communal activity (dominated by Sephardim) sooner, before the mid-eighteenth century. North Carolina, a borderlands area for both the upper and lower South, attracted few Jews and no permanent Jewish settlement until much later.

As southern civilization was transported across the mountains, the two incipient sectional patterns were transported with it. West Virginia (then still part of Virginia), Kentucky, and Tennessee (the border South) were westward extensions of the upper South. The Jews arrived relatively late, after permanent settlement was well under way in all three states. Jewish communities were not organized in any of the three until the mid-nineteenth century, when they were established by a "mixed multitude" of American-born Jews, German and Polish immigrants, and some English Jews. The lower South was extended to include the Deep South of Alabama, Mississippi, and Louisiana. These three states of the Old Southwest, like their counterparts of the Old Northwest, were originally settled by Jewish traders while the regions were still under French occupation—this despite the Black Code of 1724, which prohibited Jewish settlement in French Louisiana. Unlike their northern sisters, all three had informal but functioning Jewish communities by the end of the eighteenth century, but the first congregations in each were not established until approximately a generation later. The Sephardic influence was strong in all three states, where it persisted for some time. Florida, a world unto itself in other respects as well, displays its own settlement pattern, a mixture of early southern and later northern migrations.

Straddling both the South and the West is the next tier of southern states: Arkansas, Missouri, Oklahoma, and Texas. If there were Jews in Arkansas in 1819, as some records indicate, then all four states can claim Jews among their preterritorial pioneers. In any case, communities were organized in each about a decade after statehood, relatively sooner than in the southern states to the immediate east. Oklahoma was the last state settled by Jews, most of whom came from Arkansas and Missouri.

Until the great influx of Jews into Florida as a result of the metropolitan-technological frontier, the South had a sparse Jewish population. This was at least partly because the conditions of the rural-land frontier persisted in the southern states for a long time and the urban-industrial frontier never really became rooted until after World War II, so that opportunities for Jews were relatively limited. Jews could become crossroads merchants or modest entrepreneurs in the area's relatively small cities, but little else—and that was not enough to attract them. Moreover, this nonurban environment was culturally Christian to a far greater degree than any other in the United States. The homogeneity of the population led to the dominance of Baptists or Methodists in county after county to a degree that approximates the domination of Catholics in Ireland. Finally, the segregationist character of the South made the Jews uncomfortable, even though Jews, being white, were accepted in ways that they were not in many parts of the Northeast. Still, during the anti-Semitic years several infamous incidents occurred in the Southeast, particularly in the lower South, fanned by rabble-rousing politicians, culminating in the Georgia lynching of Leo Frank, one of the two recorded blood-libel cases in the United States.

In sum, the Jews were accepted but were not really at home. Southern Jews, like other southerners (including southern blacks), tended to develop a deep love and affection for their region, but they also remained far more conscious of being Jews despite conditions that otherwise would have promoted assimilation—small numbers, scattered populations, lack of Jewish education or institutions—because they were so clearly aware of not being part of white Protestant society. As a result, Jews built their religious institutions in a manner parallel to southern churches and linked themselves with those institutions. The pressure from the general community caused most of them to affiliate with the local synagogue or temple, so that they would be respectable in gentile eyes, as "solid churchgoing folk."

At the same time, in so highly Protestant an environment, in which religion was a matter of worship services (not simply on Sunday, but during the week as well), the Jews too centered their activities around the synagogue; since there was little incentive to, Jews did not develop other institutions (except in the larger cities), or at least did so to a much

TABLE 6 EARLY JEWISH SETTLEMENT BY STATE*

State	First Individual		First Organized Community			
	Date	Origin	Date	Name	Origin	Remarks
Alabama	1785	Sephardic(?)	1841	Mobile	mixed Sephardic	Jews first settled in Mobile area under French in early 18th century
Alaska	1855	German(?)	1904	Fairbanks	mixed German(?)	First settlement dissipated after Klondike gold rush. Second developed in Anchorage after World War II.
Arizona	1855	German	1881	Tombstone	German	German Jewish pioneers did not form stable communities though they did have quasi-communal life
Arkansas	1830	English	1845	Little Rock	mixed German	Jews spread over entire state in 1840s; individual Jews may have settled earlier
California	1837	American	1849	San Francisco	mixed German	German, American, English, and Russian Jews covered state during gold rush
Colorado	1859	German	1859	Denver	German	German Jews pioneered mining frontier; East European Jews pioneered agricultural frontier
Connecticut	1659	Sephardic(?)	1840	New Haven	German	individual Sephardic Jews settled and assimilated; permanent community created by German Jews
Delaware	1655	Sephardic	1881	Wilmington	East European	community existed briefly in early 19th century; German Jews settled in 1850s, community organized later
Florida	1819	Sephardic	c. 1850	Jacksonville	mixed German	Sephardic, French, English, and American Jews pioneered; German Jews led establishment of community
Georgia	1733	Sephardic	1733	Savannah	Sephardic	congregation organized 1774
Hawaii	INSUFFICIENT DATA		1901	Honolulu(?)	mixed German(?)	
Idaho	c. 1861	German	1895	Boise	German	German Jews pioneered mining frontier; Jews left when it passed
Illinois	1793	American	1845	Chicago	German	French Jews lived in Illinois in 1775; American Jews came from South, Germans came from North
Indiana	1814	American	1848	Fort Wayne	German	American and English Jews came from South, Germans came from North
Iowa	1833	French	1855	Keokuk	German	German and Polish Jews shared in pioneering with other groups

*Sources: Abraham J. Karp, ed., *Jewish Experience in America,* 5 vols. (New York: Ktav, 1969); Jacob R. Marcus, *Early American Jewry,* 2 vols. (Philadelphia: Jewish Publication Society, 1952); idem, "Trailblazers of the Trans-Mississippi West," *American Jewish Archives* 8, no. 2 (October 1956); *Encyclopedia Judaica.*

TABLE 6 (*continued*)

| State | First Individual | | First Organized Community | | | |
	Date	Origin	Date	Name	Origin	Remarks
Kansas	1854	German	1855	Leavenworth	German	German Jews came in with the northern influx in 1855 when the state first settled
Kentucky	1802	English	c. 1830	Louisville	mixed German	first Jews assimilated; first nonassimilating Jew came in 1827
Louisiana	1719	French	c. 1805	New Orleans	mixed Sephardic	Jews first came with French; individuals remained intermittently; first congregation in 1828
Maine	c. 1775	German	c. 1880	Portland	East European	first Jews assimilated; there was a German Jewish community in Bangor 1845–55
Maryland	1656	Sephardic	1781	Baltimore	mixed Sephardic	first Jews may have come in 1634; by 1780s non-Sephardic Jews predominated under Sephardic ritual
Massachusetts	1648	Sephardic	1842	Boston	mixed German	a quasi-community existed after 1725 in Boston; formal community established by German Jews
Michigan	1761	English	1840	Ann Arbor	mixed German	first Jews came via Canada; German Jews came up from other states to establish communities
Minnesota	1849	German	1855	Saint Paul	German	Jews came with first pioneers and were the third or fourth religious group to organize in the territory
Mississippi	1718	French	1800	Natchez	mixed Sephardic	individual Jews came under French; community established under Americans; first congregation in 1840
Missouri	1787	Polish(?)	1835	Saint Louis	German	first organized Jewish life developed by German Jews
Montana	1862	German	1864	Virginia City	German	Jews pioneered mining frontier and left when it passed
Nebraska	1855	German	1868	Omaha	German	German Jews came with first pioneers
Nevada	1859	German	1862	Virginia City	German	Jews pioneered mining frontier and left when it passed
New Hampshire	1643	Sephardic(?)	1885	Manchester	East European	first Jews assimilated; community established by East Europeans
New Jersey	1702	Sephardic	1847	Paterson	mixed German	first Jews scattered trades; settlement came with German wave
New Mexico	1846	German	1882	Albuquerque	German	Marranos in New Mexico in 17th century; quasi-community in Santa Fe after 1850
New York	1654	Sephardic	1654	New York	Sephardic	seaboard settled long before upstate, which was settled by Germans after 1830

TABLE 6 *(continued)*

| | First Individual | | First Organized Community | | | |
State	Date	Origin	Date	Name	Origin	Remarks
North Carolina	1740	German(?)	1867	Wilmington	German	bypassed by most Jews; Wilmington settlement developed before Civil War
North Dakota	1871	German	1882	Colray	German	Jews came with railroads as pioneer merchants and farmers in colonies
Ohio	1817	English	1822	Cincinnati	mixed English	"mother state" of the Jewish West; southern communities founded by English Jews, northern by German
Oklahoma	c. 1865	American	1887	Ardmore	mixed German	Arkansas Jews traded in Indian Territory after 1840; first congregation organized in 1899
Oregon	1849	German	1856	Jacksonville	German	German Jews came with gold rush and commercial boom in Portland; many came up from California
Pennsylvania	1681	Sephardic	1738	Philadelphia	mixed Ashkenazic	eastern part of state settled considerably before western part; heterogeneous from outset
Rhode Island	1658	Sephardic	1677	Newport	Sephardic	atypical New England; first community died after Revolution, revived by Germans and East Europeans 1850–83
South Carolina	1695	Sephardic	1741	Charleston	Sephardic	major Jewish community in Revolutionary era; declining in importance since
South Dakota	c. 1865	German	c. 1875	Deadwood	German	Jews came with mining frontier in West and as settlers in East
Tennessee	1838	German	1847	Memphis	mixed German	Jews came very late, mostly up Mississippi River
Texas	1821	English	1850	Houston	mixed German	individual Jews active in American settlement of Texas and war for Texas, community came later
Utah	1854	German	1864	Salt Lake City	German	Jewish community established to supply gold hunters
Vermont	1835	English	1880	Burlington	mixed German	Jewish traders worked in the area in late 18th century
Virginia	c. 1655	Sephardic	1789	Richmond	mixed Sephardic	hispanicized German and Polish Jews predominated by time community was organized
Washington	c. 1853	German	1859	Seattle	German	Jews came up from San Francisco before coming overland
West Virginia	c. 1835	German	1849	Wheeling	German	Jews came as part of Jewish settlement in the Ohio River valley
Wisconsin	1794	English	1847	Milwaukee	German	first Jews came as fur traders from Canada; permanent settlement by Jews from U.S.
Wyoming	1862	German	1875	Cheyenne	German	Jews came as pioneer businessmen with the Union Pacific railroad

TABLE 7 NUMBER OF ORGANIZED JEWISH COMMUNITIES BY STATE, 1860, 1960, 1973* (in order of rank)

No.	1860	1960	1973
90		New Jersey, Pennsylvania	
83		New York	
71			Pennsylvania (79)[b]
65			New York
38		Massachusetts	
36			California, Massachusetts
33		Texas	
31		California	Connecticut (42)
30		Connecticut	New Jersey (86)
28			Ohio
27		Ohio	
26			Texas (34)
23	Pennsylvania		
22			Florida
21		Florida	
20			
19		Illinois	Illinois (23)
18		Virginia	
17		Michigan, Wisconsin	Michigan
16		Indiana	Virginia (18), Wisconsin
15	New York	North Carolina	Indiana, North Carolina
14			
13		West Virginia	
12		Iowa	
11	California	Alabama, Maryland, Mississippi	Alabama (13), Georgia, Iowa
10	Louisiana	South Carolina	Maryland (13), West Virginia
9	Indiana, Ohio	Georgia, Louisiana	Mississippi
8	Mississippi	Maine, Minnesota	Arkansas (19), New Hampshire
7	New Jersey	Arkansas, Missouri, New Hampshire	Tennessee (9), Louisiana, Maine, Minnesota, Missouri, South Carolina
6	Georgia, Iowa	Kentucky, Tennessee	
5		Oklahoma, Vermont	Kentucky
4	Kentucky, Maryland, Tennessee, Virginia	New Mexico, Rhode Island, Washington	Washington (5), Oklahoma, Oregon, Vermont
3	Alabama, Connecticut, Illinois, Kansas, Michigan, Texas, Wisconsin	Colorado, Delaware, Oregon	Colorado, New Mexico
2	Massachusetts, Missouri, New Hampshire, Rhode Island, South Carolina	Arizona, Kansas, Montana, Nebraska, Nevada, North Dakota, Utah	Alaska, Arizona, Kansas, Nebraska, Nevada, North Dakota, Utah
1	Colorado, Minnesota, Oregon, Utah, West Virginia,[a] Florida	Alaska, Hawaii, Idaho, South Dakota, Wyoming	Delaware, Hawaii, Idaho, Montana, Rhode Island, South Dakota, Wyoming
0	Delaware, Maine, North Carolina, Vermont, Arkansas		

[a]Part of Virginia in 1860.

[b]Figures in parentheses indicate number of communities calculated on same basis as 1860 and 1960 without considering consolidations.

*Sources: 1860: *Statistical Report of the Jewish Congregations of the United States to the Board of Delegates of American Israelites*; 1960 and 1973: *American Jewish Year Book*.

TABLE 8   ORGANIZED JEWISH COMMUNITIES BY SPHERE AND
SECTION AND PERCENT OF JEWISH POPULATION, 1860, 1960,
1978

Sphere and Section	1860	1960	1978	% of Total Jewish Population	
				1973	1978
Greater Northeast	81	454	360	70.2	68.6
New England	9	92	87		
Middle Atlantic	45	266	178		
Great Lakes	27	96	95		
Greater South	52	192	165	15.4	15.2
upper South	17	69	53		
lower South	30	71	60		
western South	5	52	52		
Greater West	24	82	87	14.4	16.2
Northwest	12	41	30		
Far West	12	41	57		
United States Total	157	728	612	100	100

lesser extent than in other parts of the country. It was only with the settlement of northern Jews in selected southern centers that Jewish institutions began to multiply. This, too, was mainly as a result of the metropolitan-technological frontier.

This pattern was somewhat modified in the western South, where there was a greater sprinkling of Irish and Germans to leaven the native white population. The western South was like the rest of the South, only more pluralistic and influenced by the West to a greater extent. The Jews of the western South also tended to develop associations around their synagogues rather than communities, but they also developed other fraternal and social-welfare institutions to a somewhat greater extent than their brethren east of the Mississippi—again, in the manner of the trans-Mississippi West.

THE GEOGRAPHY OF ORGANIZED JEWISH LIFE[9]

The regional distribution of American Jewry is perhaps best illustrated by the sectional pattern of organized Jewish settlement in the United States. The pattern, which was essentially established in the past century by the Central European Jews, has remained remarkably the same over the intervening years even as the number and size of the communities increased. In the following three tables the pattern of 1860 (when the outline first became clear) is contrasted with those of 1960 (the midpoint of the postwar generation) and 1973 (the most recent data available and the year that marks the beginning of the end of the postwar generation). There is at least one organized Jewish community in every state of the Union, although the total number of separately reckoned communities has declined since 1960. In part this reflects the processes of community organization of the second half of the postwar generation: small single-congregation "communities" adjacent to one another have been coming together to create umbrella federations to serve their common needs (see Chapter 5) and thus have become, in effect, parts of larger local communities. This is particularly true in the Northeast and explains the drastic decline in the number of communities in the Middle Atlantic states. In some regions, the South and West particularly, it is a reflection of the continuing decline of small-town Jewry. Even if Jews can still be found in all corners of small-town America, fewer small towns can sustain organized Jewish life. Their synagogues close down and those Jews who wish to maintain contact with other Jews on an organized basis must affiliate with the institutions in the nearest large city.[10]

The greater Northeast has always contained the majority of the organized Jewish communities in the United States. Since 1860 its share has been somewhat more than half the total. The Middle Atlantic states dominate the sphere, with approximately 30 percent of the United States total in 1860, approximately 35 percent in 1960, and by 1973 below 30 percent. Virtually every city of any size had some form of organized Jewish life, a phenomenon that was further intensified by the growing suburbanization. By 1960 New Jersey had joined New York and Pennsylvania in heading the list of states, a lead reduced in 1973 only as a result of the combination of suburbs into regional federations. The Great Lakes states and New England fall far below their Middle Atlantic counterparts, but both still remain more densely covered than almost all other sections. Moreover, in both areas the number of organized communities has remained essentially constant since 1960, a reflection of their particular settlement patterns. In the former, the free-standing character of the section's cities makes consolidation almost impossible even where regional cooperation is encouraged. In New England the general pattern of independent towns also tends to encourage separate local Jewish communities, even in densely settled areas.

The pattern of Jewish settlement in the South also reflects the pattern of settlement indigenous to that sphere. Rather than concentrating in a few large centers, southern Jewry spread out and organized communities in a large number of medium-sized cities. This pattern was already apparent in 1860, particularly in the lower South. The persistent uniformity in the number of organized Jewish communities in each southern state, especially in relation to the South's total Jewish population, illustrates this point dramatically. By 1960 the western South was more differentiated from the rest of the South than it had been one hundred years earlier. Texas was already showing signs of becoming a special case and the other states had come to resemble more closely their sisters in the trans-Mississippi West. Between 1960 and 1973 there was a drastic drop in the number of organized communities in the South, particularly in the lower South, reflecting the continual decline of Jewish life in the crossroads settlements of that section and the concentration of Jews in the burgeoning cities produced by the postwar southern boom.

The greater part of the West was still unsettled in 1860, but where settlement had begun, the sectional patterns were already apparent. California had the third largest number of organized Jewish communities in the country (a rank it retained in 1973) and was veering sharply away from its sister states of the West as a center of Jewish life. By 1960 the patterns that had emerged were not appreciably different from those of 1860. The greater West is the only sphere to have gained in number of organized communities between 1960 and 1973, a sign of the continued attractiveness of the Far West to migrating American Jews. Many of those Jews came from the Northwest, a region of out-migration generally. As a Montana congressmen once observed: "The rural-urban migration in Montana is from rural Montana to Los Angeles." This is certainly the case as far as the Jews are concerned.

INTEGRATION AND DISCRIMINATION[11]

Despite the generally favorable climate that Jews have enjoyed in the United States, anti-Semitism in various forms has not been absent from the American Jewish experience. Its strongest manifestations have been in the form of social and economic discrimination. After the colonial era —the period between 1776 and 1815—with few exceptions, restrictions on Jewish civil and political rights were lifted; an "era of good feeling" ensued, which lasted until the 1870s. In that period social discrimination against the Jews on the part of the wealthier classes began to appear, particularly in the New York metropolitan area. Up to that time the Jews who were interested and able to do so were admitted to the best clubs, were members of integrated Masonic lodges, and took their vacations at the best resorts; but they were soon forced to found their own clubs and lodges and to seek their ease at resorts of lower prestige. During the 1880s the blight of social discrimination spread to the Middle Atlantic states and even penetrated New England, the upper South, and the Middle West at a few points. After the first stage of its expansion, this social discrimination was contained in the East until the second decade of the twentieth century. Only after 1910 did summer resorts in the Middle West and Far West show evidence of anti-Jewish discrimination, with the *Chicago Tribune* beginning to publish "gentile only" advertisements in 1913.

Colleges, too, began to discriminate, as the bright young Jews of the New York area starting leaving home in search of an education. Here again the Middle Atlantic schools were the most discriminatory, followed by those of New England. Although the private colleges of the Middle West took on exclusionary patterns, the predominance of public universities softened the extent of these practices. The West was much freer in this regard, while the South manifested very little discrimination at all. The West was almost as free of social discrimination as the South and included little in the way of religious antagonism. In the North the Great Lakes area was more discriminatory than the Far West but considerably less so than the northeastern seaboard, where discrimination centered upon New York City.

The Jews had the most difficulty achieving equality in the North (where, nevertheless, as a group they have become the most active of all in the political and civic life of the region). In both the South and West the Jews have had considerably less trouble in achieving and preserving social equality. Once equality was achieved in the South the Jews flourished as participants in their communities until the rise of populist-oriented racism in the twentieth century. In the West, the most homogeneous part of the country, the Jews have achieved less overall prominence than in the South, but have consistently maintained their positions in public life. Jewish leadership on the various American frontiers has been most pronounced in the West, somewhat less so in the South, and least in the North. Discrimination against the Jews, both social and religious, has operated in just the reverse pattern.

Social discrimination was almost everywhere accompanied by exclusion from certain occupations, a condition that persisted until the end of World War II, when the war-generated revulsion to racist and anti-Semitic views opened the door to a great equalization in American society. The occupational barriers were the first to fall, and they disappeared one by one during the 1950s. The final barriers, those in banking and the highest levels of university administration, began to collapse by the late 1960s. Jews now have virtually unrestricted access to university presidencies, and even the banking fraternity is beginning to change its policies. Formal and overt social discrimination began to crumble at the same time. Residential segregation and restricted resorts were the first to go, helped along by state and later federal legislation prohibiting such actions, but the so-called five o'clock shadow that falls on Jews and non-Jews after working hours, ushering in separate socializing, still remains in effect, though this too is changing, especially in the West.

It seems clear that social and economic discrimination, coming when they did, had an important effect on the internal organization of Jewish life in the United States. Jews who wished to dissociate themselves from the Jewish community, in a headlong rush in integrate into American society, found themselves forced to face up to their Jewishness and to create alternate institutions to take care of their individual needs and ambitions. Not only were Jewish hospitals created in large numbers during that period to accommodate Jewish patients and doctors, but the whole range of communal and welfare activities assumed a new importance, as even assimilated Jews came to recognize that they had to "take care of their own." The Jewish federation movement received a great impetus from that recognition, as well as from the fact of discrimination. At first this was reflected in the very un-Jewish quality of most of the federations' activities. It remained for a later generation to do battle with that approach and begin to transform the federations and their constituent institutions into truly Jewish instruments. But that generation would never have had the chance had it not been for the impetus provided at an earlier time, in large measure by the exclusionary practices of the larger society.

By the same token, the breakdown of the barriers of discrimination has not been an unmixed blessing for Jews. As Jews have found more doors open to them, those who have wished to move away from Jewish life have found it easier to do so. No one would sacrifice that freedom for involun-

tary restraints, even of the relatively benevolent kind of the period between 1877 and 1947, but it is also true that many Jews who could lean
in either direction, depending upon the environment in which they find
themselves, have been tilting outward rather than inward. The high
intermarriage rate represents only the tip of the iceberg in this regard.
Social integration cannot help but weaken the possibilities for living
according to a Jewish rhythm, while the prizes to be gained from economic integration usually go to those Jews who are least Jewish in their
way of life (even though most Jews who achieve prominent positions still
find it useful to maintain formal ties with the Jewish community to show
the non-Jewish world that they, too, belong somewhere).

American Jews are just now reaching the point where they must face
up to the problems of maintaining Jewish life in a truly voluntaristic and
open society, in which no significant doors are closed to Jews. It is a task
for which Jews have had little prior experience.

The Community in Its Environment

The American Jewish community must function within three environments that immediately impinge upon its consciousness and determine its affairs: American civilization, with its special features; world Jewry, particularly Israel; and contemporary technology, with its material and spiritual consequences. Each of these, with its ramifications, has a decided impact on all that American Jews do as Jews.

AMERICAN INDIVIDUALISM AND PATTERNS OF PARTICIPATION

The essentially individualistic character of American society has its effects on the organization of the American Jewish community. The nature of American society requires that Jews relate to it as individuals.[1] Jews in the United States are not considered to be members of a corporate group, as is true in some countries, because Americans do not recognize such claims. Consequently, no corporate group can make any claim upon them. Moreover, group affiliation in American society is voluntary, in the fullest sense of the word. There is an absolute minimum of compulsion to be affiliated, to stay affiliated, or, for that matter, to recognize any ties with a particular group. Strictly speaking, in American society there is no greater compulsion to associate with a particular religious or ethnic group than there is to join a camera club or a fraternal lodge, although in most parts of the country the first two kinds of association are considered likely to be longer lasting than the latter. While there are regional differences in the kinds of associationalism considered acceptable, the trend in the United States as a whole is toward even greater voluntarism and freedom of association than ever before.

The patterns of participation in American Jewish life reflect this combination of individualism and voluntarism. In a free society the Jewish community cannot live within fixed boundaries confining all (or virtually all) of those born Jews and perforce encouraging them to organize to meet their communal needs. Increasingly, American Jews, if they profess any Jewish commitment at all, feel that they are Jews by choice rather than simply by birth. The organic tie continues to undergird the fact of choice, but birth alone is no longer sufficient to keep Jews within the fold. No one is more conscious of this than the Jews themselves. As a result, the Jewish community has been transformed into what can be described as a series of uneven concentric circles, radiating outward from a hard core of committed Jews toward areas of vague Jewishness on the fringes (see Figure 1).

The hard core of the American Jewish community—one might label them Integral Jews—consists of those whose Jewishness is a full-time concern, the central factor of their lives, whether expressed in traditionally religious terms or through some variety of ethnic nationalism or an intensive involvement in Jewish affairs. For them, every day is lived by a substantially Jewish rhythm. They and their families tend to be closely linked to one another through shared Jewish interests and feelings, and they tend to associate with others of similar concern. Their Jewishness is an intergenerational affair. In short, they live, in one way or another, fully Jewish lives. Perhaps 5 percent of the Jewish population of the United States falls into this category, with the figure possibly reaching as high as 8 percent (300,000–500,000 Jews).[2]

Surrounding this hard core is a second group—the Participants— consisting of Jews who take part in Jewish life in a regular way and are considered to be much more than casually active in Jewish affairs, but to whom living Jewishly is not a full-time matter and whose rhythm of life is essentially that of the larger society. It might be said that for them Jewishness is a major *avocational* interest. They are likely to be officers of Jewish organizations, regular participants in adult Jewish-education programs of various kinds, active fund raisers for Israel, and even regular synagogue attenders. Many members of the "Jewish civil service"—

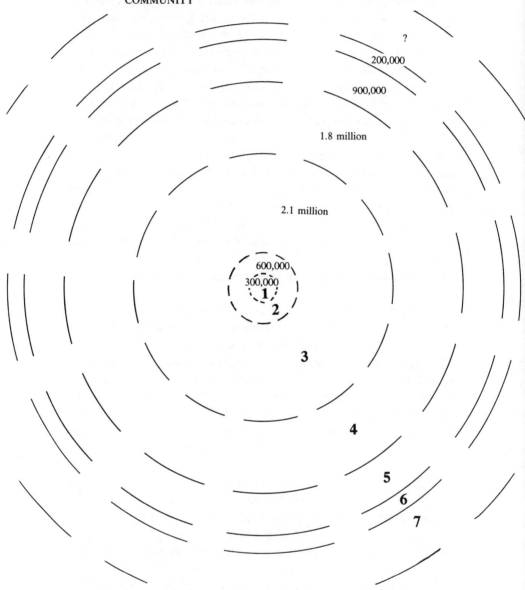

FIGURE 1 "SHAPE" OF PARTICIPATION IN AMERICAN JEWISH COMMUNITY

?

200,000

900,000

1.8 million

2.1 million

600,000

300,000

1

2

3

4

5

6

7

1. Integral Jews (living according to a Jewish rhythm)
2. Participants (involved in Jewish life on a regular basis)
3. Associated Jews (affiliated with Jewish institutions in some concrete way)
4. Contributors and Consumers (giving money and/or utilizing the services of Jewish institutions from time to time)
5. Peripherals (recognizably Jewish in some way but completely uninvolved in Jewish life)
6. Repudiators (seeking to deny or repudiate their Jewishness)
7. Quasi-Jews (Jewish status unclear as a result of intermarriage or assimilation in some other form)

professionals employed by the various Jewish agencies—fall into this category; they spend their days working in a Jewish capacity, but their nonprofessional lives are not integrally Jewish. Ten to 12 percent (600,000–700,000) is a fair estimate of the percentage of such Jews in the United States today.[3]

Surrounding the participants is a third group—the Associated Jews—which consists of those who are affiliated with Jewish institutions or organizations in some concrete way but are not particularly active in them. This category includes synagogue members whose affiliation does not involve them much beyond the use of synagogue facilities for the Jewish rites of passage or for High Holy Day services, and members of some of the mass-based Jewish organizations, such as Hadassah and B'nai B'rith, or any of the other charitable groups that are identifiably Jewish and whose membership reflects primarily private social interests rather than a concern for the public purposes of Jewish life. This is a fairly large category because it includes all those who instinctively recognize the necessity for some kind of associational commitment to Jewish life, even if it is only for the sake of maintaining a proper front before the non-Jewish community. One might estimate that it includes approximately 30 to 35 percent (around 2 million) of the country's Jewish population.[4]

Beyond that circle is a fourth—Contributors and Consumers—consisting of Jews who give money to Jewish causes from time to time and periodically utilize the services of Jewish institutions (perhaps even as members), for marriage, burial, bar mitzvah, and the like. In other words, they clearly identify as Jews, but are minimally associated with the Jewish community as such.[5] Perhaps 25 to 30 percent of all American Jews (1.5 to 1.8 million) fall into this category, many of whom have such limited incomes that they cannot develop more formal or lasting Jewish attachments in a context that makes financial expenditure a binding factor in the associational process.

Beyond the circle of Contributors and Consumers there is a circle of Jews who are recognizably Jewish in some way but completely uninvolved in Jewish life. We might call them Peripherals. While they may be married to Jewish partners and their children are unquestionably of Jewish descent, they have no desire even to utilize Jewish institutions for the rites of passage and insufficient interest even in such Jewish causes as Israel to contribute money. Perhaps 15 percent of American Jewry falls into this category.

A sixth category—Repudiators—consists of Jews who actively deny their Jewishness. At one time a large group, it has undergone a considerable decline; few of those who care are hostile and few who do not care feel the need to react hostilely to the fact of their Jewish origins. There are probably less than 5 percent in this category today.[6]

Finally, there is an unknown number of what we may call Quasi-Jews, those who are neither inside the Jewish community nor entirely out of it. They are people who have intermarried but have not lost their own personal Jewish label, or who have otherwise assimilated to a point where the fact of their Jewish birth is incidental in every respect. We have no firm knowledge of how many such people there are in the country, but can assume that between 5 and 10 percent of the known American Jewish population falls into this category, plus a number who are simply not reckoned in the conventional figures.[7]

The boundaries between these categories as well as their membership are quite fluid (as Figure 1 indicates by separating the categories with broken, rather than solid, lines). There is considerable movement in and out of all of the seven categories, though of course there is more movement along the edges of each than across separated circles. Thus Jews in group two (Participants) are more likely to move into the hard core or out into more casual membership than to drop out altogether, while the Peripherals may move into the Quasi-Jews category with some ease or under other circumstances will be easily brought into the category of Contributors and Consumers.

What this means for communal organization is that the community is built on a fluid, if not an eroding, base, with a high degree of self-selection involved in determining who is even potentially active, much less a leader or decision maker. No more than one-fourth of the Jewish population falls into the potentially active category, and by no means all of them define their Jewish concerns as public ones. For many—even those in the hard core (Hasidic Jews, for example)—the concerns of the Jewish *community* are not their concerns. They are interested in leading private lives that are intensely Jewish, but do not seek to channel their Jewishness into the realm of public affairs.

In times of crisis there will be a general movement of the circles. Thus the Six-Day War of 1967 probably increased the extent and intensity of Jewish identification in all the circles, including Repudiators, but only relative to the prior stance of the individuals involved. The Participants may have become totally preoccupied with Jewish affairs during the period of the crisis and the Peripherals may have become Contributors for the moment, but it is unlikely that Peripherals became Participants (of course we are speaking here about aggregates, not isolated cases).

There is some evidence that significant shifts are taking place in the relationship of the several circles to one another. On one hand, persons in the inner circles are closing ranks and becoming more intensively Jewish, while those in the outer circles are drifting further away from Jewish life. It is quite likely that a great gap is developing somewhere between circles two and three, a gap that is paralleled by an even greater division between circles four and five.

Immediately after the Six-Day War it was widely suggested that many Jews had "come out of the woodwork" in response to the apparent threat to Israel's survival. In fact, such research as was conducted on the Jewish response to the war indicated that even those Jews whose responses were unexpected were, for the most part, already within the third or fourth circles. That is, they were likely to be synagogue members, though very passive ones, or small contributors to the annual Israel fund-raising drives. The war transformed their passive or low-level participation into active and perhaps high-level giving, but (with relatively few exceptions) did not affect people who had never been involved before. Obviously the exceptions are more dramatic and interesting; nor does it lessen their importance to point out that they were the exceptions rather than the rule, even in a period of overwhelming American Jewish response. (This seems to have been true not only in the U.S. but also in the United Kingdom and Australia.)

The initial evidence from the Yom Kippur War of 1973 indicates that, despite all the visible excitement of the response by large segments of the American Jewish community, the spreading apart of the circles increased. It may be that some people who inhabited the outer circles were pulled into the inner circles by the crisis, but many people in the outer circles were propelled toward greater separation from the main body of the Jewish people by simply not reacting to the occasion. Those whose concern for Israel had been sharpened in the period between 1967 and 1973 became more concerned than ever before. On the other hand, those who had shown no concern evinced a greater degree of uninterest: the years had brought them more fully into the American mainstream and taken them further away from Jewish concerns, even at the survival level.

It has been estimated that perhaps as many as one-third of American Jewry were not caught up by the October crisis of 1973. If that is indeed so, it means that American Jewry stands to lose a significant share of its total population, a development that in turn will not only shift the bases of Jewish communal life in the United States, but even erode them. At the same time, there seems to be almost no question that within the inner circles the intensity of Jewish feeling increased as a result of the Yom Kippur War, and the willingness of Jews to express themselves openly as Jews became even more apparent.*

In a free and open society the drift away from Jewish life is not surprising. Indeed, the way it occurs—so casually and without deliberate intent, so unlinked to ideology, and certainly not to any ideology of assimilationism—is both a reflection on the character of American society and the reason why the model of concentric circles is the most appropriate for understanding the social structure of American Jewry. Moreover, the American Jewish model is spreading to other Jewish communities in the Diaspora, as they too find themselves in increasingly open societies that welcome the talents of Jews without holding their Jewishness against them.

The result is a community that is far different from one which exists within boundaries, the kind characterized by the state of Israel and, in the past, by the Jewish ghettos. It has become common knowledge that many of the Jews in Israel are no more knowledgeable or serious about their Judaism than those in the United States. Nevertheless, their Jewishness is unquestionably a functional element in their lives, one to which they must constantly respond. That is because they live in a Jewish state and in a Jewish society that is also a civil society, where duly constituted Jewish authorities exercise power, even coercive power, to require actions on the part of citizens directed toward serving what virtually all would agree to be Jewish purposes, if only the elemental one of Jewish survival. Even the most "assimilated" Jew in Israel must serve in the Israeli army, if he or she is eligible by virtue of age and fitness, and thus take on a task of immediate service to the Jewish people. Every wage earner in Israel, citizen or not, must pay taxes, some of which go to the support of institutions with clearly Jewish purposes, including Jewish religious purposes. This is all characteristic of a bounded society.

What characterizes a society composed of concentric circles is precisely the fact that there are no boundaries; what holds people within it is the pull of its central core, particularly as its outer edges become

*For a fuller discussion of American Jewry's response to the Yom Kippur War, see Appendix A.

increasingly blurred. Perhaps the most appropriate image for this is a magnet, able to attract iron particles that come within its magnetic field. This is the condition of American Jewry and, increasingly, of all Diaspora Jewry: a magnet at the core pulls those who contain within them the iron filings of Judaism closer to the center, more or less according to the degree of their iron (i.e., Jewish) content.

The question remains: what constitutes the magnet at the core? Prior to emancipation it was clearly the Jewish system of law, practice, and belief. Since emancipation the issue has become less clear (which is why the magnetic attraction has weakened). But whatever the magnet happens to be, it has to do with something that is authentically and totally Jewish. In this respect the American Jewish community, no matter how well acculturated to the American environment, relies upon the world Jewish environment, that which is continually and unremittingly Jewish, regardless of time or place.

THE WORLD JEWISH ENVIRONMENT

Three basic elements together compose the world Jewish environment: Judaism, the state of Israel, and world Jewry. Within this triad can be found the traditional triad of God, Torah, and Israel, a formulation that many would find preferable, but is perhaps less accurate from the perspective of contemporary Jews than the formulation suggested here.

The definition of a Jew as one who practices Judaism rather than one who lives a Jewish life is not indigenously Jewish. Rather, it was developed to explain Jews to the gentile world on the latter's terms; it first appears in the Hellenistic era, when it was necessary to somehow encompass Jewish ideas within a Greek framework. It was used, rarely, during the Middle Ages, and it did not acquire its present popularity until the modern era, when once again Jews began to define themselves and their way of life primarily in the religious terms of the Western world—this time the modern Christian West.

Given the modern emphasis on the Jews as a religious group, Judaism is generally conceived to be synonymous with the Jewish religion. Moreover, with relatively few exceptions Judaism is defined among American Jews in the way moderns have redefined the Jewish religion, namely, as a system of beliefs more than practices, and further, beliefs that are not out of harmony with the modern temper. Thus most American Jews will categorically affirm that Judaism does not include a belief in life after death, a statement that is quite problematic when one reviews the whole history of Jewish belief. Similarly, beliefs that were at one time almost universal among Jews, such as the coming of the Messiah, have simply been excluded from Judaism by most American Jews.

In any case it is difficult to determine precisely what beliefs were universal to Judaism; it is considerably easier to determine what practices were accepted by all Jews as part of being Jewish. Today even the latter dimension does not serve as a unifying point in the same way that common practice did in the past. Nevertheless there are certain common elements which Jews who consider themselves Jews in the United States accept as being part and parcel of Judaism: a certain calendar, no matter how observed; recognition of a common language and order of prayer, if only commemoratively; certain rites of passage, even though sometimes redefined; a certain belief in the God of Israel, however vague; and a certain commitment to Torah, no matter how reinterpreted.

The overwhelming majority of American Jews, by all accounts, claim to believe in a "Jewish" notion of God, that is, neither Jesus nor Mohammed nor any non-Jewish messiah or prophet figures in the belief, even in a denatured way. If they think about it at all, most Jews also accept some notion of God's covenant with the Jewish people (often interpreted metaphorically or symbolically), through which the Jewish people are conceived to have received the Torah along with a certain "chosenness." (To be sure, there are wide divergencies in what the implications of both the Covenant and chosenness are.) Finally, most American Jews who are concerned about being Jewish accept the Torah as an obligatory teaching for Jews. While few see in the Torah the system of commandments and regulations know as "halakhic Judaism," and most think of it as primarily an ethical teaching, nevertheless virtually all Jews do concede that Jews are obligated in some fashion to recognize the Sabbath, the holy days, and the festivals. Increasingly, American Jews in their collective capacity acknowledge the primacy of the dietary laws (public Jewish gatherings, for instance, are served by kosher caterers, even though 90 percent or more of those in attendance do not personally observe kashruth). There is also a growing awareness that a "good Jew" celebrates and maintains the rites of Jewish passage, from circumcision to burial in a Jewish cemetery. This, then, is Judaism for American Jews, and it remains the enduring element at the core of the concentric circles.

While Judaism provides the underlying Jewish commitment for American Jews, Israel has become the crucial operative element in shaping organized Jewish life today. To say this is not to suggest that Israel, or concern for Israel, is responsible for the panoply of American Jewish organizations in existence today: the overwhelming majority of American Jewish organizations and institutions are products of the internal Jewish impulses of American Jews. Certainly the synagogues are direct manifestations of American Jewry's conceptions of Judaism, and much the same can be said for the social-welfare and educational institutions as well. Nor do these institutions require the existence of Israel or any Israel-oriented purpose to define their central tasks, which are extensions of tasks undertaken by the organized Jewish community for centuries, if not millennia.

Israel is the crucial operative factor because it is the force that most excites Jews today in the United States as in other Diaspora communities, and best serves as a focus for Jewish aspirations in a period of weakened religious faith and practice. Ever since the decline of religion as a unifying force in the modern era, various generations of Jews have sought other rallying points. From the period of the great eighteenth-century revolutions in thought (whose chief Jewish spokesman was Moses Mendelssohn) until the end of World War II, Jews found that symbolic unifying force in a common secular liberalism. Virtually all Jews, particularly those at the cutting edge of Jewish life, sought to become linked to the increasingly secular societies around them. Whether they sought secularization as individual assimilationists or as part of a Jewish collectivity, the quest was much the same. Thus this kind of liberalism could bind together the Orthodox Jewish followers of Samson Raphael Hirsch, antireligious Jewish Bundists, Reform Jews who emphasized God and religion as the essence of Judaism while abandoning distinctive Jewish practices, and Jews who claimed no ideological interest, all in a common search for a way to enter the modern world. Each of these groups was committed to the secularization of the state and the transference of religious concerns to the private sphere, to a pluralistic state that tolerated diversity by rendering the elements causing diversity insignificant in the state's world view, and to a state based upon individualism to the extent that every individual had to make his own way within it and had his own rights as a citizen. Such was the essence of their liberalism, and in this sense Jewish socialism could be considered a form of liberalism too.

Liberalism served Jews, at least partially, as a unifying force, as long as its premises exercised a common attraction for the many who were aspiring to modernity. World War II rendered obsolete the hopes of liberalism in much of Europe, because it showed that they could not be fulfilled; the postwar period performed the same service for American Jews, because, on the contrary, in their case liberal hopes were so greatly fulfilled. What followed was not a resurgence of religious belief in place of liberalism, although that occurred in certain quarters, but the substitution of the newly created state of Israel as a new focal point for Jews, religious and secular, nationalist and assimilationist alike. Few Jews failed to be impressed with the Jewish achievement in the reborn homeland or to be excited by the novel feeling of belonging at last to a majority in at least one part of the world. There was scarcely a Jew anywhere who did not take pride in Israel's military prowess, which symbolized Jewish success in the most modern terms, i.e., in precisely those fields in which Jews had been considered inadequate for so many centuries.

Israel's role as an authoritative force in Jewish life is now taking on yet another dimension as the only locus of Jewish political sovereignty and cultural hegemony. The decisions of Israel's institutions regarding crucial aspects of Jewish self-definition are becoming increasingly authoritative for world Jewry as a whole. The recurring controversy over the question "Who is a Jew?" is perhaps the most outstanding example of Israel's new role in this regard. The Knesset (Israel's parliament), in theory a totally secular legislative body, is actually in the position of determining the religious status of a great many Jews in the world simply by the fact that it must define who is a Jew for internal Israeli purposes. Israeli forms of observance have had an impact on the Diaspora—for example, the development of Israel Independence Day as a national Jewish holiday. One can safely predict that such trends will grow more pronounced, by virtue of the increased integration of the Jewish world as a whole.

Israel thus plays a crucial role in American Jewish life both as a symbol and as a force. Jews who would deny the necessity for complete dedication to Israel's cause are, in effect, read out of Jewish communal life, while those who occupy the most important positions in Jewish communal life are usually people who can claim to be playing some significant role in the maintenance of Israel's security. Fund raising for Israel, with its constantly accelerating demands, has become the most visible Jewish communal activity and has been the stimulus for the general increase in funds raised for across-the-board Jewish purposes in the United States since the end of World War II. This has not only had certain direct effects, but also the substantial indirect effect of enhancing the Jewish federations, the organizations whose task it is to raise the funds.

Israel has always played a major role in making the decisions that affect American Jewish fund raising in its behalf. Most recently, as the Jewish world has been drawn together ever more closely into a protective relationship toward Israel and vice versa—the result of an international situation that has left the Jewish people standing more or less alone— Israel has initiated attempts to exercise direct influence over the decisions of the American Jewish community in areas beyond fund raising itself. Not only does Israel insist upon receiving the major share of money collected, but it seeks to mobilize American Jews to support its interests politically, to preserve their separate identity as Jews so as to provide the Jewish state with allies and, ultimately, with additional settlers. It seeks to make its cause the center of American Jewish interest, and in general to make American Jewry more conscious of Jewish national separatism for the sake of its interests. To date organized American Jewry has acquiesced in these demands without really examining their implications, some of which could drastically change the relationship between Jews and their fellow Americans.

Of course, Israel did not spring forth full-blown in the center of the American Jewish stage. In the prestate period there were serious conflicts between Zionists and anti-Zionists, with the great majority of the American Jewish community to be found in a camp that could properly have been labeled non-Zionist. This was true despite the fact that the American Jewish contribution to the rebuilding of the Jewish homeland was significant from the very first, when in the middle of the nineteenth century Judah Touro provided the funds for the construction of the first Jewish housing development outside the walls of the Old City of Jerusalem. The horrors of Nazism and the Holocaust rendered the majority of American Jews sympathetic to the establishment of a Jewish state, primarily out of concern for fellow Jews in need of a place of refuge. Thus from the very beginning the relationship between Israel and the American Jewish community was philanthropic in nature, based on the obligation felt by a secure community to aid its brethren in need. Israel was for "other Jews," not for American Jews, even though Israel and American Jewry were bound by a common Jewishness.

In the nineteen years between 1948 and 1967 there even developed a certain estrangement between American Jewry and Israel, as the two communities concentrated on their respective domestic concerns almost to the exclusion of anything except a casual concern with each other's problems. Israeli Jews were engaged in trying to give their state roots, and some, like the so-called Canaanites, went so far as to experiment with radical notions of severing all connections between Israelis and the Jewish people. Relatively few Israelis endorsed these ideas, but a majority of the younger generation probably came to accept the existence of an unbridgeable gap between Israel and Diaspora Jewry.

Meanwhile, American Jews were deeply involved in attaining the last measures of equalization within American society, and as such were more concerned about defining their Judaism in American terms than in seeking connections with Israel. They continued to raise money for the Jewish state, although in declining amounts, as a humanitarian activity, but did not see Israel as a source of strength or inspiration for their own needs.

The Six-Day War changed all that. Confronted with the possibility of the destruction of Israel, American Jews suddenly discovered the depths of their feeling, commitment, concern, and dependence upon the survival of the Jewish state for their own well-being. Suddenly Israel was catapulted into the very center of concern for even the Peripherals. All talk of a separate American Judaism evaporated when it became apparent that what was holding the vast majority of American Jews to Jewish identity was, in great measure, a common concern for Israel.

In the wake of the great triumph of Israel's army, especially the liberation of the Old City of Jerusalem and its cherished Western Wall, Jews in both Israel and America (and for that matter throughout the Jewish Diaspora) discovered that the links which they had perceived to be simply humanitarian actually amounted to interdependence: the various Jewish communities required one another's support in order to survive. American Jews discovered the psychic and sociological meaning of Israel as the measure of their status in the world and their own self-esteem. Israeli Jews discovered that in the crunch they could rely only upon the Jewish people, and psychically they, too, were motivated by what were after all Jewish rather than simply Israeli aspirations.

In the euphoric six and a half years between June 1967 and October 1973 the sense of Israel's importance continued to grow in the Diaspora, while the sense of Jewishness began to develop anew in Israel. The Yom

Kippur War came on the heels of those developments and had a curiously contradictory impact. On one hand, it made Jews throughout the world cognizant that they had moved from interdependence to integration, that what happened in one part of the Jewish world affected every other part almost immediately, particularly when Israel was involved. At the same time, it also brought an end to an incipient "Israelolatry" that had developed in many circles in the United States, where Israel became the be-all and end-all of Jewish existence and as a result was placed above criticism. A more balanced picture of the Jewish state began to emerge in the minds of American Jews, based upon a greater sophistication about Israel and Jewish matters in general. Between 1967 and 1973 many more American Jews had firsthand contact with Israel and Israelis, either directly by visits to Israel or through increased media coverage. Thus even at the time of the Yom Kippur War, the American Jewish response to events was made with open eyes, and in the difficult aftermath of the conflict, eyes opened further.

Even before the war broke out isolated groups of Jewish intellectuals were beginning to raise questions about the unqualified American Jewish adoration of Israel. Their questions were somewhat reinforced after the war, particularly by those spokesmen for American Jewish institutions that stood to suffer from reductions in support as a result of the tremendous financial demands that Israel was placing on American Jewry. While these criticisms were somewhat more acceptable than they were in the 1967–73 period, they still led to very harsh reactions on the part of the American Jewish establishment and were virtually neglected by ordinary American Jews; the upshot was that the basic authoritative role of Israel remained undiminished, even if Israel itself had become less sacrosanct.

While Israel is the major force in the Jewish world today, American Jewish concern with Jews the world over is in no way diminished. The recent upsurge of attention to Soviet Jewry is a case in point. Even Israel's leaders, as authoritative as they are in most spheres of Jewish life, had to bow before American Jewish pressure in behalf of the Jews of Russia: first in consenting to the launching of an all-out effort to secure the right of Soviet Jews to emigrate and, more recently, in acknowledging that this struggle would continue unabated even during such crises as the Yom Kippur War. For example, Israel's leaders were reluctant to support the Jackson Amendment to the U.S.-Soviet trade bill, which would have made the granting of most-favored-nation status to the USSR contingent upon Soviet willingness to allow Jews to emigrate freely. They communicated their reluctance to the American Jewish leadership, but the latter, forced to respond to their own constituencies, had to persuade the Israelis to consent to a strong American Jewish effort in the amendment's behalf. Similarly, American Jews feel a responsibility to assist Russian Jews who settle in the United States rather than in Israel, despite the general feeling that these Jews are somehow betraying world Jewry by coming to America. In sum, it is only in matters involving world Jewry that American Jews have been willing to challenge Israeli dominance.

The changing stature of American Jewry on the world Jewish scene has had an important impact of its own. Indeed, American Jewry has always been shaped to some degree by the worldwide vicissitudes of the Jewish people. The establishment of the American Jewish community was to a large extent a result of the impact of the fifteenth-century expulsion of the Jews from Spain and Portugal. Since the seventeenth century, pressures against Jews in various parts of the world have provided a constant impetus to the migration of Jews to the United States, as in the case of German-speaking Jews fleeing revolutionary Central Europe in the 1830s and 1840s, Jews from the Russian Empire fleeing pogroms after 1880, Hasidic Jews fleeing Nazism in the 1930s and 1940s, and Cuban Jews fleeing Castro in the 1960s. Still, until the twentieth century American Jewry was considered to be no more than an outpost of the world Jewish community. Major figures in Jewish life did not come to settle in the United States unless forced to by external events, such as persecution. Noted scholars and religious leaders considered America a wasteland.

Only as a result of World War I and the consequent drastic disruption of the great Jewish centers in Europe did the American Jewish community begin to acquire an importance of its own. Thanks to its relief efforts, led by the American Jewish Joint Distribution Committee (JDC), established in 1914 soon after the outbreak of the war, American Jewry stepped into the world Jewish picture as the principal reservoir of Jewish resources. By that time the character of the community had been substantially established by its immigrant multitudes, most of whom were themselves more or less peripheral to the mainstream of Jewish communal life. The fact that the American Jewish community, until recently at least, has been primarily a source of funds rather than of political leadership or intellectual achievement on the world Jewish scene derives from the immigrant heritage. Jews who immigrated to the U. S. were for the most part economically motivated and had to give up other activities in order to earn a living. Their talents developed commensurately.

The Nazi era enhanced American Jewry's position on the world Jewish scene beyond all expectations, economically and in every other respect. Once again world Jewry was in need of American Jewish relief efforts, and the American Jewish community rose to the highest level of prominence and leadership on the world Jewish scene, primarily through its ability to mobilize a share of America's great economic power. After World War II the organizational talents of American Jewry were also put at the service of shattered Jewish communities all over the world.

The needs of world Jewry thus became an additional factor in shaping the internal life of American Jewry. For example, the World War I watershed that led to demands for joint fund raising within the United States—the JDC—also initiated the rise of the local Jewish welfare federation to a position of centrality in American Jewish life, a rise that has been abetted by every subsequent event of significance on the world Jewish scene. Conditions in the Nazi era solidified this trend by bringing on the 1938 merger of the JDC and the United Palestine Appeal into the United Jewish Appeal (UJA), which in turn led to the reorganization of virtually every local Jewish federation as the central fund-raising body for Jewish purposes. On the other hand, the struggle over the establishment of the state of Israel briefly made the Zionist movement a major vehicle for achieving power within the American Jewish community. Once the state was established, however, the political initiative that gave the Zionist movement its role passed to those living in Israel, shattering the Zionist organizations and reducing them to a secondary role (if that) on the American Jewish scene.

Thus both Israel and world Jewry have become major components of the central core of Jewishness, alongside Judaism itself. Israel, both as a state and as the only Jewish country in the world, has become the touchstone of Jewish self-esteem and the measure of Jewish achievement for the world at large. As a result it has acquired an authoritative role in Jewish life that, for the moment at least, is unchallenged. Moreover, as the only place in the world where an authentic Jewish culture can flower (at least potentially), it exercises an unequaled attraction upon American Jews searching for a meaning in their Jewishness. Even the most peripheral of American Jews are touched by the Jewish authenticity of Israel, while the more committed find the power of Israel in this respect almost irresistible.

By the same token, American Jews are pulled by their commitments to world Jewry, even to the point of being willing to challenge the decisions of Israelis regarding the proper course of action in dealing with world Jewish affairs, as we have seen. Since World War II, and particularly since the 1960s, American Jews have tried to forge their own lines to the other Diaspora Jewish communities, partly out of necessity—there is really no one else available for the tasks at hand—and partly out of a feeling of responsibility on the part of the world's largest and most favored Jewish community toward less fortunate fellow Jews. However, the links with world Jewry and Israel involve more than links with people. They of necessity embody organization and structures that, like the people themselves, must be linked with Jewishness in the traditional sense as well. Thus part of the world Jewish environment that helps to shape American Jewish life is the relationship between traditional elements of Jewish polity and their modern American manifestations. By examining certain of these traditional elements and certain aspects of their manifestations in contemporary America, we can better understand both the unique character of the American Jewish community and the impact of the world Jewish environment on American Jewry.

TRADITIONAL ELEMENTS AND THEIR MODERN MANIFESTATIONS

While the American Jewish community is, in many respects, cut off from traditional Jewish sources in its outlook and behavior patterns, a number of elements drawn from the traditional political culture of the Jews do persist and help shape its structure and operations. One of the most important is the use of federal principles to organize Jewish communal life, a system as old as the Jewish people itself, having its origins in the federation of the twelve tribes under Moses. The very term "federal" is derived from the Latin *foedus,* which means covenant, and is an expression of the biblical idea of *brit* (covenant), which it defines the basis of political and social relationships among men as well as between man and God.[8] The covenant or federal idea, emphasizing the development of contractually defined partnerships based on mutual obligation, was translated into concrete political institutions and embedded in Jewish tradition to become part of the political culture of the Jews. Consequently, it persisted as a force shaping Jewish communal life even after external events eliminated the tribal federation as the form of government of the Jewish people.[9]

Federal principles, institutions, and arrangements persist to this day. These federal arrangements are not necessarily the same as those in modern territorially based politics, where constituent entities are united under an overarching government in such a way as to maintain the unity of the whole—especially for operational purposes—while preserving the integrity of all the partners. Frequently there are no overarching bodies, or only weak ones, to link the constituent units, but there is the linking of individuals and institutions in contractual relationships designed to foster partnership on several levels. Moreover, those partnerships take on a character of their own that is more than the sum of their constituent units.[10]

Internally, each Jewish community has always been a partnership and is so delineated in Jewish law. From earliest times local communities came into existence as a result of compacts among Jews in a particular locality and functioned according to the terms of such compacts, binding individual Jews and their families only to the extent that the compacts provided or were allowed to provide within the framework of Jewish religious law. Unlike the idea of the state in European political thought, Jewish law and political thought contain no concept of the polity as an organic or reified entity with an existence independent of its members. Nor has the Jewish polity ever been considered the private property of any particular individual or group. Rather, every Jewish community was held to be a *res publica,* the common property of all of its members, who in effect compacted or federated with one another to create specific communities within the overall framework of the Jewish people.

Beyond the limits of locality, the various Jewish communities have been linked with one another through more or less institutionalized federal arrangements that have varied in extent, duration, and significance in different periods of Jewish history. At the very least there were relationships linking the rabbinical authorities of various communities to one another for the interpretation of Jewish law. When and where conditions allowed, the relationships were made even more formal. The examples of Jewish self-government cited by Jewish thinkers and historians as the most thoroughly consonant with Jewish values and aspirations were of this nature, including the various federations of Jewish communities in the Rhineland and Spain in the High Middle Ages and the Council of the Four Lands that governed the Jews of Greater Poland in the late Middle Ages.

Today Jewish communities all over the world tend to be organized on some variation of the federal principle, unless the political and cultural framework of the societies in which they are located strongly militate against it. In Central Europe, where Jewish communities have formal status in public law, they are organized on a federal basis by that law. In the English-speaking countries they are organized that way either because they are located in countries with federal structures or because of custom. In Latin America the Jewish communities are federations of landsmanshaften, and in the United States they are federations of service agencies. Moreover, all congregations are essentially organized on federal principles to this day.[11]

In sum, wherever Jews go and whatever the adaptations they must make to local conditions, the tendency is to utilize federal principles. Only when the host society is so organized to prevent them from doing so (as in ancient Babylonia in certain periods and in modern France) do the Jews depart from this pattern, almost invariably with negative consequences for the Jewish community involved.

Federalism in the Jewish community tends to be even purer in form than that found in formally federal states, primarily because the overarching governmental body is weak or nonexistent and the federating units maintain sufficient autonomy and equality of power to require decision making on a consensual rather than a coerced basis. This means that the general pattern of community decision making is based on widespread agreement among its decision makers before action is taken —if only because there is no alternative to such an approach. There is no ultimate authority that can forge a decision out of conflicting viewpoints or impose one where there is a stalemate. Rather, decisions must be negotiated and must command the widest possible support relative to their scope; otherwise there will be no way to implement them.

The thrust toward consensual decision making that is generated by the federal arrangements among the institutions and their leaders has been raised to new heights in modern Jewish life because of the voluntary nature of the community. Obviously it is even more difficult to compel people who are associated voluntarily to accept decisions they regard as unwise or hostile to their interests than it is to deal with people who are somehow bound into the system.

This is not to say that all decisions are arrived at on an open consensual basis, in which all parties involved participate in the negotiations until a decision acceptable to all is reached. In some cases decisions cannot be made on a public basis because there is insufficient consensus in the community. In others, the general society's commitment to private decisions is so overriding as to prevent consideration of public action. Sometimes there is simply so little communication between the community's leaders and the Jewish population that the latter are not aware that an issue exists or that a decision should be (or has been) made. Many specialized decisions are made in small groups simply because of a lack of widespread interest; even some very important decisions are made that way precisely in order to avoid the difficulties of having to reach a widespread consensus. Of course, the latter situation is possible only when potential participants in the community feel that they must accept the decisions reached. This is most notable in decisions involving Israel.

The American Jewish community is so closely bound up with Israel and perceives so well that its basic interests are tied to the survival and success of the Jewish state that its members are most reluctant to challenge any decisions made in the name of Israel's best interests. This means that the coterie of leaders who, in effect, set the policies of the American Jewish community in matters affecting Israel have a great deal of leeway; they know that they are not likely to be challenged. Moreover, these same leaders are in a position to extend their power to other arenas by capitalizing on their role in relation to Israel. This ability of leaders-by-consensus to gain authority and influence through their association with the central value symbol of the community is another manifestation of the traditional political culture of the Jews, a transposition of the traditional emphasis on charismatic* leadership once derived from the Torah when it had the same kind of status in the minds of the Jews that Israel has today.

In its own way the American Jewish community relies as heavily on charismatic leaders (rather than on persons chosen by more institutionalized procedures, such as elections or heredity) as any Jewish community in the past. Jewish leadership for the most part has historically been based on forms of charisma other than personal magnetism. The biblical

---

*It should be understood that the term "charismatic" is used in its original Weberian sense of special power endowed by some external authoritative source, not as it has come to be used in popular language, where it refers to men with a particular ability to hypnotize or charm the masses.

judges and prophets were leaders by virtue of a charisma bestowed by God according to traditional understanding. Later, charisma derived from special talents of learning and scholarship and was vested in sages and rabbis. With the modern tendency of Jews to value secular above religious achievement, charisma often has come to be associated with money, a convenient measure of success. American Jewry has had some leaders, such as Rabbi Stephen S. Wise, who have had charismatic powers in the popular meaning of the term, but they were atypical. Today the ability to achieve recognition in the non-Jewish world rivals money as a source of charisma. It is noteworthy that in America the two are often connected in any case. Academicians have a charisma of their own if they are very successful. They combine recognition by the non-Jewish world with the traditional respect for the learned, however transformed and secularized it may be.

Most recently Israelis have acquired a certain charisma in their relationships with American Jewry because of their role in building the Jewish state, particularly when they have been connected with the Israeli army, a matter of great pride to American Jewry. This charisma, which reached its peak after June 1967, was somewhat tarnished by the Yom Kippur War.

Expansion of the role of professional communal servants in the American Jewish community has clearly diminished the extent to which the community relies upon charismatic leaders. With the exception of a few figures in the Orthodox camp, even American rabbis are considered successful when they inspire respect for their professional competence, rather than for any charismatic qualities. Indeed, there is a constant lament that American Jewry has no great public figures today like the leaders of earlier generations, that the men who run the community are "organization men," essentially colorless and uninspiring to the masses.[12] There is considerable truth in this, but it does not diminish the fact that there is a form of charisma operating to endow certain people with authority (particularly in the fund-raising field) in a community in which there are no clear-cut ways to legitimate authority or power.

Leadership in the fund-raising field is often denigrated by critical observers of the American Jewish community, yet in many respects its patterns and methods are closer to the most authentic elements of the Jewish tradition of leadership than those of any other segments of American Jewish leadership, comparable, in this respect, to the much-admired Israeli army or to the traditional leadership of the *gedolei ha-Torah* (the great students of the Torah). The basic principle of fund-raising leadership is leadership by example, a principle notably absent in other sectors of American Jewish life. The "follow-me" pattern is widely recognized as the only successful way to raise funds, just as the Israeli army recognizes it as the only way to lead men and halakhic Jews recognize it as the only way to encourage the observance of mitzvot. Jewish tradition recognizes that kind of leadership as the only way to build a good society.

Israel has become the principal authority-giving element in Jewish life today. The ascendancy of Israel appears to have ended a period lasting well over a century during which there was no clear-cut source of authority in Jewish life. The fact that Israel has become the new source of authority represents a break with tradition that is not without problems of its own, but this new situation nevertheless provides a means for uniting a people with very diverse beliefs.

The authoritative role of Israel functions in two ways. First, Israel is itself authoritative. Those who wish to dissent from any particular Israeli policy or demand must be circumspect. As we have said, Jews who reject Israel's claims upon them are more or less written off by the Jewish community and certainly are excluded from any significant decision-making role. Furthermore, leaders who can claim to speak in the name of Israel or on behalf of Israel gain a degree of authority that places them in advantageous positions when it comes to other areas of communal decision making. Even the synagogues, which are expected to be bastions of support for the Torah as the primary source of authority, have come increasingly to rely upon Israel and Israel-centered activities to legitimize their own positions. The shift of fund raising on Yom Kippur from fund raising for synagogue needs to the sale of Israel Bonds is an especially visible case in point.

SHIFTING BELIEFS AND COMMUNAL NORM ENFORCEMENT

Given the shifting beliefs of modern Jews and the disappearance of clear communal boundaries, the American Jewish community is confronted with the constant problem of maintaining some standard of "Jewishness."

Before the modern era, the belief system maintained by the Jewish community was quite clear-cut and involved very explicit rules which the community was capable of enforcing. During the eighteenth century—a transitional period for Jews in the Western world—the congregational communities in the United States attempted to maintain that kind of enforcement even though they did not have the weight of the governmental authorities behind them. They insisted upon the maintenance of the old belief system and the principles of Jewish law as a criterion for joining the congregation. Persons who refused were simply denied membership. Since there was only one congregation in most areas, this meant that many Jews were excluded from the Jewish community. As a matter of fact, many of the Jews who came to the United States did not much care if they were members or not, and if they were excluded because of a violation of the congregational norms they simply disappeared into the general American scene. Others, wishing to break with traditional Jewish life, never even tried to join congregations.

With the development of multiple congregations in each community at the outset of the nineteenth century, the congregations essentially gave up trying to enforce the traditional belief system and its norms as a basis for membership in the Jewish community, though individual congregations clearly set their own requirements for congregational membership and some continue to do so. During the nineteenth century there was really very little in the way of common beliefs or norms that identified a person as a member of the community or not. Perhaps the most important sign of membership was simply a willingness to affiliate in whatever way was available. By the twentieth century, however, new common elements for a belief system were beginning to develop and become implicitly accepted as the basis for defining Jewish communal allegiance. Since World War II they have crystallized for American Jewry and probably for Jews in other countries of the world as well.

It is possible to identify four major elements in the basic belief system that the Jewish community enforces today: support of Israel, a positive attitude toward Jewish tradition, acceptance of one's obligations toward other Jews, and acceptance of the obligation to take care of Jewish needs. All four are clearly rooted in Jewish tradition and stem from legitimate beliefs current in the Jewish past. However, all have been transformed and modernized in one way or another.

We have already spoken of how Israel has become the keystone to the entire Jewish belief system, the basic common denominator that virtually all Jews who do not wish to exclude themselves from the Jewish camp are willing to accept. While support of Israel may take various forms, it rests on several essentials. One is that Israel and world Jewry share an inseparable fate. From this premise it follows that Jews must support Israel materially and politically and that, while criticism of Israel is permissible under certain circumstances, one cannot be a member of the Jewish community while standing in opposition to Israel on all counts. The reaction of the committed Jewish academic Left is a case in point. They tread a very careful line between reflecting the Third-World bias of the Left and favoring the state of Israel, tending to support Israel, however critically, while simultaneously supporting the rights of the Palestinians to self-determination and taking aim at their primary target: the Jewish establishment in the United States.

Since World War II a new kind of identification with Jewish tradition has developed. In some respects it is based only on nostalgia; in others it is an active identification. In any event it would seem to be incumbent upon all Jews who wish to be part of the community to identify with some aspect of Jewish tradition. What the community does not attempt to do is to define the content of Jewish tradition or the nature of the identification. That is left up to individual determination, subject to the pressures generated by the subgroups in the Jewish community to which individual Jews belong. One may interpret the tradition in secular-nationalistic terms, in religious-ritualistic terms, or as a kind of ethnic past that in some way shapes one's own life.

Some Jews who identify with tradition, however they define it, actively attempt to maintain and transmit their particular pattern of identification. Others are content with a far more casual identification. In a sense the popular musical *Fiddler on the Roof* is a good reflection of that kind of minimal identification. Its opening number, "Tradition," tells the audience exactly what Jewish life is all about for many, if not most, American Jews. The actual Tevyes of the shtetl would not have spoken of "tradition," with its implication of sentimental attachment on the basis of individual choice, but of Halakhah (Law) with its clear sense of explicit binding norms. However, since the sentimentalized Tevye is now the father of us all, a figure with whom we can identify, he must speak of tradition, which is the point of identification of so many present-day Jews.

The acceptance of one's obligations to other Jews is also a crucial element in the belief system. This means that everyone must recognize that his fate is tied up with that of other Jews, wherever they are, and must be willing to share that fate by shouldering his obligations as part of the community. The ways in which one does so range from membership in Jewish organizations to protesting the treatment of Jews in the Soviet Union. But it is the recognition of the obligation that is crucial.

Closely connected with the idea that one is obligated to share the fate of his fellow Jews is the principle that one is obligated to care for Jewish needs no matter where they may arise. This was the first element of the modern Jewish belief system to gain wide acceptance. By and large, in the United States this is translated to mean the obligation to contribute money for Israel, for local community needs, and for the assistance of Jews in other countries of the world who need it.

The question remains as to whether a belief in God is a required element in the belief system of the American Jewish community. The answer is not clear. Certainly no positive test is ever imposed to determine a person's theological orientation before considering him to be a member of the Jewish community. Generally, the belief in God is simply not discussed. At the same time, public denial of the existence of God does not occur within the ranks of the Jewish community either. This may well be because the United States on the whole is at least nominally a "believing" society. That is, most Americans do not deny their belief in God no matter how they may define that belief. The fact of the matter is that God has become a "problem" in modern life which is not often confronted and in fact is purposely avoided. The Jewish community, which has never shown great interest in theological questions as the keystones of communal identification, is no exception.

Obviously today's American Jewish community does not lay down the law to its members and then maintain a structured system of norm enforcement even within the rather flexible parameters of belief described above. What it does do, more subtly, is to determine what minimal rules must be followed by Jews who wish to be considered members of the Jewish community.* Some of the unwritten rules that seem to be

---

*It should be clear that what we are talking about here is not "Who is a Jew?" That is a sociological matter and a religious problem that has its own validity but stands outside the political considerations which motivate us here. Here we are concerned about who is considered a member of the Jewish community, that is, who is considered to be within the Jewish camp and who is considered outside of it. Since the fact of Jewishness is in part a matter of birth (an organic or biological matter) and in part an act of identification or association (a contractual or political matter, in the sense of accepting a citizenship), the question of who is a Jew is rendered extremely complex. It is far less difficult to determine who is a member of Jewish community, which is our purpose here. There are people who would clearly be considered Jews who neither support the state of Israel, such as members of the American Council for Judaism, nor act as Jews in any identifiable way other than to dissociate themselves as Jews from Zionism. There are also the Satmar Hasidim, whose

binding upon American Jews include contributions to Jewish causes (preferably through the local federation), membership in a synagogue, marriage within the community or to a partner who has converted and thereby joined the community, and a basic commitment to avoid community conflict or at least public airing of conflict. None of these rules is absolute; it is possible to find people who do not live according to one or more of them, yet are not considered to be outside the community. However, it is extremely likely that anyone could be so considered if he violated all of them, and indeed Jews who violate any of them and are still acceptable are to be deemed special cases.

One way it is possible to avoid having to obey one rule is through the intensified acceptance of another. For example, many of the extreme Orthodox Jews do not contribute to community-wide fund-raising campaigns, but their attachment to their own religious institutions and their contributions to those institutions make it very difficult to conceive of them as standing outside the Jewish community. Conversely, an extremely large contributor to UJA will be accepted as a Jew even if married to a non-Jew.

Obviously there are many other norms that individual Jews or groups of Jews within the community consider binding on themselves as Jews, not to speak of persons who accept Jewish law as binding in one way or another. However, the community is not called upon to enforce those norms, but instead has delegated authority for their enforcement to subgroups within the community that are able to exert the requisite social pressure on their members. While it is true that social pressure is the only way to enforce any of the norms in the American Jewish community, it is no mean tool of enforcement.

THE IMPACT OF TECHNOLOGICAL CHANGE

Technological change, another environmental factor of crucial importance, is often—mistakenly—neglected in discussions of contemporary Jewish life. The Jewish people of today has been remolded by technology

---

Jewishness in one sense is clearly not in dispute, but who have by their own admission separated themselves from the Jewish community. The belief system as discussed here applies to persons who wish to be considered or who are considered members of the community. Others, although they may be clearly Jewish from a sociological or religious point of view, do not fall within our definition.

at least as much as any other people, and in some ways even more. On one hand, by enabling Western civilization to cover the globe and settle in heretofore isolated or unsettled areas, modern technology has increased the Jewish dispersion beyond anything known in the past. On the other, technology has also made possible greater Jewish unity than at any time since the destruction of the First Temple.

It is no exaggeration to say that the invention of the jet plane and the telephone have had as much influence on the patterns of American Jewish life as any more widely hailed social factors. The ability of Jews, wherever they live, to participate in the activities of the world Jewish community, to get to Israel rapidly and to send their children there for brief stays, to jet around the United States itself to attend meetings in New York, Miami, or Kansas City—all this has had a tremendous impact on who participates in the life of the community and under what conditions.

No matter how many miles separate them, Jews can be in instantaneous telephonic communication with one another and can actually be at each other's doorsteps within a day, no matter where they live. The curious and compelling phenomenon of American Jews telephoning their Russian brethren who are otherwise under virtual house arrest because of their activism, and thereby maintaining direct contact with Russian Jewry, is a dramatic example of technology as a force in contemporary Jewish life. Within the United States the telephone has radically enlarged the Jewish countrywide communications network, expanding the number, range, and geographic distribution of participants in Jewish communal life. Telecommunications with Soviet Jews is only a foretaste of the technological change and the likely impact that the telephone will have on the world Jewish community as intercontinental calls become increasingly routine.

These and other manifestations of the new technology provide an infrastructure for the political revolution that is about to engulf world Jewry and in which American Jewry will be keenly involved. Until very recently American Jewry was essentially a self-contained community, although it did have serious and profound links with the rest of the Jewish world. Internally, however, it has been minimally open to intervention by Jewish bodies from the outside and minimally involved in the organized life, much less the governance, of other Jewish communities. Circumstances are already working to transform this situation, the most important of which is technology, particularly rapid worldwide communication.

Less directly, the new industries generated by technological change have enabled Jews to improve their own economic, social, and political positions. It was technological change that made American society sufficiently expansive to allow the Jewish immigrants who arrived at the end of the great period of the country's industrialization to use their energies to get ahead and even created a demand for their talents. The Jewish immigrant pioneers on the urban and metropolitan frontiers acted to strengthen the economic base of American Jewish life and its capacity to respond to the fund-raising demands that are so crucial to it.

By the same token, shifts in technology that have made small independent businesses obsolete in a whole host of fields, and are now leading to the merger of medium-sized industries with the corporate giants, are changing the character of Jewish economic activity. These products of individual enterprise made many Jews wealthy while giving those involved in them the requisite time and flexibility for participation in Jewish affairs. Their disappearance as occupational and earnings outlets for Jews is likely to have great implications for participation in the Jewish community, if not for fund raising itself, in the very near future.

The impact of the automobile on American Jewish life has yet to be reckoned with systematically, although virtually every Jewish institution has either adapted to the automotive age or has died as a result of inability to adapt. The automobile more than any other single factor ended the neighborhood life of American Jewry, by making suburbanization possible. Thanks to the automobile, Jews, even when they live in relative proximity, are rarely within walking distance of one another and their institutions, which has transformed the character of Jewish observance and the sociological patterns of Jewish association at one and the same time. Most recently the spread of the new highway technology has enabled many Jews to live so far away from Jewish life that they find it difficult even to send their children to Jewish schools.

Today Jews have to make a conscious decision to live near one another and only the most observant seek to live within walking distance of Jewish institutions—and most Jews are not. As a result, Jewish institutions find it difficult to maintain programs day in and day out. Instead, Jews gather together only periodically, once a week for the more devoted, much less frequently for most, without even the option of having children drop in to the neighborhood community center or adults stop in for a weekly adult-education course, something that was feasible when Jews lived close to one another and such participation not only required little effort but often represented the path of least resistance, given the other leisure-time activity options.

As yet no proper study has been made of the new technology's impact on Jewish life. This is not the place to do so, but every Jew must be aware of how dependent Jewry is on technological change. In this respect, as in most others, Jews are just like everybody else only more so. As a scattered community, bound together by a communications network far more than by any authoritative institutions and certainly not by any with coercive powers, contemporary technology, which is so heavily based on communications, is made to order for the renaissance of Jewish people-hood that we have witnessed—and are continuing to witness—in the twentieth century. This is as true within the American Jewish community as in linking the American Jewish community to others. It is indeed possible to forecast not only greater interdependence among Jewish communities the world over, but greater facility for communication in the not very distant future, a fact that may very well transform the very character of organized Jewish life in the United States.

The American Environment and Jewish Religious Life

The American ethos makes a sharp distinction between the religious and the secular, confining the former to a relatively small area of private and public affairs. While this tendency is not uniformly prevalent among all groups—the exhortation to "put religion into daily life" is a common feature of American Christianity—it is effectively the case insofar as the actual behavior of most Americans is concerned. Moreover, the Jewish community is defined almost exclusively in religious terms, religious identification having proved most acceptable in the context of American pluralism. (This remains true despite the new emphasis on ethnicity that has developed in certain quarters in recent years.)

Most Jews share the cultural set of their non-Jewish fellow citizens, and given the place religious activity holds in contemporary America, they have come to feel that their Jewish activity should, in effect, remain outside the mainstream of life, should be a leisure-time activity at best. This particular way of thinking must be overcome within the Jewish community in order for the community to act at all. Within the community it has led to a certain separation between so-called religious and secular activities and groups, following the American model, a separation that is quite un-Jewish from the perspective of tradition and has profoundly affected the shape of community organization.

The result of all this has been the development of an indigenous American Jewish religious pattern—a *minhag America* (literally, American custom), which, in its several variations, is clearly identifiable as

American. This *minhag America* is based on two elements: (1) radical localization of control over Jewish religious institutions and maximum individual freedom to pick and choose one's own pattern of Jewish religious observance and behavior, and (2) a tradition of separation between those institutions and the other institutions of American Jewish life with a different set of affiliation patterns.

RELIGIOUS MOVEMENTS AS EXPRESSIONS OF JEWISH ADAPTATION TO AMERICA

Jewish life in the United States has become synagogue-centered to an unprecedented degree. Moreover, each congregation is independent in every respect, a Jewish world unto itself so to speak, at least insofar as it wants to be. Even when congregations link themselves to countrywide synagogue movements, their ties are at best tenuous and confederal.

For their first century and a half in the United States all Jews were members of some combination of congregation-community, but their numbers were so small that psychologically they regarded themselves more as members of a congregation than of a community. Since American Protestant religious life was congregation-centered, this system fitted in very well. Jews began to think of congregational affiliation as the uppermost form of Jewish identification. As other Jews with different religious customs came, they organized their own synagogues, and congregationalism was expanded and deepened. With the coming of the Reform movement and later Conservatism, "denominationalism" became entrenched and further reinforced this congregation bias. Finally, the uncompromisingly traditional synagogues succumbed to the trend, organizing themselves into Orthodox bodies.

The American synagogue has developed a character of its own even as it continues the great tradition of the synagogue in Jewish life. Before discussing that character in terms more or less common to all synagogues that have adopted American ways, we should understand the development of the three synagogue movements into which the overwhelming majority of all American synagogues are grouped.

The first synagogues established in the United States—indeed, all those established prior to the 1840s—maintained the patterns and styles of worship of traditional Judaism. They were comprehensive "congregations," designed to serve the Jewish needs of their members with no hint

of denominational or ideological divisions to pull them in different directions. The only differences among them were those that resulted from the
origin of their founders, that is, the differences between Spanish-Por-
tuguese and German–East European patterns of worship. There was no
such thing as Orthodoxy or Reform; there were simply Jews following
Jewish law in organizing Jewish congregations, whatever the level or
character of their personal observance.[1]

The Reform Movement

The Reform movement was the first to take on the characteristics of a
denomination, in the United States as in Europe.[2] Indeed, the very first
effort at Jewish religious reform occurred in the American South and
took place even before the development of German Reform itself. In
1824 Beth Elohim, a traditional Sephardic congregation in Charleston,
South Carolina, reformed its service to become the first nontraditional
congregation in the United States. Its actions had no impact beyond its
own confines, however, and Reform did not really get under way as a
movement until the arrival of the "German" or, more correctly, Central
European Jews, who arrived to the United States in the middle of the
nineteenth century.[3] The first German Reform congregations were Har
Sinai of Baltimore, founded in 1842, and Temple Emanu-El of New
York, founded in 1845. Isaac Mayer Wise, who was to become the great
leader of American Reform Judaism, arrived in the United States in 1846
and embarked on his pioneering reform efforts almost immediately.
After a brief sojourn in the East, he settled in Cincinnati, which became
the heart and headquarters of the Reform movement.

   The Reform movement developed its greatest strength in the South
and the Midwest, even though Reform congregations emerged in the
East at about the same time. Reform congregations in the East were
simply single congregations among many traditional ones, whereas in the
South and Midwest they tended to be the preeminent if not the only
congregations in their respective communities. Nevertheless, the eastern
congregations were to become strong enough within the Reform movement to challenge Wise's leadership during most of his lifetime.

   During the 1850s and 1860s Reform spread throughout the country.
Reform congregations either were founded as such or were formed by
traditional congregations that quickly converted to Reform in the wake
of the Americanization of their members. Isaac Wise published *Minhag*

America in 1857 as the new liturgy for the new movement. It is interesting to note that his approach at that time was still within the framework of Jewish tradition, for he saw himself as creating not a separate movement, but a unique pattern for all the Jews of the United States—like the different patterns that Jews of different lands of origin in Europe and the Mediterranean world had.

Wise's efforts to unite American Jewry under the banner of *Minhag America* persisted until the 1870s, when the great gaps that had appeared between traditional Jews and the Reformers on such critical matters as Sabbath observance and maintenance of the dietary laws caused unification attempts to founder. The 1870s indeed became the decade in which the work of Wise was institutionalized in Cincinnati. The founding of the Union of American Hebrew Congregations in 1873 and the Hebrew Union College in 1875 brought to fruition the work of a generation who had seen the very beginnings of Reform on the congregational plane in the 1840s and who now saw the creation of nationwide institutions for its maintenance as a movement.[4]

The Union of American Hebrew Congregations was originally designed to be an all-embracing body, as its name implies. But this was never to be, for traditional congregations refused to join with the Reformers. Hebrew Union College was already an ideologically specialized institution organized by the UAHC to produce rabbis to staff its congregations. It is important to note that in the Reform movement the congregational federation was founded before the college, because even today the congregational union dominates the college rather than vice versa (in contrast to the Conservative movement, where the college preceded the congregational federation and continues to dominate it.).

Another product of the generation of Reform was the founding in 1876 of the Ethical Culture Society, an even more "liberal" offshoot. Wise and his compatriots had secretly envisioned the day when there would be a single religion, merging Judaism and Christianity, and sought to put Reform Judaism on the right path in that direction; Felix Adler, the founder of Ethical Culture, thought that the time had come to create the institutional framework for such a synthesis, which would have the additional attraction of being separated from any particular concept of God. In fact, he attracted many of the most liberal Reform Jews, and to this day the society remains primarily a Jewish movement.

By the end of the nineteenth century the Reform movement had become the special province of German Jews (and Jews from Central

Europe who imitated German Jewry); its rabbis even felt it necessary to study for their doctorates in Germany to gain status at home, and the German language continued to be a feature of Reform congregational life. Reform, which preached a universalism that even transcended the limits of Judaism, had, in fact, become an ethnic "church" not very different from those of the Norwegian Lutherans or the Dutch Calvinists.

One result of this was a general lack of communication between the new immigrants from Eastern Europe and the Reform Jews who had come a generation earlier. The latter, who considered themselves americanized, were repelled by their brethren, whom they perceived as threats to their newly won positions in American life. But they also felt compelled to try to help the new immigrants become americanized quickly, so as to minimize the embarrassment. Thus the first contacts between the Reform Jews and the new immigrants were predicated on a gulf between the two groups, a gulf that the Reform Jews did not want the immigrants to cross, even if they had wanted to. The two groups could cooperate with one another because, for the most part, the immigrants did want to become americanized as rapidly as possible. Even though they laughed at the Reform patterns of Jewishness, they accepted guidance toward americanization from "the Germans."

Ultimately, a certain number of the East European immigrants or their children wished to americanize their Judaism along the lines acceptable to the people whom they perceived to be Jewry's upper crust in the United States: the German Reform Jews. Slowly some of them began to be accepted as members of Reform temples, and others founded new congregations that affiliated with the Reform movement. After the end of World War II this trend gathered additional momentum, and eventually the East Europeans, by their sheer numbers, overtook the German Jews and became the majority in the Reform movement— usually by forming their own separate congregations.

Three types of congregations emerged in the Reform movement in the years immediately following the war. A very small handful of congregations maintained "classical Reform" patterns, including, in some cases, holding the principal service on Sunday. Such congregations continue to exist in Chicago, Cleveland (paradoxically, the congregation of a great Zionist leader, the late Abba Hillel Silver), and San Francisco. In most cases they remained firmly opposed to Zionism. These congregations were dominated by Jews of German descent or those East European Jews who had assimilated by following German models. Some of them were actually formed after the war by splinter groups who seceded from established congregations that had turned toward support of Israel and more tradition, in order to preserve the "orthodoxy" of classical Reform.

The second and slightly larger group of congregations consisted of those old-line Reform congregations which, while retaining their essential character as congregations of the German school, moved with the times to reintroduce some of the Jewish traditions that their forefathers had abandoned, including the Saturday Sabbath. They willingly absorbed East European Jews who conformed to their ideas of prayer behavior and decorum. These congregations supported Israel as a humanitarian endeavor while carefully continuing to be non-Zionists.

Finally, there was the growing majority of Reform congregations established predominantly by East European Jews. They were considerably more traditional than either of the first two groups, even within the context of Reform Judaism, and had no qualms about Zionism. Although this last group was the largest, the middle group continued to be the bearer of Reform tradition, and the congregations within it continue to be the most prestigious. According to *The National Jewish Population Study*, conducted by the Council of Jewish Federations and Welfare Funds (CJF) in the early 1970s, some 30 percent of all American Jewish households define themselves as Reform.[5]

While the Reform movement became "more Jewish" in the traditional sense, for a long time it was unable to develop an indigenous intelligentsia of its own. For its intellectual leadership, it continued to rely mostly on Jews who had been born into other patterns and traditions and had come over to Reform after receiving their educations elsewhere. This lack of "action intellectuals," of the kind who brought a dynamic element into Conservative Judaism, has been a limiting factor in the intellectual development of the movement and may even have hindered its congregational growth. Only within recent years have young intellectuals brought up in Reform congregations become visible, but it is too soon to know what their impact will be.

The Conservative Movement

The Conservative movement was the second to emerge as an organized entity on the American scene.[6] It was created by those traditional Jews who felt the competition from Reform most keenly, that is, Jews who were themselves full-fledged participants in Western culture and who felt themselves at home in the United States. While they sought to be fully American, they also wished to maintain a more traditional brand of Judaism.

Philadelphia provided the Conservative movement with its first great source of strength and remains its strongest local center today. There, an inherent tendency to combine traditionalism with a moderate and conciliatory approach to the modern world, found among the surviving Spanish and Portuguese and some of the Central and East European Jews in the community, surfaced at approximately the same time as the Reform movement. In fact, before the Conservative movement had even begun to crystallize, Isaac Leeser of Philadelphia became the spokesman for what were later to become its central ideas. A traditional Jew in every sense of the word (the Orthodox Jews of today claim him as their own as much as do the Conservatives), he in effect antedated both movements, but the thrust of his efforts to reach a modus operandi linking traditional Judaism and the demands of American society at least edged him into what later became the Conservative camp.

Leeser was the great creative force of nineteenth-century American Jewry.[7] Among many other projects, he translated the Bible into English, created the first major Jewish newspaper in the United States, and founded the first Jewish Publication Society. In 1855 he established the first Jewish theological seminary, in Philadelphia. It failed, but a second —successful—attempt was made by Philadelphia Jewish leaders in 1886 when they started the Jewish Theological Seminary in New York.

The organized movement that is now Conservative Judaism emerged from among some of the supporters of the Jewish Theological Seminary of America. It was built around those congregations that were as well established on the American Jewish scene as those that had formed the UAHC, but whose members could not accept so violent a break with tradition. Here, too, the influence of foundings remains crucial. Unlike the Reform movement, in which the UAHC is central and Hebrew Union College is subsidiary, the Seminary has always remained central in the Conservative movement, the other organizations being subsidiary to it.

The main power center of the Conservative movement now lies in New York. In 1901 Solomon Schechter was brought in from England to breathe life into what until then had been a halting movement. He not only revitalized the Seminary, but was instrumental in creating the subsidiary institutions that make up the Conservative movement today. The United Synagogue of America, the congregational arm of the movement, was organized in 1913 to link the congregations then developing under the aegis of the Seminary.

The great growth of the Conservative movement came as a result of the americanization of the East European Jews. Those who, though becoming acculturated, still retained the desire to maintain Jewish tradition in some way, tended to seek a compromise that would preserve many of the traditional forms of worship to which they were accustomed, within a framework that made the style of worship more "American"— that is, more decorous, more theatrical, and in general more formal. They particularly wanted more formal treatment of the rites of passage, the inclusion of prayers in English, and the elimination of separate seating. The Conservative movement offered just this combination. Moreover, within the American pattern of congregationalism it offered the combination in many permutations; within a very broad range of options each congregation could determine how it would make the synthesis. Some Conservative congregations simply introduced mixed seating and greater decorum and formality, but otherwise changed nothing of the traditional service. Others substantially abridged the traditional service, introduced the organ, and concentrated heavily on the use of English and new-style ceremonials designed to appeal to the American Jewish "audience." At first some did not even eliminate the traditional pattern of separate seating for men and women. What was common to them all was an adjustment to the standards of worship prevalent among non-Jews in the United States. This included the elevation of the rabbi's role (and to some extent that of the cantor) in the service and in managing the congregation, and the introduction of accommodating devices such as late Friday night services, which enabled Jews who did not otherwise observe the traditional Sabbath to participate in weekly worship without shifting the service to Sundays.

The Conservative movement went from strength to strength to become the largest Jewish religious movement on the American scene. According to the CJF population study, 40.5 percent of American Jewish households define themselves as Conservative. The movement's success can in large measure be ascribed to its compromise nature.

If the Conservative compromise was useful to Jews who cared only moderately about expressing their Judaism in the years before World War II, it also proved very attractive to those for whom Judaism was a central concern. For the latter, Conservative Judaism offered a means to synthesize their desire for a more modern Judaism with their basic commitment to Jewishness. These Jews were virtually all products of traditional Jewish homes and were strongly imbued with Zionist ideas; they sought something more in tune with the times than the Orthodoxy they knew from their childhood, yet Reform patterns and practices were thoroughly alien to most of them, coming as they did from East European backgrounds. Conservatism had an added advantage in that it allowed them to be quite traditional in their behavior without demanding that they be Orthodox in their thinking or public discussions.

Building on Schechter's idea of "catholic Israel" (that is, a Jewish community that embraced all elements rather than confining itself to only a few), the Conservative movement quickly took the implicit position that it would avoid coming to grips with ideological problems. Conservatives were satisfied to base their movement on the idea of the peoplehood of Israel as long as the persons who accepted that idea were willing to express themselves in a moderately traditional manner religiously. Thus it became possible for the committed Jewish intelligentsia, such as it was, to rationalize their relationship with the synagogue despite theological doubts by claiming that they observed tradition for the sake of Jewish peoplehood. This idea, which reached into the highest places in the Conservative movement, was no barrier to participation in Conservative congregations. Moreover, despite very serious equivocations within the Jewish Theological Seminary itself, the Conservative movement did indeed become the movement most closely identified with the ideology of peoplehood, thereby attracting more than its share of Zionists, Jewish educators, and others whose concern with Jewish life was intense, rather than simply moderate or residual.[8]

Reconstructionism

Just as Ethical Culture was a natural outgrowth of Reform, so Reconstructionism was a natural offshoot of Conservative Judaism, taking the latter's emphasis on peoplehood and transforming it into the central focus of Jewish religious life. The Reconstructionist movement has now become virtually a fourth branch of American Judaism, but it was a long time in reaching that point. Reconstructionism first began as a system of thought designed by Mordecai M. Kaplan to reconstruct American Jewish life in light of what he perceived to be the realities of the American environment and the principles of modern thought. Its particular blend of American and Jewish thought can be said to reflect, as Charles Liebman has argued, the conventional wisdom of American Jews; most American Jews today, he suggests, if asked to define their approach to Judaism, would probably do so in Reconstructionist terms without even knowing it and certainly without acknowledging Reconstructionism.

Kaplan, however, was not satisfied with simply projecting a system of thought. As an activist and reformer by nature, he sought to develop institutions that reflected his ideas, yet to do so within the framework of existing synagogue movements and communal institutions rather than by establishing yet another sectarian body. Thus his first efforts were directed toward the development of synagogue centers as comprehensive institutions built around Jewish worship, but including all facets of Jewish existence—social, educational, and cultural. To that end he developed what he saw as a model synagogue, the Society for the Advancement of Judaism. Even its name was significant—a *society* that would join together in worship and in other Jewish activities, rather than a *synagogue* as such.

For two decades the Reconstructionists contented themselves with being a pressure group, primarily within the Conservative movement (Dr. Kaplan was on the faculty of the Jewish Theological Seminary), seeking to win adherents. However, all along there had been voices within the Reconstructionist movement urging it to institutionalize on a separate basis. In the 1950s such views began to proliferate, and by the end of the decade the first steps were taken in that direction. The emergence of the Federation of Reconstructionist Congregations and Fellowships at that time signified a new phase in the history of the movement. The next step was the establishment, in 1968, of the Reconstructionist Rabbinical College in Philadelphia. While the Reconstructionist movement remains numerically small in comparison to the other groups (many individual Hasidic groups, for instance, have more members than all the Reconstructionist congregations put together), it is becoming articulated as a fourth branch of American Judaism.

In the meantime, a change has taken within the ranks of Reconstructionists. The first adherents of the movement were Jews raised in Orthodox homes who wished to preserve more of Jewish tradition than was acceptable in Reform Judaism, but who were theologically at odds with the leading forces of the Conservative movement. Religious naturalists by and large, they sought a justification for Jewish observance in Jewish peoplehood since they could not reconcile themselves to the notion of a divinely commanded Halakhah. They have been succeeded by a generation who never experienced traditional Jewish living, who are products of assimilated homes or of the Reconstructionist movement itself. This new generation accepts Reconstructionist ideas in theory, but when applying them in practice adopts a different attitude toward observance. Thus it was possible for the first Reconstructionists—like Dr. Kaplan— to remain virtually Orthodox in their behavior while arguing that the rituals of Judaism should be performed only if they were significant to the persons who performed them; naturally these proponents found a personal significance in most traditional forms. However, the same argument applied by the present generation has led to a radical diminution of traditional observance because such practice is not part of their personal experience, and so is not meaningful to them. This in itself acts to discourage would-be adherents who, out of sentiment, might wish to retain traditional patterns of observance, no matter how inconsistently. Since the Reconstructionist movement places a high premium on reason and consistency, it has failed to gain a mass appeal. The result is that while many Reconstructionist views have entered into the consciousness of American Jewry, the movement itself languishes.[9]

Orthodoxy

American Orthodoxy was the third movement to emerge in organized fashion on the American Jewish scene. There is a seeming paradox in this because the very first congregations to be established in the United States were what later would have been considered Orthodox. But since the early groups were simply congregations in the traditional (that is, premodern) sense, they were not consciously part of any movement until the emergence of Reform and Conservatism in the nineteenth century. At that point some of the original congregations moderated their practices and became the nucleus of the Conservative movement; others refused to make what seemed to them to be major concessions to the American environment. The latter joined with the best-organized congregations created by the East European immigrants and, in self-defense, organized the Union of Orthodox Jewish Congregations and Yeshiva University.[10]

American Orthodoxy has always been centered in New York City far more than the other two movements; the bulk of its adherents as well as its leadership are located there. Even today, despite the relative decline of the New York metropolitan area in American Jewish life, perhaps 80 percent or more of Jews who live an Orthodox life (as distinct from those who are members of Orthodox synagogues but are not themselves observant) are located within a hundred miles of Manhattan. Significantly, only 11.4 percent of American Jewish households even define themselves as Orthodox, according to the CJF study.

American Orthodoxy is not neatly organized like its Conservative and Reform counterparts, since its organizational patterns reflect its internal ideological divisions. Mainstream Orthodoxy is centered around Yeshiva University and the Union of Orthodox Jewish Congregations. Besides representing the largest Orthodox group in the United States, with the most congregations and the most members, it also covers the broadest spectrum within the Orthodox community, from the most left-wing to relatively right-wing elements.

Outside the metropolitan area UOJC congregations tend to be made up primarily of Jews who do not live Orthodox lives but are members of Orthodox congregations because of family patterns or for convenience or for similar reasons. The main differences between these congregations and their Conservative counterparts lie in the slightly more traditional services of the former and their frequent (but not universal) retention of separate seating. The UOJC will accept congregations with mixed seating as members if they give some indication of moving toward adoption of separate seating. The issue of separate seating has been a big one within the UOJC since its right wing wished to maintain that condition as the minimum requirement for affiliation. Indeed, separate seating was the line that divided the Orthodox left wing from the Conservative right wing for many years.

The second major Orthodox group is Young Israel. Founded in 1912 (by Mordecai Kaplan, no less) in an effort to apply American standards of decorum and organization to Orthodoxy, Young Israel has become a nationwide movement of no little strength. Unlike the UOJC, Young Israel's congregations and members are truly Orthodox in their individual as well as collective behavior patterns. Young Israel has been moving to the right in recent years, along with the rest of Orthodoxy, and now varies between extremely right wing to moderate. As the heart of modern Orthodoxy, Young Israel continues to pride itself on its ability to combine the Orthodox way of life with the latest modern styles in other fields.

The right wing of Orthodoxy embraces two major segments: the Hasidic groups and those more or less connected with Agudath Israel.

These groups came to the United States as a result of the Nazi persecutions and the Holocaust in Europe. They are the exceptions to the American Jewish migrational pattern: they did not come in search of opportunity but because their lives were in peril. Indeed, they came with the very clear feeling that America was "not kosher" and that Jewish life in America would be unacceptable to them. From the first, they had no real desire to assimilate or to accommodate themselves to the American milieu; instead, they sought ways to preserve their separateness and keep their children from acculturating.

Orthodoxy, like Conservatism and Reform, had been moving to the left throughout the 1920s and 1930s, and even into the 1940s. But this newest group introduced truly right-wing Orthodoxy into the United States and exercised a profound influence upon the whole structure and orientation of American Orthodoxy. Their presence as bearers of Torah scholarship and upholders of the Law in its most traditional form became a source of embarrassment to the modernizing Orthodox, who were products of the earlier migrational waves and shared their desire to acculturate at least to some degree. They were instrumental in creating a network of yeshivas—institutions of higher education in the traditional manner—that have developed into repositories of traditional Jewish learning, even to the point of challenging the more americanized Orthodox educational institutions as centers of Orthodox intellectual activity.

Among the Hasidic groups the strongest are the Chabad or Lubavitcher Hasidim. The rebbe who was the head of the Lubavitcher movement at that time arrived in the United States during World War II, after an odyssey of no mean proportions, and immediately established headquarters in Brooklyn. From there he and his successor have presided over the worldwide activities of the Chabad movement.

The Lubavitcher Hasidim, like all other Hasidic groups, are characterized by their firm commitment to the traditional way of life, including the traditional dress of the East European Orthodox. However, they differ from the rest of their compatriots in their conscious and organized efforts to bring other Jews into the traditional fold. They see as one of their major purposes the "conversion" of Jews to traditional Jewish life. On this premise they have built an empire in the United States and abroad, and despite their apparent isolation from the mainstream of modern Jewish life, they are among the most active elements in the Jewish community working to counteract Jewish assimilation. One finds Lubavitcher Hasidim in small towns all over America, reaching out to the handful of Jewish families that are neglected by the organized Jewish establishment; and one finds them in the biggest communities, reaching out to Jews who have chosen to absent themselves from the ranks of organized Jewish life.

While they do not compromise in their faithfulness to the Law, they will accept Jews no matter what stage of observance they happen to be in, trying simply to encourage them to strive in the direction of greater observance. As a mystical group that sees religious significance in the performance of every ritual act, they reach out to alienated Jews by asking them to do such things as putting on tefillin or saying the proper blessings over the etrog and lulav on Sukkot. Beyond that, they maintain an educational program based on various gradations of involvement. If a person enters the program and passes through all the gradations, he should end up as an observant Lubavitcher Hasid, close to the rebbe in Brooklyn. The influence of the Lubavitcher movement should not be underestimated: in many respects it is the most dynamic Jewish movement in the United States today.[11]

At the other end of the Hasidic spectrum are the Satmar Hasidim—the most right-wing Hasidic group. Rather than reaching out to the Jewish community at large and trying to influence Jews to become more traditional, the Satmar Hasidim hold that any contact with what to them is a contaminated and assimilated Jewry can only weaken the true believers—themselves. Therefore they try to isolate themselves as much as possible from non-Satmar Jews, including other Orthodox groups. Extremely rigid in their approach to tradition, they reject the state of Israel as a secular profanation and an enemy of Jewish tradition, and they consider the bulk of American Jewry to be beyond all hope of redemption. They attempt to be self-sufficient economically so that they will have as little contact with the outside world as possible.[12]

The focal points of the non-Hasidic right wing include the alliance grouped around the Union of Orthodox Rabbis of the United States and Canada, headed by Rabbi Moshe Feinstein, the chain of yeshivas established by the late Rabbi Aharon Cutler, and the Breuer Congregation, the heir of the great German Orthodox leader Samson Raphael Hirsch. Adherents of the latter group have always prided themselves on their involvement in the intellectual economic life of the modern world, while retaining an extremely rigid traditionalism. This they transplanted to the American shore, although to their chagrin they find that their children are moving to the right and are not interested in being part of the modern world in any respect, even rejecting the secular education that their fathers believed was worthwhile. Many of the sons have moved into the yeshiva world as a result. The influence of the yeshiva world has been principally responsible for the development of a significant community of Orthodox students, with Rabbi Cutler's students spreading that world institutionally far beyond New York in the last two decades.

THE IMPACT OF AMERICA ON JEWISH RELIGIOUS LIFE

American civilization has had a substantial influence on Jewish religious life in a variety of ways that cut across all movements, although influencing them differently. Here we can note but a few of the most significant.

Status of women

Equality side by side with liberty is a cornerstone of the American dream. Especially in the twentieth century, equality in America has come to mean the elimination of all distinctions between people, including those between men and women. Jewish tradition, while according women an important place and recognizing their worth in a way that many other premodern traditions did not, nevertheless does not seek equality between the sexes. At most, Judaism attempts to enhance the separate responsibilities of the sexes, so that they complement one another and become equally important; but that is far different from the kind of equality demanded by American society. This has had a variety of consequences.

One of the first and most important manifestations of the drive to equalize the status of women was the introduction of mixed seating in American synagogues. Today mixed seating is far and away the predominant synagogue pattern. It is taken as a matter of course in all Reform and virtually all Conservative congregations, and is a fact of life in many Orthodox ones. Thus the family pew (to use the Protestant term adopted by the original advocates of mixed seating) is the standard pattern in the American synagogue.

Mixed seating brought with it the recognition that women should participate more or less equally in synagogue life, at least in its congregational aspects. From this have flowed other innovations leading to the enhancement of women's role in the ritual life of the congregation. In

Reform doctrine no real distinction is made between men and women. Women can do anything that men can in the service as a matter of right. Recently a woman was ordained as a rabbi by Hebrew Union College. Reconstructionists are equally "integrated," if not more so. For many years Conservative congregations allowed women the same rights as men except being called to the Torah and leading the service; in the movement's left wing even the latter prohibitions were dropped in the 1950s and 1960s. The onslaughts of the Women's Lib movement brought a rapid opening up of even mainstream Conservative congregations to the point where the Rabbinical Assembly Law Committee has ruled that it is now permitted to count women as part of a minyan. Only Orthodoxy continues to hold the line against women's direct participation in the synagogue service.

Perhaps more important than the role of women in the synagogue service is the growing role of women's organizations in the maintenance of Jewish life. Since the home is the center of so much of Jewish life, the woman, as manager of the home, has always played a great role in preserving Jewish tradition. Today the woman's role has grown in an organizational way as well, with women managing synagogue and other community activities and, increasingly, the institutions themselves. A generation ago, as Jewish life, following the American pattern, became a leisure-time activity, it became more and more the province of women —the principal custodians of leisure-time activity in the United States— particularly since they were acquiring more leisure while this change was taking place. Thus women's organizations acquired responsibility for everything from maintaining the youth program to raising funds for the school, in addition to their general philanthropic and social work. And the rabbi who did not have the confidence of the leadership of the women's organizations in his synagogue probably did not stay long in his job.

Ironically, the expanding recognition of the equality of women in the synagogue comes at a time when the women themselves are seeking careers and no longer have as much time for synagogue activities. Thus two contradictory trends have developed. On one hand, as in general American church practice, women are assuming positions in synagogues that were previously open only to men. On the other, the specifically women's organizations, which depended upon women seeking an outlet for their energies, are declining, as young women pursue careers and are no longer available for or interested in organizational activity.

Some male preserves remain in American Jewry, most of them holding fast except among the extreme left wing. The rabbinate is still a sphere for men, although the Reform and Reconstructionist movements are breaking down that barrier as well. Though there are some exceptions, by and large the major professional positions in the Jewish community are occupied by males, such as school administrators. The bulk of the teachers in Jewish schools are female, however. The difference is that the administrative positions are defined as full-time, while teaching is defined as a part-time position, ideal for housewives who want to earn some money on Sundays or in the late afternoon.

The official voluntary leadership of the synagogue was, until recently, predominantly if not exclusively male. Women have had some representation on synagogue boards, mostly ex officio (the president of the sisterhood is automatically entitled to a place on the board), but it has been token representation, and only recently have a few women attained board positions (and even congregational offices) on their own merits. For the moment the very basic congregational decisions remain in the hands of men, but this may well be changing.

Finally, heavy fund raising remains a mainly male activity, no doubt because the men are the ones who decide where the big money is spent.

Decorum

The drive for decorum, like the drive for greater equality for women, was an essential aspect of the break away from Orthodoxy in the United States. Abandonment of observance alone would not have caused the kind of institutional changes in American Jewish life that did occur, as is shown by the existence of large numbers of nonobservant Orthodox today. It was the people who wished to maintain some kind of Judaism who created the new institutional structures, and they did so because they were unhappy with the character of the ritual life of the Orthodox congregations they knew. The American influence favored a decorous service, one that was orderly and impressive in the way that gentile society defines these matters. Since decorum was originally introduced by German Jews, they tended to follow the models set by the Lutherans, a sect that originated in Germany, rather than the simpler forms of the American churches, emphasizing ceremony and the ministerial function of the rabbi as against the teaching function (which the American churches had originally borrowed from the Jews).

As American Jews tried to develop decorous services in the Protestant high-church manner, they usually missed the real character of Protestant decorum and created something that looked the same but was really very different. High-church Protestant services were decorous because the people who attended them brought a certain set of attitudes and behavior patterns into the congregation; it was not necessary for the minister to impose them, nor did the service have to be organized around decorum as a principle. Among Jews the striving for decorum became the central principle governing the service, but the ritual itself rarely created any inherent decorousness in the congregation. Instead, the service became a kind of staged performance in which the congregation was transformed into an audience and was expected to keep quiet. (The transfer of the focus of the service from a podium in the center of the hall to a stage up front both symbolized and concretized this shift.) Since most Jews found it difficult to keep quiet for very long, they came to the service for the shortest possible time, and even then they had to be reminded by ushers to remain solemn in the proper spirit. Instead of the impressive simplicity of the ordered Protestant service, the synagogue produced a stultifying kind of stage show that was neither worshipful in the traditional Jewish sense nor aesthetically harmonious in the traditional American sense.

In recent years there has been a reaction against decorum among the new generation. This is partly because they have internalized many of the features of Anglo-Saxon orderliness and so can be more relaxed about it. Partly it is reaction against those aspects of solemnity that have robbed the service of its "warmth." These people are looking for a religious experience that will allow them and their children to feel at home in the synagogue to a greater extent than was possible under the patterns evolved in the 1920s and 1930s. There is also a reaction against the showmanship that evolved as part of the decorous service, which alienated the service from its central purpose as a religious experience. People who attend services today tend to want to pray, and, if they know how to in any way, they want to do it themselves. Still, the reaction against decorum in this sense has come from people who are best defined as neotraditionalists, and it has not affected the broad base of synagogue membership.

The Form and Content of the Service

In the form and the content of the service, too, American life has been very influential. First, there has been a shift from the daily to the weekly service as the basic rhythm of Jewish religious observance. Most American Jews do not even think of going to pray every day as their forefathers did. For most of American Jewry today a truly observant Jew is one who tries to go to services every Sabbath. Daily services have been reduced to a once- or twice-a-year event for people who wish to commemorate the departed. Although the weekly rhythm is generally honored in the breach, it is still the accepted one.

In the weekly service itself the emphasis has shifted—stress on reading the Torah has given way to stress on the sermon. This, too, is Protestant in origin. While preaching is an ancient Jewish art, it was not until relatively late that sermons began to be delivered on a regular basis— and they certainly were never expected to supersede the Torah reading in importance. Today it is clear that the relative weight of the two has been drastically altered.

Where reform of the service has taken place, it has been in the direction of the enhancement of the rabbi's role. In the first round of reforms the role of the congregation was reduced, primarily on the (not incorrect) assumption that fewer and fewer members knew what to do in a service. This tended to strengthen the role of the cantor as well as that of the rabbi, or in Reform congregations the rabbi and the choir. Most recently there has been a shift away from choir and cantor toward a more self-contained rabbinical role. This movement was justified on the grounds that the previous change did nothing to stem the drift away from synagogue attendance, and that the task of the rabbi was to make the service more interesting. The whole effort has acquired a momentum of its own. Originally it was argued that since the congregation did not understand Hebrew, the traditional service could not help but be boring as well as unaesthetic, and that expanding the role of the cantor, choir, and, to a lesser extent, the rabbi in the service would make it more appealing. Since the cantor and choir still operated more or less within a traditional framework, this did not work; then it was further argued that more staged activities under the rabbi's direction and an increased teaching and preaching role for him would do the trick. That has been the direction of the past two decades, but without any appreciable results along the expected lines. On the contrary, there are now many congregations with members who attend services and have learned enough Hebrew to want to participate, but are prevented from doing so by the elaborate format managed from the pulpit.

Holiday Observance

The traditional rhythm of Jewish life has two focal points: daily obligations of prayer and the yearly calendar punctuated with holy days and festivals. The two are connected by the weekly Sabbath. Just as the daily rhythm has been replaced by a weekly one, so, too, has the yearly rhythm been altered to respond to the rhythm of Christian observance.

At one time the High Holy Days were almost universally observed by attendance at services. Today, with the decline in personal faith (a prerequisite for participation in the long services of collective confession and personal repentance that characterize the High Holy Days), they are being increasingly honored in the breach among the younger generation, but the rhythm is still recognized. Since the Christians have their great days in the American calendar, the Jews are entitled to theirs—provided they do not ask for too many. The three days of Rosh Hashanah and Yom Kippur are right and proper because they really do not greatly exceed the Christian demands for a day off on Christmas and Good Friday. So American society has endowed the High Holy Days with a special place on the American calendar, and in return the Jews have largely abandoned the other festivals, at least as days of abstinence from regular activity in the general society. In sum, Jews are expected to absent themselves from work on Rosh Hashanah and Yom Kippur, but are less and less likely to be found in the synagogue.

The other festivals have been reordered in priority, based upon the degree of their appeal to children, and reduced to evening activities (again, the leisure-time syndrome). Sukkot and Shavuot are practically forgotten by the majority of American Jews, but Simhat Torah has gained in importance because its principal observance takes place in the evening. Passover is observed primarily through the seder, another evening activity. In fact, Passover observance seems to have surpassed that of the High Holy Days among Jews, partly because of its timing and partly because it is a festival of freedom in a country where liberty is one of the highest values. In the 1960s the seder even became something of an American celebration as radicals and reformers developed the "freedom seder" as a central element in their ceremonial life.

Hanukkah and to a lesser extent Purim have been raised to first importance. Hanukkah has prospered because it comes about the same time as Christmas and can be used as the Jewish equivalent; Purim, because it provides a Jewish counterpart to carnival time. Both, like Simhat Torah and the seder, are overwhelmingly child-centered.

Fortunately, the new day begins at sunset in the Jewish calendar, and holiday observances traditionally begin in the evening. This gives an impetus to the spread of evening-time Judaism. Besides the seder on Passover, reading the Purim megillah and the processions with the Torah on Simhat Torah are other evening activities that work in well with the leisure-time calendar of American Jews, as does lighting the Hanukkah candles in the evening. Friday evening has come to be synonymous with the Sabbath for most Jews who recognize any kind of Sabbath observance at all; on Saturday the regular routine is restored. In sum, Jewish activity has generally become relegated to the evening hours.

The Role of the "Laity"

The very concept of "laity" reflects the American influence on Jewish life. The implicit differentiation into the rabbinate and the laity has tended to reduce the role of nonprofessionals in the synagogue (though other factors, such as the congregational character of the synagogue as an organization, have served to give the householders a principal role in congregational governance).

One major factor that has sharpened the distinction between the rabbinate and the laity is the low level of "Jewish literacy" among nonrabbis. As rabbis increasingly come to have a monopoly on Jewish education (not that theirs is so excellent but we are speaking in relative terms), it becomes far more difficult for someone who is not a rabbi to function authoritatively in the Jewish sphere. Thus in matters other than strictly business affairs having to do with the management of a particular organization or institution, nonrabbis tend to defer to rabbis, not because of the latter's experience in Jewish law, but because they are the "professionals" in a society in which professionalism is respected above all.

The Role of the Rabbis

By the same token, the role of the rabbinate has radically changed as a result of American influences on Jewish life. The early Sephardic congregations did not call their leaders "rabbis," since these leaders were not well enough educated and did not perform the traditional teaching and judging functions which they, as Jews from the Old World, understood to be essential to the rabbinical office. They were called "hazzanim" or readers, that is, they were prayer-chanters who led the service. In time the hazzan's function expanded to become much like that of the Protestant minister.

As the hazzan was transformed into the modern rabbi (and his educational standards were raised somewhat), the rabbi adapted himself to the role set out for him by his congregation, which was much like that of a minister: to be a preacher and a pastor. Since most Jews were not much interested in learning and no longer lived by the canons of Jewish law, the rabbi's traditional functions were the very ones that were least esteemed by the synagogue members who hired and fired him. This reinforced the alteration of the rabbi's role that was already in progress.

The rabbis adjusted to America's specialized society by specializing in "Jewishness" and came to serve their congregations as ministers. The people, in turn, demanded that their rabbis preach well, be good pastors, and observe the Jewish way of life according to the standard set by the congregation. To oversimplify somewhat, it can be said that an Orthodox congregation increasingly consists of observant people who expect the rabbi to observe the Law strictly; a Conservative congregation consists of unobservant people who expect the rabbi to be strong but flexible in his observance and "modern" in his demands upon his congregants; and a Reform congregation makes few ritualistic demands on its rabbi but wants him to "represent Judaism."

In sum, the rabbi has become a professional leader of his congregation like the Protestant minister, his traditional functions as scholar, teacher, and judge being replaced by those of pastor, service-conductor, and occasionally congregational administrator. This means that he is required to know much less traditional Jewish material than before, while at the same time being credited by his Jewishly illiterate congregation with knowing far more. His position has been enhanced vis-à-vis members of his congregation because of his relatively superior mastery of Jewish sources and his obligation to serve as the representative Jew for his congregation, even though his ability to be a creative rabbi in the traditional sense has diminished. To the extent that congregations feel that their rabbi holds "the keys to heaven," his status is more akin to the traditional role found in Christianity than in Judaism. On the other hand, increasingly he is expected to know the techniques of pastoral psychology and is judged by his skills in "human relations."[13]

SECTIONALISM AND JEWISH RELIGIOUS DEVELOPMENT[14]

The history of the religious development of American Jewry is in part a history of the influence of sectionalism. The first American congregation to adopt Reform was located, as we have noted, in South Carolina —appropriately enough, in the section in which the Jews integrated most rapidly. Despite this exception, all the contemporary branches of American Judaism originated as organized entities in the greater Northeast, each in a different state or section. Even today each is particularly strong or favored in some sections and weak in others.

Orthodoxy, the oldest and at the same time the youngest branch of American Judaism, originated and developed in New York and the Middle Atlantic states, both in its earliest "Sephardic" period and in its latest "East European Ashkenazic" period. Reform, on the other hand, sank only the shallowest roots in the Middle Atlantic states in its formative years. It was a product of the Great Lakes region and the South. It was not accidental that Cincinnati, the city that best served those sections in the mid-nineteenth century, became the center of the Reform movement. The Conservative movement, though now headquartered in New York, actually developed in Philadelphia, was centered there during its formative years, and still has its greatest single concentration of congregations per capita in that city. It is weakest in the South, where it has continued to play second fiddle to the Reform movement. Though its history as a congregational movement is still too brief for a pattern to be clear, there is good reason to believe that Reconstructionism, founded in New York as a religious movement for intellectuals, has gained its greatest popular following in the West, particularly in California and Colorado.

Available data allow us only to suggest why this has been so. New York City, as the largest Jewish community in the United States and as the city generally most conducive to the perpetuation of cultural pluralism, has offered the best and most extensive facilities for the development and maintenance of the Orthodox way of life and has also placed the fewest obstacles in the way of Orthodoxy. Some of the other large cities in the Middle Atlantic states may come close to New York City in this respect but cannot match it. Although small authentically Orthodox congregations have developed in most large and medium-sized Jewish communities in the other sections during the past generation, only the very largest cities can provide an environment in which a viable Orthodox community, with a full range of institutions, is able to maintain itself. Despite exceptions, such as Miami and Los Angeles, Orthodoxy in the South and West is, perforce, considerably less able to demand strict observance from its often nominal adherents and exists primarily as a reflection of the nostalgia of certain Jews for their parents' religious attachments.

Conservatism can easily be seen as a product of the moderate traditionalism of Philadelphia and Baltimore, where a tradition of managed change in conjunction with a basically conservative outlook has existed ever since the days of William Penn and Lord Calvert. As far and away the largest of the branches of American Judaism, it has since spread over the continent to such an extent that it cannot be said to have any particular area of sectional concentration. At the same time, its very size and spread have made it reflect the sectional differences in American Jewish life internally more than any other religious movement. These sectional differences form a basis for a goodly share of the internal conflict within the Rabbinical Assembly over matters of movement policy. The Conservative movement is known for its internal diversity —its "left," "right," and "center." While examples of every kind of religious adaptation present in the movement can be found in every section, there are different sectional means or modes. In the Middle Atlantic states and New England, many Conservative congregations and their leaders tend to maintain a high degree of traditionalism in ritual practice. Conservative congregations in those sections have been the last holdouts against riding on the Sabbath—even to the synagogue—and for maintaining the traditional position of women in the synagogue service. In some congregations women are not allowed on the pulpit or in the choir during services. In the South and Great Lakes states riding on the Sabbath is no longer an issue for the membership, although it may be for the rabbi. Increasingly, women are given major roles to play in the service, although their participation is still something of an issue.

By contrast, Conservatism in the trans-Mississippi West is downright radicalism. Riding on the Sabbath—even by rabbis—is virtually unquestioned west of the Mississippi, and many congregations even run buses to pick up the children on Saturday morning. The women's role has virtually ceased to be an issue. In fact, it is routine for women to be called to the Torah, and they are now being counted in the minyan in congregations throughout those sections.

The Reform movement, whose greatest strength is still in the South and Middle West, is a product of nineteenth-century American liberalism, based on the romantic, optimistic "rationalism" that flourished in the United States one hundred years ago. This nineteenth-century spirit was nowhere better expressed than in the Great Lakes states and those bordering that area, a section that combined the social values of the frontier with classic individual-enterprise economics and yet was a direct product of the most "American" influences emanating from the seaboard states. The Reform movement, then, in its search for American roots, probably could not have developed as it did in any other section. Hence it was in the Great Lakes region that its leaders developed the particular Reform synthesis combining the frontier spirit, nineteenth-century liberalism, fundamental "Americanism," and the rationalism of a transplanted German culture. The Reform movement also flourished in the South, where the Protestant-like orientation of classic Reform fit in well with the relatively successful aspirations of southern Jewry to fit into the general southern environment. Since many parts of the trans-Mississippi West were settled after the Reform idea had been elaborated, the first Reform congregations there were often created as such and did not evolve from Orthodoxy, as was so common in the greater Northeast.

While Reform congregations existed in New England and the Middle Atlantic states from the early days of the movement, in those two sections they were always overshadowed by the more traditional forms of Jewish religious expression. There was, in fact, a major sectional struggle within the Reform movement at the turn of the century, between the eastern Reform congregations (with the support of Isaac Mayer Wise) on one hand and the midwestern congregations (with southern support) on the other, over the degree of Reform to be adopted as movement policy. The eastern congregations, representing the more traditional viewpoint, lost to the midwesterners, who were led to victory by the great classical Reform rabbis of that section.

As in Orthodoxy and Conservatism, the level of traditionalism in the Reform congregations tends to diminish as one moves westward. While this seems to have always been the case, it may have become more pronounced as the Reform movement has become more concerned with the reintroduction of ritual. Again, the evidence is basically impressionistic, but the Reform congregations of New England and the Middle Atlantic states appear to be the most ritualistically traditional today, as they certainly were fifty years ago. In all parts of the Great Lakes region there appears to be an admixture of neotraditionalism and classic radicalism, as well as everything in between. The Reform congregations of the South tend to be the most radical, while those of the West are mixed, leaning toward the radical.

In general, changes in synagogue practice seem to spread from west to east, particularly when they are changes that involve a shift away from traditional practices. This has been historically true regardless of where "the West" happened to be located at the particular time, with Reform starting in the West of the 1840s and 1850s and the practice of calling women to the Torah starting in the West of the 1950s.

Sectional differences are apparent not only in religious practice but in religious organization as well. The synagogue center, with its "near-total" program of Jewish activity, is a particular feature of the Middle Atlantic states, perhaps even of New York. Elsewhere the pattern seems to be one of a few large congregations in each community that concentrate on ritual services, elementary education, and youth work, but do not seek to be all-encompassing institutions—primarily because they must compete with others already functioning outside the synagogue framework.

OTHER JEWISH INSTITUTIONS IN A
RELIGION-ORIENTED ENVIRONMENT

While the synagogue and its functions (and functionaries) have a place ready-made for them by the non-Jewish society around them, all other community institutions and functions start with the handicap of having to find their own place in the American Jewish world and to justify it within the context of American life. This has not prevented the development of institutions that are not related to the synagogue and has not kept them from achieving appropriate recognition by Jews and non-Jews alike, but they have had to reach for acceptance instead of receiving it as a right.

By and large, the organizations that found it easiest to gain legitimacy were those devoted to benevolence, philanthropy, and welfare. This was partly because these were tasks that until the 1930s were considered by Americans to be basically the responsibility of church groups; it was relatively easy for the Jews to establish their own such institutions by extension. Consequently, the major nonsynagogue organizations and institutions in the United States have developed out of efforts to deal with the social-welfare problems of the Jewish community. This includes the Jewish welfare federations (the name itself is significant) and the Jewish community centers, as well as more obvious welfare organizations. The fact that today the federations and centers have developed far broader purposes reflects the increasing maturity of the American Jewish community and American Jews' discovery of ways to build their community within the context of the American environment.

Contemporary Jewish life has been decisively shaped by the evolution of what were originally limited-purpose welfare bodies into comprehensive community organizations. Historically, the demands of World War I, the Holocaust, and World War II and the creation and maintenance of the state of Israel fitted the needs of the American Jewish community in this regard. In other words, the first great demands for overall community organization that were placed upon American Jewry were welfare demands—or at least could be construed as such. Therefore it was possible for Jews to utilize welfare institutions to meet those demands without in any way violating American ideas about subcommunities. Though the welfare organizations expanded for "philanthropic" purposes, in the process they discovered that they had to do more than provide philanthropy. They had to reorganize as something more than welfare organizations. The history of the last thirty years of American Jewish life shows how they came to cope with that discovery and react to it. The remainder of this volume therefore has as its focus that process and its contemporary implications.

The "State" of American Jewry and Its Institutional Base[1]

Within the unique polity that is the Jewish people, the American Jewish community can be conceived as a "state" of some six million people, one of several collectivities that exist in various countries of the world as religioethnic societies structured to maintain Jewish life. From this perspective the state of Israel is but another Jewish state, differing from the rest only in that it also possesses sovereignty under international law. Only certain countrywide Jewish communities in existence today—those with populations of over 120,000, plus a few others for exceptional reasons—can be reckoned as "states" with sufficiently comprehensive institutions to maintain themselves in a Jewish fashion. The others lack the wherewithal to do so, either in numbers, talent, or interest, and must be considered dependencies of one sort or another, looking to their sister communities for their basic communal needs. Although its history as a Jewish community extends back to 1654, the "state" of Jewish America was to all intents and purposes a colony of European Jewry until the nineteenth century, was a dependency even longer, and is still a polity in the process of formation.

American Jewry shares the long-standing American commitment to noncentralized decision making. Decision making in the United States is not decentralized but noncentralized. That is, there is no single center that can determine how or where decision making should be dispersed, as the notion of decentralization implies. Rather, there are many different centers of decision making, each of which exists legitimately in its own right, while the existence of each is protected within the society in some "constitutional" way. In political life even the federal government, powerful as it is, is simply one center—some would even describe it as a cluster of centers—among many.

Noncentralization is institutionalized in American society in government, religion, education, and most of the other arenas of American life (perhaps least in the economy), all of which serve to reinforce what is not only a basic social pattern but one that is culturally and ideologically accepted as the correct one.[2] This institutionalized noncentralization carries over to influence American Jewish life as well, where it is reinforced by organizational and cultural patterns well rooted in Jewish history.[3]

The "state" of Jewish America has no single overarching governing body. Action in the name of American Jewry on a countrywide basis is undertaken by a number of organizations of countrywide scope, generally with specialized fields of interest, while the real powers of communal governance, such as they are, are particularly concentrated in the 229 local Jewish federations. Chief among the countrywide bodies is the Council of Jewish Federations and Welfare Funds (CJF), the closest thing to an umbrella body that exists; its powers are growing because it represents the combined leaders of the local federations. In addition, there are bodies such as the American Association for Jewish Education (AAJE), the Jewish Welfare Board (serving the Jewish community centers), the "big three" community-relations organizations (American Jewish Committee, American Jewish Congress, Anti-Defamation League), the Synagogue Council of America, and the Orthodox, Conservative, and Reform synagogue federations plus their auxiliary bodies, and, for foreign affairs, the Conference of Presidents of Major American Jewish Organizations (more familiarly called the Presidents' Conference). The latter body has become more prominent in recent years, at least in the headlines.

Internally the "state" of Jewish America is divided into over 800 local communities (see Appendix B), organized through 229 local federations. Originally these federations encompassed single cities, but since the coming of suburbanization they have spread out to embrace virtually all organized Jewish communities within the vicinity of their original cities of jurisdiction; in that way most of the organized Jewish communities in the United States have become roughly analogous to counties. In most cases they have done so by redrawing their boundaries to embrace suburbs and small towns within their metropolitan orbit. Eighty-four of them, or nearly 40 percent, have acquired names reflecting their new scope, 28 have added appropriate wording to their original names, 9 serve two or more cities of equal size and are named accordingly. In fully suburbanized areas, such as New Jersey, or substate regions with small scattered Jewish communities like southern and central Illinois, regional federations have been organized to serve the needs of the whole area, while each local community continues to maintain its own local institutions as well (see Appendix C). There are 27 such regional federations by name and 17 more federations that are named after the counties in which they are located and that are structured in essentially the same way. The trend toward "county-ization," essentially a product of the postwar generation, is growing.

By and large American Jewish communal organization has not been based upon the state model, as is the norm in American society generally. Nevertheless, in two cases—Delaware and Rhode Island—local federations have been reorganized and renamed after the states that they now serve in their entirety, and a third, the Jewish Federation of Portland, is defined as embracing all of Oregon. Despite this relative neglect of the states for purposes of self-definition, it is testimony to the impact of the American environment that only a handful of the local federations have jurisdiction across state lines, and those are strictly responses to necessity. Washington, D.C.'s UJA serves the Maryland and some of the Virginia portions of the Washington metropolitan area; the Jewish Federation and Council of Greater Kansas City includes both the Missouri and Kansas portions of that metropolitan area; in Portland the Federation, in addition to embracing all of Oregon, also includes the narrow suburban strip across the Columbia River in Washington; and in 1973 the Jewish communities of Rock Island, Moline, Davenport, and Bettendorf in Illinois and Iowa combined their federations to establish the United Jewish Charities of the Quad Cities. It is possible that one or two other federations located in cities along state borders may reach across them to serve adjacent territories (such as Cincinnati and the neighboring Kentucky counties), but this brief list seems to be exhaustive.

In most interstate metropolitan areas Jews have divided their structures to recognize the state boundaries. Nowhere is this more evident than in the New York metropolitan region, where despite the very free movement of Jews across state lines, the federation service areas have hewed entirely to state boundaries. This is a very subtle example of the influence of American society on Jewish organization.

While the countrywide pattern of organizational diffusion is also replicated locally within each federation's area of service, the local federations tend to be more powerful umbrella bodies, which, through their great role in fund raising and community planning, have become bodies that all Jewish organizations and institutions locally must reckon with. There, too, the local Jewish community is still a polity-in-formation.

The more than eight hundred smaller communities, plus uncounted neighborhoods and suburbs, are roughly analogous to "towns," in the original American sense of the term. Organized Jewish life in these subcommunities is generally centered around one or more congregations that function as the "town" institutions, while for their more involved services and activities they rely upon the "county."

TERRITORIAL AND NONTERRITORIAL ORGANIZATION

The American Jewish community, like every Jewish community before it, is organized through a mixture of territorial and nonterritorial institutions. This fact has had some important implications in the United States, where the territorial organization of power is central to the entire political structure of the country. Territorial units delimited by political boundaries and embracing all people and institutions within them as equals are the basis of American political life. These same territorial units, with some modifications, form the basis for the organization of local Jewish communities. At the same time the ideological divisions in the Jewish community, real or putative, also provide significant points of organization, as do particular functions and certain common interests, which are then linked to the territorial community through certain common mechanisms.

The territorial organizations are invariably the most comprehensive ones, charged with providing overall direction for the community as a whole or some otherwise fragmented segment of it, while the ideological, functional, and interest organizations generally touch the more personal aspects of Jewish life. One consequence of this has been that Jewish reformers seeking to improve the organization of the American Jewish community have constantly emphasized the need to strengthen territorial organization as against other kinds, while partisans of particular interests in the Jewish community have emphasized nonterritorial forms of organization as the most appropriate forms in a voluntary community.

At the same time, because of the nature of the Jewish community, the territorial organizations rarely have fixed boundaries except by convention, and even so they are subject to revision of the kind they are now undergoing. Similarly, because ideological commitment in American Jewish life tends to be very weak, the ideological groupings have little internal strength of their own except insofar as they serve the interests of their members by taking on specific functional roles.

In many respects the territorial communities are simply aggregates of Jews living within particular political subdivisions. The ideological groupings, too, reflect historical or geographic "accidents"; thus the fact that a certain congregation is Orthodox or Conservative or Reform may not be due to its members' commitments and predilections but to its antecedent history. (Incidentally, apart from the synagogue movements, no ideological grouping has had any strong survival power on the American Jewish scene. These other groups, however, do survive as organizations that subdivide the community without providing the requisite glue to tie their members together in their commitments.)

New York City is one example of a territorial-ideological-functional mix. From a territorial perspective it is normally viewed as if it were a single Jewish community consisting of 1.84 million Jews living within the city limits; for the special purposes of UJA the 700,000 Jews who live in the adjacent counties of the New York metropolitan area are also included. From that perspective, New York is a disorganized community at best, a chaotic jumble of institutions and organizations. In fact, it is more appropriate to regard New York City as a region rather than a community, a region consisting of a congeries of communities that are organized not territorially (except in the vaguest sense), but on the basis of putative ideology (including religious ideology), function, and interest.

Although the five boroughs of New York City plus Nassau, Suffolk, and Westchester counties are organized under a single federation, which has sought to be comprehensive like those in other cities only since October 1973, few decisions are made for New York Jewry as a whole. As a region, New York is subject to all the weaknesses of regional aggregations in the United States possessing no meaningful political structure of their own. At the same time, since little has been done to create territorial communities within the region and to link the ideological, functional, and interest groupings to them, there are no subareas in which comprehensive communal decision making can take place either.

Each ideological or interest community is left to its own devices, to develop more or less effective internal decision-making mechanisms as best it can, leaving larger communal interests neglected because they are uncoordinated in any meaningful way. As a result, congregations have become "synagogue centers," and YMHA's have come to embrace religious services in an effort to develop viable subcommunities within the overall region.

Contrast the situation in New York City with that across the Hudson River in New Jersey. The state boundary and the particular organization of the New Jersey communities in question have organizationally separated the Jews there from those of New York City itself. There the various Jewish communities developed countywide, regional, or multicity territorial organizations within the metropolitan region, which substantially unite the various ideological and interest groupings for overall communal purposes, in the manner of the rest of Jewish America. They provide much more effective organization for the gamut of Jewish concerns than is available to the Jewish communities of Brooklyn, the Bronx, or Forest Hills (each with aggregations of Jews as large as or larger than those to be found in New Jersey). In other words, the myth of being part of a common community prevents various Jewish communities in New York City from developing territorial organizations of their own.

Other Jewish communities in the United States fare much better than New York in this regard too. They are manageable territorial communities that have developed a sufficient territorial basis to provide some unity among the ideological and interest groupings and institutions, although the division between territorial and nonterritorial organizations and the imperfect development of the links between them continues to be a major problem affecting the governance of American Jewry.

Still another pattern is found in the smallest communities, whether exurban or in the many small towns around the country. Their very smallness forces them to merge the territorial and ideological interests within the handful of institutions that they are able to maintain. In this respect they are closer to the "classical" pattern of premodern Jewish community organization than are their larger sisters.

Ideologically-based organizations have had more success on a countrywide basis, where until recently the absence of comprehensive territorial institutions has been marked. Countrywide organizations that developed prior to the 1930s became committed to specific ideological trends, whether they were founded that way or not. However, the impact of American life constantly serves to emphasize the territorial over the nonterritorial elements when given half a chance, and to reduce ideologically-based organizations to functional specialists responsible for specific tasks. A major result of this has been the limitation of the powers of the countrywide organizations and the localization of the primary decision-making responsibilities of the American Jewish community.

The basic institutions of the American Jewish community are essentially local and at most are loosely confederated with one another on a countrywide basis for very limited purposes. With the exception of a few institutions of higher education (and at one time a few specialized hospitals, which are now nonsectarian), all Jewish religious, social, welfare, and educational institutions are local both in name and in fact. Some are casually confederated on a supralocal basis but more are not, and those claiming national status with no local base soon find themselves without a constituency.

The overlapping local and supralocal federations that have emerged to unite these independent institutions and organizations form the basis for the communications matrix that is the countrywide Jewish community. Indeed, the major institutions of the American Jewish community —the federations and the synagogues—developed their countrywide bodies after their local institutions had become well established. Among the organizations which have been built out of a national headquarters, the only ones that have succeeded are those which have been able to develop meaningful local operations under local leadership.

The three great synagogue movements, conventionally viewed as the primary custodians of Jewish affiliation in the United States, are excellent cases in point. All are essentially confederations of highly independent local congregations linked by relatively vague persuasional ties and a need for certain technical services, such as professional placement, the organization of intercongregational youth programs, and the development of educational material. The confederations provide the requisite emotional reinforcement of those ties and the desired services for their member units. They have almost no direct influence on crucial congregational policies and behavior except insofar as the congregations themselves choose to look to them as guides. Short of expulsion from the movement, they have no devices by which to exercise authority, even in those cases where the congregation was originally established by the parent movement (which is not the usual pattern, but an occasional occurrence). Once a congregation is established it becomes as independent as all the rest.

The other great countrywide institutions of American Jewry are similarly organized. The CJF is an equally loose confederation of hundreds of local Jewish federations that have emerged in the past four decades as the most powerful institutional forces in Jewish life. The role of the CJF is definitely tributary to that of its constituents, who do not hesitate to give it direction, particularly through the Large City Budgeting Conference (LCBC), an association of the twenty-five most powerful federations within the CJF. As in the case of the synagogue movements, the power of the national organization flows from its ability to provide services to the local affiliates, generate ideas for them, and manage the flow of professionals. The key to its power lies in its ability to make those services useful and generate a demand for them.

So, too, the National Jewish Welfare Board is the countrywide service agency of the clearly autonomous local community centers, with limited operating responsibilities as their agent to serve the needs of Jews in the American armed forces. The AAJE is the service agency of the local bureaus of Jewish education and also unites the countrywide organizations that claim to have a major interest in Jewish education. The National Jewish Community Relations Advisory Council (NJCRAC) is the service agency of the local Jewish community-relations councils and the consultative forum for the countrywide community-relations agencies and organizations. Exercise of these service functions brings with it a certain power that the professionals who staff the national agencies have developed in various ways, but it is a limited power, usually more visible at conferences than in the daily affairs of the local bodies.

In recent years there have emerged countrywide leagues of national bodies such as the Synagogue Council of America, a confederation of the major synagogue movements, and, most recently, the Presidents' Conference. As leagues of confederations, their powers are even more limited. The Presidents' Conference enjoys a measure of respect as the conduit for information from Israel, but only because it can capitalize on Israel's authoritative position in the eyes of American Jewry.

Whether the federative arrangements involved are of near-universal scope and have broad-based, multipurpose goals, or are limited to single functions with rarely more than consultative or accreditative power, it is the consistent use of such arrangements that enables American Jewry to achieve any kind of structured communal unity at all. One result is

that power in the American Jewish community as a whole is institutionally shared among different loci by consent in such a way that sharing
is possible only when the ultimate power of the local community is
recognized.

American Jewish unity on a confederal basis is very different from
unity on a hierarchical one. What emerges is not a single pyramidal
structure, or even one in which the "bottom" rules the "top," as in the
case of Jewish communities with representative boards in other parts of
the world. There is no "bottom" and no "top" except, perhaps, on a
functional basis for specific purposes. Thus the absence of hierarchy is
the first element to recognize in examining the American Jewish community.

COMMUNITY SIZE, RANK, AND SPACING: SOME ROLE IMPLICATIONS

The five largest federation communities in the United States contain over
60 percent of the total Jewish population, and the top fifteen (all those
containing forty thousand Jews or more), over 75 percent. Only forty
federation communities have more than fifteen thousand Jews, and only
nine over a hundred thousand (see Table 9).

Because the locus of Jewish life and organization is in the local community, community size contributes directly to the organization of functions and decision making on the American Jewish scene. New York is
not only in a size class by itself but maintains its own—highly fragmented—organizational patterns, while holding itself substantially aloof
from all other communities. The federation system, which has become
the norm throughout the rest of the country, is limited in New York City.
Until the Yom Kippur War the major Jewish institutions and organizations, beginning with UJA, conducted their own fund-raising campaigns
and operated their own local programs outside of any overall planning
or coordinating framework, often from their own national offices.

The New York Jewish Federation served the Jewish hospitals, the
social-service agencies, and some of the Jewish Y's, but like the early
federations in other cities was rather strictly confined to the health and
welfare field. The overwhelming majority of Jewish institutions in New
York City had no contact with the Federation, nor did they see in it an
important tool for accomplishing even the general tasks of New York

TABLE 9 JEWISH POPULATION BY COMMUNITY SIZE, 1978

	No. of Communities	*Total Population*	*% of U.S. Total* 1973	1978	
Over 1 million	1	1,998,000	30.0	34.8	(GreaterNewYork)[a]
100,000–600,000	7	1,658,000	39.0	28.9	Los Angeles, Philadelphia, Chicago, Miami, Boston, Bergen Co. (N.J.), Washington, D.C.
40,000–100,000	9	623,000	7.5	10.9	Baltimore, Cleveland, Detroit, Essex Co. (N.J.), Ft. Lauderdale, Palm Beach Co., Pittsburgh, San Francisco, St. Louis
15,000–40,000	28	679,550	9.8	11.8	
5,000–15,000	46	412,650	6.0	7.2	
1,000–5,000	121	261,400	3.0	4.6	
100–1,000	360	105,500	0.3	1.8	

[a]Includes Westchester, Nassau, and Suffolk counties.

Jewry. Negotiations for a merger of the Federation and UJA on an expanded basis had begun even prior to October 1973, when the war came along to catalyze the union. A temporary unification of campaigns designed to allow UJA to raise funds for Israel during the period normally allocated to the Federation was later transformed into a permanent arrangement, so that the last major holdout has now come around to the common American pattern. It is unquestionably true that New York's great size prevented an earlier merger by allowing separate constituencies sufficient room to maneuver in and sufficient resources to enable them to ignore one another.

The major Jewish communities outside of New York are all structured so that the federations play a major, usually dominant, role in communal fund raising and decision making. All the significant ones among them are members of the Large City Budgeting Conference of the CJF. While the LCBC itself is essentially an information-gathering body, its members together represent the single most powerful influence on communal fund raising on the American Jewish scene, and the leaders of its constituent federations are the major sources of American Jewry's leadership across the spectrum of functional spheres (see below). Their names are found at the top of the leadership lists of virtually all the major Jewish organizations, even those not directly linked to the federation "family." The communications network that is generated out of the interaction of those communal leaders may well be the heart of the countrywide Jewish communal decision-making system. Significantly, New York was a member of the LCBC until the merger of UJA and the Federation.

Communities too small or too weak to be members of the LCBC stand on the periphery of the countrywide decision-making processes, no matter how well organized and active they may be locally. Occasionally, notable individuals from such communities do attain national prominence, but that is rare. Only in the last few years have the stronger of these communities begun to devise ways to enhance their national visibility in the manner of the LCBC. By and large they have been able to do so through the various "young leadership" groups, particularly of the CJF and UJA, that have been formed to recruit new talent for the Jewish community. Young leaders seem to reach positions of importance sooner in smaller communities and thus gain a voice in the countrywide councils while they are still linked to one another through the young leadership groups.

Local decision making has not been systematically studied in more than a handful of these organized communities. What we do know, however, is that there are variations among the cities in each of the categories simply as a result of the differences in scale that change the magnitude of the communications problems. The ways in which patterns of communication are organized vary in communities of different sizes, to say nothing of other cultural, historical, social, and economic factors. Size, for example, does much to determine who knows whom and how comprehensive or exclusive friendship and acquaintanceship nets are. These, in turn, determine who speaks to whom on communal matters.[4]

There is also considerable evidence that the percentage of those affiliated with and active in communal life stands in inverse ratio to community size. Since there is always a certain minimum of positions to be filled, regardless of community size, smaller communities will ipso facto involve a greater proportion of their population than larger ones, and of course there are often greater social pressures for participation in smaller communities, where people know who is and who is not participating. Various studies have shown, for example, that the percentage of synagogue members is higher in smaller communities.[5]

The size factor works in other ways as well. To some extent the number and spread of Jewish institutions is dependent upon the size of the community. A community of 10,000 Jews is not likely to have the range of institutions of a community of 100,000. Consequently it will have neither the complexity and diversity of decision-making centers or channels nor the problems of separated leadership that are likely to prevail in a very large community, where people can be decision makers in major arenas without knowing or working with their counterparts in others.

The impact of size of place also has a dynamic quality. When Jews first came to the American colonies in the eighteenth century, they lived in a number of small communities of approximately the same size scattered up and down the coast, all of which were able to support only the most rudimentary Jewish institutions, like synagogues. In the first half of the nineteenth century the Jews continued this general pattern of spreading out in many small communities, but after mid-century they began to concentrate at a few major points as a result of changing factors on the American scene. The mass migration of Jews from Eastern Europe settled in the very largest cities. At the same time, the Jews in the hinterland communities continued to migrate to those same cities because that is where the opportunities lay. It was then that the Jews became fully identified with the big cities.

Since the end of World War II there has been another shift in the scale of Jewish settlement that is only now beginning to be fully reflected in the structure of local decision making. The Jews have been moving out of the big cities into suburbs which, though nominally parts of the same metropolitan area, in fact have fully separate governmental structures and substantially distinctive socioeconomic characteristics, both of which they guard jealously. This migration is leading the Jews back once again to small communities where, unless they are involved with a great metropolitan federation, they are able to maintain only the minimum in the way of Jewish institutions locally. Scattered widely among many small towns, they are tied together at most by a common fund-raising system for overseas needs. Although the figures are buried because of the way Jewish population estimates are made, it seems that 60 percent of American Jews today live in separate suburban communities or in metropolitan communities of less than twenty thousand Jews.[6] This in itself is leading to the reorganization of Jewish life on several levels.

New Jersey is the paradigm of rampant suburbanism. At one time its

Jewish communities were concentrated in places like Newark, Camden, and Trenton, medium-sized cities or slightly larger, where the Jews passed through the same cycles of settlement that they did elsewhere. However, because they were smaller and more susceptible to pressures, once blacks began to move into previously Jewish neighborhoods those cities rapidly lost their Jewish populations to surrounding suburban areas. At the same time, there was a major influx of Jews from New York City into northern and central Jersey as part of the suburbanization process of that metropolis, and a similar, although considerably smaller, influx around Camden from Philadelphia.

As Jews moved out to the suburbs the only institution they brought with them was the synagogue. Soon New Jersey was dotted with tens if not hundreds of congregations to serve whatever Jewish needs their members required, needs that frequently were only minimal. These congregations became autonomous islands in a highly disorganized sea, leading to demands for other institutions to serve Jewish needs, not the least of which was the need to raise funds from these newly affluent suburbanites for Israel and other Jewish purposes beyond the confines of New Jersey. This led in turn to the extension of other institutions to suburban New Jersey. In some cases these represented adaptations of existing structures. Thus the Jewish Federation of Newark, which had many years before become the Jewish Federation of Essex County, became the Jewish Community Federation of Metropolitan New Jersey simply by following its former givers into the suburbs south and west of Newark. In others, new federations were established. For example, in Bergen County, outside of Englewood, the Jewish Federation of Community Services was established as early as 1953. In still others, small local federations were reorganized on a regional basis: for instance, the Jewish Federation of Central Jersey, whose origins go back to 1940, was reorganized in 1973 to include Westfield and Plainfield. By 1973 virtually all of New Jersey was included within the state's sixteen local federations, five of which were organized on a county basis (the inevitable sign of suburbanization), another five on a regional basis, and only six were still organized around a central city, all embracing suburban areas as well.

The distribution of functions in the Jewish community also follows a pattern that combines geography and population size. New York City is the de facto capital of the American Jewish community. Moreover, because New York is really a region rather than a community, one that embraces many communities organized in various ways (see below) and is also surrounded by perhaps another 15 percent of American Jewry living within the orbit of Manhattan, the Jews of New York tend to believe that they are the beginning and end of Jewish life in the United States. At the same time, what would be considered very large Jewish communities in their own right are practically buried in the metropolitan area and maintain only those institutions that meet immediately local needs.

The other very large Jewish communities are regional centers of Jewish life as well as major communities in their own right (see Table 10). Los Angeles is clearly the center of Jewish life west of the Rocky Mountains and the second city of American Jewry institutionally as well as in numbers, with branches of all the countrywide Jewish organizations and institutions located within its limits. Because of its distance from the East Coast, it has a greater degree of independence from "New York" (as a

TABLE 10   REGIONAL OFFICES OF JEWISH ORGANIZATIONS

No. of Offices	Communities
9	Chicago, Los Angeles, Philadelphia
8	Miami
7	Boston, Detroit, San Francisco, Washington
6	Minneapolis
5	Atlanta, Baltimore, Pittsburgh, Saint Louis

symbol of national headquarters) than any other regional center in the United States. Chicago is the capital of the Jewries of mid-America in much the same way, although its relative proximity to New York has prevented it from developing the same range of national institutions or local autonomy as Los Angeles. Once the great western anchor of American Jewish life, its overall position has been lost to Los Angeles along with much of its Jewish population, which migrated westward during the postwar generation.

Philadelphia and Boston, although now almost within commuting distance of New York, remain equally important secondary national centers for American Jewry because of historical circumstances. Philadelphia's old, established Jewish community has long played a national role that at one time even rivaled that of the Empire City. It continues to maintain some institutions of national significance. Perhaps more important, as the closest major Jewish community outside of the New York metropolitan area, its leaders have easy access to the national offices of Jewish organizations, where they frequently represent the point of view of the rest of American Jewry (insofar as there is any common one) vis-à-vis that of "New York." Boston Jewry, though a far younger Jewish community, has capitalized on their city's position as the "Athens of America" to create major Jewish academic institutions of national scope and to become the home of whatever Jewish academic brain trust exists in the United States.

Only in the South is the largest city not the regional center. Greater Miami, still a very new community that is the product of the post-World War II migration southward and is heavily weighted with retirees, has had little significant national impact as a community (as distinct from a location for doing the winter business of American Jewry as a whole). To the extent that there is a capital for Jewish life in the South, it remains Atlanta, the region's general capital. Despite its small Jewish population of 16,500, Atlanta possesses the panoply of regional offices associated with much larger Jewish communities in other parts of the country. The pattern of Jewish activity in Atlanta is markedly different from that of any of the other centers because of the intimacy and proximity within which the regional offices and local institutions must live. But the trend is such that Miami will probably emerge as a major regional center during the coming generation.

Jewish communities of medium size (here defined as 20,000 to 100,000 population) all play tertiary roles in the countrywide network of Jewish communal activity. This is true despite the fact that they may well be the strongest of all Jewish communities in the country, combining as they do a relatively high degree of personal intimacy with sufficient size to provide all the necessities for living Jewishly on a daily basis. They are generally able to provide the full range of local institutions and organizations found in any American community, although often in rudimentary form, but do not contain institutions serving national functions except as a result of historical accident. On the other hand, they make a major contribution to the national scene by providing a very high proportion of the leadership of American Jewry, both voluntary and professional, which is generated by the good organizational base and attractive Jewish life of communities of that size.

Table 11 represents a tentative ranking of the Jewish communities of the United States in terms of their importance on the national scene. Among the tertiary centers, national importance is determined by factors other than size. All but one of the subsidiary regional centers are located between the Mississippi and the Pacific coast, where they represent nodes of Jewish population that serve wide areas sparsely settled by Jews and thus occupy a more important role in the overall scheme of things than either their size or, in most cases, the quality of Jewish life within them would otherwise warrant. The exception is Miami, whose role we have suggested to be in the process of transformation.

TABLE 11   HIERARCHY OF AMERICAN JEWISH COMMUNITIES

Rank	*Cities*
Capital	New York (Manhattan)
Major regional (secondary) centers	Los Angeles,* Chicago,* Philadelphia,* Boston,* Atlanta*
Tertiary centers	Baltimore,* Cincinnati,* Cleveland,* Detroit,* metropolitan New Jersey (Newark),* Saint Louis,* San Francisco,* Washington
Subsidiary regional centers	Dallas,* Denver,* Kansas City,* Miami,* Minneapolis*
Significant local communities	Phoenix, Oakland, San Diego, Hartford,* New Haven, Indianapolis, Louisville, New Orleans, Springfield (Mass.), Saint Paul, Omaha, Atlantic City, Albany, Buffalo,* Rochester,* Syracuse, Columbus,* Pittsburgh,* Providence,* Memphis, Nashville, Houston,* Norfolk, Milwaukee,* Seattle

*Member, Large City Budgeting Conference of the Council of Jewish Federations and Welfare Funds.

The distribution of the main offices of countrywide and worldwide Jewish organizations and the location of Jewish institutions claiming countrywide constituencies provides a clear view of the hierarchy of Jewish communities. The 1974–75 *American Jewish Year Book* lists 224 organizations and institutions of those kinds, in seven categories (see Table 12). Of that number, 175, or over 75 percent, are located in metropolitan New York (all but two in Manhattan or Brooklyn). The

TABLE 12 DISTRIBUTION OF JEWISH ORGANIZATIONAL HEADQUARTERS IN U.S.*

Community	Total	Community Relations(22)	Cultural(35)	Overseas Aid(11)	Religious and Educational(66)	Social and Mutual Benefit(17)	Social Welfare(23)	Zionist and Pro-Israel(50)
New York	175	19	26	11	44	16	13	46
Washington	9	3	1		2		1	2
Los Angeles	8		1		6		1	
Philadelphia	7		2		4	1		
Boston	5		1		3			1
Denver	4						4	
Chicago	3				2			1
Pittsburgh	2		1		1			
Rochester	2		1		1			
Baltimore	1						1	
Berkeley	1		1					
Cincinnati	1				1			
Cleveland	1				1			
Dallas	1						1	
Hot Springs, Ark.	1						1	
Newport, R.I.	1				1			
New Brunswick, N.J.	1						1	
Saint Louis	1		1					

*Based on American Jewish Year Book, vol. 75 (1974–75).

remainder are scattered among seventeen communities, only four of which have five or more. New York dominates in every category.

Washington is in second place because as the nation's capital it is the location of a handful of community-relations and Israel-oriented bodies that need to be close to the United States government for lobbying purposes. Los Angeles, Philadelphia, and Boston rank as expected, primarily as subsidiary educational and cultural centers. Many of the communities on the list are there because of historic accident: for example, Denver has a complex of chronic-disease hospitals that originated in the days when tuberculosis was epidemic and Colorado's climate was considered curative. Other communities are listed only temporarily because heads of particular professional associations live there; after the next round of elections the list will shift.

The formidable-looking concentration of offices in New York, while significant, is much less formidable in fact because most of the organizations and institutions represent small constituencies with limited impact beyond commuting range of their headquarters. With a few exceptions, the organizations of truly countrywide scope are almost invariably limited to service functions and are far more dependent upon their local affiliates than vice versa. Most of them have emerged as significant bodies only in the past two generations, and only B'nai B'rith and the Union of American Hebrew Congregations, both of which were built on strong local bases from the first, effectively antedate the turn of the century. In short, the American Jewish polity has been and continues to be built from the ground up, from the grass roots, as it were, developing linkages, usually on a federal basis, in the process.

THE MOSAIC OF JEWISH COMMUNAL LIFE

The congregation (which is not necessarily synonymous with the synagogue) is the cornerstone of the federal structure that is the Jewish community, the first institution to be established when a sufficient number of Jews have gathered in one place to create an organized community. Indeed, the terms "congregation" and "community" are essentially synonymous in Hebrew. Jews have come together to form congregations wherever they have found themselves. In keeping with the federal principles that underlie Jewish organization, they do so by formally consenting to articles of agreement or charters that bind them together as a community in the manner defined by Jewish law and custom. The Sephardic term for such articles of congregational-communal agreement, *askamot* (articles of agreement), conveys this meaning exactly.[7]

Only in modern times did "congregation" and "synagogue" tend to become synonymous. While in the past every congregation included provisions for worship (a synagogue), it was not likely to begin and end with that function. On the contrary, since Jews do not need institutional arrangements of a synagogal nature to pray, the organization of a congregation was more likely to come about when there was a need to structure the incipient community's social-welfare or educational tasks through the establishment of a cemetery, institutions for aiding the poor, or a school. The traditional congregation was a very flexible device that could accommodate all those services and more, usually through a system of *hevrot* (committees) drawn from the congregational body as a whole.

The paradigm of Jewish communal development would suggest that as a community expands its organization necessarily becomes more complex, leading to an elaboration of the *hevrah* system or even, particularly in modern times, to the creation of other congregations or organizations within the same locality. Since the Emancipation the great migrations of Jews have brought together in the same localities people from quite different backgrounds, who have sought to preserve their respective customs through their own institutions. Increasingly, religious and ideological divisions have led to even more pronounced structural separatism. As the communities came to rest on a voluntaristic base, there was no way to prevent or even to limit the proliferation of organizations and institutions responding to these or other needs. In some cases the different bodies would develop federal or confederal links with one another (either out of choice or necessity) to create a more elaborate community structure; in others, they did not.

Under the impact of emancipation (in Europe), Protestantism (both there and in the United States), and the sheer increase in Jewish population (in both places) this process was accelerated, leading to the emergence of the modern synagogue as essentially a place of worship, though with ancillary functions. Individual synagogues came to embody specific religious-ideological trends in Judaism—Reform, Orthodox, Conservative, etc. Many of the functions formerly performed by congregations when they were entirely in the hands of volunteers were now spun off: restructured in more elaborate ways, professionalized, and given separate organizational bases of their own within the overall community.

This process appeared in its classic form in the early Jewish settlements of colonial America, where the communities grew in a leisurely enough fashion to permit the gradual development of their institutions, but it has remained generally true since then.

The rapid development of the United States and Jewish life here intensified this process. The early development of the Chicago Jewish community is a case in point. Individual Jews began drifting into Chicago in the 1820s and 1830s, before the new settlement on the shores of Lake Michigan had even acquired a political organization of its own. However, it was not until 1845, eight years after Chicago's incorporation as a city, that the first High Holy Day services were held. That same year an organized Jewish community came into existence through the creation of the Jewish Burial Ground Society, which established a cemetery. In 1846 the first congregation was founded, Kehillath Anshe Ma'arav (the Congregation of the People of the West, today known as KAM). The Jewish Burial Ground Society merged with it, and during the 1850s the congregation built its own building (1851) and established a day school (1853).

As a boomtown, Chicago began attracting Jews from other parts of Europe who wished to have their own congregational or organizational identities. Kehillath Bnei Shalom was organized in 1849 to serve the Jews of Posen, who maintained a Polish Ashkenazic ritual, while the Hebrew Benevolent Society of Chicago was organized at approximately the same time for the less Orthodox. Kehillath Bnei Shalom underwent a schism in 1876. In 1857 Ramah Lodge Number 33 of B'nai B'rith was organized, and that same year the Israelite Reform Society came into being, which in 1861 established Congregation Sinai. The United Hebrew Relief Association was established in 1859, and by the end of the decade the Young Men's Fraternity, the Clay Library and Dramatic Association, the Ladies' Benevolent Society, and the Young Ladies' Benevolent Society were all in operation, even though the Jewish population by 1860 was no more than fifteen hundred persons.

The first strictly East European congregation was organized in 1862 as Congregation Bnei Jacob. A year later Beth Hamidrash Hagadol was formed, and in 1867 the two congregations merged. The East European Jews organized many such congregations, either upon their arrival or as a result of schisms within established synagogues; at least as many mergers took place as well. The United Hebrew Relief Association opened a Jewish hospital in 1868.

Thus by the time of the great Chicago fire of 1871, at the end of the first generation of the community's existence, it already had a panoply of organizations and institutions touching upon most aspects of Jewish life, if only in a rudimentary way.

The next generation, which witnessed the great migration of European Jews, saw an almost geometrical proliferation of similar institutions and the first efforts to create community-wide linkages between them. In 1900 the principal community-wide welfare organizations federated as the Jewish Federation of Chicago, which remained the province of the German Jews for another generation and a half. The Chicago Rabbinical Association, one of the earliest attempts to create links across the myriad congregations and synagogues, was established in 1893. It was reorganized as the Chicago Board of Rabbis in 1959 with Federation support. The Zionist movement in Chicago dates back to 1886, when a branch of Hovevei Zion was established, but it received its greatest organizational boost between 1896, when the Chicago Zionist Organization Number One was formed, and World War I. In that same period, the new immigrants organized landsmanshaften, of which six hundred existed in 1948, a number that diminished to sixty by 1961 and is now approaching zero.

Citywide Jewish educational and cultural institutions came into existence in the third generation, with the two principal ones, the College of Jewish Studies (now the Spertus College of Judaica) being founded in 1925, and the Hebrew Theological College in 1922. Most of the independent Hebrew schools founded in that period have either disappeared, as the neighborhoods that supported them ceased to be Jewish, or have become part of the Associated Talmud Torah network.

By 1961 Chicago had forty-three Orthodox synagogues, twenty-five Conservative, sixteen Reform, and five traditional (a uniquely Chicago category, consisting of congregations where the service is Orthodox but mixed seating the norm). By that same year both Orthodox and Conservative rabbinical courts were in operation. The Jewish Federation and the Jewish Welfare Fund (the latter established in 1936 to meet overseas needs, something that did not interest the German Jews at the time) came together in 1968 to form the Jewish United Fund of Metropolitan Chicago, which became the umbrella organization supporting the Jewish Family and Community Service, a number of child-development and -care centers, two Jewish hospitals, and a network of Jewish community centers, as well as the Board of Rabbis and other institutions. Jewish schools were united under either the Board of Jewish Education (Conservative, Reform, and Independent) and the Associated Talmud Torahs (Orthodox). There were eight day schools in 1970, two substantial Jewish libraries, a Jewish museum, a Chicago Jewish Archives, and two Jewish city clubs (the Standard Club for the old families, dating back to 1869, and the Covenant Club, organized in 1917 for the East European Jews).

In addition to these local organizations, all the major countrywide organizations maintain regional offices in Chicago. The Orthodox, Reform, and Conservative movements maintain regional summer camps operated out of their Chicago offices, and Chicago is also the headquarters of B'nai B'rith District 6, perhaps the most powerful of all the B'nai B'rith regional groupings in the world.

As the decision to be involved in Jewish life increasingly became a voluntary one, the new voluntarism extended into the internal life of the Jewish community as well, generating pluralism—even within previously free but relatively homogeneous and monolithic community structures. This pluralism was increased by the breakdown of the traditional reasons for being Jewish and the rise of new and different incentives for Jewish association. The situation demanded new federal arrangements to achieve a degree of unity within a community larger and far more diverse than any Jews had confronted in their long history.

The pluralistic federalism that has emerged in the contemporary Jewish community substantially eliminates the neat patterns of communal organization that were common earlier, the kinds easily presented on organization charts. Certainly the model of a hierarchical organizational structure does not offer an accurate picture of the distribution of powers and responsibilities in the Jewish community today. There is no functioning organizational pyramid in Jewish life, no national organizations that can issue directives to local affiliates, and no local umbrella organizations that can order others within its "jurisdiction" to toe the mark. In sum, in most communities there is no central governing agent that serves as the point where authority, responsibility, and power converge, even in the local arena.

FROM CONGREGATIONALISM TO FEDERALISM

The combination of a very large, fully modern society that has been built from the first on individualistic principles, is pluralistic in the full sense

TABLE 13 GENERATIONAL PATTERN OF JEWISH COMMUNAL ACTIVITY; 1654–1948

Generation	Benchmark Events	Form of Organization	Dominant Groups	Frontier Situation	Challenge-Response
I (1654–85)	1654 Jews settle in New York 1658 Jews settle in Newport	single congregations	Sephardim	coastal commerce connected with land frontier	winning right to settle
II (1685–1714)	1695 Jews settle in Charleston				founding permanent institutions
III (1714–54)	1730 Mill Street Synagogue 1735 Savannah 1742 Philadelphia 1749 Charleston		Ashkenazim become majority in North America but Sephardic dominance continues		building synagogues
IV (1754–89)	1763 Touro Synagogue 1776 New York grants Jews full citizenship 1789 Federal Constitution			transition to internal interests	winning equal rights
V (1789–1816)	1795 First Askenazic congregation in U.S. (Philadelphia)	beginning of communal fragmentation	transitional period (native-born and English-born dominant)	commerce connected with westward expansion	Jewish integration into American life
VI (1816–48)	1817 Cincinnati 1825 First Askenazic congregation in New York 1837 Cleveland 1841 Chicago 1843 B'nai B'rith founded	multiple congregations	Central European ("German") dominant		spread of Jewish settlement
VII (1848–78)	1849 Jews settle in California				first mass immigration

TABLE 13 *(continued)*

Generation	Benchmark Events	Form of Organization	Dominant Groups	Frontier Situation	Challenge-Response
	1854 First YMHA 1859 Board of Deputies of American Israelites 1873 UAHC founded 1875 Hebrew Union College founded				Reform
VIII (1878–1917)	1881 Mass migration 1885 Pittsburgh Platform 1886 JTS founded 1888 JPS founded 1897 American Zionist Federation founded 1898 UOJAC founded 1906 American Jewish Committee founded 1909 N. Y. Kehillah 1913 United Synagogue founded 1913 ADL established	attempts at federal union	East Europeans become the majority but Central Europeans remain dominant	enterprise on urban-industrial frontier	second mass immigration. building Jewish institutional and religious base in New World
IX (1917–48)	1914 JDC founded 1918 American Jewish Congress founded 1932 CJF established 1933 Nazism comes to power 1938 UJA established 1939–45 WW II 1948 Establishment of state of Israel	emergence of federations	transitional period		individual and collective acculturation

of the word, and was peopled by several significantly different waves of very adventurous Jewish immigrants who shared one common commitment—that of seeking new lives as individuals—has not been conducive to the development of sufficient homogeneity to permit the emergence of a neat communal structure. Consequently, every effort to create even so much as a single nationwide "address" for American Jewry has failed. Nor is this situation without precedent. No Jewish community approaching the size of the American Jewish community has ever succeeded in creating a neat structure for itself, complete with umbrella organization and all the other accouterments. The vaunted kehillahs (organized Jewish communities) of other times and climes were all developed for much smaller communities. Since Roman times probably none has exceeded a few hundred thousand in population and most were far smaller than that. The U. S. cities with the largest Jewish populations —New York, Los Angeles, Philadelphia, Chicago, Boston, Miami—are themselves larger than all but a handful of countrywide communities that have existed over the long history of the Jewish people.[8]

As the American Jewish community grew in size, it passed by stages through the several organizational forms that English-speaking Jewries in various parts of the world have utilized at various times, moving from neat local organizations based on a modification of the traditional congregational model, to attempts at countrywide union, to the complex federalism reflected by the response of an open society to the particular set of conditions found in the New World (see Table 13).

If we were to sum up the organizational development during the first eight generations of Jewish life in the United States, the picture that would emerge would be somewhat as follows. For the first four generations Jewish America consisted of a few outpost congregations located along the Atlantic seaboard, each serving its own local population and those Jews in the immediate hinterland who occasionally repaired to the metropolis for business reasons and Jewish sustenance, the whole loosely connected through the interpersonal ties of the handful of Jews then in North America. Although after 1720 the majority of Jews in British America were of Ashkenazic origin, both the Sephardic minhag and form of congregational governance were maintained without exception until the fifth generation. Being the closest Jewish parallel to the aristocratic Episcopalian ritual and the aristocratic republicanism of colonial America, the Sephardic way appealed to a people seeking to acculturate even as they preserved their Jewishness.

Thus, in the earliest period of Jewish communal life in the United States, the small and relatively homogeneous Jewish population managed to achieve unity on the local plane through a system of local congregations not dissimilar to that presently found in countries like New Zealand (Jewish population, five thousand), whereby the Jews in each city joined together to create a common congregation that provided all the communal services (religious, social, and educational) desired, either directly or through its *hevrot*. Jews who had immigrated from all parts of the world joined these community congregations, accepting the ritual and organizational patterns of their Sephardic founders as their own. Between 1654 and the end of the eighteenth century "community" and "congregation" were virtually synonymous terms and were so recognized by Jews and gentile alike.

The fifth generation (1790–1816) was one of transition in many respects. The Jews, like their fellow Americans, began to turn their attention inward away from the Atlantic toward the new West. Jewish communities were founded west of the Appalachians, the Ashkenazim began to emerge as a distinct group with their own institutions, and Jews in general took another step forward toward integration as individuals into American life. (This was probably a generation of great assimilation, during which many of the colonial Jewish families intermarried and ceased to produce Jewish descendants.) These trends became paramount in the sixth generation (1817–47), which was dominated by American Jews or migrants who had come from or through England. This was the generation that saw the spread of Jewish settlement throughout the eastern half of the Mississippi valley and on the West Coast as well, during which time the single congregational model was replaced by that of multiple congregations. Nevertheless, organized Jewish life for the most part remained within the congregational framework.

The first break in the single-congregation pattern came in Philadelphia in 1795, when the Ashkenazim who did not want to accept the Sephardic ritual of Mikveh Israel formed their own congregation, Rodeph Shalom (appropriately enough, this first instance of a congregational schism in American Jewish history followed what is almost a common pattern in that the secessionists chose for themselves a name meaning "Pursuer of Peace"). In the course of the next generation a larger and more complex American Jewish community emerged, based on a multiplicity of congregations on the local scene, each following

TABLE 14 DEVELOPMENT OF NEW YORK CITY'S CONGREGATIONS, 1654–1851

Year	Congregation	Origins of Members	Origins
1654	Shearith Israel	Sephardic	founded by original settlers
1825	B'nai Jeshurun	Ashkenazic	broke away from Shearith Israel
1828	Anshe Chesed	Dutch, German, Polish	broke away from B'nai Jeshurun
1839	Shaare Zedek	Polish	individuals from B'nai Jeshurun and Anshe Chesed
	Shaarey Hashamayim	German	
1842	Rodeph Sholom	German	
1845	Temple Emanu-El	German	Reformers
1847	B'nai Israel	Dutch	
1851	Shaarey Brocha	French	

the ritual preferences of its founders and members (see Table 14). The new immigrants wanted their own synagogues—first to preserve their particular Orthodox traditions and later to institute reforms. Jewish organizational life was still basically congregational, but institutions independent of any congregation began to emerge by mid-century (see Table 15). In fact, many of them were dominated by leaders of particular congregations wearing different hats.

It was only in the seventh generation (1848–76), when German Jews began to dominate the community, that a trend to multiple organizations became evident. This in turn spawned the first efforts at both local and countrywide federation. Beginning in the late 1850s, the many different charitable and philanthropic associations that developed on the local scene during the previous decade or two began to unite, adopting names like United Hebrew Charities. Countrywide, the unsuccessful experiment with the Board of Deputies of American Israelites (1859) and the successful founding of the Union of American Hebrew Congregations (1873) straddled the same half generation. The emergence of Reform Judaism served as a second and continuing justification for multicongregationalism on the local scene, a far more divisive factor than country-of-origin customs, which inevitably faded after one or two generations of americanization.

From the late 1850s to the early 1880s the growing American Jewish community experimented with a representative Board of

TABLE 15 DEVELOPMENT OF EXTRACONGREGATIONAL BODIES IN
NEW YORK CITY, 1786–1860

Year	Organization	Origins	Comments
1786	Hebrah Gemilut Hasadim	Shearith Israel	disbanded 1790
1802	Hebrah Hesed Vaemet	" "	still in existence
1820	Female Hebrew Benevolent Society	" "	
1822	Hebrew Benevolent Society	independent	
1826	Hebrah Gemilut Hesed	B'nai Jeshurun	became Hebrew National Benefit Society
1841	Montefiore Society	Anshe Chesed	
1843	Independent Order B'nai B'rith	12 young Jewish men	first countrywide Jewish body
1844	German Hebrew Benevolent Society	German Jews	united with Hebrew Benefit Society by Civil War
1850	Maimonides Library Assn.		
1852	Jews' Hospital	Shearith Israel and Shaaray Tefila	became Mount Sinai in 1866
	Hebrew Young Men's Literary Society	young Jewish men	
	Philodocean Society	broke off from Hebrew Young Men's Literary Society	
1854	Touro Literary Institute	young Jewish men	merged with Hebrew Young Men's Literary Society 1858
1859	Hebrew Orphan Asylum	Hebrew Benefit Society and German Hebrew Benevolent Society	
1850s	Troop K	young Jewish men	military formations
	Empire Hussars	" " "	" "
	Young Men's Lafayette Assn.	" " "	" "
	Cultur Verein	German Jews	
	Sange Verein	" "	
	Young Men of Germany	" "	
	Harmonic Club	" "	still in existence
	Polish Young Men	Polish Jews	

Deputies of American Israelites, modeled after the Board of Deputies
of British Jews in the United Kingdom and based on congregational
units. The experiment was launched in 1859 with great difficulty.
Only an event of frightening dimensions, in this instance the Mortara

case,* could catalyze an overwhelmingly immigrant community sadly divided along country-of-origin lines and, increasingly, by a traditionalist-Reform division as well. Representatives of twenty-five congregations met in New York to form an organization that was to assume domestic as well as overseas tasks. Over the course of the next nineteen years its primary activities were fund raising for the relief of Jews in Arab lands, Palestine, and Russia, and lobbying (with no little success) for American government action to eliminate discriminatory clauses in U.S. treaties with Switzerland, Russia, and Romania. Domestically it fought anti-Semitism during the Civil War, urged the appointment of Jewish military chaplains, and sought to eliminate the last religious tests for public office in Maryland, New Hampshire, and North Carolina. In 1878 the radical reformers, who opposed the Board of Deputies as too nationalistic and traditional, secured its virtual demise by merging it with the new Union of American Hebrew Congregations.[9] Neither the Board of Deputies nor its more narrowly based successor, the UAHC, ever came close to achieving universality.

The UAHC was founded in 1873. Its very name indicates how contemporaries still conceived of Jewish life as concentrated in the synagogue and potentially unifiable on a congregational basis. Its efforts to unite American Jewry reached their peak in the 1880s, to be dashed by the now legendary "treifa banquet" of 1885, a dinner commemorating the tenth anniversary of the Hebrew Union College at which nonkosher food was served to a countrywide assemblage that included those traditionalists who still sought to work within the UAHC framework. Some of the latter actually walked out upon seeing the menu, with its seafood and meat and dairy dishes. A year later the traditionalists organized the Jewish Theological Seminary. The divisions between traditionalists and liberals were already too great for easy accommodation on the religious front and the divisions among the immigrants were to grow for two more generations.

The eighth generation (1877–1918), though the generation of the great East European migration, was still one in which German Jews dominated the community. The Jews of this generation turned away from the already-closing land frontier to concentrate in the big cities, where they

---

*In 1858 Edward Mortara, a six-year-old Jewish child, was seized by papal guards who invaded the family home in Bologna (the boy had been secretly baptized by his Catholic nurse in infancy). The child was claimed by the pope as his personal ward, was educated in Catholic schools, and subsequently became a priest. The Mortara case gave rise to widespread protest demonstrations in the United States and abroad.

developed new enterprises based on the urban industrial frontier. This was when the foundation for the present Jewish institutional and religious framework was laid on a piece-by-piece basis. It was also the time of the greatest disunity in American Jewish life—which prompted the strongest attempts at federal union, from the efforts of the Union of American Hebrew Congregations to become the all-encompassing countrywide congregational body through the unification attempts of the New York Kehillah and the American Jewish Congress. The failure of all those efforts laid to rest all attempts at union and led American Jewry to seek other, more confederal ways, to achieve the same goals.

When the mass migration from Eastern Europe created the largest and most diverse Jewish community in history, scattered over the largest area ever considered as embracing a single countrywide community, even local communities lost whatever features of unity they might have had. The new immigrants' own efforts to introduce community structures based on European models failed as fully as had the earlier efforts to introduce the Anglo-Jewish model.[10] European rabbis sent to the New World to create orderly religious institutions retreated in disorder, and even such American-generated efforts to adapt European forms as the New York Kehillah failed because of American conditions.[11] The one attempt to create a nationwide structure based on the new masses, the American Jewish Congress, had even less success.

The first experiment along these lines was the most traditional in an Old World sense. In 1887 a group of Orthodox congregations attempted to create a congregational federation that would be headed by a chief rabbi who could act as their religious authority. The following year they brought Rabbi Jacob Joseph, a major figure in the Lithuanian Torah world, from Vilna to be their chief rabbi. The key to the success or failure of their endeavor lay in securing recognition of Rabbi Jacob Joseph's authority on the part of other American rabbis and the extension of their federation's power to the regulation of kashruth. In neither case were they successful. The free-enterprise climate of the United States worked to defeat both. Since every rabbi was employed by his congregation, there was no reason for him to recognize the superiority of any other unless he personally chose to do so, and the spirit of the times was not conducive to that. Moreover, communal regulation of kashruth (which was to bring about the demise of the New York Kehillah a few decades later) ran against the American grain. Here the slaughtering and selling of meat was a matter of individual enterprise, and none of the entrepreneurs, however small, were willing to brook interference on the part of any regulatory body, particularly since not even government was significantly involved in regulation of the industry in those days. Rabbi Jacob Joseph died penurious in 1902, and with him disappeared the last vestiges of an American chief rabbinate.

In 1909, under the leadership of Judah Magnes, a San Francisco-born Reform rabbi who had found his way to a sense of Jewish peoplehood even as he was becoming one of the most prominent leaders of the Reform movement, a broader experiment was initiated in the form of the New York Kehillah. The Kehillah was a federation of local Jewish organizations linked to the American Jewish Committee (a body founded in 1906), which was to represent Jewish interests countrywide. The thought was to establish similar kehillahs in every major Jewish community in the United States, and indeed modest attempts were made to do so in Philadelphia and Detroit. What led to the establishment of the New York Kehillah was, as is so frequently the case, not an internal Jewish desire for better organizational unity but a perceived external threat, in this case the accusation by New York City Police Commissioner Theodore A. Bingham that 50 percent of the criminals in the city were Jews. The Jewish response was to organize a defense against Bingham's accusations, on one hand, and to seek organized ways to reduce crime among the city's Jews, on the other. The Kehillah was to be the vehicle for accomplishing both.

Unlike earlier (and most later) efforts at federation, which were essentially confederal in nature, designed to create relatively loose links among constituent organizations that remained internally "sovereign" in every respect, the Kehillah set out to serve directly the "citizens" of the New York Jewish community alongside its organizational constituents. The standard federal pattern on the American Jewish scene has involved a loose linkage of independent bodies under a general authority whose roles, functions, and resources have been kept limited. Tasks entrusted to it were to be generally carried out by committees constituted so as to be as representative of the constituent members as the overall governing body, so that there would be no question as to who was in the saddle. Moreover, they have been designed to function either entirely without staff or with minimal staff support, so that no headquarters with an independent outlook and powers could emerge. The Kehillah sought to link Jewish organizations of all kinds in an attempt to "form a more perfect union" in the American sense, whereby substantial powers would be transferred to the common governing body to be exercised directly by it.

Thus the work of Kehillah was carried out through four *bureaus,* a term deliberately chosen to indicate that these were to be well-staffed operating arms of the Kehillah itself and not simply committees of the Kehillah's constituent members. The bureaus included the Bureau of Jewish Education, which began operations in 1910, the Bureau of Social Morals, to deal with Jewish crime, the Bureau of Industry to focus on labor relations, particularly between Jewish employers and employees in government, and the Bureau of Philanthropy. The Kehillah attempted to accommodate the rabbis by establishing a rabbinical board parallel to the bureaus, and to create the staff necessary for the operation of the new structure by establishing a school for training communal workers.

As in the case of the abortive attempt to establish a chief rabbinate, the Kehillah met its demise over the struggle to supervise kashruth. Following the European model, it attempted to bring kashruth under the direct regulation of its Board of Rabbis. This was to serve two purposes: give the board real authority and provide an income from supervision fees, which could be used for financing neighborhood rabbinical courts and for supporting rabbis and other religious functionaries through a communal budget. In addition, funds from kashruth supervision were to be made available for the support of Jewish education. Thus a coordinated network of Jewish religious institutions was planned.

But Jewish entrepreneurs in the kosher-meat trade opposed the effort. While the Kehillah was able to make some headway with the small entrepreneurs, the larger ones threatened to sue it for violation of the New York State antitrust laws. What was considered sound public policy in Europe was viewed as a combination in restraint of trade in the United States. As a result, the Kehillah was forced to abandon its effort; the loss of revenues that this entailed meant that it was unable to acquire a proper financial basis from which to compete against all the centrifugal forces that worked against it. By 1916 the Kehillah's financial problems led it to separate the bureaus from the parent body so that each would be in a position to secure its own funding.

World War I turned Jews' attention to overseas relief and at the same time Magnes's own pacifism rubbed off on the Kehillah during a period of extraordinary patriotic fervor in the U. S., to the latter's disadvantage. The Kehillah survived nominally until 1922, but had ceased to be of significance after America's entry into the war. Of all its institutions only the Bureau of Jewish Education continued to exist, becoming the Jewish Education Committee of New York, a reflection of the community's return to the more confederal arrangements that had become the norm in American Jewish life.

The exigencies created by World War I led American Jewry to make one attempt to create a countrywide elected Jewish assembly, the American Jewish Congress of 1918. In 1917 that segment of American Jewish leadership which opposed the American Jewish Committee, led by Rabbi Stephen S. Wise and including the Zionists, capitalized on the still-great gap between German and East European Jews to challenge both the Committee and the Kehillah on democratic grounds. They sought to organize an American Jewish Congress in an effort to replace the Committee with a countrywide body that they themselves would lead. The very calling of the Congress involved complicated negotiations among the various groups on the American Jewish scene. The American Jewish Committee, for example, opposed the idea as incompatible with the proper Jewish role in American society. Moreover, the struggle between German and East European groups and between the anti-Zionists and the Zionists became focused on the Congress question, since it was clear that the Congress would be largely dominated by the East Europeans and the Zionists, or at least their spokesmen. In the end it was agreed that the Congress would be convened as a special wartime effort and would be limited to a single session. Countrywide elections were held, and the delegates assembled in Philadelphia in December 1918 with the purpose of formulating a postwar program for the Jewish people and naming a delegation to the peace conference.

The still-unsettled conditions of the immediate postwar period led to an agreement that a second session would be held. It also met in Philadelphia, in 1920, where it received a report from the peace conference delegation and then disbanded. Rabbi Wise immediately reconvened the delegates representing the East European and Zionist blocs and laid the foundations for a new and continuing body, also named the American Jewish Congress (the present organization). Despite the hopes of Wise and the Zionists, it did not become a representative body that could speak in the name of the whole community. The two Congresses represented the high tide of the Zionist effort to assume control of the American Jewish communal structure; since 1918 there has never been another comparable effort.

During that same generation, however, the new immigrants, stimulated by their new surroundings, began to develop the beginnings of a system of Jewish communal life that turned out to be more suited to the American environment, one that despite appearances to the contrary has been able to mobilize American Jewry for its great tasks. That system had its origins in the closing years of the nineteenth century, but its development is essentially a twentieth-century phenomenon.

The present system of American Jewish communal life derives directly from the response of the already-established, predominantly German-speaking Jews to the needs of the new immigrants at the time of the mass migration, as they perceived those needs, a response then modified by the organizational demands generated by the immigrants for and by themselves. This in turn led to the creation of welfare federations, defense agencies, congregational umbrella organizations, and seminaries. The immigrants themselves established synagogues, landsmanshaften, and fraternal organizations. Organizations such as B'nai B'rith expanded to become mass-based, and new mass-based organizations such as the American Jewish Congress and the Zionist groups were formed. A welter of "national" and local bodies sprang up to meet the special political, cultural, and social interests of the new arrivals.

One of the consequences flowing from this organizational free-for-all was that any group could undertake any service and was even encouraged to do so if the service seemed needed. For example, over the years B'nai B'rith provided a string of services unusual for a fraternal body, including several chronic-disease hospitals, vocational counseling to assist Jews in finding employment, and the Anti-Defamation League. It also became the principal sponsor of Jewish religious and communal services on the campus through its Hillel Foundations—all this in addition to its women's and youth divisions. B'nai B'rith assumed these tasks in a period when it was the largest countrywide Jewish organization in existence and the one best able to mobilize the voluntary support necessary for activities that transcended their local communities.

In the meantime a gradual change was taking place in the social-service realm. Organizations that had begun as charitable committees through which volunteers collected money and perhaps even provided some services for the beneficiaries of their largesse were transformed first into philanthropic organizations with clear-cut programs and then into social-welfare agencies and institutions, with buildings, professional staff, and the like—in other words, institutionalization and bureaucratization took place. This led to a more systematic rendering of services but also created the need for more funds, thus contributing substantially to the Jewish communal leaders' interest in setting up similarly institutionalized and bureaucratized fund-raising mechanisms—in short, the federations. The connections between these multifarious organizations and groups were at best minimal. No real communications network existed on either the countrywide or local planes.

World War I brought the first real steps toward the creation of such a network. The unification of overseas welfare activities under the newly formed JDC was the first successful effort to link old-line (i.e., "German"), Orthodox, and secularist elements into a common framework. While, as noted, the war also produced an abortive attempt at creating Jewish unity on a mass basis countrywide, in the aftermath of the failure of the American Jewish Congress, new efforts were generated on the local plane to link the diverse elements in the community for at least limited welfare and defense purposes. During the 1920s the welfare federations and community councils, the institutions that best embodied these efforts, took root locally and began to coalesce on a countrywide basis.

The first Jewish federations appeared on the American scene during the eighth generation, beginning with the establishment of the Boston Federation of Jewish Charities in 1895. By the time the United States had declared war on Germany, twenty-three such local federations had been organized, including one in New York City in 1917, after it became apparent that the New York Kehillah was foundering. These federations linked existing Jewish social-service and philanthropic institutions, primarily for the purpose of joint fund raising. Their roots went back to the 1860s, when, following the first wave of Jewish charitable efforts outside the congregational framework, there had been a period of unification of what had become a multitude of small operations into larger, more formally organized and staffed bodies. At least one Jewish community, Memphis, traces the organization of its central social-welfare agency, the Jewish Service Agency of Memphis, back to 1864 (although it should be noted that its Jewish Welfare Fund was founded in 1934). In many cases these bodies formed the nuclei of the expanded Jewish federations that emerged in the following generation.

The difference in nomenclature between the united charities of the 1860s and the federations of the next generation was significant. The former were indeed unions and represented the unification of diverse groups under a single governing body, even if the individual entities maintained some separate identity. The federation movement, on the other hand, was explicitly federal, providing an additional dimension of governance without eliminating or changing the governing bodies of their constituents.

Cleveland's Federation of Jewish Charities, organized in 1903, was typical. It was founded by the established leadership of the community to develop a joint fund-raising effort in behalf of its eight charter member agencies. They included the Hebrew Relief Society (founded 1875), the Jewish Orphan Asylum (founded by B'nai B'rith in 1868), the Kesher shel Barzel Montefiore Home for the Aged (1881), the Cleveland Section of the Council of Jewish Women (1894), and the Council Educational Alliance Settlement House (1898). In the Federation's first campaign 1,217 donors contributed $41,350. In Cleveland, as elsewhere, the early federations by and large remained the province of the German Jews (even though many of the services they provided were directed toward assisting the East European immigrants). As a result, the East Europeans began to create their own institutions, often duplicating those under the Federation. In Cleveland the Jewish Relief Society (founded in 1895), the Jewish Orthodox Home for the Aged (1906), and the Orthodox Orphan Home were all created at the same time that the Federation was coming into existence. There was even an attempt to federate some forty-five immigrant-sponsored societies and organizations during the early 1900s under Orthodox auspices.

Of the fourteen Jewish communities now having Jewish populations of forty thousand or more, at least eleven established united benevolent or relief associations or united Jewish charities prior to the establishment of their federations. (Six of these eleven established theirs between 1859 and 1871. In the case of four of the other five, as well as two of those that apparently went directly to the federated structure, there was no significant local Jewish population until well after the Civil War.) For most of the Jewish communities in the next size category the attainment of a sufficient Jewish population came at a time when the federation movement had already begun to take on momentum, so that most of them moved directly into federative arrangements (see Table 16).

The original federations rarely embraced Jewish institutions outside the social-welfare sphere. In exceptional communities, like Detroit, the

TABLE 16   UNIFICATION OF PHILANTHROPIC EFFORTS IN SELECTED
LARGE JEWISH COMMUNITIES

Community	Date	Philanthropy
Boston	1864	United Hebrew Benevolent Association
Chicago	1859	United Hebrew Relief Association
Detroit	1899	United Jewish Charities
Essex Co.	1903	United Hebrew Charities
Los Angeles	?	United Jewish Welfare Fund
Miami	c. World War I	United Jewish Aid Association
New York	1859	?
Philadelphia	1869	United Hebrew Charities
Pittsburgh	Civil War	United Hebrew Relief Society
Saint Louis	1871	United Hebrew Relief Association
Washington	1882	United Hebrew Relief Society

Talmud Torah system (there the United Hebrew Schools) was included
in the federation family from the first. It was not until the 1930s that the
first tentative links between the federations and the synagogues were
forged, and those were rare indeed. Table 17 shows how local federations
were established across the country. Major Jewish communities that had
not established at least rudimentary federations before World War I did
so in the 1920s, but it was not until the mid-1930s and the rise of Nazism
that the federation movement became truly nationwide, reaching into the
smaller Jewish communities as well. By the end of the ninth generation
almost all Jewish communities with sufficient organizational complexity
had established local federations.

In many cases, particularly where the original federations had come
into existence on a restricted basis, parallel Jewish welfare funds were
created in the 1930s to raise money for overseas purposes. It was during the
tenth generation, particularly in the 1950s, that the two parallel bodies
were merged in community after community and the federations themselves were reorganized to become more comprehensive community-planning, financing, and initiating bodies. While there are still some holdouts
that maintain the dual system (Memphis is one), with the unification
of the New York Jewish Federation and UJA in 1973 on the heels of the
Yom Kippur War, it is possible to say that this task has been accomplished.

TABLE 17 SPREAD OF LOCAL JEWISH FEDERATIONS

1895	1896	1897	1898	1899
Boston, Mass. (reorg. 1961)	Cincinnati, Ohio (reorg. 1967)			Detroit, Mich. (reorg. 1926)

1900	1901	1902	1903	1904
Chicago, Ill.: Federation (merged with Welfare Fund as Jewish United Fund in 1968)	Phila., Pa. (reorg. 1956) Saint Louis, Mo.		Cleveland, Ohio Buffalo, N.Y. Omaha, Neb.	

1905	1906	1907	1908	1909
Atlanta, Ga. (reorg. 1967) Indianapolis, Ind.	Lawrence, Mass.	Toledo, Ohio (reorg. 1960)		

1910	1911	1912	1913	1914
San Francisco, Marin Co., and peninsula, Calif. (reorg. 1955)	Dallas, Tex. Little Rock, Ark.	Los Angeles, Calif. Pittsburgh, Pa. (reorg. 1955)	New Orleans, La. (reorg. 1967) Manchester, N.H.	Des Moines, Ia.

1915	1916	1917	1918	1919
Saint Joseph, Mo.		New York (including N.Y.C. Nassau, Suffolk, and Westchester cos.): Federation (merged with New York UJA in 1973)	Alameda and Contra Costa cos., Calif. Syracuse, N.Y. Oakland, Calif.	Portsmouth, Va.

1920	1921	1922	1923	1924
Baltimore, Md. (reorg. 1969) Portland, Ore. (reorg. 1956) Altoona, Pa. (reorg. 1940)	Fort Wayne, Ind. Sioux City, Ia. Davenport, Ia.	Camden Co., N.J. San Antonio, Tex. Terre Haute, Ind.	Metropolitan N.J. (Essex Co.)	Lafayette, Ind. Atlantic City, N.J. (reorg. as shore area N.J. in 1971)

1925	1926	1927	1928	1929
Columbus, Ohio (merged 1959) Newburgh, N.Y.	Seattle, Wash.	Sheboygan, Wis. Spokane, Wash.	New Haven, Conn. Lancaster, Pa. York, Pa.	Trenton, N.J. Champaign-Urbana, Ill. Minneapolis, Minn.

1930	1931	1932	1933	1934
San Jose, Calif. (reorg. 1950) Montgomery, Ala. Grand Rapids, Mich.	Lincoln, Neb. Chattanooga, Tenn.		Kansas City, Mo. Northern Jersey (Paterson) Passaic-Clifton, N.J. Harrisburg, Pa. Tri-Cities (Florence), Ala. Peoria, Ill. Utica, N.Y. Ohio valley Wheeling, W. Va.	Memphis (Shelby Co.), Tenn. Louisville, Ky. Ardmore, Okla.

TABLE 17 (*continued*)

1935	1936	1937	1938	1939
Washington, D.C.	Chicago, Ill.:	Norfolk, Va.	Miami, Fla.	New York: UJA
San Diego, Calif.	Welfare Fund	Houston, Tex.	Milwaukee, Wis.	(merged with
Delaware	(merged with	Rochester, N.Y.	North Shore	Federation in 1973)
Jacksonville, Fla.	Federation as	Augusta, Ga.	(Marblehead), Mass.	Brockton, Mass.
Saint Paul, Minn.	Jewish United Fund	Rockford, Ill.	Kenosha, Wis.	Jersey City, N.J.
Akron, Ohio	in 1968)	Duluth, Minn.	Tyler, Tex.	El Paso, Tex.
Richmond, Va.	Denver, Colo.	Broome Co., N.Y.	Sioux Falls, S.D.	Austin, Tex. (reorg.
Youngstown, Ohio	Bridgeport, Conn.	Charleston, W. Va.	Johnstown, Pa.	1956)
Wyoming valley	Salt Lake City,		Butler (Butler Co.),	Knoxville, Tenn.
(Wilkes-Barre), Pa.	Utah		Pa.	Uniontown, Pa.
Reading, Pa.	Galveston Co., Tex.		Allentown, Pa.	Easton, Pa.
Pottsville, Pa.	Fort Worth, Tex.		Waterbury, Conn.	Huntington, W. Va.
Birmingham, Ala.	Norristown, Pa.		Ventura Co., Calif.	Topeka-Lawrence,
mid-Kansas	Evansville, Ind.		Elgin, Ill.	Kan.
(Wichita)	Flint, Mich.		Joliet, Ill.	Fitchburg, Mass.
Lima, Ohio	Troy, N.Y.		Rock Island, Ill.	Holyoke, Mass.
Niagara Falls, N.Y.	Nashville, Tenn.		Central La.	Leominster, Mass.
Canton, Ohio	San Bernardino,		(Alexandria)	Lansing, Mich.
(reorg. 1955)	Calif. (inc. 1957)		Northeastern La.	Saginaw, Mich.
	Vicksburg, Miss.		(Monroe)	Glens Falls, N.Y.
	Port Arthur, Tex.		New Bedford, Mass.	Middletown, N.Y.
			Perth Amboy, N.J.	
			Albuquerque, N.M.	
			Schenectady, N.Y.	
			Steubenville, Ohio	
			Warren, Ohio	
			Tulsa, Okla.	
			Palm Beach Co.,	
			Fla.	
			Springfield, Mass.	
			Albany, N.Y.	

1940	1941	1942	1943	1944
Central N.J.	Northwestern Ind.	Decatur, Ill.	Dayton, Ohio	Meriden, Conn.
(expanded 1973)	(Gary; reorg. 1959)	Pensacola, Fla.	Hollywood, Fla.	Hampton, Va.
Phoenix, Ariz.	Tampa, Fla.	Southern Me.	Savannah, Ga.	Bay Cities, Calif.
Shenango valley	Columbus, Ga.	(Portland)		
(Sharon), Pa.	Lynn Co. (Cedar	Elmira, N.Y.		
Madison, Wis.	Rapids) Ia.	Tucson, Ariz.		
Pittsfield, Mass.	Springfield, Ill.	Newport News, Va.		
Northeastern Mich.	Southern Ill.			
(Bay City)	Waterloo, Ia.			
Charlotte, N.C.	Shreveport, La.			
N.C. Triad	Port Chester, N.Y.			
(Greensboro)	Poughkeepsie, N.Y.			
	Oklahoma City,			
	Okla.			

1945	1946	1947	1948	1949
Jackson, Miss.	Erie, Pa.	Southern Idaho	Raritan valley, N.J.	Central Fla.
Hartford, Conn.	New Britain, Conn.	(Boise)	Sacramento, Calif.	(Orlando)
Rhode Island	Annapolis, Md.	Lewiston-Auburn,	Stockton, Calif.	Bangor, Me.
Scranton-Lacka-	Saint Joseph Co.	Me.	(reorg. 1961)	Fall River, Mass.
wanna Co., Pa.	(South Bend), Ind.	Hudson, N.Y.		Kalamazoo, Mich.
Muncie, Ind.	Racine, Wis.	Worcester, Mass.		Waco, Tex.
Danbury, Conn.	Norwalk, Conn.			Charleston, S.C.
	(reorg. 1964)			
	Long Beach, Calif.			

1950	1951	1952	1953	1954
New London, Conn.	Kingston, N.Y.	Englewood, N.J.	Bergen Co., N.J.	
Saint Petersburg,			Corpus Christi, Tex.	
Fla.				

TABLE 17 *(continued)*

1955	1956	1957	1958	1959
	Lower Bucks Co., Pa.			Sarasota, Fla.

1960	1961	1962	1963	1964
Hazelton, Pa. Somerset Co., N.J. Columbia, S.C.		Birmingham, Ala.	Clearwater, Fla.	Orange Co., Calif.

1965	1966	1967	1968	1969
	Mobile, Ala.	Kern Co., Calif. North Broward, Fla. Beaumont, Tex.	Framingham, Mass.	Central Ill.

1970	1971	1972	1973	1974	1975
	Palm Springs, Calif. Baton Rouge, La. Vineland, N.J.		Las Vegas, Nev. Quad Cities, Ill.-Ia. Stamford, Conn.		Northern Middlesex Co., N.J.

Beginning in 1960 there was another modest spurt in the creation of new federations, primarily in response to the Jewish migrations of the metropolitan frontier. Eighteen of the twenty-one federations organized in that period were organized either in areas of new or greatly expanded Jewish settlement, where there had been no need for such institutions before. The federations originated as a very pragmatic—one is moved to say typically American—response to a set of needs. Yet the form of the response was fully consonant with Jewish political culture as well as the American environment. Perhaps it was that combination that led to the development of a "federation perspective," a justification of the federation approach that was something less than a coherent ideology but had certain articulated theoretical premises of its own, which emphasized the necessity to seek Jewish unity, communal responsibility, organizational efficiency, and comprehensive community planning within the context of the inevitably loose matrix of organized Jewish life.

The development of the federations can be seen as passing through three stages. In the first stage the federations were *leagues* of individual operating agencies for joint fund raising. The allocation of funds collected was essentially based on balancing the sources of contributions so that every agency received more or less the same proportion of funds that it might have received through independent fund raising, but the amount was larger. In the second stage the federation structures were tightened; they became *confederations* of their operating agencies and began to assume a role in allocating funds based on some overall planning, as well as balancing the sources of contributions. Many have now entered a third stage, becoming *federations* with important community-planning functions entrusted to them, so that their power stems from a combination of fund raising *and* planning. Their new powers include anticipatory planning and the generation of new functions and agencies on the basis of their planning work. Allocations, while continuing to follow historical patterns, are increasingly subject to at least significant incremental changes based upon decisions made by the federation leadership.

Thus we have seen that the demands placed upon the American Jewish community beginning in the late 1930s have led to a growing recognition of the need to reconstitute the community's organizational structure at least to the extent of rationalizing the major interinstitutional relationships and generally tightening the matrix. These efforts at reconstitution received added impetus from the changes in American society as a whole (and the Jews' place in it after 1945). They signaled the abandonment of earlier efforts to create a more conventional organizational pyramid in imitation of foreign patterns, which would have been quite out of place, given the character of American society as a whole.

TRENDS IN JEWISH ORGANIZATION AFTER WORLD WAR II

The aftermath of World War II brought with it an expansion of the trends already noted in Jewish organizational life in the 1930s, now radically intensified as a result of the new conditions of what had become, in effect, the postmodern world. American Jewry had become the foremost Jewish community in the world, larger by far than any other functioning Jewish community; indeed, it was ten times larger than its nearest functioning counterpart. It owned the bulk of the wealth that world Jewry could mobilize to undertake the tremendous tasks of relief and reconstruction confronting it as a result of the Holocaust, tasks which increasingly came to be concentrated in the development of the new state of Israel as the initial demands of postwar relief were satisfied.

At the same time, American Jewry confronted a new situation at home: barriers against full participation in American society rapidly fell away to be replaced by what Will Herberg was to call the "triple melting pot," that is, the recognition of Judaism and Catholicism along with Protestantism as "legitimate" American faiths. Finally, the opening of the metropolitan frontier, with the resultant suburbanization of America, saw the Jews in the vanguard of the movement out of old neighborhoods to the suburbs or to suburbanlike areas within the central cities, requiring institutional adaptations to new life-styles.

All these factors influenced Jewish organizational development between the end of the war and the mid-1960s. In the first place, some institutions began to centralize, or at least began to structure properly the governmentlike functions undertaken by the Jewish community. These were generally the federations and their constituent organizations. Locally and then nationally, through the CJF, the federations and their constituents gained in strength, emerging as the dominant fund raisers in the Jewish community.

Pioneering in "single-drive" fund raising in the style of the United Fund (the most important reason for their founding), the federations became the motive force behind an unprecedented voluntary effort. The exciting tasks of raising funds for postwar relief and for the rebuilding of Israel, which captured the imaginations of American Jews, stimulated a phenomenal increase in the amount of money contributed for all Jewish communal purposes. The impetus provided by fund raising for Israel redounded to the benefit of domestic Jewish needs as well, since the larger sums forthcoming from the coordinated drives were so allocated as to increase their resources too.

Between 1939 (the first full year of operation of UJA) and 1974, the local Jewish federations in the United States raised approximately $5.7 billion, approximately $2.6 billion of which has been raised since the Six-Day War. Well over half this amount has been transmitted to UJA, primarily for use in Israel, although during the Nazi era and immediately following a large share went to the relief of Jewry in Europe. Yet federation fund raising is but the tip of the iceberg. Since the Six-Day War, Jewish communal services linked to the federation have received four times as much support from other sources than from the federation campaigns themselves, virtually all of which comes from user fees (of which hospitals provide the lion's share). What is important, however, is that together the federations and their constituent agencies control about 75 percent of the public expenditure of the American Jewish community. Another 20 percent—roughly the equivalent of what the federations raise minus the Israel Emergency Fund—is raised primarily by synagogues for their operating expenses. (Unfortunately, the synagogues do not publish budgetary reports, so that we can only estimate the amounts involved.) Perhaps 5 percent is raised independently by various organizations.

With a few exceptions, the federations from the first did not (and do not) subsidize synagogues or functions that come under the synagogue's wing. By common agreement the latter were left to raise their own funds, and in the first half of the postwar generation they did so with remarkable success. Nevertheless, though large amounts of money were raised for the construction and maintenance of synagogues in the same period, synagogue fund raising offered neither the excitement nor the continuity of the annual federation drives. The synagogues' great fund-raising efforts were necessarily one-time affairs and the annual needs of each congregation remained relatively limited.

The substantive quality and the recurring nature of the federations' tasks also served to strengthen their hands in other ways. They attracted leadership, both voluntary and professional, of the highest caliber available to the Jewish community. In time that leadership, because of the nature of the tasks which confronted it, came to regard Jewish communal problems as interconnected. Federation leaders thus began to concern themselves with the broad range of Jewish needs, not simply with overseas relief or with the welfare functions that had been traditional to the federations in the period before World War II.[12]

By 1960 most of the major Jewish federations were engaged in community planning of some sort, were supporting Jewish educational and cultural programs as well as welfare, defense, and overseas services, and were beginning to think of themselves as the central bodies for Jewish communal endeavor within their respective areas of jurisdiction. After 1960 federations increasingly began to define the range of their interests as embracing virtually the total Jewish community, excluding only the synagogues. At the same time, on the countrywide plane the CJF began to strengthen its position, often providing the impetus for local federations to become involved in areas that had previously been considered outside their purview.

During this period there was also a sorting out of roles among the previously existing countrywide organizations, many of which had at one time or other aspired to the central role being assumed by the federation movement. Thus the American Jewish Committee, the American Jewish

Congress, B'nai B'rith, and the Zionist organizations began to edge away from the task of actually providing governmentlike services and to redefine themselves as mass-based organizations whose task it was to capture the federations, or at least to be their animating spirit. This shift, begun gradually, is only now beginning to gain momentum.

Here a word about the structure of the local federation is in order. While there are variations from community to community, and community size does have a bearing on the degree of complexity to be found in each, a more or less common pattern has emerged. (See Table 18 for the structure of one local federation, the Federation of Jewish Agencies of Greater Philadelphia.) Legally every federation is a membership organization. Anybody who makes a certain minimum contribution to the annual appeal is automatically enrolled as a member. Technically, the ultimate power to manage the federation's affairs rests with the membership, which is invited to an annual meeting to take up such business as the election of a board and officers, the presentation of an annual report, and changes in the constitution. In fact, however, only a small fraction of the membership participates in these annual meetings (an attendance of fifteen hundred in even the largest community would be considered extraordinary); by and large, those who do show up merely ratify actions already approved by a nominating committee and by the board.

Occasionally the existence of the mechanisms of the annual meeting does lead to its use as a forum for handling community conflict. In the late 1950s, for example, there was one last effort on the part of the Detroit Jewish Community Council to capture the central position in the community from the Jewish Welfare Federation. In this the Community Council was aided and abetted by the city's leading Conservative rabbi, then one of the most eminent rabbis in the United States. They put forward a rival slate to the one officially submitted by the federation nominating committee. An intense public campaign utilizing the local *Detroit Jewish News* and other means of publicity ensued, preparatory to its being brought before the federation's annual meeting, as called for in the bylaws. Both sides saw to it that hundreds of their supporters turned out for the annual meeting and the election was held as scheduled, with the federation slate winning.

Most federation boards meet monthly and serve as institutionalized sounding boards and ratifying agents for decisions taken by the officers and leadership. In most cases the boards are partly elected by the mem-

TABLE 18 STRUCTURE OF FEDERATION OF JEWISH AGENCIES OF GREATER PHILADELPHIA

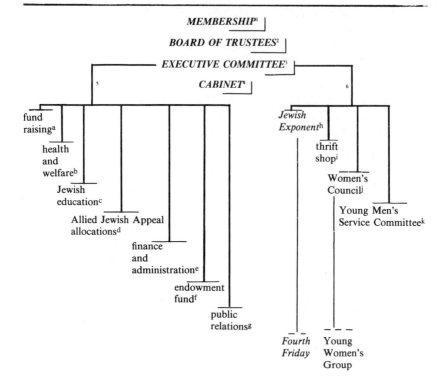

1. Defined in the bylaws as any Jewish individual over eighteen years of age in the Greater Philadelphia community who contributes at least ten dollars a year to any Federation activity. The membership votes annually to elect trustees, and provision is made for them to call special meetings and to nominate trustee candidates.
2. The board is the chief decision-making, policy-setting body in the Federation. It is comprised of no more than 210 elected members (on a rotating basis), presidents of all local constituent agencies, and several individuals in special categories. It meets at least ten times each year.
3. The executive committee reviews matters prior to board consideration and makes recommendations to the board. It serves as the board during July and August. It consists of the elected officers, appointees (by the president with board approval), and the chairmen of all standing committees. There is also a group of special invitees who serve unofficially.
4. The cabinet is basically an advisory and consultative group around the president. It has, however, been vested with certain administrative authority (within board policy), such as negotiating the annual agreement with UJA, distributing Federation endowment income, and determining financial procedures in the Building Fund program. It consists of the elected officers, past Federation presidents, and a small group who occupy key positions, such as the chairman of planning, the chairman of Allied Jewish Appeal, the building fund chairman and the president of the *Exponent*.
5. These seven sections are basic operational divisions of Federation, each with a variety of responsibilities, and all coordinated into a single operation:
   a. Involves Allied Jewish Appeal–Israel Emergency Fund, United Fund, building fund, thrift shop.
   b. Involves health, family and children, group activities, budgeting guidance, and a wide variety of special programs and functions. Works closely and constantly with appropriate agencies.
   c. Covers both the planning and budgeting aspects of this field. Continuous involvement with appropriate agencies.
   d. Covers all Allied Jewish Appeal agencies except UJA and Jewish education, as indicated elsewhere.
   e. Involves all fiscal, management, personnel, real estate, kitchen, etc. matters.
   f. Covers every phase of endowment planning—letters of intent, foundation, special programs, etc.
   g. Serves Federation as a whole, every department separately, and most of its agencies.
6. h. The *Exponent* has its own board and staff, but is owned by the Federation, which serves as publisher.
   i. Thrift shop is a division of Federation with its own board and staff. It sells contributed merchandise only and supplements United Fund income for health and welfare purposes.
   j. A division of Federation conducting a wide variety of programs and involved in practically all phases of Federation work. Supervises the Young Women's Group.
   k. Conducts programs, recruits participants, participates in Federation affairs, and trains young men for deeper involvement and potential leadership.

bership at large and partly designated by the federation's constituent bodies, in some combination. Federation nominating committees usually seek to present slates that include spokesmen for the widest possible range of interests and institutions in the community, so that every acceptable point of view will be presented. Thus, the boards tend to be rather large bodies, numbering in the hundreds in the larger communities.

While the boards by and large accept policies developed by the leadership, they play a balancing role and from time to time exercise veto power. Matters brought before a federation board generally have been designed so as to meet any possible objections of the people sitting on it and the groups they represent. Where that has not been done, or the board has not been persuaded, proposals have been rejected or returned to committee for revision. On occasion boards even initiate the development of new policies and programs. In many respects the board's function is similar to that of the limited town meetings of New England: a community that is too large to assemble at frequent intervals in its entirety delegates the task to a broadly representative body of its citizenry, whose role is not so much to govern actively as to speak in the name of the community on the proposals of those who handle the community's day-to-day business.

The struggle over whether to endorse the establishment of the Institute for Jewish Life and provide monetary support for its operations that took place in one major Jewish community demonstrated how the board can very effectively overrule decisions taken by the other bodies. As in most communities, the professional leadership in this one was generally opposed to the establishment of the Institute, viewing it both as a potential source of duplication of existing services and as a threat to local control of educational and cultural functions. Moreover, they perceived it as competing for limited funds, which they thought could be put to better use within their own communities.

To develop support for the proposed institute the CJF committee that suggested it sent representatives to meet with the executive committees of federations around the country, to answer their questions and try to persuade them to back it. In this particular community there was very strong and vocal opposition from the heads of affected local agencies (who also had been invited to attend the meeting to present their case) and from the older leadership, whose general conservatism saw the Institute as a risky endeavor. Only a few of the younger members of the executive committee spoke out in its behalf. When a vote on what recommendation was to be placed before the board was taken, it went two to one against the Institute.

In the period between the executive committee's vote and the next meeting of the board, a few of the younger members tried to persuade some of the more prestigious leaders who were known to be open-minded on the subject, but to little avail. At the board meeting the executive committee's recommendation was presented in the most forceful terms. Then at the last moment one of the federation's inner circle, who had a reputation as a maverick, attacked the pending rejection of the Institute as going against the trend of the times and as sabotaging American Jewry's efforts to raise its educational and cultural sights. To everyone's surprise, he was supported by one of the most prestigious members of the community, who had up until that time been silent on the issue. He indicated that as an officer of the CJF he had had occasion to see that younger leaders in smaller communities were strongly behind the Institute, seeing in it a chance to enrich the quality of Jewish life in their communities, something which this particular community was large enough to do on its own. This led him to believe that perhaps it was important to conduct such a project on a countrywide basis. His support led other members of the board to voice theirs as well, people who might have been hesitant to go against the established leadership. Once the momentum began, it soon became clear that a majority of the board would back the proposal; the president recommended that it be returned to the executive committee for reconsideration, which it was. At the next board meeting the executive committee had a positive recommendation, which was accepted unanimously.

The day-to-day business of the federation is entrusted to an executive committee, or, in the larger communities, to a cabinet made up of the officers and the committee chairman, which reports to an executive committee. The federation's professional staff works with that body, which meets with considerable regularity to oversee the federation's operations, make policy, decide on programs, and recommend the allocation of funds (of course, the decision in all these matters is the prerogative of the board).

The executive committee (or cabinet) is assisted in its work by a network of standing and special committees entrusted with specific tasks.

These usually include an allocations committee, committees to oversee the various functional groupings of the federation agencies, committees responsible for the various fund-raising activities (including the annual campaign and the endowment fund), and one or two housekeeping committees. In addition, most federations have women's and young leadership divisions that are linked to them but have their own organizational structure and leadership. One of the characteristics of most federation committees is that their membership includes people who are not otherwise federation officers or board members. In fact, the committee structure has become a way for federations to introduce other people into the processes of communal governance and to recruit new people for board and executive-committee positions by first testing them in concrete situations.

Where federations perform certain functions directly, these are also linked organizationally to the overall federation structure. In Philadelphia, for example, the Federation of Jewish Agencies is the publisher of the *Jewish Exponent,* the community's leading weekly newspaper and one of the three largest Jewish weeklies in the world. Sometimes a federation will experiment with a new function by incorporating it as a committee or division until such time as it becomes a constituent agency. Thus, while the Jewish community's campus programs were undergoing reorganization in Philadelphia, a Commission on Campus Affairs was established as a committee of the Federation. Once the reorganization was completed, the Commission was made a committee of the reorganized Jewish Campus Activities Board, a constituent agency. Similarly, when the Federation began experimenting with ways to deal with the problems of Jews left behind in changing neighborhoods, it did so through a committee; then as certain functions became institutionalized, the operation was transferred to the Jewish Community Relations Council.

An outstanding example of this trend is the shift that is taking place with regard to the maintainance and control of the B'nai B'rith Hillel Foundations. The Hillel movement was founded in the late 1920s by Abram Sachar on the campus of the University of Illinois, prompted by an awareness that Jewish students away from home had no collective way to express their Jewishness and no source to provide them with Jewish contacts or services of any kind. Recognizing this situation as a missed educational opportunity, Dr. Sachar initiated a program at his university and turned for support to B'nai B'rith, which at that time was by far the most powerful Jewish group in the Middle West. The initiative of B'nai B'rith District 6 (encompassing that area) led to the program's adoption as a countrywide project.

As Hillel Foundations were established on other campuses from coast to coast, a modus vivendi was developed whereby B'nai B'rith provided financial support channeled through its national office, local B'nai B'rith committees handled the capital needs and housekeeping tasks for individual foundations, and the Hillel directors—increasingly, men with rabbinical backgrounds—became virtually autonomous in matters of program. This latter situation was helped along by the fact that a superb group of dedicated young men went into Hillel service during its first two decades, often directly from their seminaries, and were able to gain significant control over the substantive aspects of Hillel's work. As recently as the early 1960s they had the last word in all programing and personnel matters, with B'nai B'rith having adopted a policy of strict noninterference at the insistence of the Hillel directors themselves.

Meanwhile, the expansion of the program to over two hundred campuses in the United States and Hillel's first tentative extensions abroad rendered its financial demands too heavy for B'nai B'rith to bear alone. The services Hillel was providing were on a scale that required the intervention of the governmental surrogates of American Jewry, namely, the federations, and B'nai B'rith members began to use their influence within their local communities to secure federation allocations for the program. The federation response was modest but good. Soon a substantial share of Hillel's national budget was being obtained from local federation sources but was still channeled through Hillel's national office, which effectively controlled the allocation and use of funds in the local foundations. Since this was the standard pattern with regard to all countrywide organizations, it was accepted as a matter of course by both the federations and B'nai B'rith, which remained Hillel's parent organization.

In the mid-1960s, at the height of the campus revolt against "the system," Jewish students naturally were in the forefront of the action. Those who took their Jewishness seriously used this as an opportunity to take issue with the Jewish aspects of the system, most particularly the Hillel Foundations. In many cases the charges were justified. The Hillel program, plagued by limited resources despite federation allocations and dominated by an aging professional leadership, had failed to adapt to changing circumstances. Consequently it could be seen as failing to reach even the committed Jewish youth. Since many of those same students were the children and grandchildren of the leaders of the federations, the latter were easily aroused to undertake a reexamination of Jewish campus activities and the role of the Jewish community in providing campus services.

By the late 1960s the federations and most major Jewish communities were undertaking a serious reevaluation of Jewish campus services and their own role in providing those services, with the Hillel Foundations undergoing the severest criticism. In almost every major community where there were substantial concentrations of Jewish students, the local federations set up alternate devices for providing campus services with direct federation allocations to support them. Where local Hillel leadership, voluntary and professional, was strong and competent, as in Los Angeles, Hillel remained involved in the new forms and reorganized itself to meet the new challenges. In communities like Philadelphia, where the local Hillels were undergoing changes in leadership, a separate Jewish Commission on Campus Affairs was established as an interim measure, pending a final reorganization. On a countrywide basis the CJF established a Commission on College Youth and Faculty, to which federations from all over the country sent members; through its voluntary leadership and professional staff, this commission was entrusted with the tasks of fact-finding, stimulating new forms of local federation activity on the campus, conciliating students to bridge what appeared to be a growing gap between them and the organized Jewish community, and negotiating with establishment organizations (such as Hillel) to ease the way toward a reorganization of campus services.

The Hillel response to all this was that much more money was needed in order for an effective campus program to be mounted. Regardless of whether Hillel was the agency best suited to carry out that program, its request was a legitimate one. The campus services had been underfunded for years, primarily because they were conceived to be the province of B'nai B'rith, with the federation role being peripheral. Once the federations began to acknowledge the need for greater financial support, they made it clear that they would make the effort only if the effective governance of campus programs within their areas of jurisdiction was transferred to the local community, where it would be lodged in one of their constituent agencies. Given the situation, Hillel had no choice but to agree. By the mid-1970s, reorganizations were increasingly being effected in the various local communities, creating local partnerships between the federation (representing the Jewish community), on one hand, and the local B'nai B'rith, on the other—often with campus representatives and faculty and students representing a third and balancing element—to form a new agency responsible for all Jewish campus services. Within these bodies the locus of control was clearly local and lay with the federations. The national Hillel office was increasingly becoming a service agency instead of an operating body, thereby following the pattern long since established with regard to other countrywide bodies. Its task was to recruit or train personnel and serve as a placement service to assist localities in meeting their personnel needs, to provide technical assistance on programing, and to maintain those countrywide activities that the Hillel movement required.

In the manner of the American Jewish community, this reorganization took place with a minimum of overt conflict. The Hillel organization survived because the federations were not interested in engaging in the sort of struggle with B'nai B'rith that would have been necessary to eliminate it. Hillel was transformed to accommodate the new demands. It adjusted to the fact that control had passed from a voluntary body no longer able to fund its activities, to the one set of Jewish institutions in the United States capable of mobilizing the necessary support. B'nai B'rith's role in all this was also transformed. Slowly abandoning their efforts to provide even the semblance of governance for its Hillel Foundations, B'nai B'rith members sought to retain the Hillel Foundations within the formal confines of the organization and to strengthen the program.

The result of all this was the creation of a network of institutions and organizations along the lines discussed above. This network functioned best on the local plane, where the tasks were most concrete, the needs most apparent, and the resources most easily mobilized. Its capacities were more limited on the national plane, where symbolic issues and matters of personal and organizational prestige often dominated Jewish communal politics, causing interpersonal and interorganizational rivalries that often obscured and limited the real organizational strength of the American Jewish community.

THE SYNAGOGUE IN THE NEW COMMUNITY

The only organizations willing to challenge the federation movement in the postwar period were the congregational arms of the three synagogue movements, both in an individual capacity and jointly, as members of the Synagogue Council of America. The 1950s was a particularly propitious decade for them to assert themselves. These were the years of the so-called religious revival, and the attempt in certain quarters to define Jewishness exclusively in religious terms served to strengthen the authority of the religious spokesmen.

While the federations were expanding their operations community-wide, the synagogues were becoming preeminent within the community. Of all the existing Jewish institutions and organizations, the synagogues had the greatest opportunity to reach out to a new generation who, though largely estranged from the traditions of Jewish observance, were still seeking institutionalized ways to express their Jewishness. The synagogues' growing monopoly over the celebration of the Jewish rites of passage insured them of a steady and even growing constituency.

The synagogues' importance was further enhanced by the growing shift from city to suburb. The Jews who had flocked to the great cities during the heyday of the urban frontier settled in neighborhoods where organic links were as strong as, if not stronger than, associational ones. This was as true of the more assimilated Central European Jews as it was of the East European immigrants in the swarming ghettos. Whether he formally joined a synagogue or not, in both those neighborhoods a Jew was surrounded by family and friends, businesses and institutions, all operating within an essentially or substantially Jewish milieu.

The move to the suburbs changed all this. The old neighborhoods broke up, and Jewish life in the suburbs grew progressively more attenuated. The immediate environment was no longer as thoroughly Jewish as before; Jews no longer lived in the same proximity to each other. Under such conditions Jews who once maintained their Jewishness through organic relationships had to seek more formal associational ties simply to keep those relationships alive. The local synagogue offered the easiest means of making the transition, and given the American context, the most acceptable one.

Consequently, synagogue membership soared in the 1950s (paralleling similar developments in the churches). Whether the membership gains represented a "return to Judaism," as was assumed at the time, or simply a transition to more formal affiliation on the part of those already committed, as demanded by changed circumstances, is a question that remains unanswered.

The resurgent synagogues capitalized on their position by reaching out to embrace a variety of functions. They became the primary custodians of Jewish education, establishing religious schools on their premises as a means of attracting additional members, adapting those schools to the new conditions of suburbia, creating an ideology to justify the new trends they initiated, and virtually eliminating the private and communal Hebrew schools of the previous era. They became the chief organizers of Jewish youth, either on a congregational basis or through their national organizations—in effect replacing both the Zionist organizations and B'nai B'rith. They began to undertake recreational and social-service functions that had been the province of the Jewish community centers and the local Jewish welfare agencies. To accommodate their expanded role, synagogues developed into large institutions, often with memberships of over one thousand families. Indeed, synagogues with fewer than several hundred families came to be considered as less than viable.

This growth in the local communities was accompanied on the countrywide plane by attempts on the part of the national synagogue bodies to lay claim to a larger voice in the affairs of the American community than they had heretofore commanded. Though the challenge that the national synagogue bodies threw out to the federations was only marginally successful, this struggle for supremacy bespoke a continuing area of contention within American Jewish life. As the leaders of the synagogue bodies sought to bring additional functions into their synagogues (i.e., under their jurisdiction), they increasingly came into conflict with the leaders of the federation bodies, whose conception of the tasks of the community as a whole was expanding at the same time.

This conflict reflected a confusion of roles as much as a clash of interests, which in turn was a product of the accidental patterns of growth of American Jewish institutions. In some ways the conflict marked the end of the pioneering period of organized American Jewry, the point where haphazard growth brought jurisdictional and functional overlap that could be rationalized intellectually and ideologically but required harmonization institutionally. Organizationally speaking, the first task of the American Jewish community for the final quarter of the century is to deal with the problems brought on by this conflict. To do so requires an understanding of the latent roles of the various institutions and organizations of the community in order to sharpen them and make them manifest.

Organizing Jewish Activity

CATEGORIES OF COMMUNITY ORGANIZATION

The politylike characteristics of any society are expressed through its institutional structure and dynamics. The more complete its set of institutions is, the more truly can it be defined as a comprehensive polity. As for the American Jewish community, its organizations and institutions can be grouped into four categories, based on the kinds of roles they play within the community as a whole: (1) governmentlike institutions, (2) localistic institutions and organizations, (3) general-purpose, mass-based organizations, and (4) special-interest institutions and organizations.

Governmentlike Institutions

Governmentlike institutions play roles and provide services on a countrywide, local, or regional basis that under other conditions would be played, provided, or controlled by governmental authorities, either predominantly or exclusively.

COMPREHENSIVE-REPRESENTATIVE ORGANIZATIONS

The most clear-cut examples of governmentlike institutions in the American Jewish community are to be found on the local plane: the Jewish federations, which provide comprehensive services to the community either directly or through their constituent agencies. They reach virtually all Jews in the community through their central fund-raising activities.[1] While some organizations remain outside the scope of the federations (the synagogues, for example, are linked with them tenuously if at all), most significant organizations maintain some connection with them, whether as constituent agencies, affiliates, or beneficiaries. Indeed, the federations are in the process of becoming the comprehensive-representative organizations of the community.

The first comprehensive communal organizations generally adopted the term "charities" or "philanthropies," as in Boston, where the federation to this day is known as the Combined Jewish Philanthropies. After World War I the tendency was to substitute the term "welfare" (e.g., the Jewish Welfare Federation of Detroit) for "charities," in recognition of the changing attitude toward assistance for those in need, but still reflecting the essentially social-service orientation of these bodies. Federations that were developed or reorganized after World War II have increasingly come to use the term "federation" unqualified by any adjective other than "Jewish" (e.g., Greater Phoenix Jewish Federation), an indication of the progressive expansion of the intended role and scope of these comprehensive-representative organizations.

As we have mentioned, the first federation was founded in Boston in 1895, and altogether twenty-three were established before World War I. Their primary concerns were the provision of philanthropic services to an immigrant population and charitable services to the needy of the earlier immigration. While most of the major Jewish communities had established federations by the mid-1920s, the majority of the 237 federations were founded in the middle and late 1930s, apparently as part of American Jewry's response to Nazism and anti-Semitism (see Table 19).

In the 1930s the emerging role of the federations as the central agencies of Jewish communal life was challenged by the Jewish community councils. This came about at a time when the federations themselves still considered their scope to be primarily limited to philanthropy. In no small measure, the challenge was a reflection of the efforts of the rising East European Jewish leadership to provide what they believed to be a more appropriate "central address" for the Jewish community than that afforded by the federations, which were still dominated by Central European Jews. It was their contention that the umbrella body of the Jewish community should be based upon the membership organizations rather than the service agencies, an arrangement that would lead to a more representative body. They suggested that the federations serve as fund

**TABLE 19 COUNTRYWIDE JEWISH ORGANIZATIONS NOW IN EXISTENCE
(CLASSIFIED BY FUNCTION AND DATE OF FOUNDING)***

Institutions— Organizations	1840–60	1870
Comprehensive- Representative		
Religious		1873 Union of American Hebrew Congregations 1875 Hebrew Union College (HUC)
Educational and Cultural		
Community Services		
Community Relations		
Professional Associations		
Zionist and Israel-Related		
Multicountry		
Social and Fraternal	1843 B'nai B'rith 1846 United Order True Sisters 1849 Free Sons of Israel	

*Source: *American Jewish Year Book*

TABLE 19 (*continued*)

Institutions—Organizations	1880	1890
Comprehensive-Representative		
Religious	1886 Jewish Theological Seminary (JTS)	1896 Rabbi Isaac Elchanan Seminary (RIETS) 1898 Union of Orthodox Jewish Congregations (UOJC)
Educational and Cultural	1886 Yeshiva University 1888 Jewish Publication Society	1892 American Jewish Historical Society 1895 Gratz College
Community Services	1884 United HIAS Service	1899 National Jewish Hospital 1893 National Council of Jewish Women
Community Relations		1893 Jewish Chautauqua Society
Professional Associations	1889 Central Conference of American Rabbis	1899 National Conference of Jewish Communal Service
Zionist and Israel-Related		1897 Zionist Organization of America
Multicountry		1891 Baron de Hirsch Fund 1897 International Jewish Labor Board
Social and Fraternal	1883 Beth Abraham	1896 Jewish War Veterans 1897 B'nai B'rith Women

TABLE 19 *(continued)*

Institutions— Organizations	1900	1910
Comprehensive-Representative		
Religious	·	1912 National Council of Young Israel 1913 National Federation of Temple Sisterhoods 1913 United Synagogue of America 1918 Women's League for Conservative Judaism
Educational and Cultural	1904 Jewish Museum 1905 Yeshivath Chaim Berlin 1907 Dropsie University 1909 JTS Teachers Institute	1916 Histadruth Ivrith 1918 Jewish Teachers Seminary 1918 Sholem Aleichem Institute 1918 Yeshivath Torah Vodaath
Community Services	1904 American Medical Center at Denver (formerly JCRS) 1907 National Asthma Center	1913 City of Hope 1914 Leo N. Levi Memorial Hospital 1917 National Jewish Welfare Board
Community Relations	1906 American Jewish Committee	1913 Anti-Defamation League 1918 American Jewish Congress
Professional Associations	1900 Rabbinical Assembly 1902 Union of Orthodox Rabbis of U.S. and Canada	1910 Jewish Ministers and Cantors Association of America 1918 Association of Jewish Center Workers
Zionist and Israel-Related	1901 Jewish National Fund (JNF) 1903 United Charity Institutions of Jerusalem 1909 Hashachar (Young Judea and Junior Hadassah) 1909 Mizrachi-HaPoel Ha-Mizrachi (merged 1957) 1909 B'nai Zion	1912 Hadassah 1913 Labor Zionist Alliance
Multicountry		1914 Joint Distribution Committee
Social and Fraternal	1900 Workmens Circle 1905 B'rith Shalom	1915 Sephardic Jewish Brotherhood of America

TABLE 19 (*continued*)

Institutions— Organizations	1920	1930
Comprehensive-Representative		1932 Council of Jewish Federations and Welfare Funds (CJF)
Religious	1922 Hebrew Theological College 1922 Jewish Institute of Religion (JIR) 1923 National Federation of Temple Brotherhoods 1923 UOJC Womens Branch 1926 Synagogue Council of America 1929 National Federation of Jewish Men's Clubs	
Educational and Cultural	1920 American Academy for Jewish Research 1921 Hebrew College (Boston) 1921 Herzliah Hebrew Teachers Institute 1923 B'nai B'rith Hillel Foundations 1923 UAHC—CCAR Committee on Synagogue Education 1925 YIVO 1925 College of Jewish Studies (now Spertus College of Judaica) 1927 Jewish Academy of Arts and Sciences	1930 United Synagogue Commission of Jewish Education 1933 Ner Israel Rabbinical College 1937 Yiddisher Kultur Farband (YKUF) 1938 Central Yiddish Culture Organization (CYCO) 1939 Conference on Jewish Social Studies 1939 American Association for Jewish Education (AAJE)
Community Services	1920 Jewish Conciliation Board 1925 Leadership Conference of National Jewish Women's Organizations 1926 National Jewish Committee on Scouting	1931 Jewish Braille Institute 1938 B'nai B'rith Career and Counseling Service 1939 Jewish Occupational Council
Community Relations		1933 Jewish Labor Committee
Professional Associations	1923 Rabbinical Council of America 1926 Jewish Teachers Association 1926 National Council for Jewish Education	1937 American Jewish Correctional Chaplains Association
Zionist and Israel-Related	1923 National Committee for Labor Israel 1925 American Mizrachi Women 1925 HaShomer HaTzair 1925 Herut-USA (formerly United Zionist Revisionists) 1925 Pioneer Women 1926 PEC Israel Economic Corporation 1927 United Israel Appeal 1928 Women's League for Israel 1928 American Israel Lighthouse	1931 American Friends of the Hebrew University 1935 Habonim 1937 Womens' Social Service for Israel 1938 League for Labor Israel 1939 United Jewish Appeal 1939 American-Israel Cultural Foundation
Multicountry	1925 American ORT Federation 1926 World Union for Progressive Judaism	1935 Freeland League 1939 World Jewish Congress
Social and Fraternal	1921 Jewish Socialist Verband 1924 B'nai B'rith Youth Organization (BBYO)	

TABLE 19   (*continued*)

Institutions— Organizations	*1940*	*1950*
Comprehensive- Representative		1955 Conference of Presidents of Major American Jewish Organizations

Religious	1940 Jewish Reconstructionist Foundation
	1940 Machne Israel (Lubavitcher)
	1940 JWB Commission on the Jewish Chaplaincy
	   1947 Association of Orthodox Jewish
	      Scientists
	     1948 Society of Friends of Touro
	       Synagogue
		1950 HUC-JIR (merger)
		1951 United Synagogue Youth
		   1954 Reconstructionist Federation of
		      Congregations and Havurot
		   1954 National Conference of Synagogue
		      Youth

*Educational and
Cultural*
	1940 United Lubavitcher Yeshivoth
	1940 Merkos L'Inyonei Chinuch
	1940 Jewish Book Council
	1941 Brandeis Institute
	1941 Jewish Peace Fellowship
	1941 Research Institute of Religious Jewry
	1941 Yeshivath Beth Joseph
	1941 Telshe Yeshiva
	   1944 Torah Umesorah
	   1944 National Jewish Music Council
	   1945 National Council of Beth Jacob Schools
	   1947 Mirer Yeshiva
	   1947 American Jewish Archives
	   1947 HUC School of Education and Music
	   1947 University of Judaism
	   1948 Congress for Jewish Culture
	   1948 Brandeis University
	   1948 National Association of Hebrew
	      Day School PTAs
		1952 Hebrew Arts School for Music and
		     Dance
		1952 National Hebrew Cultural Council
		1953 American Jewish Historical Center
		1953 West Coast Talmudical Seminary
		1953 National Yeshiva Teachers Board of
		     License
		   1955 Hebrew Cultural Foundation
		   1955 Leo Baeck Institute

Community Services	1949 American Jewish Society for Service	

*Community
Relations*
	1943 American Council for Judaism
	   1944 National Jewish Community Relations
	      Advisory Council (NJCRAC)
		1953 Commission on Social Action of
		     Reform Judaism

*Professional
Associations*
	1941 National Association of Temple
	     Administrators
	1943 American Jewish Press Association
	1944 Rabbinical Alliance of America (Igud
	     Harabbanim)
	   1946 Association of Jewish Chaplains of the
	      Armed Forces
	   1947 Cantors Association
	   1948 National Association of Synagogue
	      Administrators (United Synagogue)
	   1949 International Association of Hillel
	      Directors
		1950 Association of Jewish Community
		     Relations Workers
		1951 Educator's Assembly
		   1955 National Association of Temple
		      Educators
		   1956 National Association of Yeshiva
		      Principals
		   1956 American Conference of Cantors
		   1957 American Jewish Public Relations
		      Society

*Zionist and
Israel-Related*
	1940 Federated Council of Israel Institutions
	1941 American Red Magen David
	1942 Ampal-American
	   1944 American Committee for the Weizmann
	      Institute
	   1946 World Confederation of General
	      Zionists
	   1947 American Trade Union Council for
	      Histadrut
	   1948 Society of Israel Philatelists
	   1948 Women's Organization of HaPoel
	      Ha-Mizrachi
	   1948 Poale Agudath Israel
	   1948 Israel Music Foundation
	   1948 Americans for a Progressive Israel
	   1948 Dror
	   1948 American Committee–Sports for
	      Israel
	   1949 American Committee for Shaare
	      Zedek Hospital
		1950 RASSCO
		1950 American Committee for Music Library in
		     Israel
		1950 American Physicians Fellowship for Israel
		     Medical Association
		1951 American Zionist Youth Council
		1951 State of Israel Bond Organization
		   1954 Theodore Herzl Foundation
		   1954 Hebrew University Technion Joint
		      Appeal
		   1954 American Israel Public Affairs
		      Committee
		   1955 American Friends of Tel Aviv
		      University
		   1955 Bar Ilan University in Israel
		    1956 American Society for Technion
		     1957 American Jewish League for Israel

Multicountry	1946 American Friends of the Alliance
	      (Israelite Universelle)
	   1946 Consultative Council of Jewish
	      Organizations (CCJO)
	   1946 Ozar HaTorah
	   1947 Coordinating Board of Jewish
	      Organizations
	   1947 World Federation of YMHA's and
	      JCC's
		1951 Conference on Jewish Material Claims
		     against Germany
		1951 Pe'ylem

*Social and
Fraternal*
	1940 Association of Yugoslav Jews in United
	     States
	1942 National Federation of Jews from Central
	     Europe
	   1948 Council of Jewish Organizations in
	      Civil Service
	   1949 American Veterans of Israel
		1951 American Sephardic Federation (reorg.
		     1972)
		   1954 Ezrath Nashim
		   1956 Rumanian Jewish Federation of
		      America

TABLE 19 (*continued*)

Institutions—Organizations	1960	1970
Comprehensive-Representative	1965 North American Jewish Youth Council	
Religious	1960 National Jewish Information Service for the Propogation of Judaism 1960 Atid 1960 Yavneh 1968 Reconstructionist Rabbinical College 1968 Kadima (Pre-USY)	1973 National Jewish Hospitality Committee and Information Centers
Educational and Cultural	1960 National Foundation for Jewish Culture 1961 Society for the History of Czechoslovak Jews 1962 Magnes Museum 1963 Jewish Liturgical Music Association 1965 National Commission on Adult Jewish Education 1966 Association of Jewish Libraries 1967 Herzliah-Jewish Teachers Seminary 1967 HUC-JIR School of Education in Los Angeles 1968 HUC-JIR School of Jewish Communal Service 1969 Association for Jewish Studies 1969 North American Jewish Students Network	1970 Jewish Students Press Service 1970 Touro College 1970 Yeshiva University West Coast Teachers College 1970 Center for Jewish Community Studies 1971 National Center for Jewish Policy Studies 1971 Associated American Jewish Museums 1971 Association for the Sociological Study of Jewry 1971 Research Foundation for Jewish Immigration 1972 Institute for Jewish Policy Planning and Research 1974 American Society for Jewish Music 1974 National Jewish Conference Center 1974 Center for Holocaust Studies 1977 Yeshiva University of Los Angeles
Community Services	1960 National Association of Jewish Homes for the Aged 1965 Home Center for the Retarded 1965 National Association of Jewish Family, Children's, and Health Services 1965 National Commission on Law & Public Affairs (COLPA) 1969 Jewish Rights Council	1971 North American Jewish Students Appeal
Community Relations *Professional Associations*	1960 National Association of Hebrew Day School Administrators 1964 National Organization of Orthodox Synagogue Administrators	1970 Independent Rabbinate of America
Zionist and Israel-Related	1963 American Friends for Religious Freedom in Israel 1964 American Histadrut Cultural Exchange Institute 1969 American Friends Haifa University	1970 American Zionist Federation 1971 World Zionist Organization—American Section 1973 American Zionist Youth Foundation 1973 American Associates of Ben-Gurion University
Multicountry	1961 International Council on Jewish Social and Welfare Services 1964 American Jewish Conference on Soviet Jewry 1964 Student Struggle for Soviet Jewry 1964 Memorial Foundation for Jewish Culture 1965 International Conference of Jewish Communal Service	1971 National Conference on Soviet Jewry
Social and Fraternal		

raisers for the community councils to enable the latter to function as the spokesmen and policy makers for their communities.

Where Jewish community councils were organized, a struggle of greater or lesser intensity developed between them and the federations, which lasted from the mid-1930s to the mid-1950s. In about three-quarters of the cases the community councils ultimately had to concede, and in all but one of the other cases they absorbed the fund-raising function to become federations in all but name. In some places there was a merger of the two bodies: in Los Angeles the Jewish Federation–Council of Greater Los Angeles was created. In others, like Detroit, there was a standoff, with the Jewish Community Council withdrawing to public-relations activity almost exclusively. In still other places, Philadelphia, for example, there was a reorganization: the Jewish Community Council became the Jewish Community Relations Council, a constituent agency of the federation, and became responsible for the community's external relations. In no case did the community councils emerge as the comprehensive-representative organizations, as their proponents had hoped, primarily because the federations were able to capture two decisive areas of communal activity: fund raising and financial support for Israel.

Elsewhere we shall discuss the question of whom the federations represent, but here the general point can be made that while the problem of representation is in some respects far from being solved in American Jewish life, it is clear that it is part of the struggle that transformed the federations from fund-raising mechanisms for social-service institutions into comprehensive-representative bodies. American Jewry, perhaps in tacit recognition of the difficulties presented by an unbounded community of concentric circles, has not relied upon competitive elections as a means for making their institutions representative. Although formal elections are held regularly, generally a previously agreed-upon slate, put together by a nominating committee appointed by the incumbent officeholders, is presented for what usually amounts to unanimous ratification by the electors. The occasional contested election usually involves a factional fight with one group seeking more representation than it has had in the past. In spite of this—or perhaps because of it—the great majority of the federations have sought to devise ways for a very wide range of Jewish groups and interests within the community to be represented within their structures, at the very least in relatively nominal fashion on their boards, and with increasing frequency in meaningful fashion on their executive, planning, and working committees.

The federations' central position is enhanced by the fact that they are dominated by people who are involved in the total life of the community and who therefore tend to see its problems from a perspective based on a conception of the community as a whole.[2] These people are also usually the representatives of the local Jewish community to countrywide and worldwide Jewish bodies.

Other governmentlike institutions at the community level include bureaus of Jewish education, the Jewish community-relations councils, and the community-services organizations and institutions. While these bodies serve more narrowly defined functions than the federations, they also must adopt a broader perspective, looking at the community as a whole because they are extensively involved in all its relevant parts. Appropriately, the bureaus of Jewish education, local community-relations councils, Jewish community centers, communitywide welfare institutions, and the like—all of which perform functions that would otherwise be performed by government—are generally linked to the federation.

It is hard to point out a single comprehensive-representative organization on the countrywide plane. The Council of Jewish Federations and Welfare Funds, the Conference of Presidents of Major American Jewish Organizations, the Synagogue Council of America, the National Jewish Welfare Board, the National Jewish Community Relations Advisory Council, and the American Association for Jewish Education make claims in that direction. But in fact the Jewish communities of the United States are only leagued together; they are not sufficiently federated on a countrywide basis to have generated comprehensive institutions comparable to those on the local scene. The closest analogous body to the local federations is the CJF, which sometimes leans in the direction of becoming an umbrella organization with considerable scope and at other times pulls back from any such tendencies in order not to offend other powerful countrywide organizations, such as the umbrella organizations of the synagogue movements or the powerful membership organizations such as B'nai B'rith or the American Jewish Committee. The annual General Assembly of the CJF has become the most important meeting of the American Jewish community, a gathering of over two thousand Jews— delegates from all the local federations and representatives of every organization and institution that has business with them.

TABLE 20 COMPREHENSIVE-REPRESENTATIVE ORGANIZATIONS*

State	Jewish Federation/ (Community Federation) (67)	Jewish Welfare Federation/ Federated Charities/Agencies (42)	Jewish Welfare Fund/Agency (28)	United/Combined Jewish Appeal/ Philanthropies (21)	Jewish Community Council/Center (54)	Federated/Fund and Council (16)	Jewish Federation and Council (3)
Alabama	Montgomery	Tri-Cities	Mobile				Birmingham
Arizona	Phoenix				Tucson		
Arkansas			Little Rock				
California	Long Beach Sacramento San Diego San Jose	Alameda Palm Springs San Francisco	San Bernardino Stockton		Ventura Co.	Kern Co. Los Angeles Orange Co.	
Colorado					Denver		
Connecticut	Danbury Hartford New Britain Stamford Waterbury		Meriden		Bridgeport New Haven New London Norwalk		
Delaware		Delaware					
District of Columbia				Washington			
Florida	Miami North Broward Palm Beach Co.	Hollywood Pensacola	Clearwater		Jacksonville Central Florida Saint Petersburg Sarasota Tampa		
Georgia		Atlanta Augusta Columbus			Savannah		
Idaho				Southern Idaho			
Illinois	Decatur Central Illinois Southern Illinois Springfield	Champaign-Urbana	Elgin Joliet	Chicago Quad Cities Illinois-Iowa	Rockford	Peoria	

State	Jewish Federation/ (Community Federation) (67)	Jewish Welfare/ Federation/ Federated Charities/Agencies (42)	Jewish Welfare Fund/Agency (28)	United/Combined Jewish Appeal/ Philanthropies (21)	Jewish Community Council/Center (54)	Federated/Fund and Council (16)	Jewish Federation and Council (3)
Indiana	Fort Wayne	Indianapolis Lafayette Northwestern Indiana	Michigan City Muncie		Evansville	Saint Joseph Co.	
Iowa	Sioux City Waterloo	Des Moines	Linn Co. Davenport				
Kansas	Topeka-Lawrence	Mid-Kansas					
Kentucky	Louisville						
Louisiana	Shreveport	Baton Rouge New Orleans		Northeast Louisiana		Alexandria	
Maine	Lewiston-Auburn				Bangor	Southern Maine	
Maryland			Annapolis Baltimore				
Massachusetts	Fitchburg Framingham North Shore Springfield Worcester	New Bedford		Boston Brockton Haverhill Holyoke	Lawrence Leominster Pittsfield		Fall River
Michigan	Kalamazoo	Northeastern Michigan Detroit Lansing Saginaw			Flint	Grand Rapids	
Minnesota		Minneapolis				Duluth Saint Paul	
Mississippi		Vicksburg	Jackson				
Missouri	Saint Louis			Saint Joseph		Kansas City	
Nebraska	Omaha	Lincoln					

*Total federations listed: 229; source: *American Jewish Year Book*, vol. 75 (1974–75)

TABLE 20 (*continued*)

State	Jewish Federation/(Community) Federation) (67)	Jewish Welfare Federation/Federated Charities/Agencies (42)	Jewish Welfare Fund/Agency (28)	United/Combined Jewish Appeal/Philanthropies (21)	Jewish Community Council/Center (54)	Federated/Fund and Council (16)	Jewish Federation and Council (3)
Nevada				Las Vegas			
New Hampshire					Manchester		
New Jersey	Camden Co. Central New Jersey Metropolitan New Jersey North New Jersey Raritan valley Shore Area Somerset Co. Trenton	Atlantic City Bergen Co.		Englewood Jersey City Morris and Sussex cos.	Passaic-Clifton Perth Amboy Vineland		
New Mexico					Albuquerque		
New York	Broome Co. Buffalo Niagara Falls Rochester	Syracuse New York City	Elmira Glens Falls Hudson Poughkeepsie	Middletown Newburgh	Albany Kingston Port Chester Schnectady Troy Utica		
North Carolina	North Carolina Triad	Charlotte			Asheville		
Ohio	Akron Canton Cincinnati Cleveland Columbus Warren Youngstown	Toledo Lima District			Dayton Steubenville		
Oklahoma	Ardmore				Oklahoma City Tulsa		
Oregon		Portland					

State	Jewish Federation/ (Community Federation) (67)	Jewish Welfare Federation/ Federated Charities/Agencies (42)	Jewish Welfare Fund/Agency (28)	United/Combined Jewish Appeal/ Philanthropies (21)	Jewish Community Council/Center (54)	Federated/Fund and Council (16)	Jewish Federation and Council (3)
Pennsylvania	Allentown Pittsburgh Shenango valley Uniontown	Altoona Philadelphia	Butler	Harrisburg New Castle Pottsville Wyoming valley York	Easton Erie Hazelton Johnstown Lancaster Lower Bucks Co. Norristown Reading Scranton-Lackawanna		
Rhode Island	Rhode Island						
South Carolina		Columbia	Charleston				
South Dakota		Sioux Falls					
Tennessee	Nashville	Chattanooga	Knoxville Memphis				
Texas	Beaumont Fort Worth	Dallas Tyler San Antonio			Austin Corpus Christi El Paso Houston	Galveston Waco	
Utah						Salt Lake City	
Virginia	Newport News Norfolk–Virginia Beach				Hampton Portsmouth Richmond Roanoke		
Washington					Spokane	Seattle	
West Virginia	Ohio valley	•Charleston Huntington					
Wisconsin	Milwaukee	Green Bay Kenosha Racine		Appleton		Madison Sheboygan	

COMMUNITY-SERVICES ORGANIZATIONS

Community-services organizations generally include those agencies that originally joined together to constitute the Jewish federations, including Jewish community centers, Jewish family services, homes for the aged, Jewish hospitals, immigrant aid societies, and the like. Also to be found in this category are the burial and free-loan societies, which may or may not be affiliated with the federation network. As a general rule these agencies originated independently and federated to conduct joint fund-raising campaigns when they reached the point where their budgetary needs exceeded the capacities of their separate fund-raising mechanisms. Today they pride themselves on their commitment to serve the entire Jewish community and frequently the non-Jewish community as well— at times to the point where their Jewish connection is nominal.

These organizations tend to be structured along highly professional lines. They are governed by a coalition of social-work professionals and cosmopolitan voluntary leaders still heavily drawn from Central European backgrounds, or else by men and women who have accepted the particular outlook of such people as modified by time. As institutions, they combine the sense that they speak for the community as a whole (within their specific areas of competence) with their primary mission of service to individuals. This is true even of the Jewish community centers, which in recent years have been struggling with the problem of how to serve families.

While most of these institutions have had to confront only peripheral challenges from other institutions regarding their role in the Jewish community, they have had to undergo serious reevaluations of their character as Jewish agencies as their clienteles have changed, to say nothing of the communal demands placed on them both from within and without the Jewish community.

The federations remain the source of the Jewish public funds that these agencies receive, although most also receive allocations from their local United Fund. By and large, however, they are supported by user fees, which, except in the case of the Jewish community centers, increasingly involve government reimbursements.

COMMUNITY-RELATIONS ORGANIZATIONS

As we have seen, community-relations organizations have consistently sought a role in the "governmental" sphere of the Jewish community.

Today the local community-relations councils have acquired a role as the "external-relations" arm of the federations, while the local branches or chapters of the major countrywide defense organizations are increasingly taking on subsidiary or different roles. The sorting out of these organizations and the creation of the community-relations sphere in its present form represents a long-drawn-out struggle of twentieth-century American Jewish life, one that has confused many people who have taken that struggle to be a reflection of the real character of the American Jewish community. This erroneous view was able to gain great currency because the major skill of the community-relations organizations has always been public relations, and they have tended to spread their particular concerns and conflicts over the front pages of the Jewish press, where they have attracted far more attention than their activities might have objectively warranted.

If the matter of image and public relations has played a very real role in fostering the impression that the community-relations organizations *are* the Jewish community, there was also a substantive dimension to be considered, namely, that at certain periods B'nai B'rith (the parent organization of the Anti-Defamation League), the American Jewish Committee, and the American Jewish Congress did have aspirations to that role, just as their local parallels—the Jewish community councils—had in their communities. We have already suggested how the latter were forced to settle for the role that they presently have.

The adaptation of the countrywide organizations to the present situation involved an even stormier transition. The American Jewish Committee, the American Jewish Congress, the Anti-Defamation League of B'nai B'rith, and to a lesser extent the Jewish War Veterans and the Jewish Labor Committee were founded to serve the Jewish community as a whole before they developed a local presence. Like the federations, but even more so, the community-relations organizations grew out of the context into which they were born. All five of the countrywide bodies were established around the turn of the century, when the emancipationist ideology was still running at high tide and Jews wished to minimize the degree to which they organized themselves as a people. This meant that their primary concerns were the defense of the Jewish good name vis-à-vis the non-Jewish world and intervention with foreign governments in behalf of less fortunate "coreligionists" who did not have the benefits of equal rights and opportunity that American Jews enjoyed by virtue of living in a free society.

As was the pattern in that period, these tasks fell to a handful of affluent and influential individuals whose prestige and position placed them at the forefront of the community, what were in other times referred to as shtadlanim. The American Jewish Committee, the oldest of the three great community-relations organizations, was the very embodiment of this approach, but the others shared it to a greater or lesser degree. What was characteristic of the three organizations was that in one way or another they connected their external-relations work with what they saw as a potential mandate for providing the entire American Jewish community with leadership in all the spheres they considered to be important. Thus the American Jewish Committee was closely involved in the effort to establish kehillahs in New York and Philadelphia, with the hope that such bodies would be developed in other cities as well and would find their place within the Committee's framework. The American Jewish Congress, born at the very end of this period, just after World War I, saw itself as mobilizing the masses of American Jews in the direction of a coherent countrywide representative body. The Anti-Defamation League was an offshoot of B'nai B'rith, the oldest countrywide Jewish organization in the United States, which until World War I still had visions of itself as the integrating factor in American Jewish life.

This particular combination of activities and aspirations had two immediate consequences: it meant that the focus of the community-relations organization was countrywide rather than local, which in turn meant that they inevitably came into conflict with one another as they sought to work within the same field and on the same issues. These conflicts came to a head in the 1930s, in the fight against the anti-Semitism of those years, and led to the famous MacIver Report and the struggle of the 1940s to create some kind of order in the community-relations field. The result was the creation of the National Jewish Community Relations Advisory Council as a coordinating body that embraced most, but not all, of the defense organizations, local and national.

Significantly, the American Jewish Committee stayed out of the new body. The implications of this were not simply organizational but went far beyond that. The MacIver Report was stimulated by the federation movement through the CJF, as one of its first efforts to extend its influence beyond the communal-welfare sphere. The federations' leverage came, in no small measure, from the fact that their allocations to the community-relations groups had assumed significant dimensions. The fact that the community-relations groups accepted that effort, whether willingly or not, reflected their abandonment of claims to comprehensive leadership. That is one of the reasons why the American Jewish Committee, which was not yet ready to concede its claims, remained aloof.

On the other hand, it also raised the power of the federation-related local community-relations groups. The emergence of the NJCRAC was paralleled by the creation of Jewish community-relations councils locally, with federation support, to coordinate common activities on the local scene. These bodies helped shift that significant segment of community-relations activities which had a local dimension from the countrywide organizations to a new network of local organizations, each of which was tied to the local federation to a greater or lesser degree. Within that sphere the Jewish community-relations councils became very strong indeed. Moreover, the countrywide organizations found it necessary to develop local branches or chapters in order to survive. The American Jewish Committee and the Anti-Defamation League both perceived this, each in its own way, and successfully made the transition from being simply "national-office" organizations to being organizations with constituencies around the country.

When the American Jewish Committee came to realize that it needed to build a local base, it went about the task seriously. As a result, in at least some cases its local chapters have begun to acquire the role of the mass-based organizations as defined here. In Philadelphia, for example, the local American Jewish Committee chapter inaugurated an unparalleled string of innovative programs in the decade following 1965, including a program designed to help Jewish storekeepers caught in changing neighborhoods, a monthly literary and opinion supplement to the local Jewish newspapers, a Jewish free university, and a community archives. Each of these projects came under federation sponsorship or obtained substantial federation funding, but the initiative arose from the Committee chapter in question, functioning as a combination pressure group and active leadership force, with many people who wear hats in both the Committee and the federation participating in the transformation of ideas into programs.

The American Jewish Congress, which was somewhat late in shifting its direction, had considerably less success in this regard and has suffered accordingly. Nevertheless, there has been a proliferation of local branches or chapters of the countrywide organization, which feed the national office as well as undertaking certain kinds of local programs.

Localistic Institutions and Organizations

Localistic institutions and organizations (primarily synagogues, now that the landsmanshaften have virtually disappeared) have the foremost task of meeting the primary personal and interpersonal needs of Jews. By their very nature, synagogues are geared to be relatively intimate associations of compatible people. While the growth of the large American synagogue has led to a confusion of functions (which has contributed to the present difficulties of the synagogue as an institution), it still retains primary responsibility for meeting those needs. Even large congregations, which do not seem to provide for any apparent intimacy among their members, serve essentially localistic purposes. Their concerns are with the immediate social, and to some extent psychological, needs of their members. Any institutional interest in the larger community tends to be strictly related to that primary purpose.

By and large, the active officers of synagogues tend to be men and women whose prime communal activities are restricted to local concerns. Though one sees persons with cosmopolitan interests listed on synagogue boards and in some cases even assuming synagogue presidencies, for the most part this does not reflect any abiding interest on their part in synagogue affairs. Rather, the task is accepted as a duty which must be borne, not as an arena within which one can achieve communal recognition. By the same token, congregational rabbis, no matter how "cosmopolitan oriented" they might have been in other positions and how much they personally can perceive the interests of the community as a whole, must necessarily serve localistic ends.[3]

The localistic character of the synagogue explains why synagogue movements have tended to narrow the definition of what constitutes the area of concern for American Jews and why they have not functioned to broaden American Jewish interests. It is not in their nature to do so, nor is it their task. Problems arise only when they wish to confine the totality of Jewish existence within their particular localistic limits.

General-purpose, Mass-based Organizations

General-purpose, mass-based organizations function to (1) articulate community values, attitudes, and policies, (2) provide the energy and motive force for crystallizing the communal consensus that grows out of those values, attitudes, and policies, and (3) maintain institutionalized channels of communication between the community leaders and the broad base of the affiliated Jewish population to deal with the problems and tasks facing the community. In political structure these mass-based organizations parallel the governmentlike and localistic institutions, bridging the gaps between them, providing a motivating force to keep them running, and determining their respective roles in the community as a whole. In a sense these organizations function as the equivalent of political parties (indeed, in some Jewish communities in other countries they *are* political parties) to aggregate and mobilize interests in the community.

There are three varieties of these organizations in the American Jewish community. First, there are the quasi-elite community-relations organizations that have begun to reach out to develop a larger membership base —but in such a way that only people with special interests or backgrounds are likely to find their place within them. The American Jewish Committee is perhaps the best example and in many respects is the most important. Beginning as a small, self-selected group, it has developed a considerably larger membership base (estimated at twenty-seven thousand) as the American Jewish community has become more democratized. Although it actively recruits members, its ranks still include only a relatively select group of people. At the same time it is very powerful, since the implicit criterion for membership seems to be that a person be an influential or potentially influential leader. More than that of any other organization, its membership is strategically placed among the leadership of the governmentlike institutions and the major synagogues.

The American Jewish Congress is another organization of this type, but its history has followed exactly the opposite pattern from the Committee's. Intended as a mass-based organization, it has instead become the preserve of a self-selected group, increasingly interested in a particular kind of civil-libertarian approach to Jewish communal affairs. Today its "mass" membership is about the same as the Committee's.

The second variety consists of ideologically-based organizations that have sought to become political parties, and as such to dominate the community's institutions. The Zionist organizations in the United States (with the exception of Hadassah) are the principal examples of this group. They remain open to all types of Jews but have not been able to develop the mass base they desire.[4] Not only have they fallen short of their basic aim, but they have also failed to develop the kind of elite cadre that would place them in the first group. After the Six-Day War, Hadassah, the Zionist Organization of America, Mizrachi-HaPoel HaMizrachi, the Labor Zionist Alliance, and the United Zionist-Revisionists federated on a countrywide and local basis to form the American Zionist Federation and local Zionist federations in the major local communities, in an attempt to restore the Zionist "presence" on the American Jewish scene.

The Zionist organizations, too, have their origins at the turn of the century, but their history has taken a different turn. They reached their peak at the very beginning of the generation now coming to an end, when the struggle over the establishment of the state of Israel was at its height, and they have been more or less in decline ever since. There was some infusion of life following the Six-Day War, when the Zionist organizations, adapting to the changed situation, sought to become the forces for the articulation of programing in behalf of Israel, at least within the larger local communities. There are also a few Zionist fraternal bodies that still struggle along in attenuated form. They were organized within the framework of the Zionist movement at the turn of the century to provide social and fraternal benefits as well as to mobilize Jews for the political tasks of Zionism.

Special note must be taken of Hadassah in this connection. Hadassah, despite some setbacks, probably remains the largest single Jewish organization in the United States. It is truly a mass organization of Jewish women, with chapters in far-flung corners of the United States as well as in the main centers. In fact, Hadassah and the synagogues are the two most widespread phenomena of organized Jewish life in the United States. The reasons for this are to be found in the particular place that women have played in American Jewish life. While Hadassah is officially known as the Women's Zionist Organization, in many parts of the country the organization plays down its Zionist connection and functions simply as a prestigious Jewish women's group that happens to be interested in Israel-connected projects. This way Hadassah can capitalize on the tremendous drawing power of Israel without tarring itself, in the minds of many, with the Zionist brush.

SOCIAL AND FRATERNAL ORGANIZATIONS

Social and fraternal organizations should be included in this category only insofar as they serve public or communal purposes in addition to private social functions. This is characteristic of the major bodies. In what can be described as a typically Jewish manner, B'nai B'rith and the

National Council of Jewish Women seek to combine both sets of functions in one set of activities.

Both are among the oldest Jewish organizations in the country, founded in 1843 and 1893 respectively, and both at one time had hopes of providing American Jewry with a common membership base. In the late nineteenth century B'nai B'rith tried to build its private social function into one of providing comprehensive countrywide Jewish leadership, taking on such tasks as representing Jewish interests to the outside world and offering social-welfare and health services for the countrywide community. When the Jewish community of the United States was small, only one Jewish orphans' home was needed to service the entire countrywide community. Indeed, almost no local community except New York could afford to maintain an orphanage of its own. Recognizing the need, B'nai B'rith established an orphans' home in Cleveland, which served the bulk of American Jewry for several decades. However, in the 1890s, when the major Jewish communities began creating their own institutions, B'nai B'rith adapted its programs to serve communities lacking certain services. Today orphanages are out of fashion and care for children without parents is a responsibility of the Jewish agencies, so the B'nai B'rith program has become tangential to the American Jewish enterprise.

The Anti-Defamation League, the B'nai B'rith Hillel Foundations, the B'nai B'rith Vocational Service, and the Leo N. Levi Memorial Hospital in Hot Springs, Arkansas, are survivals or offshoots of those early efforts. However, as the Jewish community articulated itself organizationally in the course of its development, this combination was slowly recognized as the mismatch of functions that it was. As a result, there has been a progressive shift of those tasks to other communal agencies. Today B'nai B'rith is less in the business of providing institutionalized services to the Jewish community and more concerned with mobilizing its membership for certain public activities more compatible with its structure.

The National Council of Jewish Women went through a similar phase, although never achieving the institutionalization of services that B'nai B'rith has. Today both have memberships of over 100,000 and reach out to the rank and file of the American Jewish community, while at the same time addressing themselves to the most sophisticated and complex communal needs. As such, they most fully meet the criteria set forth in the definition of general-purpose, mass-based organizations and play an especially important role on the American Jewish scene. Where their leadership is strong they make important contributions; where it is weak, they still serve as powerful veto groups that can prevent other organizations from acting in the name of the community.

We have already seen how B'nai B'rith acquired a responsibility for the Hillel Foundations. When the Hillel programs as constituted came under attack in recent years, the Hillel leadership, which had otherwise more or less ignored their B'nai B'rith sponsors, turned to the local districts and even lodges for support in their battle with the federations over the future of the program. That support was forthcoming, and in whatever each federation did, it acted in such a way as to conciliate the B'nai B'rith members, or at least their leaders, before proceeding with any changes.

Besides the specific social and fraternal organizations, a number of other groups, such as Women's ORT (Organization for Rehabilitation and Training), which is organized to provide additional support for the ORT vocational school system around the world, have definite social colorations, despite their very specifically defined public missions. The people who join them usually do so because a particular local chapter is composed of their friends or of those whose friendship they aspire to gain. Thus they might better be classified as social and fraternal groups.

Special-interest Institutions and Organizations

Special-interest institutions and organizations, as their name indicates, reflect the multitude of special interests in the community, either by maintaining programs of their own or by mobilizing concern and support for various programs conducted by the governmentlike institutions. The number of special-interest organizations is myriad, and they cover the gamut of interests that any Jewish community could possibly possess, from hospitals to free-loan societies to assorted study groups. They concentrate on specific issues and try to raise those issues before both the larger Jewish public and the leaders and decision makers of the Jewish community. No one special-interest group is likely to have a great deal of influence in the community as a whole, though some will be decisive in those specific areas in which they are involved. A whole host of them can wield some influence on communal decision making, depending on the character of the interest they represent, the degree of sympathy it invokes among community decision makers, and the caliber of leadership attached to the special-interest group.

PROFESSIONAL ASSOCIATIONS

Professional associations of Jewish civil servants have emerged as a very special kind of special-interest organization. They are a relatively new phenomenon on the American Jewish scene, reflecting the great increase in the size, scope, and quality of the Jewish civil service in the past generation. During the first two centuries of American Jewish life the only Jewish professionals were the few hazzanim (prayer leaders) who were employed to conduct services, perhaps teach a little, and perhaps also double as shochetim (ritual slaughterers) and mohelim (performers of the rite of circumcision). The first rabbis came upon the scene in the middle of the nineteenth century, in most cases replacing the hazzanim (whose functions they assumed in place of the traditional rabbinical functions of the Old World) and in others relegating the hazzanim to roles as cantors or cantor-teachers. A generation later the first social-work professionals appeared, and their numbers increased in the interwar period. Professional Jewish educators emerged at the beginning of the twentieth century. However, the real growth in number and variety of Jewish professionals did not occur until the years after World War II.

The rabbis were the first to organize professional associations, countrywide with the Central Conference of American Rabbis (1889), the Rabbinical Assembly (1900), the Union of Orthodox Rabbis of the United States and Canada (1902), and locally through boards of rabbis (around World War I). The Jewish social workers organized in 1899 and the Jewish educators in 1926, with their greatest proliferation coming in in the late 1940s. Today these groups are becoming a major force on the American Jewish scene, setting standards of admission into the various fields of Jewish communal service, establishing the norms for service in those fields, and even setting communal standards of Jewishness in many ways. Given the enhanced roles of professionals in the present-day American Jewish community, their influence is great and is likely to grow.

As their numbers increase each group is beginning to acquire a local dimension as well, with chapters that are often crucial links between otherwise unconnected local institutions. The primary connection between synagogues, for example, is through their rabbis' involvement in their local rabbinical associations, both intramovement and transmovement. The higher civil servants of the federations and their constituent

TABLE 21 SPHERES, INSTITUTIONS, AND ORGANIZATIONS*

Sphere	Institutions and Organizations		
	LOCAL	COUNTRYWIDE	WORLDWIDE
Religious-congregational	synagogues rabbinical associations boards of rabbis rabbinical courts kashruth councils Orthodox outposts	Synagogue Council of America synagogue confederations and the men's, women's, and youth affiliates seminaries and yeshivas rabbinical associations	Israeli rabbinate Knesset international synagogue confederations
Educational-cultural	synagogues communal, secularist, and day schools colleges of Jewish education central agencies of Jewish education Jewish studies programs in universities local cultural institutions and groups Jewish community centers Jewish federations	AAJE National Foundation for Jewish Culture–Joint Cultural Appeal Torah Umesorah Jewish Welfare Board B'nai B'rith Hillel Foundations Jewish colleges and universities scholarly associations educators' associations Jewish cultural institutions and organizations Jewish foundations	Jewish Agency and subsidiaries Memorial Foundation for Jewish Culture
Community relations	Jewish community-relations councils local chapters or offices of American Jewish Committee, Anti-Defamation League, American Jewish Congress, Jewish War Veterans, Jewish Labor Committee Jewish federations	NJCRAC Presidents' Conference CJF American Jewish Committee Anti-Defamation League American Jewish Congress Jewish Labor Committee Jewish War Veterans professional associations special-purpose groups (e.g., for Soviet Jewry)	World Jewish Congress Israeli government Consultative Council of Jewish Organizations Coordinating Board of Jewish Organizations

Institutions and Organizations

Sphere			
	LOCAL	COUNTRYWIDE	WORLDWIDE
Communal-welfare	Jewish federations social-service agencies Jewish community centers local Jewish press hospital health care	CJF Jewish Welfare Board B'nai B'rith American Jewish Committee American Jewish Congress United HIAS Service	Israeli government Jewish Agency international professional/functional associations
Israel-overseas	Jewish federations local Zionist chapters local Zionist offices local "friends" chapters	Presidents' Conference CJF UJA Zionist organizations Israel Bonds Organization United HIAS Service "friends of Israel" or overseas institutions JDC Jewish Welfare Board Otzar HaTorah B'nai B'rith American Jewish Committee world Conservative and Reform synagogue bodies	Israeli government Jewish Agency Jewish National Fund ORT Claims Conference World Jewish Congress Conference of World Jewish Organizations (COJO)

*For the most complete available listing of countrywide institutions and organizations, local Jewish federations, and the Jewish press, see the annual directories in the *American Jewish Year Book.*

agencies and the local Jewish educators have also organized locally to give themselves a common forum in many communities.

THE FIVE SPHERES OF COMMUNITY ACTIVITY

Overlaying the structural or organizational matrix of the American Jewish community is a functional matrix, consisting of five primary spheres of activity: (1) religious-congregational, (2) educational-cultural, (3) community relations, (4) communal-welfare, and (5) Israel-overseas (see Table 21). These serve in place of ideology to provide Jewish America with a substructure, collectively and in its various territorial divisions. The relationships between these spheres have followed a pulsating pattern. At first they were essentially undivided because American Jewry was institutionally primitive and unformed. As the communal structure became increasingly articulated, the spheres not only took on discrete characteristics of their own but began to separate from one another as well. The element of competition entered into the situation, based upon each sphere's claim to preeminence. Most recently the spheres have begun to reintegrate on a new basis, as the complexities of the contemporary world force them out of their isolation.

Religious-Congregational Sphere

Since the ideological commitment of American Jews to a particular synagogue movement is very weak, except at the extremes of Orthodoxy and Reform, they expect their synagogues to provide certain immediately personal and interpersonal ritual-cum-social functions on a congregational basis. The synagogues have an essential monopoly on those functions locally, while the synagogue confederations, rabbinical associations, seminaries, and yeshivas maintain a parallel monopoly over the community's theological and ritual concerns countrywide. Among the supplementary bodies that function in this sphere locally are rabbinical associations, which usually embrace representatives of all branches of Judaism; kashruth councils, usually in Orthodox hands; local rabbinical courts to handle matters of personal status—particularly conversion and divorce—for those who maintain halakhic norms, usually Orthodox but increasingly paralleled by Conservative bodies as well; and, in the larger community, intercongregational regional organizations for each movement and boards of rabbis that embrace them all. In some communities there are also what may be called "Orthodox outposts": yeshivas or branches of the Lubavitcher movement that serve (and seek to develop) special constituencies.

Countrywide, the three great synagogue confederations dominate the religious-congregational sphere. Over the years each has expanded its scope and intensified its efforts, creating new congregations in suburbia, developing spin-off organizations and institutions to tie their congregational members more closely to the movement and recruit and train leaders for them, and attempting in general to make an impact on the American Jewish community as a whole. In their common quest for an expanded role in American Jewish life, they have leagued themselves into the Synagogue Council of America, which for a few years during the height of the "religious revival" of the 1950s tried to capture the leading role as spokesman for American Jewry and now seeks to be the Jewish counterpart to the National Council of Churches and the National Catholic Welfare Association.

There are three forms of local congregations in the United States. The first are the mainstream congregations affiliated with one of the national religious movements: Orthodox, Conservative, Reform, or Reconstructionist. Then there are the congregations that, for whatever reason, are unaffiliated with any of the major movements. These tend to fall into two groups: (1) traditional congregations (found in abundance in Chicago and New York), which lie somewhere between Orthodox and Conservative positions but choose not to affiliate officially with either movement, and (2) congregations that are not acceptable in any of the countrywide movements (usually because of some infraction of the relatively few rules or standards that the national bodies maintain). The third group consists of congregational bodies that are continuing in character but are not organized as synagogues in the formal sense. These include small Orthodox houses of prayer *(shtiblach)* and, more recently, religious fellowships *(havurot),* groups that are not prepossessing in an institutional sense but often have a great deal of impact on the community because of the quality and the intensity of commitment of their worshipers.

Each of the synagogue confederations has a seminary of its own that, because of its academic character, projects itself on the American Jewish scene in a quasi-independent way. Even with the growth of Jewish-studies programs in academic institutions, these seminaries remain the backbone of organized Jewish scholarship in the United States. Their alumni lead the congregations of American Jewry and, through their rabbinical associations, link the seminaries and their confederations. In addition, a growing number of yeshivas in New York and many of the other major Jewish communities reflect the proliferation of the new ultra-Orthodox elements in the community. They preserve and extend traditional Jewish scholarship on a scale never before experienced in American Jewish history.

Since World War II there has been an increasing involvement of power centers outside the United States in the religious-congregational sphere. While the international federations tied to the various synagogue movements are, in reality, so much window dressing—established, maintained, and directed from the United States—and have no power of their own, the Israeli rabbinate is a growing force on the American scene by virtue of its role in determining the personal status of individual Jews. In an age of jet travel between Israel and the Diaspora, such decisions have ramifications that reverberate throughout the Jewish world. In this connection, the Knesset is also acquiring influence in the religious-congregational sphere and indeed is the first secular body anywhere to do so, simply because of its central role in defining who is a Jew in a country where there is no separation of religion and state.

The synagogues remain the most independent institutions in the American Jewish community, fiscally self-sufficient, subject to no communal discipline (except in the subtle ways that influence all Jews), and barely required to maintain even minimal standards within their respective movements. American synagogues have traditionally considered themselves (and have been considered) private institutions, like clubs or fraternal lodges, accountable to no one but their own members. This, indeed, is their status in American law and has simply been carried over unquestioningly into Jewish communal affairs. This means, in effect, that a very large share of Jewish activity—involving perhaps half the total revenue and expenditure of American Jewry for internal purposes—is managed outside of any communal decision-making system. We shall have occasion to examine the implications of this in subsequent chapters.

Educational-Cultural Sphere

The synagogues also play a major role in educational matters, having acquired that role in the 1950s after a contest with nonsynagogue schools of some forty years' duration.[5] Today the great majority of Jewish Sunday and afternoon schools at the elementary level, and a large number of those at the secondary level, are housed in and controlled by synagogues. Synagogue control is so complete where it exists that we do not even have reliable estimates of how much is spent on Jewish education, since synagogues do not make their budgets public.[6] Presently, however, the tide seems to be running against the current highly fragmented system and toward new forms of intercongregational or communal arrangements. Outside the synagogues there are a few surviving secular schools, usually Yiddishist in orientation, managed by secularistic equivalents of congregations. The Sholem Aleichem School in Detroit is one of the best examples of this kind of school, providing as it does a complete set of localistic activities for the parents as well as the children —in effect it functions as a surrogate congregation. In a number of cities parents with secular backgrounds have joined to create similar schools for their children.

There are also some remnants of older noncongregational school systems, generally confined to serving the long-established areas of Jewish residence: an example is the system of the United Hebrew Schools and Yeshivoth of Philadelphia. The outgrowth of a number of independent neighborhood Talmud Torahs that served Jews in the "old neighborhood," its schools languished when they lost their natural clientele to the world of the large American congregation. When they sought to expand, in the years immediately following World War II, congregational pressure on the federation and the communal leadership effectively cut them off. With their minimal budgets, they could maintain neither the necessary staff nor an adequate plant. They survived by servicing the community's gleanings in various old neighborhoods, often children of immigrant families who had yet to adapt themselves to American congregationalism. In this they were more successful than most of their counterparts in other cities, which simply closed their doors as the neighborhoods they served were evacuated. Significantly, in the early 1970s discussions were reopened regarding the expansion of the United Hebrew Schools into the Philadelphia suburbs, perhaps a reflection of the problems being faced by the synagogue schools.

Finally, there are a handful of full-blown communal school systems —the largest of which are in Detroit, Minneapolis, and Saint Paul—that function as the comprehensive educational arms of the Jewish community and dominate Jewish educational activity locally. These schools are true school systems, integrated vertically and horizontally and maintained with strong federation support. In every case they were able to survive that critical moment after World War II when the challenge of the synagogues was at its height, because of either exceptional leadership or devoted support on the part of a major segment of the community. Where Talmud Torahs were able to define or redefine themselves as communal rather than neighborhood institutions, maintain a near-monopoly over afternoon schools, extend themselves into the secondary realm and perhaps beyond, and secure an alliance with the federation that recognized their role as the community's major educational force, they survived and even prospered. However, this rarely came about without opposition from the congregational rabbis, who had to be neutralized—often by their own membership, whose educational commitments were to the communal system.

The only new movement in Jewish elementary and secondary education that stands generally outside the synagogue is the day-school movement. Even when nominally attached to one of the religious movements, day schools tend to develop with communal support by default. However, because few communities have any well-defined way to deal with them, they are not necessarily tied to the central institutions of communal governance, but remain nominally private schools that receive subsidization to some degree. The relatively limited enrollments of the day schools, coupled with their high standards, make them prohibitively expensive for all but the wealthiest congregations to maintain. At first, federations were reluctant to provide assistance to day schools, in no small measure for ideological reasons. Recalling the difficulties their forebears in Europe had had in gaining admission to institutions providing secular education, American Jews were extremely grateful for the fully equal opportunities afforded by the American public schools. Their response was to become ideologically committed to the principle of public education. Hence to them day schools represented a step backward to parochialism.

In time this attitude began to change, partly because the federation leaders became interested in more intensive Jewish education to meet the clearly pressing problems of assimilation and in part because of changes in the public schools themselves. The trend today is not only in the direction of federation support, but toward the incorporation of the day schools as federation constituents as well, with full rights and obligations as members of the federation "family." In 1974 for the first time more than half the federation subsidies for Jewish education were allocated to day schools.

On the high-school level the communal role is generally greater and is increasing. Today Jewish high schools other than Sunday schools increasingly are being sponsored and funded by the Jewish community as a whole, either as communal high schools or as intercongregational ones. They are usually under the aegis of the central agency for Jewish education and receive federation funding.

Central agencies of Jewish education in the larger Jewish communities do have some formal responsibility for developing curriculums and setting professional standards for the synagogue schools. Occasionally they even maintain experimental schools that provide whatever intensive supplementary Jewish education exists in a given community. While their operational role is limited, they usually represent the only links between the synagogue educational programs and the central institutions of the local Jewish community.

Most recently, rising costs and declining memberships have led some synagogues to join together to establish intercongregational schools. They are generally stimulated to do so by the central agencies for Jewish education, which see the educational advantages involved. This trend is developing slowly, given the synagogues' reluctance to relinquish their schools—but necessity creates its own conditions.

Higher Jewish education is also divided into three segments: the colleges of Jewish studies, the seminaries and yeshivas, and the emerging Jewish-studies programs in general colleges and universities.[7] The larger Jewish communities provide higher education through colleges of Jewish studies or their equivalent, which are almost invariably communal unless they are branches of national seminaries (as in Los Angeles) or represent efforts on the part of the very largest and most powerful synagogues to provide their own comprehensive educational facilities. There has also been a proliferation of *yeshivot gedolot* in recent years. These are yeshivas that, while they tend to be nominally private and independent, are usually part of some countrywide network linked by a leadership that has graduated from the same "mother" yeshiva and bound by the halakhic decisions of the same rabbi. While having the least formal ties to any outside bodies, in many respects these yeshivas may be bound more tightly by a common discipline than any other Jewish institutions except those of the Hasidic groups.

The Jewish-studies programs in the universities, whatever their name and format, are beginning to acquire a certain measure of importance in the overall scheme of Jewish education locally and are even beginning to affect the character and content of the traditional institutions of Jewish education. Their status is enhanced by the fact that the men who staff these programs are generally independent of the Jewish community in any formal way and at the same time possess high status in the community's eyes (as Jewish scholars who have "made it" in the general university). Although these programs are formally outside the Jewish community, for many purposes they function as parts of the local Jewish education "package." Graduates of local Jewish educational programs find them a useful means for continuing their Jewish studies, and their faculties often serve as an important communal resource. It would be wrong, however, to overestimate their importance—as compared to the seminaries and yeshivas as sources of Jewish scholars or the colleges of Jewish studies as influences on local communal life.

The colleges of Jewish studies, whose core is the program to train Hebrew teachers, are as locally rooted as the elementary and secondary schools, but because of their specialized character and limited clientele they are generally operated by the central agencies for Jewish education with heavy federation subsidies. Originally tied entirely to the local Jewish education network, many of these colleges are now trying to develop links to the universities as well through joint programs. The seminaries and yeshivas generally appeal to specialized countrywide clienteles and are supported by their respective constituent groups.

Most communities also have some adjunct and informal education services through institutions such as the B'nai B'rith Hillel Foundations and the Jewish community centers. Some can boast special institutions and programs, such as the Brandeis Camp Institute that serves the Los Angeles metropolitan area. Adult education is generally the province of the synagogues and centers, with more advanced courses being provided by the local college of Jewish studies in the larger communities. Finally, there are various cultural groups, such as Hebrew-speaking societies, discussion groups, Yiddish clubs, and the like, which usually are formally independent in organization but actually are linked through their members to one of the local institutions; their function is to provide a meeting place for the local Jewish intelligentsia.

If anything, Jewish educational activities are even more localized than the religious-congregational activities. The AAJE, the umbrella body for the central agencies and itself a confederation of local and countrywide groups, is limited in the technical services it renders to studies of local needs and problems. The Orthodox day schools are somewhat more clearly linked to their countrywide bodies, particularly the Torah Umesorah schools. The Conservative day schools are nominally linked to an umbrella body that exists in name only, and many such schools have no extracommunity ties at all. The most important ties linking any Jewish schools are the professional associations linking Jewish educators.

It is also in the educational-cultural sphere that most of the independent constituencies serving countrywide—colleges and universities, yeshivas, scholarly associations, and philanthropic foundations—function. Even here, however, the trend is toward greater integration. The chief integrating instrumentality is the National Foundation for Jewish Culture. Established in 1960 by the CJF, it had a slow start, but the inauguration of the Joint Cultural Appeal under its administration in 1971 gave it a new impetus. The Joint Cultural Appeal was established at the initiative of the CJF to consolidate the individual appeals of the country's major Jewish cultural institutions, in an effort to increase the total "pot" made available to them by the local federations. Its nine constituent agencies run the gamut from the American Jewish Historical Society to the YIVO Institute for Jewish Research.

That same year the CJF established the Institute for Jewish Life, a foundationlike body whose task was to stimulate new initiatives in the fields of Jewish education and culture. The Institute emerged as the federations' response to the student protests of the late 1960s, whose chief target was the ostensible lack of federation support for Jewish education. In general, its creation was opposed by the established countrywide and local bodies operating in this sphere, who felt that their roles were being challenged and that money they needed would be diverted to yet another agency. Its champions were the young leadership of the federation movement, and indeed its establishment represented their first success on the countrywide scene. The original proposals called for massive funding for the Institute, in the millions of dollars, but in fact the final result was measured in the low hundreds of thousands, with a concomitant reduction in the Institute's proposed scope. After some early modest but real successes as a quasi-independent body, the Institute was abolished and its major projects transferred to established countrywide bodies—ostensibly because the Institute's pioneering tasks were completed, but in fact as a result of pressures within the CJF.

Worldwide bodies in the educational-cultural area include the Jewish Agency, which represents the Zionist point of view and Israel's interests and works most extensively to promote adult education (through the Herzl Institute and the Herzl Press) and to link Jewish students with Israel (through the American Zionist Youth Foundation). The Memorial Foundation for Jewish Culture, a worldwide body with headquarters in New York, has become the most important source of support for Jewish scholarly and cultural activities, for its resources, derived from German reparations funds, exceed those of any other institution. Its allocations for American purposes are relatively modest; it sees its role to be a provider of funds for the rest of the Jewish world, which has fewer local resources.

Among the scholarly associations and research institutes, YIVO and the American Jewish Historical Society are probably the most potent independent bodies actually engaged in projects. Yet even their activities are distinctly circumscribed, if only because of monetary limitations. In general these bodies are small, independent, and outside the mainstream of American Jewish life. The American Academy for Jewish Research, the Conference on Jewish Social Studies, the Association of Professors of Hebrew, and the Association for Jewish Studies link scholars in Jewish fields on a professional basis. Only the last-named, which has become the professional society of Jewish academics, has made any significant contact with the central decision makers of the Jewish community.

As for book publishing, this is conducted on a private-enterprise basis, except for the Jewish Publication Society (JPS) and the small seminary and movement publication programs. Only recently has the publication of Jewish books for profit expanded much beyond the textbook business. Today publishing houses like Behrman House and Ktav have increased their programs, Schocken remains a major source for Jewish books, various universities sponsor special series of Judaic studies, and many general publishing houses are receptive to Jewish titles. In sum, the "Jewish market" has been recognized to be a profitable one. Still, there is a far greater demand for popular works than for serious scholarship, which must rely upon such traditional outlets as JPS and the university presses.

The important thing to recognize about the cultural activities of American Jewry is how peripheral those engaged in them are in the context of American Jewish public affairs. Since the cultural institutions do not even have the advantage of feeling needed by the decision makers, as is true of Jewish education, and rarely have the prestige of Jewish academics in general universities, they are at a great disadvantage in a community that is not much oriented to scholarly or cultural concerns.

Community-Relations Sphere

Most major Jewish communities have a community-relations council that considers itself the central agency for handling community-relations problems. In addition, communities often have local offices or chapters of the American Jewish Committee, the Anti-Defamation League of B'nai B'rith, the American Jewish Congress, the Jewish War Veterans, and the Jewish Labor Committee that also engage in community-relations work, whether in cooperation with the local community-relations council or independently. Indeed, the classic pictures of fragmentation in American Jewish life usually depict the community-relations field, and it has been in that field that the most publicized countrywide efforts have been made to bring order out of chaos, beginning with the development in the 1940s of the National Jewish Community Relations Advisory Council, a confederation, as we have seen, of independent agencies combining both local agencies and countrywide bodies in one common league. Of course its role is limited precisely because it is a confederation of powerful and independent bodies.

In the educational-cultural and religious-congregational spheres the situation is so structured that the many separate organizations engage in relatively little direct competition. In the community-relations sphere, however, the smaller number of separate organizations overlap because they deal with the same problems, often the same explicit issues. Except in the case of organizations with special referents, such as the Jewish Labor Committee, this problem is an ever-present one. The effects of that competition are potentially great because they are directed toward matters that reach outside the Jewish community and directly affect its relations with the larger world. Consequently, a considerable amount of self-policing and specialization has developed within the sphere in the past two decades.

In contrast to the interorganizational situation in this field, the American Jewish Committee, the Anti-Defamation League, and the American Jewish Congress, the "big three" in community-relations, are the most centralized of all countrywide Jewish organizations.[8] Their role in American Jewish life was originally enhanced by their centralized structures at a time when the local Jewish communities were barely organized and the individual institutions within them were too parochial to reach out to the general community. Today the situation is reversed, and only those that have managed to decentralize are thriving. The American Jewish Congress, perhaps the most centralized, has not properly taken root on the local plane and as a result is suffering tremendously as a countrywide organization. The Anti-Defamation League and the American Jewish Committee began earlier and with greater success to achieve substantial decentralization, though in both cases the national office still plays a very great role even in local activities. The American Jewish Committee, whose own centralized origins reflect an earlier oligarchical stage in American Jewish life, has gone the furthest in developing strong local chapters—in essence trying to replicate its now expanded membership of influential personalities on the local scene as well as countrywide.

The Jewish Labor Committee and the Jewish War Veterans are smaller replicas of the "big three," each with a special constituency and a more specialized function. The Jewish War Veterans reflects the changing fate of veterans' organizations in general in its inability to attract members. It should be noted that the JWV is perhaps the most democratically run of all Jewish organizations: its national body is a true federation of its state bodies, which in turn are federations of their local posts; elections for the higher offices are usually contested.

More recently, the synagogue movements have attempted to enter the community-relations field as part of their drive toward dominance in American Jewish life. Bodies such as the Synagogue Council of America, the Commission of Social Action of Reform Judaism, and the National Commission on Law and Public Affairs (COLPA) of the Orthodox reflect this. However, they still play a relatively limited role on the overall scene. In addition, there are several special-purpose groups dealing with particular aspects of Jewish community relations, most of which have not been linked with the NJCRAC, if only in self-defense. Finally, the CJF and its constituent federations have been in the picture for many years because of the support they provide for the community-relations agencies.

Increased American Jewish involvement in the concerns of the Jewish people as a whole has sharpened the need for a communal voice that speaks as one, at least in the field of foreign relations. This has led to the establishment of the Presidents' Conference, which, as noted, consists of representatives of some thirty major countrywide Jewish organizations who meet to receive briefings and decide on common courses of action. Since the role of the Presidents' Conference is confined to overseas activity, it will be discussed in the section on the Israel-overseas sphere.

Support and assistance for Israel now being key items on the community-relations agenda, the Israeli government has become a prime mover in this sphere. Despite occasional disclaimers, official American Jewish action in behalf of Israel in the public-relations field is conducted in close consultation with and in response to the initiatives of the Israeli authorities. In certain respects Israel's role in the community-relations sphere may well be greater than its role in any other sphere of decision making in the American Jewish community.

Meanwhile, federation allocations to all the groups involved, for national and local purposes, have been stepped up, increasing the local group's budgetary dependence upon the comprehensive-representative organization. Thus while the community-relations sphere remains distinct, during the course of the generation now coming to an end it has become increasingly tied into the communal-welfare sphere and the federations which dominate that sphere.

Communal-Welfare Sphere

The communal-welfare sphere has undergone the greatest change in the past generation. As late as the 1950s it was simply another functional grouping among several, although considerably better organized internally, since the various Jewish social-service and welfare agencies and the Jewish community centers had federated with each other a generation or more earlier. While the local Jewish federations had already expanded to include fund raising for overseas needs, their pretensions to centrality in the community were limited by the fact that, on the domestic scene, they remained primarily concerned with the traditional social-service functions.[9]

By the end of the 1950s the federations had been transformed into the major fund-raising bodies in the community and stood on the threshold of a whole new world of responsibilities. The latter transformation came as federations realized that proper execution of their role as allocating agencies necessitated greater involvement in community planning of a scope that at least touched all the community-wide activities in any given locality. At the same time, the old German leadership in the communal-welfare field was being broadened to include East European elements as well, selected from the same income, occupational, and observance levels.

The 1960s saw the federations undertake community planning on a large scale, beyond what was required for the simple allocation of funds. They also took greater responsibility for and interest in Jewish education as well as continuing and even deepening their relationships with their constituent social-service and welfare agencies. In the process, most made strong efforts to broaden their leadership base to include new segments of the community, although even this broadening took place within certain limitations which omitted or failed to reach certain constituencies (see below).

The key to the growth of the local federations' power lies in their role as the major fund-raising bodies on the American scene. Even though money and influence are not necessarily correlated on a one-to-one basis, there is unquestionably a relationship between them. As local agencies become more dependent upon the federation for funds, they are more likely to be included in the ambit of federation planning and policy making.

The same pattern has repeated itself on the countrywide plane, though in a less clear-cut way. The difference is that the CJF does not have the fund-raising power of the local federations, and consequently has no comparable monetary power to exercise over the parallel national associations. The Jewish Welfare Board, for example, is funded the way the CJF is—by grants from its local constituents and the local federations directly, thus limiting the possibilities of CJF influence on indirect grants. The national community-relations and religious organizations are even more independent. Still, the work of the CJF in reviewing the budgets of these groups on behalf of their constituent federations is a lever of some importance.

The role of the CJF has been growing, primarily because it is able to offer a forum that none of the other groups can. The CJF General Assembly, as we have seen, has become a major gathering place for people at the highest level of communal decision making in American Jewry, including representatives of organizations only tenuously connected with it on a formal basis.

A new addition to the communal-welfare scene is the Israeli element —the government of Israel and the Jewish Agency—as a result of the large role played by the federations in raising funds for Israel's needs. The government of Israel has its special concerns in American Jewish life, which it pursues in many ways but is increasingly finding it advantageous to pursue within the communal-welfare sphere. The Jewish Agency, particularly since its recent reconstitution, has virtually co-opted the federation leadership as its "non-Zionist" representatives, creating a tighter bond than ever before between the institutionalized representatives of the World Zionist movement and the American Jewish community. In both cases, the institutionization of relationships is still in its incipient stages.

Other institutions in the communal-welfare sphere include the traditional social-service agencies, hospitals, and community centers on the local plane and their parallel countrywide bodies, plus those other organizations that maintain residual functions in the field. The Jewish hospitals, most of which were founded during the era of heightened American anti-Semitism to provide places where Jewish patients could feel comfortable and Jewish doctors could find employment, have increasingly become institutions serving the general public—a Jewish contribution to American society, as it were. Historically this has been how the hospital field has been organized in the United States, with hospitals primarily under religious auspices but open on a nonsectarian basis.

With the introduction of government subsidization of hospitals and medical care, these hospitals, including the Jewish ones, began to receive ever-larger shares of their budget from government sources. So today the Jewish community may retain control of the Jewish hospital, but it does so by virtue of providing a mere fraction of its total budget. In Philadelphia, for instance, the community directly contributes only 1 percent of a total budget that runs into tens of millions of dollars and channels another 4 percent in through its share of the United Fund receipts. The remainder is covered by user fees (now for the most part paid by the federal government) and government grants and contracts.

Except for the level of care provided—traditionally high in Jewish hospitals—there is little to identify present-day Jewish hospitals as Jewish. Their medical staff may be more heavily Jewish, but other personnel are hired on a nondiscriminatory basis. Since only a few Jewish hospitals were ever kosher and most simply provide kosher food for those who request it, even that is not a distinguishing characteristic. (Following the practice of the airlines, which offer frozen packaged kosher dinners to Jewish passengers who so request, many non-Jewish hospitals, especially in the larger cities, now provide a similar service.)

The maintenance of separate Jewish hospitals has been a bone of contention in the Jewish community for many years, with the partisans of increased communal support for Jewish educational and cultural activities attacking communal expenditures for hospitals on the grounds of misplaced priorities. In fact the issue has become a symbolic one: little attention is paid to the amounts allocated. In some communities, hospitals do absorb a disproportionate share of federation allocations for local purposes, particularly considering their present functions. At the same time, even communal leaders who have previously opposed malapportionment of funds have increasingly come to recognize the utility of the Jews maintaining a stake in a full range of social-service institutions, even a relatively small one. The general feeling today is that withdrawal from the field would mean abdicating an accepted role in the general community.

The Jewish family services and vocational agencies, like the hospitals, have undergone considerable transformation since their early days. In some cases, like that of the hospitals, they have virtually ceased to serve Jewish clienteles. Even in those cases where they have not, the Jewish content of their programs is open to question. Professionally trained social workers, often among the most competent to be found in their fields but with minimal Jewish backgrounds, have little in the way of Jewishness to give to the clients who come to them, other than the feeling that they are helping to keep intimate matters "within the family."

Recently there has been a very modest effort to increase the amount of Jewishness in these agencies as a justification for continued communal support. Since the federation dollar usually covers a larger share of their budgets than in the case of the hospitals, they do need the Jewish community for the maintenance of their programs, and the Jewish community itself is likely to feel that the issue of Jewishness is more relevant in their cases. After all, there is no particularly Jewish way to provide medical care, at least from the technical point of view. Family problems are a very different matter, however. There it is possible to identify some clearly Jewish approaches and even to suggest that the Jewish tradition is a relevant element in the assistance provided.[10]

The immigrant-aid societies continue to function at a much reduced level because immigration has dropped so greatly. Nevertheless, there is a continuing trickle of Jewish immigrants to the United States, and the Jewish communities do maintain an apparatus to receive and assist them. Today most immigration is by Jews from the Soviet Union, and the immigrant-aid societies have been geared up to deal with them.

The Jewish community centers, too, have begun to grapple with the problem of their Jewishness in a serious way. The centers had their origins in the Jewish desire to provide facilities for new immigrants that were equivalent to the YMCA's but in a more compatible setting. Later they took on the roles of settlement houses to assist in the americanization of the great migration. In both cases, the Jewishness of the institutions lay in the fact that they maintained whatever Jewish social milieu their members brought with them. They themselves had no particularly Jewish purposes to serve.

By the interwar generation, when both original purposes had diminished in importance, the Jewishness of the centers became barely noticeable. This situation persisted until the 1960s, when the centers began to discover that they had lost their raison d'être, which could come only through fostering honest Jewish expression. Since then, the trend has been toward more Jewishness, although no clear direction can be said to have been established yet—partly because the professionals themselves, no matter how willing or how interested they may be in enhancing the Jewish side of their programs, tend to have minimal Jewish backgrounds and relatively little personal involvement in authentic Jewish life, and partly because the centers' voluntary leadership is still divided on the subject.

We have already noted the existence of associations of local social-service agencies on the countrywide plane. In addition, the United HIAS Service (the result of a merger between the Hebrew Immigrant Aid Society and the United Service for New Americans) is entrusted with responsibilities for handling immigration matters and immigrants. Given the nature of its activity, it is one of the few countrywide bodies in this sphere with operating responsibilities; immigration, which ultimately has local ramifications, requires a central Jewish address to handle the details and sometimes even to handle the dispersal of populations. For example, at the beginning of the 1960s when Jewish refugees began to leave Cuba in large numbers, the United HIAS Service developed a major operation in the Miami area, through which it helped resettle Cuban Jewish refugees in various parts of the country. Most recently, it has been doing the same with Soviet Jews. Its funding comes through the federation system as well.

Israel-Overseas Sphere

This area is the best organized and the best integrated of all the spheres. Its integration dates back to World War I and the founding of the American Jewish Joint Distribution Committee. In general, the sphere has two interlocking wings: one concerned with fund raising and the other with political-cum-educational activities. Responsibilities for fund raising are divided between the federations that handle UJA, the Israel Bonds Organization, the Jewish National Fund, and the various "friends of Israel" or overseas institutions. Political-cum-educational activities are conducted primarily through the Zionist organizations, which are now at least nominally united into the American Zionist Federation, locally and countrywide.

Since the potential for competition among these organizations is great, despite the felt need to cooperate for the common good of Israel and the Jewish people, a system of negotiated sharing has been developed: a network of agreements dividing the funds or the campaign arenas or both. The basic agreements are reached nationally between the representatives of the federations working through the CJF and UJA on an annual basis, dividing the funds raised in the local campaigns. A second agreement, among UJA, the Israel Bonds Organization, and the various "friends" groups, more or less spells out their respective jurisdictions and claims to various methods of fund raising. Thus Israel Bonds has been allocated the right to make synagogue appeals, while direct solicitation is a province of UJA through the federations. The "friends" chapters normally work with big givers through personal contacts, but in the years immediately after 1967 they were asked virtually to suspend their activities (except the raising of funds for capital expenditures) in order to support the Israel Emergency Fund. This arrangement was terminated in the summer of 1971 and then renewed at the outbreak of the Yom Kippur War in October 1973.

The offices of the Israel-oriented institutions—the Jewish National Fund, the American "friends" of the various institutions of higher learning in Israel, the American-Israel Cultural Foundation chapter, and, in a somewhat different category, the Israel Bonds office—have a much more limited role to play on the local Jewish scene. Their business does not involve membership or local activity except in connection with the specific tasks at hand. They are very closely linked with their national offices and should be considered as no more than local branches.

Aside from the Israel-oriented bodies the following organizations are also involved in the worldwide activities of the Jewish people: the JDC, ORT, Otzar HaTorah, and the Conference on Jewish Material Claims against Germany (Claims Conference). They have played significant roles in the postwar period. The JDC in particular has become the bearer of American Jewish expertise, as well as money, to Jewish communities in need of redevelopment everywhere—in Europe, Asia, North Africa, and Israel. More than any single body, it was responsible for the restoration of Jewish communal life in Europe after World War II.[11] ORT—originally founded in the last century in Russia but subsequently transferred to the United States—maintains training schools in Israel and in North Africa, and has worked under United Nations auspices to establish vocational-training programs for underdeveloped countries. Otzar HaTorah was founded by a wealthy American Jew of Syrian birth after World War II to create a network of Jewish day schools in North Africa and the Middle East that would provide Jewish children with a general and traditional Jewish education. For a while its efforts were quite successful, but with the liquidation of Jewish life in the Muslim world, the schools have dropped in number.

Several American organizations whose primary concerns are domestic also play a role in overseas activities. Thus B'nai B'rith has become a worldwide organization, the first American Jewish body to attain that status. Its local chapters play a role in major Jewish communities everywhere, including Israel, and its international office has sought a corresponding role on the international scene, principally, in the foreign-relations sphere. The American Jewish Committee has also expanded its range of interest to include overseas activities, especially after World War II. Although it has not established chapters outside the United States, it maintains offices in Europe, Latin America, and Israel, where it seeks to work with local Jewish communities in matters of common interest. Its Latin American office has concentrated on fighting anti-Semitism and assisting in the development of Jewish intellectual life, particularly in Argentina. Its European office has worked closely with other bodies in the reconstruction of Jewish life on the Continent and has been very active in the Jewish negotiations with the Vatican to secure changes in Catholic attitudes and policies toward the Jewish people. Its Israel office concerns itself with building bridges between Israel and Diaspora Jewry.

Both the Conservative and Reform movements have organized world synagogue bodies that have sought to foster congregations linked with those movements in other countries, or to enroll existing local congregations under their respective banners. The Conservative movement has been particularly active in Argentina, where, thanks to good leadership, it has created a large Conservative congregation and even a theological seminary to train Spanish-speaking Conservative rabbis. It has also been successful in winning over the major congregations in Stockholm and Copenhagen, and has established a small network of congregations in Israel, founded mostly by Conservative Jews who have settled there. The Reform movement has actually transferred its world headquarters to Jerusalem, although in a nominal manner, and has persuaded most of the European liberal congregations to join with it. As a result of Conservative and Reform efforts, Orthodox Jews have also sought to build a World Council of Synagogues, but in their case much of the initiative has come from Israel, or at least from American Jews residing in Israel.

At the initiative of the director of the Israel office of the American Jewish Committee, in 1974 the American Jewish organizations in Israel established an informal association to develop ways that might better present the American Jewish viewpoint to Israel's leadership. The founding members, in addition to the American Jewish Committee, included the American Jewish Congress, the AAJE, the Jewish Welfare Board, and the Conservative and Reform synagogue movements.

The most important organizational development in the Israel-overseas sphere within recent years has been the emergence of the Presidents' Conference as a body of growing significance. Originally called into existence in 1955 to prevent the overlapping of response on issues affecting Israel, it languished until the Six-Day War, primarily because there were not that many American Jewish organizations clamoring to act on matters concerning Israel. Given new impetus by the growing "alliance" between the United States and Israel and the necessity for Israel to strengthen its own American lobby, the Presidents' Conference has become an important vehicle for consultation between Israeli officials and American Jewry.

Internally, the Presidents' Conference remains a consultative and coordinating body in which all decisions must be made unanimously. Thus it is limited in the degree to which it can take an active role, but it has brought some order into the American Jewish foreign-relations picture, primarily in matters relating to Israel. Since it is the conduit for Israeli government decisions, virtually all American Jewish organizations have been willing to follow its guidelines. When it comes to other matters, Soviet Jewry for example, the Presidents' Conference is much less strong because there is no single authoritative voice capable of speaking for world Jewry on that issue.

Separate organizations have developed in the United States to support the cause of Soviet Jewry, and as single-interest organizations, they are willing to do whatever is necessary to advance their cause with fewer constraints than those placed on organizations with many different interests. Hence they have managed to force the American Jewish community to adopt more extreme positions in behalf of Soviet Jewry than either it or the Israelis might have wished. During the Yom Kippur War, for example, both the American Jewish leadership and the Israeli authorities sought to place a moratorium on activities in behalf of Soviet Jewry, on the grounds of "first things first." The partisans of Soviet Jewish emigration refused to allow this and threatened to bring public pressure. They won the day.

The overlapping of activities that characterizes community relations in American Jewish life also prevails in connection with international Jewish community-relations organizations and has its own impact on American Jewry. So many Jewish bodies have consultative status before the United Nations and its agencies that there are *two* councils of Jewish organizations designed to coordinate their activities: the Consultative Council of Jewish Organizations and the Coordinating Board of Jewish Organizations. Finally, the World Jewish Congress periodically attempts to play a role on the American scene. For a long time its links with the American Jewish Congress (which was its official American affiliate) prevented it from extensive involvement in American Jewish affairs. It recently severed those links and established its own American office, through which it is now trying to develop a program.

The problem of cooperation among the Zionist organizations has consistently been more difficult. Since—with the exception of Hadassah—they are tied to the great national (read: worldwide Jewish) Zionist parties that participate in the political life of Israel, they were unwilling to cooperate on the local scene until very recently. After agreements reached in Jerusalem in 1970, they responded to their growing weakness by creating a countrywide Zionist federation paralleled by local Zionist federations, in which each of the parties preserves its own identity but functions under a common umbrella, based on federal principles, for common purposes. How this new federative effort will shape decision making within the Zionist movement is as yet unclear, since the country-wide and local federations are themselves still more formal than real in many cases.

Naturally, the Israel-overseas sphere is substantially influenced by sources outside the United States. The Israel government and the Jewish Agency take a very active role in the fund-raising process and interact very closely with the CJF and UJA in the matter of allocation and use of funds. Consequently, this has become the major decision-making arena linking the American Jewish and Israeli partners. Similarly, the Jewish National Fund and the Keren Hayesod are active participants, both through the Jewish Agency and, in the case of the Jewish National Fund, to some extent directly on the American scene as well. These representatives of Israel are also involved in the educational sphere.

THE SPHERES AND THE LINKS BETWEEN THEM

The postwar generation has witnessed the increasing integration of the communal-welfare, Israel-overseas, and community-relations spheres and, as the generation progressed, certain linkages between the communal-welfare and the educational-cultural spheres as well. Thus in multiple-dimension, fragmented New York the local federation and UJA merged in the aftermath of the Yom Kippur War and are now beginning to lay plans for substantially increased activity in the field of Jewish education, which inevitably will bring the new communal body into closer contact with the synagogue centers. At the same time, new thrusts in the social services are also creating bridges even within that framework.

In the other categories federation roles are being extended. Intercongregational linkages and those between synagogues and federations are growing in response to current conditions. Declining synagogue membership and support necessitate new responses after a twenty-year boom. Now that normalization has set in, the sense of privateness that has characterized most congregations is beginning to give way to a recognition of their dependence upon and role in the community as a whole. Federations and synagogues are finding new activities that they must conduct in common. Even the already-linked communities are deepening their linkages, often through new mechanisms of institutionalization. While no trend is unidimensional, and it should not be assumed that because there is greater interaction there is a lessening of tension, the trend does seem to be toward linkage and partnership, even if sometimes on an antagonistic basis.

The organized Jewish community is constructed out of these building blocks and exists as a result of the network of linkages that they have developed with one another. Since those linkages are, at least in their initial stages, entirely voluntary in origin, they do not follow any single pattern. Rather, they have developed in each community in accordance with certain factors that have influenced communal life locally. Moreover, even after circumstance limits the possibility for severing established linkages or of crossing over to form radically different ones from those that have developed over the years, the element of consent continues to play an important role in determining whether a particular linkage is pro forma or significant.

Overall, the complexities of contemporary American Jewish life are leading to greater linkage among all the spheres. Now that the federations have staked out a real role for themselves in the educational-cultural sphere, that too is being drawn into the overall orbit. The last holdout is the religious-congregational sphere. Linkage between it and the others has become one of the primary items on the American Jewish community's agenda for the coming years. It is no accident that both the Synagogue Council of America and the CJF set up committees to investigate the federation-synagogue relationship at approximately the same time in 1973. In community after community similar explorations are taking place, accompanied by concrete actions. In this respect, developments in the American Jewish community parallel those in other polities throughout the world in the twentieth century: a clear movement from separated spheres toward increased integration, with all the problems of coordination that such integration brings.

7

*The Major Communities**

The American Jewish polity includes six basic forms of local communal structure that can be identified: (1) communities fragmented regionally along multiple dimensions, (2) communities fragmented along a single (congregational-communal) dimension, (3) communities segmented into congregational and communal spheres, (4) communities in which the congregational and communal spheres are linked, (5) communities in which the two spheres are integrated, and (6) communities that revolve around single congregations. Table 22 represents a preliminary classification of all Jewish communities of over five thousand population.

NEW YORK: A REGION FRAGMENTED ALONG MULTIPLE DIMENSIONS

New York City, properly speaking, is not a community at all but a region. However, since it is a region that is densely populated and whose institutions are very close to one another, even its subareas—boroughs, neighborhoods, adjacent suburbs—share the same characteristics of fragmentation along multiple dimensions. This extreme fragmentation is a natural consequence of the density and diversity of the Jewish population. New York's multiple dimensions result from the fact that the city is also the headquarters of the great countrywide Jewish organizations

*Sources for this chapter will be found in Appendix D.

Population Size	Fragmented		Segmented	Linked	Integrated
	Regional	Congregational-Communal			
over 1 million	New York				
100,000–600,000		Bergen Co. Washington	Baltimore Chicago Miami Philadelphia	Boston Los Angeles	
40,000–99,000			metropolitan N.J. Saint Louis San Francisco	Cleveland Detroit Pittsburgh	
15,000–40,000		Central N.J. North Jersey North Shore Mass. Shore Area N.J.	Atlanta Buffalo Cincinnati Denver Kansas City Lower Bucks Co., Pa. Milwaukee New Haven Orange Co., Cal. Raritan valley Rhode Island Rochester	Dallas Hartford Houston Long Beach Minneapolis Oakland	Camden
5,000–14,999			Akron Albany Atlantic City Bridgeport Brockton Dayton Delaware Englewood, N.J. Framingham Jacksonville Jersey City Louisville Memphis Morris Co., N.J. New Orleans Norfolk Northwest Indiana Norwalk Orlando Palm Beach Co. Passaic Richmond Saint Petersburg San Antonio San Diego San Jose Scranton Seattle Springfield, Mass. Stamford Syracuse Toledo Trenton Tucson Worcester Youngstown	Columbus Indianapolis Las Vegas Omaha Phoenix Portland Saint Paul	

and institutions, all of which have a direct local influence because of their location and relatively easy accessibility for the Jews of the metropolitan area. It is a situation not without disadvantages. Among other things, it makes for severe leadership problems locally; under the circumstances, the national bodies are able to skim off the best regional talent for their own purposes.

The synagogue center is the basic form of localistic organization in the New York area, and indeed was invented in New York primarily to meet indigenous needs. This particular institution came into being because there the synagogue is almost the only point of linkage for most of those who wish to be affiliated with a comprehensive Jewish institution (albeit a minority of all Jews in the area). As such, the synagogue center also has been called upon to provide more comprehensive services than would have been the case had there been other institutions available capable of serving the entire community, of the kind that have developed in virtually every other sizable local Jewish community in the United States. It is significant that the synagogue centers' major competition in the older New York Jewish neighborhoods are those YMHA centers that have synagogues attached to them.

One of the characteristics of the synagogue center is that it seeks to be all-encompassing, in terms of providing a full range of religious, educational, cultural, and even certain basic social services to its members. As a result, the synagogue center is almost totally detached from any lateral or vertical links within New York City. Such ties as it has are with the national office of its umbrella organization—one of the three synagogue movements or the Jewish Welfare Board—to which it will turn for any required external assistance.

The communitywide organizations serving greater New York tend to be limited in scope and neither comprehensive nor representative. The best example is the New York Jewish Federation, which until recently embraced only those social-service and welfare agencies (particularly hospitals) that could not be supported by local institutions and required a region-wide effort. It should be noted that these are precisely the institutions that over the years increasingly made their services available to the general community, to the point where in many instances their Jewish aspect has become quite nominal. As a result, the links between organizations that in other communities function comprehensively and those that provide community services are relatively attenuated. Moreover, many of the subregional communal-service institutions are substantially independent of the federation, either through linkage with other countrywide groupings or through location in a synagogue center.

Fragmentation of communal activities and services proceeds up and down the line, no doubt as a result of the convergence of two factors. We have suggested that the presence of the national headquarters of most organizations in New York exercises a detrimental influence on local development. In addition, the very size of the Jewish community allows every special interest to find ample expression, thus rendering its members more self-sufficient and less eager for the company of others.

The community-relations organizations do have New York chapters, but they are subordinated to their respective national offices by virtue of proximity and the incomparably greater resources of the latter. Their local programing is essentially provided through the national offices. New York is the center of Zionist and Israel-related organizations for all of American Jewry, each of which maintains its own structures and programs within the metropolitan area, almost without reference to anything outside the Zionist sphere and—until recently, when the American Zionist Federation was created—with minimum reference to one another. The focal point of Zionist activity is the Jewish Agency building on Park Avenue, which houses the Jewish Agency–American Section, the Herzl Institute (an adult-education service of some magnitude), and a wide variety of offices of Zionist and Israel-oriented groups. Similarly, the National Jewish Welfare Board has its own offices and program activities. All three synagogue movements maintain seminaries and major offices in New York City, which have a direct impact on their respective farflung constituencies.

The educational and cultural groups—which in any case tend to fragmentation, even under the best of circumstances—find in New York the ultimate opportunity for separation. On one hand, they are institutionally separate, since each organization maintains its own education program. Even the Jewish Education Committee, because of its historic origins as an outgrowth of the kehillah experiment, was separated from the federation until its recent reorganization. The very existence of a critical mass of Jews for almost every kind of cultural activity makes it possible for a variety of Jewish groups to function, each totally independent of the others and not driven by the need that impels Jews with cultural interests in smaller communities to seek one another out for mutual sustenance.

Needless to say, the diversity on the fraternal front is even greater. For many Jews, fraternal associations are the only points of contact with organized Jewish life, and in New York such groups tend to be far more private and less oriented toward public or social purposes than elsewhere. In part this is because New York still has room for country-of-origin associations (landsmanshaften) and for strictly social clubs composed of people who feel no necessity to define their Jewish purposes in more public terms. Moreover, as a continuing center of Jewish immigration, New York is able to retain much of its Jewish diversity; and as the center of Hasidic life and separatist Orthodox groups in the United States, it also offers more opportunities for comprehensive Jewish living on the fringes of the Jewish mainstream.

Jewish ethnicity is at its most thriving in New York, with its northeastern location and its special position as the port of entry for most Jewish immigrants since 1654. The subtleties of Jewish ethnicity add to the fragmentation of the region as a whole and provide a surrogate for organized unity. In short, ethnicity inhibits the drive toward communal organization. The general feeling of Jewishness that prevails among the majority of Jews in New York City and is reinforced by the ethnically oriented pluralism of the Northeast means that Jews here can feel Jewish without taking any active steps to participate in organized Jewish life. It is precisely the low level or absence of ethnic feeling in other parts of the country that has led Jews to work so hard at their organizations, substituting associational for organic ties in an effort to survive as Jews. At the same time, Jewish ethnic consciousness as a whole also stimulates a certain consciousness of the subdivisions of Jewish life—such as the differences in country of origin, particularly among more recent immigrants, which tend to frustrate efforts at unity based on associational ties that perforce consider Jews as Jews, no more and no less.

The original Sephardim and those who have been "galvanized" into their ranks constitute New York's congregationalists par excellence; indeed, Shearith Israel, New York's oldest and most prestigious congregation, seeks to be a kind of comprehensive kehillah in its own right. This is also the pattern of the later Sephardic arrivals, who came to New York at the time of the mass immigration and more recently after World War II. They, too, tend toward congregationalism or some equivalent form, to the extent that they remain linked with organized Jewish life at all.

In accord with their traditions, the descendants of the Central European Jews, particularly those of German origin, are still most closely connected with such communal institutions and organizations as hospitals, social-service agencies, and the federation itself, as well as with the American Jewish Committee. While by now they are probably a minority in all of these, for a great percentage of Jews of German and Central European descent such association forms their primary point of Jewish affiliation, perhaps coupled with linkage to a Reform temple, in a continuation of the pattern established by their nineteenth-century forebears. The exceptions among this group are the German Orthodox element, who have formed congregations almost as separate in their own way as Shearith Israel.

While the East European Jews have come to dominate the community by dint of sheer numbers, they are still to be found more in the Conservative synagogue centers, the Zionist organizations, and the American Jewish Congress, where they have implanted their own patterns of behavior, as modified by their respective American experiences. East European Jewry also dominates New York Orthodoxy in all its variety, including the Hasidic communities, each of which is as separate and self-contained as it can possibly be, even when, as in the case of the Chabad movement, they seek to reach out to influence Jewry as a whole.

Finally, there are the Israeli emigrants, who have come to form a new kind of ethnic subculture within New York Jewry. Its members group around a sense of shared Israeli culture rather than any Jewish religious or ideological identification. As in the case of earlier immigrant groups, Israelis have actually created their own territories in various sections of the city—certain apartment complexes in Forest Hills, for instance— where they can share and practice their "native" culture.

The existence of strong localistic pulls, weak comprehensive organizations on the local plane, and the attraction of the national offices all serve to create serious leadership problems for New York Jewry. Persons who aspire to Jewish leadership beyond the localistic institutions are almost immediately drawn into the vortex of national Jewish organizational life and politics, leaving few to man the ramparts of New York, as such. Only in the federation and its constituents, where national leadership is dependent upon the achievement of status among the local leadership cadres, has this problem been somewhat overcome. In the case of the rabbinate, where local ties are of the utmost importance, a pulpit in one of the great metropolitan area congregations is indeed the springboard to national leadership, but rabbis can take advantage of that situation only by limiting their local involvement to the immediate boundaries of their respective congregations.

COMMUNITIES FRAGMENTED ALONG A SINGLE DIMENSION

The communities that fall into this category are to be found primarily in the suburban areas of the Northeast, particularly around Greater New York but outside the immediate New York City orbit, as well as in Washington, D.C. (for somewhat different reasons). Here too the synagogues are virtually the only points of connection with organized Jewish life. The congregations in question may or may not be synagogue centers per se. In some cases they are extensions of the New York City pattern, with appropriate suburban adaptations. In others, they strive for comprehensiveness but serve clienteles that do not demand the range of services that a synagogue center in the metropolitan area has come to provide.

By and large, the synagogues are within the orbit of some larger representative organization, a federation or a Jewish community council, but the attachment is minimal. In turn, the larger organization provides little in the way of services to the Jews in the area, functioning primarily as a means of fund raising for Israel or of handling relations with the local non-Jewish community. Thus these are also communities with strong localistic organizations and weak community-wide ones. Leadership tends to be confined to the synagogue or, where men and women of exceptional talent are present, is siphoned off to the national offices, which are still within easy traveling distance of the majority of these communities. Within the congregations, rabbinical leadership tends to be very strong, to the point of overshadowing the voluntary leadership on most occasions. This is at least partly because the voluntary leadership consists of people who happen to have moved into a particular suburb for reasons extraneous to their Jewish concerns, while the pulpit is frequently occupied by a rabbi who aspires to national position but does not want actually to live in New York, only within striking distance of its many communal opportunities.

Bergen County

Bergen County, New Jersey, affords a good example of a community fragmented along a single dimension. Located just west of the George Washington Bridge but across the state line, it is within relatively easy commuting distance of New York City, although outside the metropolitan area as defined by the U. S. Census Bureau and generally by Jewish organizations as well. Thus it has developed its own independent institutions to a greater degree than have the suburban counties north and east of New York City. Jews make up some 10 percent of the county's total population and have congregations in most of the county's seventy different independent municipalities.

Settled initially by East European Jews (principally from Lithuania and Russia) in the 1880s and 1890s, Bergen County has a Jewish community that is essentially a product of post–World War II suburbanization. While there was a small boom in Jewish settlement immediately after World War I and another migration after 1931, when the George Washington Bridge was completed, the greatest influx arrived only after World War II. By 1950 Bergen County had 20,000 Jews in a general population of 540,000. By 1970 the Jewish population had quintupled while the overall population had only doubled.

The community grew along congregational lines from the start—a congregation was organized in the municipality of Englewood in 1896 —and did not develop the kinds of communal institutions that marked areas of German Jewish settlement. The smallness of the Jewish population prior to the postwar years also discouraged institutionalization outside the congregations. It was not until 1952 that Englewood established its own United Jewish Fund, which also embraces some of the immediately adjacent municipalities. The Jewish Federation of Community Services of Bergen County, which came into existence a year later, would like to claim jurisdiction over the entire county, and in some respects it does overlap with the United Jewish Fund. Its primary purpose, however, is to raise funds for strictly local needs. Fund raising for Israel and overseas needs, as well as for the major regional Jewish institutions, is handled separately by the United Jewish Appeal of Greater New York.

Today Bergen County boasts twenty-five Conservative, nine Reform, and five Orthodox congregations, a day school, and over one hundred identified Jewish organizations. Not only did each of these develop independently, but it was only in the late 1960s that any real efforts were made even to begin to coordinate activities in the Jewish community. The organization of the Bergen County Rabbinical Association in 1968 may have marked the turning point. In 1969 the Community Relations Council was established, primarily to combat manifestations of anti-Semitism that still flared up in a county which in the 1930s had been a center of the German-American Bund. That same year the federation began a movement to consolidate its separate local drives into a single campaign and to reach out to UJA to establish links with it as well. While considerable progress has been made since then, it is still fair to say that Bergen County—like most of the other Jewish communities in New Jersey—is essentially a fragmented community that may be moving to better linkages but has yet to achieve them (see Table 22).

Washington

The Jewish community of Washington, D.C., is equally fragmented—for different reasons, however. Washington's small size as a city, coupled with its relative unimportance until the days of the New Deal, meant that few Jews were attracted there prior to the 1930s. The burgeoning federal establishment brought tens of thousands of Jewish settlers to Washington, most of them government employees, as well as some who came to take advantage of the boom in the service economy that accompanied the federal expansion.

The Washington Jewish community is thus still a comparatively recent one. Moreover, given the revolving-door nature of federal employment, Washington is not a city that encourages people to sink roots. The effects are felt in the Jewish community, which is perhaps the most socially fragmented Jewish community in the United States, surpassing even Los Angeles and Miami, other contenders for the title. The sheer lack of Jewish interest among so many of Washington's Jews limits the possibilities for vibrant communal life. One consequence of this seems to be that even concerned Jews are insufficiently motivated to seek out communal expression for their interests; instead, they establish their own personalized Jewish attachments and let matters rest there.

Washington's first congregation, the Washington Hebrew Congregation, was not organized until 1852. Its founders were German Jewish settlers who joined forces with some Jews in government service at the time. (Whatever there is of "old" Jewish Washington is descended from this company.) A schism between Reformers and traditionalists led to the secession of a group from the Washington Hebrew Congregation, who founded Adas Israel, now a Conservative congregation. Its first synagogue structure was erected in 1876. Even after the East European migration there were only four thousand Jews in Washington. The three small Orthodox synagogues founded at that time have now been merged into two.

A B'nai B'rith lodge was established during the Civil War and another in 1869. In 1882 a United Hebrew Relief Society came into being. Other institutions grew slowly from 1890 until World War I, but an attempt to create a community Hebrew school in 1910 failed for lack of financial support. Supplementary Jewish education in Washington remains exclusively in the hands of the congregations. The day-school picture is equally fragmented. The Hebrew Academy (ultra-Orthodox) was founded in 1944, and Solomon Schechter Day School (Conservative) in the 1960s, as was a yeshiva high school; all three are entirely independent. A YMHA was formed in 1912. Today its lineal descendant, the Jewish Community Center in suburban Maryland, is probably the single most active institution in the community.

The great boom in Washington's Jewish population came after World War II, with the number growing from about 20,000 in 1945 to the present estimated 110,000. At the same time, the changing character of the city led to a Jewish exodus to the suburbs, to the point where 85 percent of the total Jewish population now resides outside the city limits, 75 percent in neighboring Maryland. The community's forty-one congregations probably do not include even half the total number of Jewish families. The physical center of communal life is the Jewish Community Center–Home for the Aged–Jewish Social Service Agency Complex in Rockville, Maryland.

In the 1930s the Washington Jewish Community Council was founded and the United Jewish Appeal began operations strictly as a fund-raising agency; the two remain separate. The Board of Jewish Education, a rather weak body attached to the Jewish Community Council, sponsors a community Hebrew high school, Washington's first venture into communally sponsored Jewish education but one that is by no means comprehensive in scope. UJA originally confined its role to fund raising for Israel and other overseas organizations, plus the few countrywide organizations that were its beneficiaries in New York. More recently it has begun to allocate funds to local institutions as well, to become a community instrumentality without becoming a federation. Today UJA funds support the Jewish Community Council: the two now reinforce one another rather that compete. But these institutional gains have been more than offset by the suburban migration of Washington's Jews, who have dispersed over so wide an area that geography works against greater linkages.

SEGMENTED COMMUNITIES

The form of communal organization most prevalent among American Jewish communities today is the segmented one. A list of the communities that fall within this category would almost constitute a roster of the major Jewish communities in the United States, as well as of a majority of the medium-sized ones. Included here are Baltimore, Chicago, metropolitan New Jersey (Essex and Union counties), Miami, Philadelphia, Boston, Saint Louis, San Francisco, Atlanta, Denver, Kansas City, and many others (see Table 22).

The major feature of this form of organization is that while it permits multiple points of affiliation within the community (principally related to size), there is also a loose network that has been formed around two main nodes: the congregation and the comprehensive-representative organization. Thus it is expected that a "good Jew" will belong to a synagogue or the equivalent and will also contribute to the local Jewish federation through the annual combined appeal. The federation is likely to have constituent bodies linked to it through funding and planning arrangements. At the same time, the congregational and communal sectors remain substantially separated; they are certainly without formal links, although there may be some informal or even semiformal ties that do reach across the gap between them.

In general, organizational life in these communities is well articulated, and the two principal nodes very much so. While the congregations are rarely synagogue centers in the style of New York, they do provide a wide range of activities and seek a central position in the Jewish life of their communities as a matter of course. By the same token, the comprehensive-representative organizations are also well developed, with strong links between them and their constituent agencies that embrace virtually every sphere of Jewish communal life, except perhaps the religious-congregational. Their boards tend to be broadly representative of the community, by design, although the representation is co-opted rather than selected by any grass-roots method, and their leadership tends to be more or less open to those who wish to play an active cosmopolitan role. By and large, the leadership of the cosmopolitan and localistic sectors is separate, except perhaps in the case of the most prestigious congregations in the community, where persons who might otherwise not aspire to congregational leadership will accept it out of a sense of obligation.

The segmented congregational-federation community, it should be noted, is marked by a relatively high degree of hostility between the spokesmen for the two nodes. This is so because both tend toward aggressiveness in the performance of their particular tasks. Moreover, both frequently find themselves competing for the same people—and for their time and money. However, in this form of community the conflict between the federations and their agencies and the congregations is acted out within a common framework, which, while not necessarily promoting close relations, does not allow each sector to go its own way either.

Boston and Philadelphia

Boston and Philadelphia, the principal cities in this category, are the major subcenters of American Jewry and the only cities besides New York that serve as headquarters for any significant countrywide institutions. They are at the same time major Jewish communities in their own right. Philadelphia is the third largest Jewish community in the United States and Boston is the fifth. (When its suburban areas are included Boston may well be the fourth, slightly larger than Chicago.) Boston has now begun to rival New York as the intellectual center of American Jewish life, while Philadelphia steadily maintains its position as a well-articulated Jewish community serving countrywide, regional, and local needs in a balanced fashion.

The Jewish communities of both Philadelphia and Boston are of sufficient size to cover the gamut of Jewish concerns without particular strain —a characteristic of this size community generally (but not manifest, as we have seen, in Washington and Bergen County, for reasons already noted). Both are located in the Northeast and are near enough to New York City for their leaders to be involved in countrywide Jewish activities, but far enough removed from New York's magnetic field not to suffer from the leadership drain described above. While both are being strongly influenced by metropolitanization, in both instances there are still strong anchors within their central cities—or for Boston, in the inner ring of towns that has long since replaced Boston as the focal point of Jewish life—to overcome the many deleterious effects of metropolitan population dispersal. Thus both are able to retain critical masses of Jews in key neighborhoods for the maintenance of an active Jewish life on a daily basis, without recourse to car pools for commuting to synagogues or community centers once or twice a week.

Two major differences between these communities are the respective periods in which they were settled and their sources of settlers. Philadelphia is an old Jewish community by American standards, dating back to colonial times. It received much of its character in the nineteenth century, when for many years it was the center of organized Jewish life in the United States and the pioneer in the development of the first countrywide Jewish institutions. It has a number of old, distinguished congregations that have managed to survive for a century or two and to develop loyalties that span the generations. Their strength is made even greater by the fact that Philadelphia tends to be a relatively stable community, with little in-migration or out-migration to upset established patterns. Philadelphia's federation grew as a federation of local social-service organizations and remained just that until the 1950s. As in so many other large communities, the Allied Jewish Appeal emerged as a separate organization and was only later merged with the federation, after which the newly enlarged federation began to concern itself with the problems of Jewish education and thus to build bridges to the synagogues through Gratz College, its educational arm.

Boston, on the other hand, had only the slightest Jewish presence before the great migration from Eastern Europe, and its Jewish community is primarily of East European origin. Influenced by New England culture, Boston Jewry soon became known for its pioneering role in the development of communal structures—its federation is the oldest in the country—and in the high level of its communal concern, as reflected in its patterns of financial contribution. While Boston did not have many ties across the communal and congregational spheres, its communal sphere was quite comprehensive in scope, even reaching into Jewish education in a significant way, to the point where congregations found it necessary to link themselves to the Bureau of Jewish Education. On the other hand, suburbanization has increased segmentation in the community. As the population has fanned outward from the central areas, new congregations have been formed outside the service orbit of communal institutions. Boston is presently trying to overcome that development and to restore the earlier pattern.

Boston began to develop into a major Jewish intellectual center as Jews moved increasingly into the mainstream of American society. For a long time New York, with its greater ability to maintain isolated Jewish cultural and intellectual activity, remained preeminent. However, once the best Jewish minds could find places in the American university world

—and indeed began to fill such places without surrendering their Jewish concerns—Boston, with its abundance of prestigious academic institutions, emerged as an important Jewish intellectual center. The shift marks a new phase in American Jewish intellectual life, which is no longer lived in isolation from the American mainstream but is integrated into it. The location of Brandeis University in nearby Waltham added an institutional focus to this development. By achieving this new status in the Jewish world, Boston has acquired a certain independence vis-à-vis New York, given the importance of intellectual life in the Jewish scheme of things.

Chicago

Chicago, the Jewish capital of the Midwest, is another segmented community. Its Jewish community is a product of the nineteenth century and achieved its initial form as a result of the settlement of German and Central European Jews during the days of city's first boom. Its oldest and most prestigious congregations stem from that period and have survived numerous moves and social changes by means of judicious mergers. As in the case of most of the large cities, the Jewish settlers were a polyglot group from all parts of Europe. While the Germans and Central Europeans helped set a certain tone on one level, on another there was no overall pattern established because of the great diversity of the mass of East European Jews who arrived subsequently. It was only in the 1960s that Chicago began to unify its institutions on the communal plane, and it is still much closer to New York than to Boston, Los Angeles, or even Philadelphia in the nature of relationships between communal and congregational areas.

As we have noted, the first generation of organized Jewish life in Chicago spans the period from the founding of Congregation KAM in 1846 until the fire of 1874 (not to be confused with the Great Fire of 1871), which burned out the East European ghetto. During the following generation, from 1874 to World War I, the Jewish population of Chicago grew from 10,000 to over 200,000, as East European Jews continued to pour in. Even so, by 1920 only 85 percent of Chicago Jewry was of East European birth or descent, an indication that German and Central European Jews still formed an important element. The East European arrivals came into a situation marked by intense congregationalism and congregational factionalism. It was a situation they were very familiar with from experience, and they entered the fray in their new home with much zest. Tales of legendary synagogue fights form the heritage of Chicago Jewry to this very day.

The third generation, the period between world wars, witnessed the high point of communal activity in the field of Jewish education to date, with the development of the Board of Jewish Education, the College of Jewish Studies, the Associated Talmud Torahs (Orthodox), and several major neighborhood Hebrew schools not linked to any synagogues. Following World War II, however, supplementary Jewish education passed entirely into the hands of the synagogues, except for the small Orthodox element affiliated with the Associated Talmud Torahs.

Meanwhile, the division between German and East European Jews persisted and may even have intensified. One way this was reflected was in the formation of the Covenant Club in 1917, to provide a downtown luncheon facility for the successful East Europeans, to parallel the Standard Club (incorporated in 1869), which maintained its German Jewish exclusivity.

Chicago's Jewish Federation was founded in 1900 to provide joint fund raising for the hospitals and social-service institutions of the community. It never became interested in overseas and Zionist needs, however, and the Jewish Welfare Fund came into being for that purpose in 1936, supported primarily by the East European community. The two were not merged until 1968, when the Jewish United Fund of Metropolitan Chicago was established; even so, both retained their separate identities within the framework of the latter. Prior to the merger the two bodies were not only separate but also maintained the limited roles characteristic of pre-World War II days; however, since the merger their community-planning dimension has developed with a vengeance.

The Chicago Jewish community's segmented style was maintained in the post–World War II generation as well. In the late 1940s and early 1950s the Jews evacuated Chicago's West Side, which had been the heart of Jewish activity in the city for two generations, and then, in the 1950s and 1960s, they began to abandon the city altogether, scattering over the northern and western suburbs and even into the southern suburbs in small numbers, so that geography intensified segmentation. By the 1970s the frontiers of settlement of Chicago's Jewry were forty miles distant from the Loop, with the majority of Jews concentrated in West Rogers Park, within the city limits, and Skokie just beyond.

Most institutions serve only a small segment of the Chicago area's

Jewish population. Synagogue affiliation in 1969 was less than 50 percent in the city and reached about 60 percent in the suburbs, where it was generally the single point of affiliation for those Jews desiring any association at all. The rabbis in the city were either members of the Chicago Board of Rabbis, the heir to the Chicago Rabbinical Association, or the Orthodox Merkaz Harabonim. There were separate Orthodox and Conservative rabbinical courts. Orthodox rabbinical training was provided by the Hebrew Theological College and a branch of the Telz Yeshiva, while the division between Orthodox and non-Orthodox schools continued to be institutionalized through the Associated Talmud Torahs and the Board of Jewish Education. Even the emergence of the Jewish United Fund, an obvious attempt at linkage and integration, led to new kinds of segmentation in the Chicago pattern, as the Fund established a Jewish Education Planning Department in what seemed to be direct competition with the Board of Jewish Education, its own constituent agency.

At one time the third largest Jewish community in the United States, Chicago has been dropping in size in both absolute numbers and in position since the end of World War II, when many Chicagoans began migrating westward. As a community, the division between German and East European Jews remained pronounced until the postwar period, with the institutional balance reflecting the division. Its size tended to work against integration in the first place, although its regional location somewhat canceled that out, since the Midwest, with its emphasis on a pluralism of associations, has tended to promote more integration than the Northeast. Chicago's general environment, with its tendencies toward individualism, also did not help the cause of integrated communal organization. Most recently, the metropolitanization of Chicago Jewry has added to the possibilities for segmentation rather than linkage among the local Jewish institutions.

Greater Miami

Greater Miami, the only large Jewish center in the South, is also a segmented community—for very different reasons. It is the newest of the very large Jewish communities, even newer than Los Angeles. Its official founding took place in 1896, but the first real influx of Jews did not arrive until the 1920s. There was another influx after World War II, and yet a third in the 1960s. Miami claims about 200,000 Jews, which places it no lower than sixth among the American Jewish communities, perhaps even fifth. The great bulk of its Jewish settlers came from the Northeast, principally New York, and they brought with them many of the characteristics of New York Jewry, including a penchant for fragmentation. However, because of Miami's much smaller size, the local Jewish federation has been able to establish some kind of overall framework to make the community a segmented rather than a fragmented one.

As in the case of most new Jewish communities, the locus of organized Jewish life is the congregations, but because Miami is so new the congregations themselves do not have multigenerational histories. Rather, most of them represent first-settlement efforts with all that this implies, including domination by the founders, reliance upon publicly attractive rabbis to draw members, minimal congregational loyalty, and the like. The community-wide institutions have only begun to develop in the past ten years as serious forces in the community. Their position is rendered more difficult by the fact that many of the potential leaders are only part-time residents of the area, maintaining residences in their cities of origin to which they return for substantial portions of the year. Unlike Los Angeles, the Miami community has not developed the network of educational and cultural institutions needed to transform its raw numbers into a significant force in Jewish life. Perhaps this is simply a question of its newness, but in part it has also to do with the character of the general environment, which is far less oriented in that direction than is the West Coast.

Miami's role as a winter retreat for residents of colder climates has also given it an interesting place in the countrywide scheme of things. Although national institutions do not have branches there, it is in a way the winter headquarters of American Jewry, the site of many important meetings that are held in Miami and environs because of the Jewish leadership's presence in the area. This may actually have had a retarding effect on the development of the local community, since national affairs monopolize community time without providing any corresponding local benefit.

Metropolitan New Jersey

Metropolitan New Jersey's segmentation is strongly influenced by its location in the Northeast on the border of New York and in a highly suburban area. Essentially a community settled directly by East European Jews in the late nineteenth and early twentieth centuries, its Jewish life reflects its origins. The out-migration from New York did not engulf it until after World War II. Until the 1950s the community was concentrated in Newark, where Jewish neighborhoods plus a certain separation from New York encouraged the development of local institutions in the general American Jewish pattern. However, in recent years Newark has become a virtually all-black city and the Jews have scattered not only to other parts of Essex County but beyond, thereby weakening the hold of communal institutions and strengthening suburban congregations.

Saint Louis and San Francisco

The Jewish communities of Saint Louis and San Francisco, on the other hand, are products of mid-nineteenth-century German-speaking immigrants, and in both cities circumstances have tended to reinforce the patterns established by the original German and Central European Jewish settlers, even in the face of the subsequent migration from East Europe. In addition, in the last several years the Bay Area of San Francisco has become something of a center for contemporary Jewish mystical cults, attracting large numbers of rootless Jewish young people in search of life's meaning.

San Francisco's special character is further enhanced by the fact that not only were Jews among the city's founders—*two* congregations were organized in 1849, the first year of American settlement in the city—but also Jews integrated rapidly into the general society, rising to the heights of social rank while retaining their Jewish ties. Thus the San Francisco Jewish establishment, which has dominated the communal institutions, for a long time resisted the countrywide trend toward more intensive Jewish activity. While the same was often true for San Francisco's congregations as well, so that there was little conflict between the communal and the congregational spheres, it also meant that the patterns of segmentation characteristic of nineteenth-century Judaism, which divided the spheres, have continued to do so. This situation began to change at the beginning of the 1970s, however.

In Saint Louis, Jews were slow to organize themselves. Between the city's founding by the French in 1764 and its transfer to the Americans forty years later, no Jews were allowed to settle within the city limits. Another thirty years or so elapsed before organized Jewish life made an appearance. In 1837 a High Holy Day service was held for the first time;

in 1840 a cemetery was acquired; a congregation was founded in 1841, which combined Jews of Prussian, Bohemian, and English background; and a Benevolent Society was started in 1842.

The efforts to overcome early schisms in the religious sphere are attested to by the congregation's name, United Hebrew Congregation. (Significantly, by the mid-1840s its services followed the Polish tradition.) Nevertheless, the effort at unity failed, and German and Bohemian Jews founded their own congregations in 1847 and 1849 respectively, both less traditional in their religious policies. Isaac Leeser, at the time the acknowledged leader of American Jewry, tried to effect a merger of the three congregations during his visit to Saint Louis in 1851, but the religious disagreements could not be overcome. All that resulted was a merger of the two less traditional congregations in 1852. Two years later a schism in the United Hebrew Congregation led to the formation of still another synagogue.

The first Reform congregation in Saint Louis was established in the mid-1860s. Of the three Orthodox synagogues formed in the 1870s, only one has remained Orthodox. Even the original Reform congregation, Shaare Emeth, split in 1886 in a struggle over the rabbi's religious views, with the dissidents departing with their religious leader to organize Temple Israel. That same decade saw the formation of new congregations by immigrants from Eastern Europe. At present there are five Reform, three Conservative, and seven Orthodox congregations serving the Jewish community.

In order to care for the refugees from Chicago's Great Fire of 1871, the various relief associations that had sprung up in the 1850s and 1860s merged into the United Hebrew Relief Association. In the 1890s services were established to assist the new immigrants, particularly night classes and day nurseries. These efforts were combined under the Jewish Alliance, and then in 1899 it and the United Hebrew Relief Association merged to become the United Jewish Education and Charitable Association, later to become the Saint Louis Jewish Federation. At the same time, the Jewish hospital and YM-YWHA were established. A Jewish orphanage was founded in 1907. Until that time Jewish orphans had been sent to the B'nai B'rith Home in Cleveland. In that same period the Orthodox Home for the Aged came into existence, soon to replace a pioneering agency of the first settlers, the Home for Aged and Infirm Israelites, which had been established in 1882.

As in Chicago, the interwar period was the time of greatest effort at communal integration to date. In 1924 Orthodox and Conservative rabbis and voluntary leaders joined to form the Vaad Ho-ir (City Council), primarily to handle matters of kashruth. In 1926 five independent Hebrew schools were united as the Associated Hebrew Schools (although intensive Jewish education nevertheless remained confined to a relatively small minority). After World War II the synagogues moved in to preempt the domain of the Associated Hebrew Schools, and Jewish education passed into their hands. The small Orthodox community found that it had little in common with the predominantly Reform Jewish establishment and began to develop separatist patterns of its own, establishing a day school in 1943, to which boys' and girls' high schools were added in the early 1960s. When the Rabbinical Association in Saint Louis was formed in 1954, only Reform and Conservative rabbis joined. In a pattern characteristic in Reform-dominated communities, the YMHA became a major factor, filling roles that synagogues were more likely to do in communities with strong Conservative leanings. In 1968 over thirteen thousand families were listed as members of the YMHA.

LINKED COMMUNITIES

In terms of the organizational structures of the various local institutions, there is little surface difference between the segmented and linked communities; nor is there likely to be any less coolness or hostility between the congregational and communal sectors, which must be recognized as the natural rivals they are. However, only when the rivalry serves divisive ends, as it does in the three forms described above, can it be said to have gotten out of hand. The virtue of the linked form lies in the way the two sectors interact with one another, so as to transform natural rivalries into what sometimes comes close to being creative tension. That is a potentially great achievement, good for the entire community and for both sectors as well.

The patterns of leadership in these communities also resemble those found in segmented ones. By and large, there is a sharp division between those who accept leadership positions in synagogues and those who seek such positions within a broader context of communal activity. Within the professional sphere these communities tend to have very strong rabbis and the most able federation leaders. In both cases there is at least a reasonable chance that the very ability of these men allows them to transcend the rivalries imposed upon them by their respective roles. Having ability, they feel less threatened by moving out of the normal channels and by accepting the existence of tension as part of the environment. Thus they are able to work with each other on specific tasks to everyone's benefit, even though they may simultaneously maintain the sense of rivalry and even a certain critical orientation toward their counterparts.

Cleveland and Detroit

The situation in Cleveland and Detroit reflects this well. The combination of factors has worked in both cities to maximize the quality of organized Jewish life. Both communities are of a proper size to maintain a well-articulated organizational structure, lacking in no features available elsewhere in the United States except the most specialized groups found only in New York. At the same time, neither is too large to limit widespread links between leaders and members of the community, and among the leaders of the various spheres themselves. The location of both, in areas originally settled by Yankees from New England, has also contributed to the strong sense of communal responsibility. Both communities are known for their generosity to philanthropic causes, Jewish and otherwise.

Their location in the Great Lakes states places Cleveland and Detroit in a cultural climate different from that of the Northeast, yet at the same time they are within an hour's flight of New York. The Jews of Cleveland and Detroit also combine some sense of ethnicity with a strong commitment to the associational pluralism that is characteristic of the Great Lakes section—the awareness that every person must link himself to a group by formal association and maintain the affiliation for the duration of his life unless there is some good reason for changing it. Thus people are freer to choose whether or not to be Jews in that section, but once committed they are likely to manifest that commitment by joining a Jewish organization and retaining the association.

The Jewish communities of both Cleveland and Detroit were founded by German Jews in the middle of the last century and received the bulk of their Jewish population during the course of the East European migration at the turn of the century. Both cities benefited from the organizational skills and strengths of nineteenth-century German Jewry, while at the same time their organizations were infused with the kind of Jewish content provided by the East European migrants. Moreover, both were fortunate in acquiring some truly exceptional individuals in the pioneering stages of the communities' development, whose imprint gave each community a special tone. The fact that they were settled in a particular period added another benefit. Neither community became exclusively congregationalist in character, but rather saw the development of communal and congregational institutions side by side, with the same people —many of them the same exceptional figures—playing prominent roles in the development of both, which ultimately helped to bring the two sectors closer together than in most American Jewish communities. Finally, while neither city has been in a position to build major national institutions, both have provided important leaders for the professional and voluntary spheres for all of American Jewry and are known as sources of talent for the entire Jewish community.

Another common characteristic of the two cities is that suburbanization in both has proceeded to the point where there are almost no Jews residing in either Cleveland or Detroit proper. This situation, which is still relatively unusual in the larger American Jewish communities, despite strong tendencies in that direction in virtually all of them, is now beginning to have an influence on the character of Jewish life in both. In one sense it has stimulated already-active federations to engage in even more planning and intervention into the location of Jewish institutions than is true in the case of any other communities. The Cleveland Federation is making a major effort to preserve a critical mass of Jews in Shaker Heights, where the principal Jewish institutions are located; for Shaker Heights has now become an inner suburb and is beginning to suffer from the same problems of out-migration that transformed Cleveland proper a decade and a half earlier. The Detroit Federation has attempted to influence the direction of the movement of the Jewish population by buying land and locating institutions very early in the resettlement process, thereby not only holding down costs but also influencing Jewish settlement patterns by locating institutional complexes in key places. At the same time, there is no question but that increased suburbanization and fragmentation of the Jewish population among a number of suburbs has served to enhance congregationalism in both communities and to deplete the communal leadership pools as well.

Despite their many points of similarity, Cleveland and Detroit have taken different paths toward communal integration or the linkage of the several spheres. In Detroit only two congregations emerged from the nineteenth century as multigeneration institutions capable of maintaining the loyalty of members across the years, one Reform and one Conservative. The principle communal agencies, on the other hand, have been in existence since the turn of the century, separately but cooperatively. Each has developed a substantial constituency of its own, including both supporters and users. The Detroit Federation was created by the coming together of constituent agencies, which included the central agency for Jewish education, so that from its earliest days Detroit Jewry had established the principle of communal responsibility for Jewish education with proper community support.

In linked communities the congregational and communal sectors have developed common programs, formal and informal, that link them together in permanent and constructive ways. In both Cleveland and Detroit certain functions are performed jointly by the synagogues and the federation or its agencies, such as neighborhood rehabilitation in Cleveland and Jewish education in Detroit. The Detroit Federation has also developed an ambitious advance-planning program.

The characteristics of a linked community are best demonstrated by the Jewish educational situation in Detroit. There the United Hebrew Schools, the Federation's educational arm, has provided afternoon supplementary education for the community since 1919, serving the majority of those who avail themselves of Hebrew-school education at all levels. While their schools are part of a centrally directed system, many are conducted on synagogue premises and in partnership with the congregations. In the postwar period the United Hebrew Schools helped subsidize synagogue construction by prepaying on long-term classroom leases, thus providing funds for the congregations to build new buildings. In time the UHS began to provide synagogues with centralized purchasing and computer facilities on an informal basis, plus ancillary services at cost, to enable them to maintain their programs. In turn, synagogues that have entered into a partnership with the United Hebrew Schools do not maintain their own Hebrew schools but instead send their children to the appropriate branches of the United Hebrew Schools, whether on their own premises or not. Thus it was through the community's involvement in education that institutionalized links were formed with most of the synagogues in the city, links that held fast until suburbanization began to lead to the proliferation of independent congregational schools.

By contrast, very strong congregations substantially antedated the

Cleveland Federation and many of the communal institutions; education there followed the general American Jewish pattern and became segmented among the synagogues, except on the higher levels, where the central agency did come in to provide common services. On the other hand, the federation supplied some neighborhood services, supervision of kashruth, and the like, which have linked its work very closely with that of the congregations in ways that would still be deemed unusual in most communities.

Los Angeles

Los Angeles is a community that is in the process of tranformation from the segmented to the linked form. While only a fraction of that of New York, Los Angeles's size, when combined with the dispersed character of the city, does generate a certain tendency toward diffusion in Jewish ranks. However, the organized Jewish community has been influenced by other factors to create a network of institutions more closely linked to one another than in any other Jewish community of over 100,000.

The Los Angeles Federation came into being in its present form in 1959, through a merger of the original philanthropic federation (established in 1912) and the local Jewish community council (hence its name: Jewish Federation–Council of Greater Los Angeles), which ended a protracted conflict between the two bodies. So complete was the merger that the community-relations function is now undertaken by a standing committee of the Federation-Council. In the 1960s the Federation began to provide subsidies for synagogue schools. Then in 1973 it established a broadly based committee on Jewish life, with strong synagogue representation, to plan how to increase these interinstitutional linkages across the board. The committee has proposed far-reaching changes designed to give the Federation a key role in the overall development and management of all aspects of Jewish communal life, including those in the religious-congregational sphere, in a federal manner. Many of these proposals are now in the process of being implemented.

Los Angeles's geographical location resulted in its being settled primarily by American-born Jews, who came with the organizational skills characteristic of the American culture and did not have the tendencies toward fragmentation usual among Jewish immigrants from the Old World. Moreover, the fact that the local community never depended upon a compact inner-city neighborhood to provide a framework for organized Jewish life, but had to build its institutions from the first on the model that has now become common in a metropolitan era, enabled the community to start its development from the point that others are just now reaching. Having never established institutions that require neighborhoods for survival, the community is able to experiment with institutions that are built upon dispersed patterns of living and to seek to forge links within that context rather than adapt institutions designed for other patterns of settlement. Further, the fact that Los Angeles was transformed as a Jewish community by the huge migration of Jews to the area after World War II has made it into one of the Jewish frontiers of the contemporary world, where openness to innovation has consistently been greater than in more established regions.

Los Angeles has gained a certain strength from being the West Coast headquarters of the great countrywide Jewish institutions, although their presence has served to retard the drive toward unity, primarily because they bring East Coast quarrels into the Los Angeles community. Nevertheless, as the leadership of those branch institutions becomes increasingly rooted in Los Angeles, the institutions themselves are pulled more closely into the local orbit.

Denver and Minneapolis: A Study in Contrasts

A preliminary survey indicates that in Jewish communities of fifteen to forty thousand persons, the most important factors shaping their organization seem to be the presence of unusual individuals who have been able to forge links across the several spheres. If we contrast Denver, a segmented community, with Minneapolis, a linked community, we will get a good picture of how these two forms of local communal structure differ. The communities are essentially the same size and age, both are located west of the Mississippi River, and both serve as centers of Jewish life for large surrounding areas. They differ, however, in the quality of the leadership that developed in each community in its formative stages.

Denver is an extremely segmented community in which community-wide institutions barely existed for many years. Jewish life was primarily confined to a handful of congregations with little communication between them, each functioning almost as a separate community but offering a minimal program for its members. Communal institutions have emerged primarily since World War II, during which time Denver's

Jewish population has been at least partially transformed by in-migration. However, these have not become umbrella institutions but instead have developed specialized constituencies much like the congregations. The Jewish Community Center is the closest thing to a linking institution that exists in the city, since the federation confines itself to a very narrow range of activities, and even the Center has become more like a secular congregation than an all-embracing communal institution. In the realm of Jewish education, only recently has a central agency been established, but it is too soon to evaluate its role in the community.

Minneapolis, on the other hand, had the benefit of leaders with a strong communal outlook, who sought to create communal institutions that would link the community from the first. The community's leading Conservative congregation was actually founded by products of the communal Talmud Torah. Moreover, no Minneapolis congregation was able to develop the kind of loyalty in its early years that characterized the three principle congregations in Denver. Thus none was able to compete for the attention of the Jews in the way that the communal institutions were attempting to do. Even now, when the surviving congregations have acquired very serious multigeneration constituencies, they have had to retain their commitment to communal institutions and goals because it is expected of them. Their leaders have had to follow their congregations in this, however reluctantly at times. Thus Jewish education in Minneapolis has always been primarily a communal function. The federation has consistently been strong and the community has consistently supported community-wide institutions, most recently a Jewish community center that has made every effort to break out of the "secular-synagogue" pattern. Moreover, synagogue leaders, including the rabbis, are significantly involved in all phases of the community's activities as a matter of course, not necessarily without tensions but in meaningful ways nonetheless.

INTEGRATED COMMUNITIES

In a few communities in the United States a communal superstructure has emerged in such a way that the congregations are formally linked into it. The Jewish Federation of Camden County, New Jersey, is a prime example. It is a multipurpose operating agency rather than simply a fund-raising and planning body, with the various communal functions provided through Federation committees or divisions. At the same time the synagogues, though maintaining formally independent structures, are built into the same Federation network, having representation as such within the Federation's governing structure and providing certain services as arms of the community (read: Federation) with appropriate funding from communal sources. This arrangement comes closest to being a kehillah in the American framework. It has managed not so much to eliminate rivalry and tension between the two main sectors as to force the management of tension into a single framework more or less across the board. In such integrated communities, there is probably a wider sharing of leadership, since it is harder to draw a distinction between communal and congregational organizations and functions, thus making both equally attractive to the same cadres.

CONGREGATIONAL COMMUNITIES

Only the very smallest Jewish communities remain congregational communities, although, in fact, most Jewish communities had their origins in this form. As the term implies, a congregational community is one in which the entire range of communal activities is contained within a single congregation. Even where a nominally independent Jewish organization, such as a B'nai B'rith lodge or Hadassah chapter, exists, all tend to be members of the single congregation, since it offers the only point of religious affiliation locally. This is naturally a phenomenon of very small communities, where there are only enough Jews for one congregation and where, as is usually the case in small cities and towns, local citizens are expected to maintain some form of religious tie.

Until the recent influx of Jews from Philadelphia settling in its outer reaches, Norristown, Pennsylvania, was a prime example of such a congregational community, in which the congregation saw itself as the Jewish center and covered the entire gamut of Jewish activities, from the Allied Jewish Appeal to community relations. Its rabbi holds the title of executive director, and the synagogue-center is a member of the CJF.

The early colonial communities were all congregational communities in this sense: they embraced the entire range of activities at any given time, including social welfare, cemeteries, education, and the like. Recently there has been a trend toward the revival of the congregational community in smaller cities, where the congregation created by the first wave of Jewish settlers was later supplemented by another founded by the second wave, usually after the first turned Reform. Now, with the shrinkage in numbers and level of traditionalism in those communities, the tendency is to combine both the traditional and Reform congregations under a single roof and within a single organizational structure, with due provision for both manifestations of Jewish tradition to the extent that there is any desire for them.

Thus, for example, Decatur, Illinois, united its two synagogues in the early 1960s and built a new edifice for them, which is used to accommodate the entire range of Jewish communal activity. The B'nai B'rith lodge and Hadassah chapter, while nominally separate, draw their membership almost exclusively from the congregational pool, perhaps including a few people who do not otherwise identify with the congregation.

Because this form of community is usually found in very small cities, the tendency is for the voluntary leadership to overshadow the rabbinate or any other form of professional leadership. Small communities rarely have their pick of rabbis and frequently find themselves having to make do with those who are unable to achieve success in larger communities. The major exceptions to this occur in communities located near metropolitan centers, where rabbis with other interests find "easy" congregations, or near major universities, which are often able to obtain bright young rabbis pursuing their doctorates. These rabbis frequently have a great impact, although by the very nature of their individual interests they are not always committed to exerting their utmost for the local community, and in any case they tend to move on after earning their degrees.

The voluntary leadership, on the other hand, may well consist of people of considerable talent drawn to the community for business or professional reasons, who must make a Jewish life for themselves. This is particularly true in university communities, where substantial numbers of Jewish academics are available for communal life. Because of the very smallness of the place they are drawn into more active Jewish living and Jewish service than might be the case were they located in larger communities where their needs would be satisfied by others, including more specialized organizations.

While some communities in all six categories are thriving, there seems to be an overall tendency toward greater integration within each category and even some movement in that direction across categories. The expansion of communal activities and the very complexity of contemporary life have combined to force this trend. As in the world generally, it is becoming increasingly difficult to separate activities and functions into different sectors or spheres, and somehow order has to be forged out of potentially chaotic competition. Thus the situation today differs from that of the 1930s, when everybody went his own way and did whatever he or she wanted, a situation that could be tolerated in a less complex era even if it was not efficient or pleasant. Today organizations and institutions must work out reasonable arrangements for living together. Moreover, the high cost of providing services is beginning to be an added incentive for collaboration.

8

Institutions
and Decision Makers

FOUR BASIC DIVISIONS

The relationships among the institutions and activities of the organized American Jewish community have been shaped by certain accepted canons that serve to divide them: into so-called religious and
secular spheres on one hand, and into public and private sectors, on
the other. The protagonists of that community are divided by their
roles into "cosmopolitans" and "locals," as well as into professionals
and volunteers.

"Religious" and "Secular"

The organization of the functions of the American Jewish community
and how those functions are perceived by its members reflect patterns
absorbed from the American Protestant environment. On one hand,
there are ritual-oriented activities seen as belonging to the synagogues
and their confederations. These have been labeled "religious" and are
rarely touched by the community functioning in its capacity as a whole.
On the other hand, there are the welfare, social-service, and Israel-
oriented concerns of the community, which have been treated as "secular" and, with few exceptions, are located in those institutions of the
community outside the province of the synagogues. In between are the
educational and cultural functions, which are sometimes treated as reli-

gious and sometimes as secular—and often suffer because they fall between the two stools.

This division developed out of the American milieu with its emphasis
on the separation of church and state, and was enhanced in the early days
of the twentieth century by the relatively sharp division between those
Jews who concerned themselves with their shuls and those who, while
members of synagogues and temples, were really far more interested in
welfare and community-relations activities, which they saw as divorced
from religion per se. This led to the rise of two separate groups of
decision makers, a development reinforced by the fact that the other
divisions tended to enhance the separation between "religious" and
"secular." The synagogues were conceived of as private activities—in
effect the exclusive province of their members—and the so-called secular
activities were increasingly regarded as public, that is, as belonging to the
whole Jewish community. Moreover, professionals in the synagogues
were recruited from a very different group from those serving the secular
organizations. The former were trained as religious functionaries in seminaries, while the latter were primarily social workers drawn from highly
secularist environments.

Despite all the forces for separation, the division could not and did not
remain a hard and fast one. Indeed, it has been breaking down since the
end of World War II. First, there was the great expansion of certain
educational and cultural functions that could not be neatly divided between the two. In effect they were divided functionally over the course
of time, but the division could not be made complete because the activities themselves suffered in the course of being divided. Moreover, as the
synagogues grew in power in the 1950s and began to see themselves as
the true custodians of American Jewish life, they began to claim authoritative roles in areas previously reserved to the secular side, particularly in community relations and social services for middle-income families who were synagogue members or potential members. Although they
have since pulled back from their forward positions in most of these
areas, the residue of involvement remains—the wall, as it were, has been
breached.

Finally, the whole thrust of Jewish tradition militated against such an
artificially enforced separation. As those concerned with the secular side
became more involved in Jewish life, they began to consider their services
to the community to be not merely social aid and welfare but rather as
functions that had a traditional Jewish content, no less so than those of

the synagogues. Nevertheless, while ideologically and functionally the lines between the two are weakening, structurally the separation between religious and secular institutions remains as strong as ever.

"Public and "Private"

The division of the Jewish community into religious and secular sectors has been substantially reinforced by implicit notions as to what is public and what is private in American Jewish life. Unlike the religious-secular division, which is perceived in at least a commonsense way by the leaders of the community, there is little conscious perception of the public-private distinction—partly because there is some notion that where governmental activities are concerned, all Jewish communal activities are private. Nevertheless, the distinction does exist and decision makers do operate in light of it.

The activities sponsored or funded by the federations and their constituent agencies are understood to be the public activities of the American Jewish community. Synagogue activities are regarded as private, the exclusive domain of their members. Decisions regarding the establishment of synagogues, their location and relocation, the amount of money charged for the right to participate in their programs, the physical plant constructed to house them—all these remain the prerogative of congregational members or leaders regardless of overall community interests or needs.

Only in the last few years has the notion of the synagogues being private enterprises been questioned within Jewish communal circles, and then only privately, in a belated recognition that the modern American congregation, which may have one or two thousand member families and usually provides a range of services that goes far beyond simple maintenance of the weekly and yearly worship schedule, is not the same as a collection of twenty or forty men gathered together primarily for purposes of daily prayer. In part this recognition is a response to the synagogue's encroachment upon the traditionally communal sector. In part it is a reflection of the suburbanization of American Jewry: synagogues have become the major, if not the only, centers of community activities in their respective suburbs, and movement of a large synagogue from one neighborhood to another affects the whole course of Jewish life within a particular locale.

Even if the synagogue is eventually absorbed into the public sphere of the Jewish community, there will still be a private sphere, comprising the social clubs, chapters, and lodges that to a large extent serve the associational needs of American Jews. In traditional Jewish fashion, which does not recognize a completely autonomous private sphere, these groups either are organized for ostensibly communal or charitable purposes or are swept up into aspects of the community's public life, as witness their role in the annual campaign. Despite their involvement in charitable activities or communal service, however, the various lodges, fraternal associations, and country clubs belong to the private sphere. Policy making in and for this private sphere undoubtedly does have some effect on the Jewish community, but it is relatively minor, something that is not true in the case of the synagogues, despite their claim to private status.

"Cosmopolitans" and "Locals"

The distinction between public and private, as it is implicitly recognized in organized American Jewish life today, follows very much along the lines of the division into what social scientists have described as "cosmopolitans" and "locals." Briefly, cosmopolitans regard the community as a total entity and maintain connections and involvements across all of it. While their cosmopolitanism is first defined in relation to a particular local community, after they develop a cosmopolitan outlook toward the local community they almost invariably also take a cosmopolitan view of the larger world of which that community is a part. Locals, on the other hand, are persons whose involvement and connections are confined to a small segment of the total community—a neighborhood, a particular social group, or, in Jewish life, a particular synagogue, organization, or club—and do not extend to the community as a whole, except indirectly. Moreover, their perceptions of the larger world are also quite limited, based as they are on localistic involvements.

Everybody, it might be said, is either a cosmopolitan or a local. To a very real extent this is a natural social division. Yet all cosmopolitans have clearly localistic needs and seek more intimate ties than are afforded by connections to the community in the abstract or even to a set of institutions, which must inevitably be depersonalized to some degree. Moreover, locals can be mobilized for essentially cosmopolitan purposes when those purposes strike home. Thus every community needs institutions devoted to serving both cosmopolitan and local needs, plus the local needs of cosmopolitans and the cosmopolitan needs of locals.

In the Jewish community the organizations and agencies that fall within the federation family generally represent the cosmopolitan interests, and consequently attract cosmopolitans to leadership positions. The synagogues, on the other hand, represent localistic needs and interests first and foremost. As a result, the leadership they attract consists of a very high percentage of locals. The exceptions are the cosmopolitans who lead synagogues with predominantly cosmopolitan memberships and cosmopolitan rabbis who are leaders of locals because they need a congregational base.

Most institutions combine cosmopolitan and local representation, and functions are generally sorted out between them to reflect cosmopolitan and local interests. In some cases the functions are not easily allocated, leading to conflict along cosmopolitan-local lines. The evolution of the management, content, and character of Jewish education in America affords an example.

The first professional Jewish educators in the United States had a pronounced cosmopolitan outlook. Imbued as they were with the spirit of Jewish nationalism, developed at the turn of the century and manifested most clearly in the Zionist movement, they regarded the Jewish community as a totality. Accordingly, they attempted to develop community-oriented schools designed to teach the Jewish cultural heritage to American-born children through a broad-based curriculum that was rooted in a knowledge of the Hebrew language and included both the ritual and national components of Jewish life. The schools they established educated only a small number of children but produced the only native-born Jewishly literate element that American Jewry has ever known, at least until the recent development of day schools.[1]

While the educators in question succeeded in laying the foundation for an American Jewish educational system, they failed substantially in their primary goals. The majority of American Jews were more interested in effecting a successful integration into the general society than in submitting to an intensive Jewish educational process. Moreover, with a few notable exceptions, local communities were rarely in a position to provide the kind of institutional or financial support necessary for the establishment of true community schools. Most of the embryonic federations were interested in social-welfare services of a secular nature but not in Jewish education, with its "foreign" or "religious" overtones. Only occasionally did the cosmopolitans among the voluntary leadership in the community evince a concern for Jewish education to match that of the professional educators.

In the 1920s and 1930s responsibility for Jewish education began to pass into the hands of the synagogues. This was in part a natural development. As American Jews moved from their original settlements in the large cities into second-generation neighborhoods, they founded synagogues, often Conservative in affiliation, to satisfy their immediate Jewish needs. Prime among these needs was the Jewish education of their children, and before long each new synagogue boasted its own congregational school. Despairing of any other alternatives, many professional educators abetted the transfer of Jewish education to the synagogues on the ground that there was no one else to do the job; they also hoped that the Conservative movement would echo their cosmopolitan sentiments regarding the Jewish community. The educators settled for the establishment of central agencies for Jewish education which represented the community's interest, such as it was. But these bureaus of Jewish education, dominated by cosmopolitans, were confined to an advisory role.

While the Conservative movement did endorse a cosmopolitan outlook, the individual Conservative synagogues, being primarily localistic institutions, pursued their own local interests. Modern Orthodox synagogues, following the trail blazed by the Conservatives, did the same, as did the Reform temples when in time they extended their Jewish educational programs beyond the Sunday school. Thus the synagogues gradually whittled away at the cosmopolitan orientations of Jewish education.

The rabbinical leadership, in particular, advanced the postulate that American Jewish children were not likely to identify with a Jewish national culture, and the curriculum of the congregational schools was shaped accordingly. The hours and days of instruction were reduced. In place of an emphasis on Hebrew the schools stressed the teaching of "synagogue skills" and congregational loyalty, on the assumption that the dominent concerns of Jewish children in America were likely to be religious, like those of all other Americans. Increasingly, Jewish education moved in localistic directions, as congregational rabbis made it clear that their primary interest was in fostering loyalty to their own institutions.

The growth of synagogue membership in the 1950s confirmed the triumph of congregational control over Jewish education, and by the early 1960s Jewish education had become a localistic preserve in virtually every Jewish community. But as the sixties wore on, Jewish young people, like their counterparts in the larger society, began to seek a broader view of life than that afforded by their suburban environments. In the process they turned away from Jewish identification—more precisely, from congregational life. Since they had been taught that Judaism was, in effect, limited to the synagogue (which they now associated with the privileged provincialism of suburbia), when they "lost their faith" they had no other points of Jewish identification and concluded that their Jewishness was irrelevant.

The Six-Day War, coupled with the emergence of the black-power movement, reawakened Jewish ethnic impulses in many of these young people, leading them to see for the first time other possibilities inherent in Jewish attachment beyond those of the synagogue and its ritual. Ironically, it was precisely those elements of Jewish civilization that their fathers had rejected as unlikely to reach American Jewish youngsters—the national-cultural elements revolving around Israel—that proved to have real drawing power in the end.

Jewish educators and the Jewish community at large are beginning to respond to this new thrust from both cosmopolitan and local perspectives. The cosmopolitans in the community look at this as an opportunity to foster a greater community role in the Jewish educational process at all points. Many are seeking a broader Jewish curriculum than that current in the synagogues, often through day schools that at least nominally have closer ties to the cosmopolitan elements in the community than do the afternoon Hebrew schools. The locals have come to realize that Israel is one of the few forces capable of inspiring their children, and hence are embracing a more cosmopolitan orientation simply in order to serve their own localistic goals.

This new concern, in turn, has led to new demands for community responsibility in Jewish education, demands that are still resisted by most synagogues. However, the problem of soaring educational costs has prompted an increasing number of synagogues to explore communal subsidization of their schools, although without communal control, opening another wedge for the discussion of a reorientation of structures and priorities. Today Jewish education remains the primary battleground between cosmopolitans and locals in the Jewish community. The outcome of that battle will undoubtedly be tied to the question of whether the synagogues will continue to be regarded as private institutions or will be absorbed more fully into the public sphere.

Professionals and Volunteers

In addition to the division between cosmopolitans and locals, leadership in the American Jewish community is split into professionals and volunteers. The professionals are subdivided according to whether they were trained in religious or secular institutions. It is safe to say that the American Jewish community boasts the most professional leadership of any in the world, probably the most professional of any in Jewish history. (The roots of this undoubtedly lie in the commitment to professionalization that is a hallmark of the larger American society.) The United States became enamored of professionalism in the 1840s, and since then true professionalism has become as much a mark of the American approach to doing the world's work as splendid amateurism was of the British approach. The Jewish community has imbibed that commitment to professionalism and has consistently moved to professionalize its own organizations and institutions.

The day-to-day business of the Jewish community is now almost exclusively in the hands of professionals—or at least people who are paid for their services, even if they do not meet professional standards or consider themselves as forever committed to Jewish careers. Because these professionals are involved on a daily basis with the problems of the community, are to a greater or lesser extent committed to such involvement for the course of their adult lives, and are more or less trained to occupy the positions they hold, they exercise great influence in the policy-making processes of the community.

On the other hand, the number of voluntary leaders has not diminished. Parallel roles for professionals and volunteers have developed in virtually every Jewish organization and institution, allowing for extensive participation by both. What is not fixed is how professionals and volunteers relate to each other. Generally speaking, there is at least an underlying tension between the two, though not necessarily a counterproductive one.

This tension is most noticeable in the synagogues, where from time to time it is likely to erupt into confrontation. The essential intimacy of the leadership circle in the synagogue creates a potential for conflict that might not exist in other institutions. Moreover, the gap in interests and values between the chief synagogue professionals—rabbis, cantors, executive directors—and the voluntary leadership is likely to be greater in the synagogue than elsewhere. The tension is further aggravated because both the professionals (the rabbis, in this instance) and the volunteers can lay special claim to a central, authoritative role. The rabbi's claim is based on his role as spokesman for the transcendent goals of Judaism, while that of the voluntary leadership is based on the nature of congregational government in both the Jewish and American traditions (to say nothing of the fact that they provide the financial support for the institution). Since both sources of authority are institutionalized (and necessary) within the congregational framework, conflict is inevitable—and indeed there have been instances where it attained legendary proportions.

In some cases the rivalry between professionals and volunteers is accommodated by a separation of functions and in some, by a mixing of functions. As a general rule, wherever the requirements of the profession are most exclusive and demanding, and the need for professional expertise has been established, separation of functions tends to be the norm; wherever the line between professional competence and volunteer talent is least distinct, sharing tends to be the norm. Thus in Jewish education and certain Jewish social services not only are operations placed in the hands of professionals, but so is policy-making power. Voluntary leadership tends to confine itself to ratifying policies suggested by professionals, stating general organizational goals and principles, and finding the necessary financial and community support for their enterprise.

On the other hand, the lines that divide professionals and volunteers tend to be relatively weak in community-relations and federation work. Professionals are simply people who work full time at what they are doing and cannot claim to have very much expertise (other than experience) for handling what are essentially political tasks. They become influential because they do spend all their working time at what they do and consequently know the situation better than the voluntary leadership. At the same time, some volunteers may have special talents, capabilities, or positions—particularly political positions—that place them in strategic positions vis-à-vis the professionals and give them major roles in the decision-making process in those arenas where their talents, capabilities, or positions are useful.

This relatively undefined situation prevails in the communal arena primarily because the American Jewish community has no class of "professional politicians" like that of Eastern and Central Europe before the Holocaust or Latin America today. However, lack of a recognizable group of politicians does not eliminate the need for people to fill political roles. Thus it falls to people drawn from ostensibly nonpolitical channels to perform the functions of political mobilization and decision making that are the province of politicians in other systems, without their being perceived—or perceiving themselves—in that light. As a result, social workers, rabbis, businessmen, and occasionally academics have to take up the tasks of professional politicians without either being chosen for that role through normal political means or being recognized for what they are in a positive way.

The very sources of the professional and volunteer leadership help to mark the division. By and large the volunteers are recruited from among the affluent elements in the community. This is partly because the hierarchy of influence among the voluntary leadership is often determined by the size of their contributions and partly because the costs of playing a leadership role are so great that only the well-to-do can afford the time and money to do so. The only exceptions to this are organizations like the Jewish War Veterans, which, because they draw their membership from a population having relatively modest incomes, have traditionally provided subsidies to enable their leadership to function in that capacity.

To be a voluntary participant in the Jewish community one must be able to spend time—often a great deal of time—away from one's career or business and be prepared to pay for travel and maintenance out of personal funds, because voluntary leaders are not expected to take money from the organizations they serve. Aside from successful businessmen and professionals and perhaps young lawyers associated with law firms where there is a tradition of participation in Jewish communal life, the only people who can contribute the requisite time are academicians, and they are limited by their inability to spend the money required to maintain an active role. Thus, of necessity wealth becomes an important factor in determining who the voluntary leadership will be.

However, the situation is not quite as stark as it seems. Obviously it is least true in the case of small synagogues and clubs (the most localistic institutions) and most true in the case of UJA (the most cosmopolitan). Even in situations where wealth is an important factor, it is not the only measure of leadership. The wealthiest are not necessarily the most important leaders. There is apparently some threshold of prosperity past which most persons are relatively equal in the pursuit of leadership roles. A man of relatively modest means may choose to contribute a high portion of his resources to the Jewish community and be recognized accordingly, while a very wealthy man who is unwilling to make an equivalent allocation will be denied recognition.

Moreover, the willingness to give must be coupled with a willingness to serve. Large contributors may or may not choose to be active participants, while smaller contributors may be willing to donate their time, energy, and talents. Evaluation of a person's contribution is usually based on the norm in the group to which he belongs. Thus an academician can be considered a large contributor by giving what is, in absolute terms, a small amount of money. Finally, certain old families who have a tradition of responsibility for communal affairs are recognized as community leaders on the basis of long-standing precedents, even when they cannot compete in wealth with newer elements.

With important exceptions, professional American Jewish leadership historically has been recruited from two sources: immigrants to the United States and the lower middle class. For both, Jewish professions have been at the very least the means to make a decent living and at best have provided an opportunity for advancement up the socioeconomic ladder. Except in the field of social case work, there is actually no tradition of noblesse oblige that draws people from well-to-do backgrounds into full-time communal service. But as the Jewish community becomes more affluent, young men and women from such families are beginning to enter the Jewish professions for reasons of personal interest. This is particularly true in the communal-welfare and community-relations fields.

In part this pattern is a legacy of the emancipation ideology that has dominated Jewish communal life for the past several centuries, whether implicitly or explicitly: the view that a person is successful only if his accomplishments are attained in the general world. If he goes into specifically Jewish occupations, it is taken as a confession that he cannot succeed outside the limited arena of the Jewish community. Jewish activities were not deemed to be serious or deserving of the attention of talented people; in fact, the more Jewish the occupation, the less attractive it was to Jews seeking careers. Many of the most able Jewish professionals today did not set out to become members of the Jewish civil service but in effect "backed into" their careers. This is a problem that Jewish professionals have had to overcome in order to gain status in the eyes of the voluntary leadership and to maintain their own self-esteem.

Nevertheless, it should be noted that the American Jewish community has done very well in attracting professional talent and is in no way inferior to other polities in that respect. It has even been able to compete with the American government, as evinced by the existence of some lateral movement of personnel from Jewish service to the federal service and vice versa.

THE DECISION MAKERS: THEIR ROLES AND FUNCTIONS

The pattern of leadership in American Jewish life can be seen in the roles of influential (or potentially influential) groups in the American Jewish community today. These categories, in turn, fall into three divisions: congregational decision makers (rabbis, congregational boards), communal decision makers (communal workers, cosmopolitan volunteers), and peripherals (academics, youth, and women). Finally, there is the Jewish press, which stands in a class apart.

Congregational Decision Makers

RABBIS

At the very least, rabbis function as decision makers within their congregations, while the more talented, important, well known, or cosmopolitan among them are able to build upon their rabbinical roles to become influential in the larger arena of Jewish communal life. By and large, rabbis tend to be restricted to their congregations or to their synagogue movements by the communal sector and by their own reluctance to venture outside the area in which their authority is rarely questioned.[2]

There are many reasons for the restrictions implicitly placed on rabbinical leadership. In part they have to do with the fact that rabbis play such a central role in their own religious-congregational bailiwick that they hesitate to participate in other communal areas of activity, where their roles might not be as prominent. Since there is generally little shifting of leadership roles from area to area, except in the case of the most important voluntary leaders or in exceptional circumstances, rabbis would be discouraged from doing so in any case.

Rabbis are further deterred from broader participation because of the particular way in which they are regarded in the American Jewish community. Rabbis traditionally functioned as interpreters of the Law, and as such were naturally involved in the entire range of communal activities; they formed the judicial branch, so to speak, of the Jewish polity.

However, most American Jews now consider rabbis as "ministers" in the Protestant sense, which means that they are set apart from the laity— a non-Jewish concept, incidentally—by virtue of their special pastoral functions and special responsibilities to maintain Jewish tradition, in itself an isolating factor in the contemporary Jewish community.

When they leave the congregational setting it is difficult for rabbis to shift roles, as they would have to do were they to participate in, say, communal-welfare activities. They would have to participate as if among equals, with neither the special competence of professionals nor any claim to special recognition by virtue of their rabbinical positions. Equality in such a situation is uncomfortable for both sides, since neither knows how to respond properly to the other. Thus it is more convenient for a rabbi simply not to participate. The few men who transcend this limitation are more often than not Reform rabbis, who, though they suffer the disabilities of having a special pastoral function, are at least not expected to be very different from laymen in their patterns of Jewish observance. Moreover, some Reform congregations—usually the distinguished "first congregations" that serve the community's old families— expect their rabbis to be moderately active. However, even the involvement of such rabbis seems to be declining.

In recent years the CJF has made an effort to overcome this division by attracting rabbis to their annual General Assembly, perhaps the most important gathering of the American Jewish community as a whole. They have induced local federations to provide special grants to rabbis from their communities (and also to college professors and students), thus encouraging their attendance. The hope is that this will stimulate them to participate in federation activities in their local communities. Whatever its other implications, this effort is another reflection of the growing breakdown between the religious and communal divisions.

The field of education and culture is perhaps the one area in which rabbis can participate fully, although rabbis are not especially eager to become professional leaders in this area for at least two reasons. First, Jewish education tends to enjoy a relatively low status in the eyes of the voluntary leaders who control their destinies as rabbis—all the preachments about the importance of Jewish education to the contrary. The fact is that a rabbi simply cannot advance in prestige in the community through an involvement in Jewish educational and Jewish cultural activities, which are generally relegated to the young or to specialized constituencies. Second, American rabbis rarely have the training or time to develop the degree of excellence in Jewish scholarship that would give them the status they demand—and receive—in the pulpit. Professors of Judaic studies, and even simple Hebrew teachers, are frequently more knowledgeable Jewishly than are congregational rabbis. Thus it is far better for rabbis to speak in behalf of Jewish education to nonparticipants in the educational process than to attempt to become teachers themselves.

Beginning in the 1950s rabbinical training came to be an accepted and even desirable prerequisite for major positions in Jewish education. Young men seeking to be Jewish educators saw rabbinical training as important for their own education and the rabbinical title as a means of substantially enhancing their status. The seminaries, in turn, encouraged this trend in an effort to increase their own dominance of the educational-cultural sphere.[3] Today an increasing proportion of bureaus of Jewish education, day schools, Hillel Foundations, and Jewish educational camps are led by men with rabbinical training who have chosen to specialize in Jewish education rather than serve in the pulpit. Nevertheless, the two fields of specialization have remained quite separate.

A few rabbis are able to use their congregational bases to move into broader community politics. Generally these are the men who under other circumstances might have become professional politicians and who chose the rabbinate because it offered the opportunities to enter the larger arenas of Jewish communal politics. Such rabbis—for instance, Stephen S. Wise and Abba Hillel Silver—were more common a generation ago, when the organized American Jewish community was structurally far less institutionalized than it is today and professional workers were less common. Now it is more difficult for rabbis to make the move. Congregations are more complex than they used to be and make greater demands on their rabbis, leaving them less time for outside activity. Moreover, the overwhelming institutionalization of communal activities has increased the amount of time and energy necessary to move into communal leadership circles, and professionalization has created leadership cadres that rival the rabbis for roles as central decision makers. When the Jewish community was smaller, its leadership was concentrated in fewer hands, and its functions (and finances) were more limited, a few dynamic rabbis could rise to positions of great eminence by dint of their virtuosity. None of those conditions prevail today, and the virtuoso rabbi has gone the way of other virtuoso leaders.[4]

Another reason why rabbis are not found in the forefront of American

Jewish leadership is that synagogues are essentially localistic institutions, and rabbis, no matter how cosmopolitan their outlook, must adapt themselves to localistic needs and interests in order to maintain their congregational bases. Many rabbis are themselves simply locals and therefore have no problem serving as leaders of locals. Others are cosmopolitans by nature and inclination, but recognize that their role in the community depends upon their maintaining a local base. Such rabbis tend to become spokesmen for localistic interests at a time when "communal responsibility" has become the watchword of the central leadership, which further alienates them from the cosmopolitans in the community and drives a wedge between them and the community's other leadership cadres.

This problem tends to come to a head in two very practical ways: fund raising and community planning. Rabbis, as leaders of their congregations, must place congregational financial needs at the forefront of their concerns, often bringing them into implicit conflict with the local federation drive. While the common commitment to Israel acts to prevent overt conflict in this area, the tension is frequently there. It has been exacerbated since the Yom Kippur War, as Israel's need for funds took a jump upward even as its image was tarnished.[5] Squeezed by the diversion of funds toward the Jewish state, local institutions also faced great inflationary pressures, leading to open questioning of priorities for the first time in years. Within the local community, the rabbis' interest in preserving and even expanding congregational services to bind their members more closely to them often comes into conflict with the federations' interest in communalizing services on the principle of avoiding duplication, cutting costs, and providing more comprehensive coverage.

CONGREGATIONAL BOARDS

Since synagogues account for so much of Jewish activity in the United States today, the men and women who constitute the congregational boards of trustees are important decision makers, though they are rarely recognized as such. This lack of recognition stems from the fact that there are so many congregations in the United States, each controlling its own budget, hiring its own personnel, establishing its own program, and building its own facilities with little reference to any outside body.

These congregations spend at least $300 million a year and perhaps as much as $500 million. (Nobody knows the exact figure or even how to make a proper estimate.) This is equal to the amount of money that is contributed to the federations and UJA in the best years of their drives.

There are over forty-five hundred Jewish congregations in the United States, according to the fragmentary figures available. If the average congregational board consists of ten members (probably a low estimate), this would mean there are at least forty-five thousand congregational board members. In fact, the number is probably larger than that. When we add in the men who serve on congregational committees, the number of those involved increases even further, and our knowledge of what they do and how they do it diminishes even more.[6]

Every form of decision making is to be found in the government of Jewish congregations in America, ranging from the most autocratic—in which one man decides all congregational policy, hires, fires, and decides as he pleases on all issues—to situations where the most open forms of town-meeting democracy prevail, and the congregation governs itself without the mediation of any board.

In the larger congregations, with boards of thirty or more, actual policy making may be confined to an inner circle within the formal board. Let us assume that decision making is shared among five people in each congregation—again, probably an underestimate. That means there are twenty thousand significant decision makers governing the synagogues of the United States. At this stage of our knowledge it would be difficult to describe the typical congregational board member or even the typical congregational board. What unites them is their essentially localistic commitment to the primary needs of their own particular congregations. It is rare to find a congregational board that, in its official capacity, will concern itself with the needs of the larger community, even when its members may otherwise be major communal leaders.

This fragmentation of outlook has great consequences for the community as a whole, particularly as regards the largest congregations, which have memberships of a thousand families or more. Its consequences are obviously far less important in congregations of fifty families. What is most important is that even congregations of medium size, whose actions are not likely to jolt the Jewish community as a whole the way those of the largest ones do, have a tremendous impact on the character of the community by virtue of their control over the education of their children. (While congregations are frequently formed because of a desire to provide Jewish schooling for the children of potential members, once they come into existence they take on a life of their own that relegates education to a secondary position. The maintenance of the congregation in a manner appropriate to the social and economic status of its members then becomes the prime concern, and Jewish education sinks to a lower rung in the hierarchy of priorities.)

Relations between rabbis and congregational boards stand at the heart of the congregational decision-making process. The variety is great here too, but three general models can be found. The congregational board or the most influential person in the congregation may simply dominate the rabbi, confining him to a role that involves conducting services and carrying out similar ritual chores. In some cases rabbis are not even allowed to attend congregational board meetings. Sometimes the diametrically opposite state of affairs prevails: the rabbi is so strong that he dominates the congregational board and leadership, which exists primarily to mediate between him and the congregation as a whole or to carry out his wishes whenever he does not want to be directly or extensively involved.

Normally, however, some kind of division of functions is worked out between the congregational leadership and the rabbi, with decision making shared in certain relatively clear-cut areas. This kind of modus vivendi will persist for years in many congregations, though every so often an issue will come along that does not fit easily into the established pattern; if the rabbi wins the ensuing conflict there will be a revised distribution of power in his favor, and if he loses the result will usually be his departure from the congregation.

Communal Decision Makers

COMMUNAL WORKERS

Communal workers gain their power on the basis of either expertise or day-to-day involvement with the problems of the community. Those who are employed by specialized agencies—Jewish community centers, hospitals, old-age homes, vocational services, family services, and the like —generally have suitable professional qualifications that give them the status of experts in their fields, with all that such a status implies in American society. Those who work in federations—managing the campaign, planning community operations, and so on—do not have that particular advantage but enjoy a position of control over the flow of information that reaches the voluntary workers. Their technical knowledge and perennial availability give them important decision-making roles unless they are directly challenged by the voluntary leadership.

This rarely happens because in most cases the voluntary leadership is not interested or does not feel competent enough to challenge them.

From time to time communal workers are challenged by members of the voluntary leadership on some basic issue. When that happens the challengers are frequently eased out of their positions, either by the professionals themselves or by the voluntary leadership, which seeks to avoid controversy of this sort. To some degree the professionals actually control the selection of the top leaders from the voluntary sector. Obviously they have relatively little control over who is to be made available for leadership positions, but among those who offer themselves for leadership, they can do a great deal of grooming and pruning.

The majority of today's communal workers outside the educational sphere have been trained as social workers, with legal training probably in second place. In relatively few cases are the senior civil servants of the Jewish community trained specifically for Jewish positions; usually they simply fall into such positions by chance—although this is less true among the younger workers. In an effort to overcome the personnel problem, Jewish agencies have tried to provide their recruits with the funds to attend secular schools for social-work training on condition that they serve the agencies for a specified period of time. In the past few years, several joint programs have been established by the CJF in cooperation with the local federations to recruit and train new personnel for junior executive positions in the federation movement. Programs have been initiated in Boston (Brandeis University), New York (Yeshiva University), Baltimore (University of Maryland and Baltimore Hebrew College), Cleveland (Case Western Reserve University), and Los Angeles (Hebrew Union College and University of Southern California).

What is notable about Jewish communal workers as a group is that so many of them came from relatively left-wing backgrounds. They originally entered the social-work field out of a desire to improve society, and they moved into the Jewish field at least partly because it afforded a means of advancement. Equally notable is their general lack of Jewish education. Indeed, for a long time the bulk of the Jewish communal workers were not even concerned with the specifically Jewish aspects of their programs. It has only been since the early 1960s, when they began to recognize that it was the Jewish aspects which gave their agencies a raison d'être, that they have become more concerned with their own Jewishness and the Jewish content of their programs.

For the most part, the communal workers are not well grounded in traditional Jewish learning or even in rudimentary knowledge of Jewish history, law, society, and customs. Consequently their deficiencies are most glaring when it comes to making decisions involving the Jewishness of their programs—in sharp contrast to their great expertise in other respects. Although many of them have become seriously interested in fostering the Jewish aspects of their work, they are in a difficult position when it comes to translating attitudes into concrete programs.

There is unquestionably a degree of rivalry between the rabbis and the Jewish communal workers, although the fact that they fill distinctly different roles prevents the competition from reaching excessive proportions except where there are direct conflicts of interest. Such conflicts of interest tend to arise when either side attempts to encroach upon what the other has determined to be its own sphere. In the 1950s and 1960s the synagogues were the chief aggressors in this regard, moving increasingly into social-service areas. At the same time, Jewish communal agencies began to compete with the synagogues in the areas of education and youth. Both thrusts have generated appropriately hostile responses. In some communities the struggle for control of particular areas of activity has become so significant that overt hostility has broken out between synagogue and communal workers. In others, the points of conflict are relatively intermittent, and hostilities are latent rather than manifest for the most part. The tensions are not as apparent among the voluntary leadership on either side, partly because of overlapping and partly because of the fact that professionals in general have become the initiators in the American Jewish community—as they so frequently are in the general American community—and hence the lion's share of conflict will naturally be generated by them.

JEWISH EDUCATORS

Jewish educators represent still another category of Jewish civil servants. They generally pass through different forms of training and pursue different career lines. While some men trained as rabbis become Jewish educators, most of them decided upon Jewish education as a career before entering rabbinical school. They seek a rabbinical degree because they perceive that, on the American Jewish scene, the rabbi has a position far exceeding that of an "ordinary" Jewish educator, no matter how talented the latter or how limited the former. Consequently they acquire rabbinical titles to protect themselves, to give them as authoritative a voice in the community as the congregational rabbis with whom they must serve.

It can fairly be said that the educators' decision-making role is confined to the sphere of Jewish education, that is, to schools or camps where they exercise authority as professionals. Their authority in such situations is that of experts and is given the respect that experts generally receive in the American Jewish community. However, their authority is limited by various external factors. Chief among these are the problems inherent in Jewish education in the United States: the ambivalence of parents as to the amount of Jewish education they wish their children to acquire, the problems of obtaining qualified teachers and adequate financial support, and the fact that most educational facilities are lodged in the synagogues, the leadership of which has other priorities.

Still, within this framework there is usually little interest in what the Jewish educators teach except on the part of the rabbi, who may intervene to assure that "loyalty to the institution" is given first priority. Beyond that, even the rabbis tend to pay little attention to the day-to-day operations of "their" schools. A Jewish educator may more or less do what he pleases in his school with little outside interference, provided he does not do anything that openly violates the Jewish communal consensus.

COSMOPOLITAN VOLUNTEERS

We know very little about the cosmopolitan voluntary leadership of the American Jewish community, but one thing that does mark them is their relative affluence, although wealth is by no means the only criterion of leadership or advancement. Cosmopolitan volunteers—serving preponderantly in the spheres of community relations, communal welfare, and Israel-overseas affairs—are a group for whom Jewish activity is a means for expressing Jewishness, as synagogue worship or observance of Jewish tradition is for others. In effect, their activity becomes their religion, and their observance is conditioned by the demands of communal life. Thus they do not necessarily see any need to observe the Jewish holidays or festivals, the dietary laws, the Sabbath, and the like. But their maintenance of the forms, traditions, and activities connected with Jewish communal work is every bit as systematic as that of traditionally observant Jews in the other sphere. Some of them are involved in communal leadership primarily for the honor of it, the traditional *koved,* but many others work as persistently and almost as many hours as their professional counterparts for little recognition. Moreover, they lay out large sums of money—in the form of contributions and in expenses—for the pleasure of participating on the highest planes of organized Jewish life.

Money and energy are thus key sources of such influence over decision making as the cosmopolitan volunteers have, although neither replaces talent when it comes to the actual decision-making process. Money may buy a man the presidency of an organization or agency and energy may put a man in a leadership position, but some kind of talent is necessary if a person is actually to have a share in making decisions. This is true only because of the role of the professionals in screening the advancement of the voluntary leadership. That is not to say that money does not wield some clout in and of itself. If the major donor to a local federation is interested, say, in a particular hospital, then the hospital may get a larger allocation than it might otherwise have received. But that kind of situation is more likely to arise in smaller communities, where one man can wield a great deal of influence over the campaign.

In at least one area—fund raising—volunteers are the dominant decision makers. No matter how much professional help is provided, only the voluntary leadership, the men who give the money, are able to influence others to give money. Moreover, they usually feel that they have as much expertise about fund raising as anyone else, and therefore they are less likely to defer to the ideas or demands of the professionals. By and large, the professionals recognize this and are content to leave major decision-making responsibilities in the area of fund raising to the volunteers. Volunteer leaders may also play a role equal to that of the professionals in areas primarily requiring political finesse because there, too, no particular expertise can be called into play except that of talent and experience.

Peripheral Participants

ACADEMICS

Academics are here treated as a separate factor in Jewish communal life, not because as a group they exercise any particular role in the community, but because they represent a special category that weaves in and out of the American Jewish communal structure. Academics enjoy great prestige among American Jews, synthesizing as they do the traditional Jewish concern for learning with success in the larger world. Furthermore, Jews are heavily represented, indeed overrepresented, in the academic field (this for a whole host of reasons, having to do in many respects with the very fact of their being Jewish).

Some academics, although relatively few to date, find the Jewish community an appropriate outlet for their desire to be active in public affairs and to seek the implementation of their ideals. Thus while there is a general complaint within the Jewish community that most academics are alienated from it (a complaint the evidence shows to be untrue, or at least highly exaggerated), there has always been a handful of very important communal leaders drawn from academic ranks.[7] By combining the resources at their disposal with a willingness to serve the Jewish people, they become very influential indeed, particularly since they are almost the only leaders in the community who do not gain power because they are employed by the community or give large sums of money to it. Perhaps the biggest problem of academics in pursuing leadership roles is that their universe of discourse is so often alien to the majority of the communal leadership. Only academics who can overcome this communications gap can rise to positions of importance.

In localistic situations, like the synagogue, academics tend to associate with like-minded people in the quasi-academic professions—scientists, engineers, and such—with whom there is a shared interest. Such congregations often appear snobbish to the outsider, but from another perspective they can be regarded as a continuation of a traditional phenomenon, that of forming congregations according to occupation, to serve immediate localistic needs. Indeed, one may argue that that is precisely the function of localistic institutions—to provide an intimate framework for the fulfillment of highly personal social needs. The fact that there are relatively few groups within the American Jewish community that have developed such specialized frameworks makes the academics stand out, but the phenomenon in itself is not a new one. Moreover, it is now increasing as a result of dissatisfaction with the very large congregations, which, by their very nature, cannot fill the requirements in question.

This pattern first became evident in the 1950s, among academics with Orthodox leanings who formed their own congregations in those major cities where they could be found in sufficient numbers to do so. In the 1960s some secularist academics banded together to create schools for their children that also provided a social dimension. Most recently, in the 1970s, non-Orthodox academics have taken the lead in developing *havurot,* either connected with synagogues or as independent groupings.[8] On the other hand, when academics become involved in Jewish affairs beyond the immediate personal level, they tend to gravitate toward the most cosmopolitan institutions of the community. One rarely finds academics in synagogue leadership positions; rather, they will be found in the federations, the American Jewish Committee, or the American Jewish Congress, where they tend to have an impact beyond their numbers.

YOUTH LEADERS

Youth leaders must be treated as separate from the main body of community decision makers because of the American tendency to consider youth as a class by itself. In fact, however, young people are more often than not close copies of their parents, and the careful observer can almost invariably predict what the future of particular youth leaders is likely to be on the basis of their present interests and performance.

Youth leaders are not directly responsible for any particular share of the decision-making process in the American Jewish community, but at certain times when the voice of youth tends to attract more attention from adults, they can influence decision making indirectly by making their demands felt within the larger community. The late 1960s and early 1970s were one such period. The demands youth made were not necessarily new, but they were taken more seriously than usual by the adults, giving youth a greater influence than the same age group enjoyed ten or twenty years ago, even though many of the same demands were being made then. Nevertheless, their influence is confined to the diversion of a small share of communal resources and does not bring about any major changes in the community as a whole—this despite the verbal excitement generated in all segments of the community by the youthful demands.

WOMEN

With some exceptions, women decision makers in the Jewish community function in environments segregated from male decision makers. The exceptions are significant for what they reveal. Very wealthy women who have a record of independent activity are admitted to the governing councils of major Jewish institutions and organizations.[9] So, too, are the top leaders of the women's groups in an ex officio capacity, which is sometimes translated into meaningful participation but frequently remains simply ex officio.

This is not to say that women's role in American Jewish life is insignificant; quite the contrary. Not only are women leaders to be evaluated as decision makers of greater or lesser importance in their own right, but the women's organizations play a significant if subordinate role in the constellation of Jewish communal institutions. The most powerful women's organization is Hadassah, whose leaders are also the ones taken most seriously in the community as a whole and whose work has great impact within the various segments of the community. The other women's Zionist organizations, plus the National Council of Jewish Women, play similar if slightly less visible roles because they are smaller in size. Probably the least important of the women's organizations devoted to public purposes are the sisterhoods, whose functions are clearly localized in the synagogues.

Women have been given custody of much of the direct social-welfare and popular-cultural activity of the community—a phenomenon that parallels developments in American society as a whole. From the beginning of organized Jewish life in the United States, women have provided much of the personnel for fund raising for specific health and welfare institutions (except those that are linked to the federation drive) and the energy for developing the popular-cultural programs provided by synagogues and similar organizations. In recent decades the rising costs of social-welfare activities have led to a reduced role for women in that field, for they cannot raise the kind of money that is needed to make a significant difference to more than a few institutions. They now raise money to provide subsidiary or needed fringe benefits for the institutions of their concern.

In the realm of popular culture women reign practically unchallenged. Here their importance is so great today that in effect they determine what will be of cultural interest to the bulk of American Jewry. They buy the books that make certain Jewish books into best sellers and the theater tickets that make certain plays of Jewish interest into hits. They invite the authors to lecture to the congregations. They decide much of the content of the adult-education programs. Since these popular-cultural activities probably contribute more to determining the level of literacy of the American Jewish population than any other factor, the women's role in the community is a very important one indeed.

This central role is due to the fact that "culture" is defined as a leisure-time activity in American society and hence is the province of women. To the extent that living Jewishly as a whole is increasingly being defined as a leisure-time activity, the role of women in other spheres of Jewish life is also growing. Women are becoming more visible among the leadership of synagogues, especially in the smaller Jewish communities, where the pool of available leadership talent is limited. Only the residue of a traditional outlook that viewed such activities as serious and hence the province of men, coupled with the few traditional limitations on women as participants in synagogue rituals, has prevented a great shift of decision-making power in the domestic functional spheres into the hands of women. As the Women's Lib movement grows in influence, even these barriers are rapidly falling. Outside the Orthodox camp ritual limitations on women have virtually disappeared, and women are beginning to take part in congregational leadership roles to a greater extent than ever before. The Reform and Reconstructionist movements now ordain women as rabbis, and women are being elected to congregational presidencies in synagogues of all but the Orthodox wing.

At present women in large numbers staff the lower echelons of Jewish communal life, as both professionals and volunteers. They do so through their women's groups, as religious-school teachers, and as the secretarial "top sergeants" in the offices of Jewish organizations and institutions, where their impact is great. But there are many signs that Jewish women, like their counterparts in the larger society, will no longer be content with the limits heretofore placed on their activity.

The Jewish Press

In a community as diffuse as that of American Jewry, where organizations are not comprehensive in their membership even though they represent the sum of Jewish life as a polity, the press plays a special role in decision making, by determining the kinds of information about Jewish life presented to different audiences, controlling its flow, and shaping the channels of information flow within the communications network as a whole. (To be sure, the American Jewish press carries only a share of that load, perhaps even a decreasing share.) The four components of the American Jewish press are (1) weekly newspapers, (2) monthly house organs of Jewish organizations and institutions, (3) independent publications, and (4) quality magazines such as *Commentary, Judaism,* and, most recently, *Moment.* The first group represents the only grass-roots journalism in American Jewish life. The second reflects the views of the Jewish organizational establishment. The third expresses a variety of interests and opinions, whereas the fourth gives the American Jewish community its intellectual voice.

THE WEEKLIES

The weekly newspapers—collectively known as the "Anglo-Jewish press" and for the most part publisher-owned—wield considerable influence within their respective Jewish communities, to the extent that they in effect control the sources of publicity. Their publishers (who usually double as the papers' editors) are treated as figures of some importance. Since there is rarely more than one newspaper in any community, their power is unchecked by competition. For the most part, they wield power in a highly personal manner that reflects their own idiosyncrasies and interests.

In an increasing number of communities, local federations now own and operate the weekly paper. The trend toward federation ownership is a product of complex factors, including the general tendency for family-owned businesses to pass into corporate or institutional hands as the original generation dies out and their children choose other fields of endeavor. In addition, in all but the largest communities cost factors require weekly newspapers to seek subsidization, a burden that only the federations are likely to assume. The federations also require some medium of communication and find it advantageous to acquire newspapers of their own, especially since this enables them to "manage" the news as much as any powerful individual editor might. In such cases, the editors tend to be functionaries with limited powers.

The major functions of the local Jewish press are, in order of importance, to disseminate information of social interest (news of births, bar mitzvahs, weddings, funerals, and the like), to provide information about Israel of a sort that will reinforce the Jewish image of that country, and to maintain a running commentary on current Jewish problems consonant with the community's myths. There is every reason to believe that Jews get most "hard news" about Israel and the Jewish world from the general rather than from the Jewish press, particularly in the Northeast, where the *New York Times,* with its own correspondent in Jerusalem, provides far more extensive coverage of the Israel scene than any Jewish weekly newspaper. The community's primary internal news source is the Jewish Telegraphic Agency (JTA), and its dispatches are generally superficial. JTA's coverage of Jewish news is broader than that of the *Times,* in the sense that its bulletins catalog more information, but as a public instrumentality supported by communal funds, it is hesitant to probe too deeply. Nevertheless, its daily dispatches are indispensable to

Jewish communal workers, although they are rarely seen by the voluntary leadership.

For the most part, the Jewish newspapers rely on publicity handouts and serve up a heavy diet of photographs of local worthies being honored for one reason or another. Controversy is avoided at all costs. Only the most careful reading of the weekly press, and much of that between the lines, might yield an understanding of what is really happening in the community. This is true despite the fact that there are presently three community-supported international wire services devoted exclusively to Jewish affairs.

THE HOUSE ORGANS

Most of the information about Jewish issues that is obtained by the Jewish leadership from internal sources comes mainly from the institutional periodicals that abound on the American Jewish scene. Some of these, such as the *Reconstructionist* (published by the Jewish Reconstructionist Foundation), *Congress Monthly* (published by the American Jewish Congress), and *Hadassah Magazine,* attempt to cover (with varying degrees of success) most current topics of Jewish interest. They have substantial followings and over the years have played an important role in shaping the beliefs and attitudes of Jewish communal leaders.[10] Others, such as the synagogue movement periodicals, enjoy a more limited influence, but this may change as these magazines seek to improve their format and content. Some periodicals in this category, such as the *National Jewish Monthly* and *Jewish Heritage* (both published by B'nai B'rith), have come to play an important educational role by serving as sources of Jewish knowledge, particularly for Jews with minimal Jewish backgrounds. Others, such as the Zionist periodicals, preach to the already-converted. All in all, the institutional periodicals provide a steady diet of popular information about current Jewish life and problems. The perspective, to be sure, is that of the sponsors, but on the whole the approach is more subtle than overt.

THE INDEPENDENT PUBLICATIONS

Independent publications, such as the *National Jewish Post,* the *Jewish Spectator,* the *Jewish Press,* and *Sh'ma,* form the main competition to the house organs. Predominantly creatures of their editors, these journals are vehicles of freewheeling criticism whose frequent target is the American Jewish establishment. They have had some impact on the American

Jewish scene if only because they are free enough to be forceful and have needed to be flamboyant and controversial to attract readers.

The *National Jewish Post,* a weekly, tends to provide behind-the-scenes news in sensational form. It is more forthright than any other paper in covering the controversies of American Jewry—except that it emphasizes the trivial controversies that break out among American Jews rather than the important issues confronting the community as a whole. The *Jewish Spectator* constitutes the most persistent critic of the American Jewish establishment, and the *Jewish Press* is the voice of militant Orthodoxy. *Sh'ma,* a recent entry in the category, has become a prime forum of the American Jewish avant-garde.

THE QUALITY MAGAZINES

The single most influential periodical on the American Jewish scene is unquestionably *Commentary* (sponsored by the American Jewish Committee). Its power and prestige derive, apart from its intrinsic excellence, from the fact that it is influential in American society as a whole, particularly among the intellectual community. This is not to imply that the majority of American Jewish leaders read *Commentary,* although a substantial and growing percentage of the younger and more intellectually attuned leadership do. Whatever *Commentary* publishes, especially on American Jewish topics, invariably attracts attention and filters down, in one form or another—as a feature in the local Jewish press, as a subject of comment in the house organs—to the Jewish populace. Thus in many respects *Commentary* helps shape the agenda of domestic concerns of American Jewry.

Most recently, the editor of *Commentary* committed his journal to fighting for the political interests of American and world Jewry, implicitly recognizing the corporate character of the Jewish people. One feature of this policy has been a heavy focus on Israel-related issues. This has had the curious result of lessening the overt Jewish content of the magazine, even as it has become more "Jewish." Thus *Commentary,* quite properly, has sought to lead the Jewish battle over such matters as the American defense budget, rather than attempt to maintain its Jewish credentials by concentrating on more "parochial" concerns. In effect, *Commentary* functions as a barometer of Jewish self-esteem and, as such, is more influential within the Jewish community than its original editors may have intended it to be.

Commentary is only one of a number of journals, albeit the most successful, appealing to an American Jewish elite. *Judaism,* a quarterly published by the American Jewish Congress, addresses itself to the philosophic and cultural concerns of the Jewish community in somewhat academic terms. *Tradition,* a journal sponsored by the Rabbinical Council of America, performs a similar function for the Orthodox intellectual community. *Midstream,* a monthly published by the Herzl Foundation, is a forum for discussion of the "problems of Jewish existence," particularly questions affecting Israel and Zionism. Together, these and similar journals work at shaping the intellectual framework within which decision making takes place in the American Jewish community.

HOW REPRESENTATIVE IS THE JEWISH LEADERSHIP?

The question has been repeatedly raised as to how representative the leadership of the American Jewish community is. This is not easy to answer, for it is tied in with such questions as elections and their meaning, the level and forms of participation in the process of choosing leaders, and the larger question of whether the American Jewish community is sufficiently well defined that we can even know who would be representative of it.

By and large, the cosmopolitan volunteers are probably representative of the more Jewishly committed elements in the mainstream of the American Jewish community, despite the fact that they are rarely elected, in any meaningful sense of the term, to the offices they occupy. Though not always formalities, the elections are usually simply means of formally ratifying the choices of nominating committees, and even when contested they are rarely contested by candidates representing seriously different characteristics or points of view. (This varies according to community and organization; in a few, contests are by no means rare or unproductive.) They are representative because there is a certain sameness in American Jewry: their desires, tastes, attitudes, interests, and educational backgrounds probably depart very little from the norm among the majority of American Jews.

Ideologically, most leaders in the American Jewish community share a common liberal bias.[11] The sources of this liberalism have been a matter of considerable discussion in recent years, but there is general agreement that the Jewish response to emancipation lies at the root of much of this commitment, which extends throughout the Jewish community. In this respect the leadership is representative of the Jewish public. In recent years there seems to be a breaking away from unquestioning liberalism in certain quarters of the community, however, and we may be witnessing the end of an epoch in this respect. The shifts are taking place among segments of both the leadership and the Jewish public.[12]

In this connection, the changes in the character of the voluntary leadership reflect the changes that have taken place in the American Jewish community. The first generation of voluntary leaders consisted of immigrants who had prospered but retained a regard for the Jewish life they remembered. The second generation, comprising their americanized sons and daughters, had learned of Jewish communal responsibility from their parents but themselves had little to remember in the way of authentic Jewish life. The present generation is the most acculturated of all, is also the best educated secularly, and thus is better able to make intellectual contact with Jewish culture. If nothing else, these changes have made Jewish communal activity a more sophisticated affair, a trend that is accelerating.

By and large, lower-middle-class Jews do not rise to positions of importance (as distinct from achieving nominal representation) among the community-wide voluntary leadership—in part because they cannot afford it and in part because their localistic outlook limits their ability to make contact with the cosmopolitans. Their chances for leadership in the Jewish community are confined almost exclusively to synagogue boards, B'nai B'rith lodges and JWV posts, and similar private clubs, lodges, or chapters that are dominated by lower-middle-class Jews. To a certain extent, then, the cosmopolitan voluntary leaders represent an oligarchy, but it is a voluntary one as much as or more than it is self-perpetuating. Nor is it an oligarchy that extends itself through all spheres of Jewish life. It is as confined in its own way as are any other of the elements of Jewish communal leadership, professional or voluntary.

Handling the Tasks
of the Jewish Community

DEFENSE, EDUCATION, AND SOCIAL SERVICES: THE
CENTRAL TASKS OF THE ORGANIZED COMMUNITY

There are certain tasks, or functions, that are binding on every Jewish community. These are all ultimately geared to the question of Jewish survival, undoubtedly the most urgent issue confronting the Jewish people as a polity. Whereas Jewish survival was once thought to be the almost exclusive concern of Diaspora Jewry, we now see that it is a matter also affecting Jews living in a Jewish state. As for the American Jewish community, being a voluntary group it finds it necessary to stress the importance of survival and to make this an ideological point rather than taking survival for granted.

One consequence is that the closer a particular issue is to the heart of the question of Jewish survival, the greater the importance that is attached to it by the American Jewish community. This is not out of the ordinary. It is taken for granted by every nation that survival is the first task of its leadership and governing institutions. Other tasks, equally important, may or may not be assigned to these agencies, but matters affecting survival must be. Indeed, the question of survival has become so central and so problematic an issue in American Jewish life that there are those who claim that the American Jewish community should do nothing more than to concentrate on the fight to assure its survival. Given this overriding interest, the community's two most important concerns are defense and education. Other vital tasks that the American Jewish community performs are in the fields of social services and welfare, communal finance, and the maintenance of a common belief system.

Defense

The major defense concerns of the American Jewish community have changed radically within recent years. From the 1870s to the 1930s domestic anti-Semitism was the dominant defense concern of American Jews, with overseas involvement slowly growing at the same time. Beginning in the 1930s, this was gradually replaced by efforts to defend Jews in other parts of the world. After the establishment of the Jewish state in 1948, however, Israel became the major focus of Jewish communal attention. Especially since the Six-Day War of 1967, insuring the survival of Israel has become the heart of the defense function of the American Jewish community. Even the community-relations agencies are now spending a high proportion of their time and resources seeking to increase support for Israel in the United States. Since as a result the most important factors in the community are persons and groups who are connected with the defense of Israel, there has been an effort on the part of many groups to climb on that particular bandwagon.

While the effort to safeguard Israel has continued to occupy the major share of American Jewish energies devoted to defense, other forms of community-relations activities proceed apace. The fight against anti-Semitism is still of prime concern, although since the end of World War II (except in response to sporadic outbreaks) it has taken a different turn. In the 1950s the community-relations organizations began to storm the bastions of social and economic prejudice, by and large effectively. The campaign of the American Jewish Committee to admit Jews into hitherto barred executive suites and the attack of the American Jewish Congress on expressions of Christian religion in the schools are two of the better-known examples of this effort.

With the spread of the civil-rights revolution, the Jewish community-relations organizations began to form broad alliances with other community-relations groups, so that by the mid-sixties there was a united front of Christians and Jews, black and white, that focused on attacking the inherited prejudices of the past. A feeling developed of a band of brothers struggling to obliterate universal ignorance and obscurantism. However, all this changed in the wake of the Six-Day War and the rise of the black-power movement. Jews now discovered that they were no longer welcome in the very civil-rights coalition they had been so instrumental in shaping. Further, as Israel began to draw increasing criticism, it became clear that, all ecumenical protestations to the contrary, the non-Jewish leadership did not understand the importance of the land of Israel to the Jewish people and failed to support Israel's cause at critical moments. Once again the community-relations groups found themselves engaged in a battle to protect Jewish interests as such. The situation has only intensified in the intervening years. If there has been some rapprochement between Jews and blacks and between Jews and the churches —and it seems that there has—it is because the American Jewish community has rediscovered its own interests and pursued them vigorously. Nor does Israel's new centrality in defense matters mean that the fight against anti-Semitism has ceased. It is simply being conducted on a new level.[1]

Education

Education is now recognized to be an equally essential concern. In fact, it was not until Jewish education was explicitly associated with Jewish survival that it came to be regarded as a vital task in all quarters of the community. Meeting Jewish educational needs is a somewhat problematic matter for the community, however, since this exposes the root ambivalences of contemporary Jewish life. Here the desire for survival as a people clashes with the desire for full integration into the general society or, perhaps more accurately, into the new worldwide cosmopolitan culture that has proved so attractive to the middle and upper classes, particularly to students and intellectuals. Jewish education therefore requires a greater measure of commitment to the notion that Jews are different and must educate their children to be different.

Serious Jewish education has as its goal the creation of a "counterculture," at least to some degree. This is hard for people to accept in the modern world, with its bias toward universalism. The experience of the American Jewish community in this regard is typical. Nobody who is considered an important communal figure is likely to deny the importance of Jewish education; but the character of the commitment to Jewish education is a different matter. American Jewish education reflects all those ambiguities, and that is one reason why major decision makers rarely play any real role in the educational field and why professional Jewish educators are not major decision makers in the community.

Since these ambivalences are not easily overcome there is not likely to be any dramatic change in the foreseeable future, although there has been a consistent and gradual increase in support for Jewish schools over the last twenty years. The federations' newfound concern for Jewish day schools is one strong indicator of this trend. It is now clear that the major decision makers are willing to provide some kind of minimum base support for Jewish education locally through the federations and their appropriate constituent agencies, and for Jewish culture countrywide through the Joint Cultural Appeal and otherwise. This minimum base is progressively being defined upwards, but it remains a base line, not an aggressively advancing one. Moreover, the federations are discouraged from moving beyond the minimum by the unresolved struggle over control of Jewish education between the community as a whole and the individual synagogues.

The biggest development in Jewish education in recent years is the spread of day schools. While enrollment in other forms of Jewish education stabilized by 1962 and then began to decline, the enrollment of the day schools continued to rise, although it too now seems to have leveled off. By 1971 nearly seventy thousand students were registered in Jewish day schools, in contrast with forty-three thousand in 1969 and four thousand (all in New York City) in 1935. In 1971 day-school students constituted slightly over 14 percent of all pupils in Jewish schools of any kind. In that year, day schools in some forty-six large and middle-sized cities received federation allocations. In that same year, too, New York counted 173 day schools with over forty-six thousand students, representing some 38 percent of all Jewish-school enrollment. Chicago and Los Angeles, with 9 day schools each, ranked next, with over seventeen hundred students in Chicago and over sixteen hundred in Los Angeles. Three more cities had Jewish day schools with enrollments of over one thousand: Boston (5 schools), Miami (8), and Philadelphia (4). The largest federation allocations for those schools were in Chicago ($321,000) and Philadelphia ($242,000).

It should be noted that one form of Jewish education, if it can be called that, has attracted great support from the most important decision makers, as well as the community as a whole. That is the use of Israel as an educational resource for Jewish teenagers and college students. By virtue of its symbolic value, Israel, the focal point of the Jewish defense effort, has become the central focus of American Jewish educational effort as well. Many American Jews, including the top leadership, who are distressed and alarmed by the intensity of the assimilation of Jewish young people, believe it is possible to reverse the assimilatory process by exposing the youth to the positive influence of Israel. The result has been the creation of a number of work and study programs to facilitate the encounter of American Jewish youth with Israel. There is no question that American Jewry will pay increasing attention to Israel's importance to education.

Social Services and Welfare [2]

While the Jewish community remains committed to providing a range of social services for Jews and non-Jews alike, this function has lost some of its importance on the communal scene. This is partly because the social services themselves have become progressively less Jewish—in appearance, if not in fact—and partly because the rise of the welfare state has reduced their significance in American Jewish life. In many cases the social-service agencies under Jewish auspices are strictly nonsectarian, accommodating non-Jews as well as Jews. For example, the Jewish hospitals, as we have mentioned, are simply institutions sponsored by the Jewish community as one of its contributions to the welfare of American society as a whole. The Jewish community maintains its stake in such institutions because it is a customary way of contributing to the life of the general community, because it provides a bridge to other minority groups with whom the Jewish community wants to maintain good relations, and because there is some strong, if unspoken, sentiment in the Jewish community that it is well for Jews to have such instrumentalities under their supervision "just in case."

Pressures are also mounting for the social-welfare agencies to give representation on their governing bodies to their non-Jewish clients. While most Jewish communities have resisted those pressures and intend to continue to do so, the fact that the institutions are supported only partially by Jewish funds and heavily by United Fund and government contributions or grants makes it more difficult to hold that line. Clearly, where non-Jews have been allowed into the governing bodies, the institutions become even less important in the Jewish decision-making constellation. This is particularly significant because the social-welfare agencies still serve as vehicles for initiating new communal leaders, testing them out, and developing them for more responsible positions in the local Jewish community.

Certain institutions presently considered to be within the social-service sphere are now seeking to broaden their interests, usually by moving into the educational-cultural sphere as well. This is particularly true of the Jewish community centers, whose social-service functions have been reduced as their educational and cultural functions have increased. Some Jewish community centers have sought to become secular rivals of the synagogues, as they attempt to serve the localistic needs of their members. By and large they have not succeeded in so doing because they cannot provide their members with the facilities and ambience necessary for the proper observance of the Jewish rites of passage. Only the synagogues are able to fill this function. The centers' strength derives from their ability to mobilize sufficient funds to provide more sophisticated recreational and cultural facilities that might attract Jews on the basis of special interests—health clubs, theater, and the like. This ability reflects the overlapping character of the center and federation leadership in many communities, a carryover from an earlier period when Reform Jews made use of both as instrumentalities for extrasynagogal activities. Where this has been the case the centers have developed roles and channels of influence somewhat different from those of other social-service institutions.

By and large, as the centers become more overtly Jewish they also become more cosmopolitan institutions, seeking to serve specialized Jewish cultural needs as the justification for their claim on substantial community funds. Such needs include sponsoring assorted Jewish cultural programs, community summer camps with Jewish content, and coffeehouses for Jewish college students. To some extent this has led to a sorting out of roles between the centers, the synagogues, and the schools. No such sorting out can ever be complete, nor should it be—healthy competition on a reasonable basis enhances the possibilities for Jewish communal life by providing alternatives through services in depth. What is important is that each of the three sets of institutions has its own basic tasks for which it is responsible and that the overlapping be at the peripheries of each, not at the core.

THE POLITICS OF COMMUNITY FINANCE[3]

Community finance is obviously a central task of the American Jewish community, as it is in any polity—money is ultimately needed to sustain communal activities—and fund raising is a continuing and unrelenting activity. Its importance in determining the organization of Jewish communal life is such that, from a strictly organizational point of view, it has often been considered the most important task of all. The effort to raise the funds to sustain communal activity is a constant one and the annual campaign therefore plays a major communal role; determining the hierarchy of the voluntary leadership and the reputation of professionals across the whole gamut of Jewish organizational life. It is no accident that the very beginnings of comprehensive community organization on the American Jewish scene stemmed from the necessity to organize and to systematize fund raising.

In those days synagogues were more or less immune from the terrific pressures generated by the problems of finance. They were small and could rely for their maintenance upon the traditional pattern of soliciting donations in return for the distribution of honors during the service. The rise of the large modern congregation, with its voracious need for funds to sustain a multifaceted program, has placed them in basically the same position as any other agency in the community.

Two major struggles that developed in the area of fund raising, but have essentially been resolved, have had significant consequences for the organizational structure and patterns of decision making in the community. The first was the struggle within each locality over whether to centralize the raising of funds for Jewish communal purposes. By and large, the decision has been to centralize fund raising for all purposes except those that fall within the religious-congregational and education-cultural spheres. The struggle over the latter sphere is still under way and the tide is flowing toward centralization. Whether the religious-congregational sphere will be next in line is unclear, but it is no longer a foregone conclusion that it will remain separate, as it was a few years ago.

The second struggle was between local and countrywide organizations over who should be responsible for raising funds. The local organizations won the lion's share of the victory, gaining control over fund raising even for most countrywide and international purposes. The local federations were particularly successful in this regard, almost eliminating all nonlocal fund raising by participants in the arenas they have come to dominate. Even UJA, backed as it is by all the prestige that Israel can bestow, has come to terms with this fact and has become almost totally dependent upon local machinery for mobilizing the huge sums it does every year. This victory has substantially strengthened the power of the local communities in the overall framework of American Jewish life.

Not unexpectedly, the allocation of funds is the arena in which most conflict is generated and real issues are ventilated. The politics of the budget is the most vital politics of all in setting the real priorities of any polity. At the same time, reality dictates that the annual budgetary process in the Jewish community, as in any other public body, involves decisions about marginal changes only. Most budget items are fixed by prior commitments evolved over long periods of time and reflect the balance of interests within each allocating body. Many are fixed costs that not only cannot be shifted but also tend to consume any increase in available revenues. Even before the inflation of the mid-1970s, the increase in established fixed costs in Jewish institutions was approaching 10 percent annually—perhaps not incidentally, that was the average annual increase of fixed costs at that time. This rate increases substantially in inflationary periods. Thus most if not all of the campaign increment each year must be "taken off the top" before new allocations can be made. Since major shifts in allocations among institutions are rare, given the balance of forces on allocating bodies, budgeting tends to be incremental.

The present balance of forces on budget-making bodies may or may not be representative of the public each body purportedly represents (although there is no particular reason to believe that they are not). In any case, there does seem to be a correlation between the allocations and the level of interest in a particular program or institution shown by the most effective members of the allocating body. "Effectiveness" in this case may have to do with level of giving, level of activity, or general ability to influence committees. Clearly, the programs and institutions closest to the hearts of big, active givers have an advantage. The more comprehensive the purposes of the institution are, the wider and more balanced its allocating body is likely to be and the more difficult it will be to gain additional support for pet projects. Conversely, the narrower the purposes of the institution, the more likely that allocation powers will be concentrated in a few hands. Thus a synagogue with fifteen hundred member families (over five thousand people) will probably have a less balanced allocations process than a federation in a Jewish community of three thousand.

While it is not possible to ascertain precisely the total amount spent by the American Jewish community for public purposes, it apparently exceeds $2 billion a year, a sum equal to or greater than the budgets of many American states. The size of this sum marks its seriousness. For all too long certain people in the Jewish community looked upon Jewish public finance as a matter of philanthropy, or the voluntary contribution of sums for the relief of the less fortunate. But a $2 billion expenditure for the panoply of purposes covered by American Jewish institutions is not simply philanthropy; it is serious business.

Tables 23 and 24 summarize our limited knowledge about the present state of Jewish public finance in America. Table 23 shows the estimated annual receipts of the Jewish community for its communal services in 1970, the latest year for which a full estimate is available. The nearly $1.5 billion shown in the table does not include the income of congregations and other localistic organizations and institutions, except for those con-

TABLE 23   ESTIMATED ANNUAL INCOME OF JEWISH COMMUNAL
SERVICES IN U.S., 1970*

	(in millions of dollars)†
1. Welfare fund contributions (excluding capital funds)	$ 174.9
Plus: Israel Emergency Fund of UJA	124.0
2. Grants by United Funds	24.0
3. Other contributions to national and overseas agencies (including capital funds)	106.3[a]
4. Other income of national and overseas agencies	120.2
5. Hospital income including research funds (excluding 1 and 2)	688.2[b]
6. Family service income (excluding 1 and 2)	5.2
7. Child care income (excluding 1 and 2)	18.1
8. Jewish vocational service (excluding 1 and 2)	5.1
9. Aged care income (excluding 1 and 2)	103.7
10. Center income (excluding 1 and 2)	31.3[c]
11. Jewish education income (excluding 1)	75.3[d]
TOTAL	$1,476.3

[a]This sum includes operating funds, restricted funds, and capital funds.
[b]Excludes some nonreporting hospitals.
[c]*JWB Year Book,* vol. 20, 1971.
[d]Approximate; based on revision of estimate in *National Study of Jewish Education,* less welfare-fund allocations.
*Source: *American Jewish Year Book,* vol. 73; prepared by S.P. Goldberg.
†This excludes mainly endowment income in most communities, local capital-fund campaigns, and internal congregational operating expenses.

nected with Jewish education, nor does it include endowment income in most communities or local capital-fund campaigns. It is safe to suggest that another $500 million should be added to this total, reflecting a $2 billion annual revenue even before the inflationary period of the mid-1970s.

The largest single source of revenue shown in Table 23 is hospital income, which includes government subsidies, grants and reimbursements, and private fees, all of which are used within the institutions into which they flow. The largest general revenues are those of the welfare-fund contributions, which in 1971 amounted to some $360 million all told.

Table 24 shows the amounts raised in central Jewish community campaigns from 1939, the first year that complete figures were available, through 1971. Examination of the table shows how these campaigns grew to become the major source of general funding for the Jewish communities of America. An examination of the table shows how Israel's wars have played a decisive role in establishing new plateaus of giving within the American Jewish community. The first two major increases did indeed precede the establishment of the Jewish state, coming in quick order at the end of World War II, when the dimensions of the Holocaust became known. The great increase of 1948 stabilized on a new plateau, which then eroded in the early 1950s, only to shift upward again after the Sinai Campaign of 1956. The greatest increases came, however, as a result of the 1967 and 1973 wars, the latter of which is not reflected on this table.

The key element in the central Jewish community revenues is the regular welfare fund, since all of the Israel Emergency Fund is passed on directly to Israel. Table 25 profiles the pattern of federation allocations of welfare funds by function. It will be noted that over 55 percent of the regular welfare-fund collections is allocated to Israel and other overseas needs, overwhelmingly to Israel. A mere 4 percent (meaning some 7 percent of the total domestic allocation) is allocated to country-wide agencies. Thus some 40 percent of all funds raised by the federations are used for local needs. This proportion varies considerably from community to community, by community size (see Table 26). Thus in the largest Jewish communities—those with Jewish populations of forty thousand and over—as much as 47 percent of the regular campaign collection is retained for local use, while in those with under five thousand Jewish population, whose networks of local Jewish services are

TABLE 24 ESTIMATED AMOUNTS RAISED IN CENTRAL JEWISH
COMMUNITY CAMPAIGNS, 1939–71 *(in millions of dollars)**

Year		Total[a]	NEW YORK CITY NYUJA	FJPNY	Total	Other cities
1939		$ 28.4	$ 6.6	$ 6.0	$ 12.6	$ 15.8
1940		27.0	5.2	6.1	11.3	15.7
1941		28.2	5.0	6.4	11.4	16.8
1942		29.3	4.7	7.1	11.8	17.5
1943		35.0	7.0	6.6	13.6	21.4
1944		47.0	9.2	9.7	18.9	28.1
1945		57.3	12.6	9.8	22.4	34.9
1946		131.7	32.8	11.8	44.6	87.1
1947		157.8	38.2	13.2	51.4	106.4
1948		205.0	56.2	13.2	69.4	135.6
1949		161.0	41.9	12.1	54.0	107.0
1950		142.1	36.6	13.5	50.1	92.0
1951		136.0	34.6	13.6	48.2	87.8
1952		121.2	29.8	13.3	43.1	78.1
1953		117.2	28.2	13.5	41.7	75.5
1954		109.3	25.7	14.0	39.7	69.6
1955		110.6	25.7	15.3	41.0	69.6
1956		131.3	33.1	15.6	48.7	82.6
1957		139.0	33.9	15.2	49.1	89.9
1958		124.1	28.8	16.9	45.7	78.4
1959		129.1	28.4	17.2	45.6	83.5
1960		126.0	27.2	17.5	44.7	81.3
1961		124.4	26.8	17.7	44.5	79.9
1962		128.1	26.6	17.3	43.9	84.2
1963		123.4	24.9	17.6	42.5	80.9
1964		125.2	24.1	18.7	42.8	82.4
1965		131.3	25.6	19.4	45.0	86.3
1966		136.5	26.2	19.8	46.0	90.5
1967	Regular	144.5	27.7	22.1	49.8	94.7
	Emergency[b]	173.0	49.0	—	49.0	124.0
1968	Regular	152.6	29.3	22.8	52.1	100.5
	Emergency[b]	80.0	20.0	—	20.0	60.0
1969	Regular	162.9	31.3	22.4	53.7	109.2
	Emergency[b]	99.0	22.0	—	22.0	77.0
1970	Regular	174.9	33.9	23.4	57.3	117.6
	Emergency[b]	124.0	27.0	—	27.0	97.0
1971	Regular	196.8	41.3	23.8	65.1	131.7
	Emergency[b]	163.0	32.2	—	32.2	129.8
TOTAL		$4,533.2	$1,019.3	$492.6	$1,511.9	$3,020.3

[a]Total *regular* pledges are shown at the end of each campaign year, prior to shrinkage
and adjustments. Israel Emergency Fund amounts were apportioned between New York
City and other cities in relation to total pledges, exclusive of some expenses and shrinkage.
IEF totals for other cities include some amounts raised in smaller cities without welfare
funds. Pledges exclude amounts raised annually in smaller cities having no welfare funds,
but include some multiple-city gifts which are duplications, as between New York City and
the remainder of the country. Excludes capital-fund campaigns of the Federation of Jewish
Philanthropies of New York: $3 million in 1943: $13.5 million in 1945, and $16.5 million
in 1949, and about $168 million in 1961–71, including other noncampaign income and
endowment funds of beneficiary agencies. Also excludes some endowment funds and
capital fund raising by federations for local agencies outside New York City (FJPNY data
include unrestricted legacies and earnings on investments).

[b]Provisional Estimates; excludes Israel Education Fund of UJA, with pledges of about
$32 million in 1965–70. Total for both regular and IEF campaigns in 1967 was $318
million; $233 million in 1968; $262 million in 1969; $299 million in 1970, and $360 million
in 1971. Data are subject to adjustment for intercity duplications.

*Source: American Jewish Year Book, vol. 73; prepared by S.P. Goldberg.

TABLE 25 ESTIMATED DISTRIBUTION TO BENEFICIARIES OF FUNDS RAISED BY JEWISH FEDERATIONS* *(in thousands of dollars)*†

	Total		New York City[a]		Other Cities	
	1970	1969	1970	1969	1970	1969
Total amount budgeted to beneficiaries[b, c, d]	$140,001	$133,765	$41,590	$40,849	$98,411	$92,916
Percent	100.0	100.0	100.0	100.0	100.0	100.0
Overseas Agencies	77,414	73,756	23,050	21,225	54,364	52,531
Percent	55.3	55.1	55.4	52.0	55.2	56.5
United Jewish Appeal	74,050	70,566	22,500	20,750	51,550	49,816
Percent	52.9	52.8	54.1	50.8	52.4	53.6
Other overseas	3,364	3,190	550	475	2,814	2,715
Percent	2.4	2.4	1.3	1.2	2.9	2.9
National agencies	5,569	5,267	570	500	4,999	4,767
Percent	4.0	3.9	1.4	1.2	5.1	5.1
Community relations	2,846	2,745	—	—	2,846	2,745
Percent	2.0	2.1	—	—	2.9	3.0
Health and welfare	21	23	—	—	21	23
Percent	g	g	—	—	g	0.2
Cultural	685	625	—	—	685	625
Percent	0.5	0.5	—	—	0.7	0.7
Religious	326	303	—	—	326	303
Percent	0.2	0.2	—	—	0.3	0.3
Service agencies	1,691	1,571	570	500	1,121	1,071
Percent	1.2	1.2	1.4	1.2	1.1	1.2
Local operating needs	54,003	52,336	17,970	19,124	36,033	33,212
Percent	38.6	39.1	43.2	46.8	36.6	35.7
Local refugee care[e]	1,018[f]	707	—	—	1,018[f]	707
Percent	0.7	0.5	—	—	1.0	0.8
Local capital needs	1,991	1,698	—	—	1,991	1,698
Percent	1.4	1.3	—	—	2.0	1.8

[a]Figures for New York include the United Jewish Appeal of Greater New York and Federation of Jewish Philanthropies. Local refugee costs in New York City are borne by NYANA, a direct beneficiary of UJA nationally. Most overseas and domestic agencies, which are normally included in welfare funds in other cities, conduct their own campaigns in New York. The New York UJA includes the following beneficiaries (in addition to the National UJA): United HIAS Service and National Jewish Welfare Board). Data for New York UJA based on estimates of distribution of 1969 and 1970 campaign proceeds, regardless of year in which cash is received.

[b]Based upon communities which are currently CJF members and some smaller cities which are not CJF members, but which were included in the base group of communities used in 1948, when this statistical series was started. Minor differences in amounts and percentages due to rounding. United Fund support excluded from this table.

[c]The difference between this amount and "total raised" in Table 23 represents mainly "shrinkage" allowance for nonpayment of pledges, campaign and administrative expenses, elimination of duplicating multiple-city gifts, and contingency or other reserves.

[d]Includes small undistributed amounts in "total" and "other cities" columns.

[e]NYANA is included in UJA totals.

[f]Rise results from variations in reporting; on a comparable basis, refugee-care allocations were about $960,000 in 1970, and about $890,000 in 1969.

[g]Less than .05 of one percent.

*Does not include Israel Emergency Fund. For gross estimated collections see Table 23. Net amounts comparable to data in this table become available after actual shrinkage and collections are determined by experience.

†Source: *American Jewish Year Book,* vol. 73; prepared by S.P. Goldberg.

	Total[a] 1970	Total[a] 1969	Under 5,000[b] 1970	Under 5,000[b] 1969	5,000–15,000[b] 1970	5,000–15,000[b] 1969	15,000–40,000[b] 1970	15,000–40,000[b] 1969	40,000 and Over[b] 1970	40,000 and Over[b] 1969
Total amount budgeted[c]	$98,411,378	$92,916,434	$11,593,958	$10,445,569	$14,318,818	$13,085,815	$15,426,768	$14,947,948	$57,071,834	$54,437,102
Percent	100.0	100.0	100.0	100.0	100.0	100.0	100.0	100.0	100.0	100.0
Overseas agencies	54,364,328	52,530,772	8,694,027	7,910,940	8,881,697	8,102,210	9,326,973	9,191,632	27,461,631	27,325,980
Percent	55.2	56.5	75.0	75.7	62.0	61.9	60.5	61.5	48.1	50.2
United Jewish Appeal	51,550,396	49,816,066	8,389,189	7,619,928	8,469,721	7,696,865	8,682,695	8,571,074	26,008,791	25,928,199
Percent	52.4	53.6	72.4	72.9	59.2	58.8	56.3	57.3	45.6	47.6
Other overseas	2,813,932	2,714,706	304,838	291,012	411,976	405,345	644,278	620,558	1,452,840	1,397,791
Percent	2.9	2.9	2.6	2.8	2.9	3.1	4.2	4.2	2.5	2.6
National agencies	4,999,359	4,766,669	547,373	531,352	753,960	734,603	869,792	846,930	2,828,234	2,653,784
Percent	5.1	5.1	4.7	5.1	5.3	5.6	5.6	5.7	5.0	4.9
Community relations	2,845,783	2,744,751	240,677	227,431	402,320	398,071	507,411	504,799	1,695,375	1,614,450
Percent	2.9	3.0	2.1	2.2	2.8	3.0	3.3	3.4	3.0	3.0
Health and welfare	21,279	22,725	12,224	12,941	7,822	7,235	1,233	1,549	—	1,000
Percent	d	0.2	0.1	0.1	0.1	0.1	d	d	d	d
Cultural	685,103	624,784	69,825	66,668	92,468	80,379	127,485	116,862	395,325	360,875
Percent	0.7	0.7	0.6	0.6	0.6	0.6	0.8	0.8	0.7	0.7
Religious	326,405	303,488	122,769	123,729	88,164	91,666	35,972	32,343	79,500	55,750
Percent	0.3	0.3	1.1	1.2	0.6	0.7	0.2	0.2	0.1	0.1
Service agencies	1,120,553	1,070,929	101,642	100,583	163,186	157,252	197,691	191,377	658,034	621,709
Percent	1.1	1.1	0.9	1.0	1.1	1.2	1.3	1.3	1.2	1.1
Local operating needs	36,033,235	33,211,664	2,155,650	1,835,745	4,253,081	3,898,567	4,652,287	4,254,711	24,972,217	23,222,641
Percent	36.6	35.7	18.6	17.6	29.7	29.8	30.2	28.5	43.8	42.7
Local refugee care[e]	1,018,351	706,882	—	—	46,330	40,605	137,202	126,684	834,819	539,593
Percent	1.0	0.8	—	—	0.3	0.3	0.9	0.8	1.5	1.0
Local capital needs	1,990,601	1,697,750	195,228	166,705	380,789	308,342	439,651	527,609	974,933	695,094
Percent	2.0	1.8	1.7	1.6	2.7	2.4	2.8	3.5	1.7	1.3

[a]The difference between totals budgeted for beneficiaries and gross budgeted for all purposes represents "shrinkage" allowance for nonpayment of pledges, campaign and administrative expenses, and contingency on other reserves. The difference between what a community may budget for all purposes (its gross budget) and totals raised may also reflect the extent that the budgeted amounts may include funds on hand from previous campaigns (reserves, etc.). Minor differences in amounts and percentages due to rounding.

[b]Jewish population.

[c]Includes small undistributed amounts.

[d]Less than 0.05 of one percent.

[e]Rise results from variations in reporting; on a comparable basis, refugee care allocations were about $960,000 in 1970 and about $890,000 in 1969.

*Does not include Israel Emergency Fund.

†Source: American Jewish Year Book, vol. 73; prepared by S.P. Goldberg.

TABLE 27 DISTRIBUTION OF FEDERATION ALLOCATIONS FOR LOCAL SERVICES IN 112 COMMUNITIES, 1969, 1970 (*excludes New York City*)*

	1969			1970			
	Amount	Percent of Total	Percent of Total Federation Allocation	Amount	Percent of Total	Percent of Total Federation Allocation	Percent Change
Health	$ 6,949,941	13.2		$ 6,606,195	11.6		− 5.2
Family service, child care	12,096,672	23.0		12,881,740	22.7		+ 6.5
Centers, camps, youth services[a]	15,009,121	28.5		16,701,458	29.4		+11.3
Aged care	5,513,766	10.5		5,774,341	10.2		+ 4.7
Employment and guidance	1,833,048	3.5	5.6	1,987,821	3.5	5.5	+ 8.4
Jewish education	7,792,229	14.8	23.8	8,741,525	15.4	24.3	+12.2
Refugee care[b]	702,064	1.3	2.1	1,005,835	1.8	2.8	+43.3
Community relations	1,417,449	2.7	4.3	1,658,013	2.9	4.6	+17.0
Other	726,435	1.4		870,424	1.5		+19.8
United Fund to federation for local administration[c]	576,170	1.1		605,100	1.1		+ 5.0
TOTAL	$52,624,970	100.0		$56,832,452	100.0		+ 8.0
Sources of income							
Federations	$32,781,090	62.3		$35,934,769	63.2		+ 9.6
United Funds	$19,843,880	37.7		$20,897,683	36.8		+ 5.3

[a]Includes Hillel college youth programs.
[b]Rise results from variations in reporting. On a comparable basis, refugee allocations were $959,835 in 1970 and $891,065 in 1969 (1.7 percent in each year).
[c]Includes United Fund allocations for administration of local services which are part of total administrative and fund-raising costs ($16,418,340 in 1970 and $14,696,075 in 1969) reported for these 112 cities. Federation allocations for administration of local services are not shown in this table, except for income from United Funds.
*Source: *American Jewish Year Book*, vol. 73; prepared by S.P. Goldberg. Includes United Funds and Hillel college youth programs.

TABLE 28   PERCENTAGE DISTRIBUTION OF FEDERATION ALLOCATIONS* FOR LOCAL SERVICES IN 112 COMMUNITIES, 1969, 1970†

	(112) Total		(46) Under 5000a		(35) 5,000–14,999a		(18) 15,000–39,999a		(13) 40,000 and Overa	
	1969	1970	1969	1970	1969	1970	1969	1970	1969	1970
Health	13.2	11.6	d	d	0.8	0.7	6.0	5.5	17.7	15.5
Family service, child care	23.0	22.7	12.6	12.2	23.6	23.9	21.5	21.8	23.7	23.2
Centers, camps, youth servicesb	28.5	29.4	65.4	63.1	45.4	45.9	37.3	37.5	21.7	22.9
Aged care	10.5	10.2	7.3	7.9	12.0	9.4	7.5	7.5	11.0	11.0
Employment and guidance	3.5	3.5	—	—	1.0	0.9	3.3	3.4	4.2	4.2
Jewish educationc	14.8	15.4	11.1	12.7	12.5	14.0	15.5	15.3	15.3	16.0
	(23.8)	(24.3)	(17.2)	(18.5)	(22.5)	(24.7)	(29.2)	(27.6)	(23.3)	(24.0)
Refugee caree	1.3	1.8	0.2	d	0.6	0.5	1.5	1.6	1.5	2.1
Community relations	2.7	2.9	1.5	2.2	1.4	2.0	3.4	3.4	2.8	3.0
Other	1.4	1.5	1.9	1.9	1.5	1.7	1.0	1.2	1.4	1.6
United Fund to federations for local administrationsc	1.1	1.1	—	—	1.1	1.0	2.9	2.9	0.7	0.7
TOTALf	100.0	100.0	100.0	100.0	100.0	100.0	100.0	100.0	100.0	100.0
Sources of income										
Federations	62.3	63.2	64.6	68.4	55.7	56.7	53.1	55.2	65.4	65.9
United Funds	37.7	36.8	35.4	31.6	44.3	43.3	46.9	44.8	34.6	34.1

aJewish population.
b, cSee Table 27.
dLess than 0.05 of one percent.
eFigures in parentheses are percentages of Jewish Education allocations to total federation allocations.
fSlight difference due to rounding.
*See Table 27.
†Source: American Jewish Year Book, vol. 73; prepared by S. P. Goldberg. Includes United Funds.

TABLE 29 ESTIMATED DISTRIBUTION OF FEDERATION AND UNITED
FUND ALLOCATIONS TO LOCAL SERVICES, 1965, 1970
(in millions of dollars)

Field Receiving Chest Support	Total 1965	Total 1970	New York City 1965	New York City 1970	Other Cities 1965	Other Cities 1970
Centers, camps, youth services[a]	$14.3	$22.3	$ 3.9	$ 5.6	$10.5	$16.7
Family and child care	14.2	18.4	5.0	5.5	9.2	12.9
Hospitals and health	13.5	11.6	5.8	5.0	7.7	6.6
Aged	4.1	7.3	0.9	1.5	3.2	5.8
SUBTOTAL	$46.1	$59.6	$15.6	$17.6	$30.6	$42.0
Less: provided by United Funds (exclusive of administration)	$17.5	$22.5	$ 1.9	$ 2.2	$15.6	$20.3
Provided by Federations	$28.6	$37.1	$13.7	$15.4	$15.0	$21.7
United Funds to Federation for local administration	$ 0.9	$ 0.9	$ 0.4	$ 0.3	$ 0.5	$ 0.6
Receiving only federation support						
Employment services (including free loans)	$ 2.1	$ 2.9	$ 0.7	$ 0.9	$ 1.4	$ 2.0
Jewish education	6.1	9.7	0.8	1.0	5.3	8.7
Refugee aid	0.7	1.0	[b]	[b]	0.7	1.0
Community relations	1.0	1.7	[c]	[c]	1.0	1.7
Local capital[d]	1.5	2.1	[d]	[d]	1.5	2.1
Other	1.1	1.7	0.6	0.8	0.5	0.9
SUBTOTAL	$12.5	$19.1	$2.1	$2.7	$10.4	$16.4
TOTAL	$59.5	$79.6	$18.0	$20.7	$41.5	$59.0
Provided by Federations	$41.1	$56.2	$15.7	$18.1	$25.4	$38.1
Provided by United Funds[e]	18.4	23.4	2.3	2.5	16.1	20.9
TOTAL[f]	$59.5	$79.6	$18.0	$20.6	$41.5	$59.0

[a]Includes Hillel college youth programs.

[b]About $1.0 million provided annually by NYANA, financed by UJA.

[c]Provided mainly by national agencies.

[d]Most capital campaigns are excluded because they are conducted apart from annual campaigns; United Funds in nonfederated cities are also excluded.

[e]Includes in NYC grants by Greater New York Fund and United Hospital Fund to federated agencies. In addition, nonfederated agencies receive about $0.4 million annually.

[f]Data for other cities are understated by about $1 million in 1970—compared with total estimates in Table 25 because functional distributions are not available in all smaller cities.

Source: *American Jewish Year Book,* vol. 73; prepared by S.P. Goldberg.

minimal, less than 20 percent is retained for local use, with the very smallest communities retaining minuscule amounts. The cities in between retain approximately one-third of their total regular campaign contributions for local services.

The distribution of funds by function within local communities is shown in Tables 27 and 28. The tables include United Fund contributions as well as money raised directly by the Jewish community since both are handled by constituent agencies of the federation and involve some federation role in their allocation (see Table 29).

The relationship between the Jewish federations and the local United Funds dates back over fifty years. Indeed, Jewish philanthropic bodies, either the federations or their predecessors, were often instrumental in developing United Fund and community-chest organizations for the general communities in which they were located. Jews were the pioneers in united giving and helped transmit that approach to the general community of which they were a part. In some communities the United Funds are actually fund-raising and community-planning confederations of the Protestant, Catholic, and Jewish federations, with each of the three constituent federations having an institutionalized role in the governance of the overall United Fund. In others there is general cooperation, but the United Fund stands as a separate organization that makes allocations to Protestant, Catholic, and Jewish institutions on the grounds that they provide services to the overall community or to some significant segment of it. As a result, Jewish federation leaders usually make a great effort to promote Jewish giving to the United Fund and are expected to make significant contributions to it themselves. In many communities the United Fund raises approximately the same amount from the entire community as the Jewish federation does from the Jews, and of that amount, Jews are disproportionately high givers.

Relations between the Jewish community and the local United Fund have become more difficult in recent years, particularly with the increased pressure on the part of nonwhite minorities for community assistance. These pressures on the United Fund have worked in two ways. First, they have led to the diversion of United Fund money to projects that are more likely to benefit the nonwhite communities than Jewish institutions, thereby making it necessary for the Jews to struggle harder to even retain their previous allocations, much less maintain their share as inflation alters the value of the dollar. Moreover, in response to the demands of blacks (which are fully in line with the American ethos and one of the points at which that ethos comes into conflict with Jewish interests), the United Funds have increasingly insisted that beneficiaries' facilities be open to all members of the community and include representation from all segments of the community on their governing boards.

Most of the Jewish beneficiary agencies were prepared to undertake

TABLE 30 ALLOCATIONS TO LOCAL JEWISH EDUCATION BY 86

Jewish Population	Federation Allocation to All Local Jewish Needs				Total Local Allocation[a]			
	1966	1970	Increase 1966–70[c]		1966	1970	Increase 1966–70	
	Dollars	Dollars	Dollars	Per-cent	Dollars	Dollars	Dollars	Per-cent
Less than 5,000[c]	572,388	825,617	253,229	44.2	825,050	1,153,532	328,482	39.8
		855,640				1,206,455		
5,000 to 14,999	2,228,216	3,492,867	1,264,651	56.8	4,551,166	6,182,644	1,631,478	35.8
		3,764,462				6,606,191		
15,000 to 39,999	3,189,770	4,671,315	1,481,545	46.4	6,347,620	8,207,171	1,859,551	29.3
40,000 and over (excluding New York)	34,728,765	43,437,013	8,708,248	25.1	46,800,849	58,540,987	11,740,138	25.1
	18,809,893	25,817,964	7,008,071	37.3	29,183,566	38,870,293	9,686,727	33.2
TOTAL	40,719,139	52,426,812	11,707,673	28.8	58,524,685	74,084,334	15,559,649	26.6
		52,728,430				74,560,804		

[a]Includes community-chest funds.
[b]Figures in parentheses denote the number of reporting communities in the population category.
[c]Increases were not made by all cities during each of the intervening years.
[d]Per-capita allocation to Jewish education was computed by dividing total allocation to Jewish education by Jewish population of the community.
[e]Figures do not include Norristown, Pa., since complete data were not available for 1970.
*Source: *American Jewish Year Book*, vol. 73.

to open their facilities across the board. For the hospitals it was no problem, since they have traditionally been open to all. The social-service agencies have been moving in that direction for many years. The major problem lies with the Jewish community centers, whose dual role as places of recreation and bastions of Jewish identity come into conflict when such issues are raised. On the other hand, the same agencies have been extremely reluctant to surrender any element of Jewish control over their governance. This has led to a certain amount of tension between the federations and the United Funds, and probably marks the end of the period when Jewish institutions could expect significant United Fund assistance for their activities.

Among other things, Tables 27 and 28 reveal that between 1965 and 1970 federation support for Jewish education rose by over 50 percent,

FEDERATIONS AND WELFARE FUNDS, BY COMMUNITY SIZE,* 1966, 1970

			Allocation to Local Jewish Education						Per Capita[d] 1970
	1966		*1970*		*Increase 1966–70*[c]		*Percentage of Change*		
Aggregate Jewish Population[b]	*Dollars*	*Percent of Federation Allocation*	*Dollars*	*Percent of Federation Allocation*	*Dollars*	*Percent of Federation Allocation*	*Federation Allocation*	*Total Allocation*	*Dollars*
54,700 (19)	146,745	25.6	241,286	29.2	94,541	66.4	37.3	28.8	4.41
57,805 (23)			250,786	29.3					4.34
265,770 (28)	592,781	26.6	1,003,931	28.7	411,150	69.4	32.5	25.2	3.78
301,145 (32)			1,015,431	27.0					3.37
383,630 (18)	926,755	29.1	1,276,604	27.3	349,849	37.7	23.6	18.8	3.33
4,476,000 (14)	4,800,273	13.8	7,165,060	16.5	2,364,787	49.3	27.2	20.1	1.60
2,095,000 (13)	4,002,806	21.3	6,117,968	23.7	2,115,162	52.8	30.2	21.8	2.92
5,180,000 (79)	6,466,554	15.9	9,686,881	18.5	3,220,327	49.8	27.5	20.7	1.87
5,218,580 (87)			9,707,881	18.4					1.86

from \$6.1 million to \$9.7 million. This pattern of increase has been maintained into the 1970s, so that by 1973 the total reached \$16 million (up 127 percent over 1966). Perhaps 50 percent of all Jewish education expenditures today comes from federation sources. Moreover, Jewish education allocations represent about 25 percent of the total federation and local allocations. The different patterns of distribution by community size are shown in Table 30. The allocations of federations to country-wide and overseas agencies are shown in Tables 31 and 32.

As indicated, general data on synagogue finances remain unavailable, the gaping hole in our knowledge of the expenditures of the American Jewish polity. The fragmentary information that we have suggests that the total of all funds raised by individual synagogues approximately equals the amount raised by the federations. Data from Baltimore, Maryland, and Philadelphia and Erie, Pennsylvania, confirm that synagogues, combined with other local organizations outside the federation orbit, raise as much or more than those communities' federations. In 1970–71 the Baltimore Federation raised a total of $7.3 million, of which just under $3 million was budgeted for local services. The thirty-two synagogues within the Baltimore Federation's service area raised $4,345,000, virtually all of which was expended locally for congregational purposes (a small amount represents dues paid to their national affiliates). Three of the thirty-two congregations had budgets exceeding half a million dollars, the largest of which was $642,000. Another nine had budgets of over $100,000, while nine had budgets of under $10,000. The average synagogue budget in Baltimore was slightly in excess of $137,000. Assuming that this approximates the national average, the total budget for the roughly forty-five hundred congregations in the United States would be $630 million. Therefore, a cautious estimate of $500 million is not excessive.

In calculating the total Jewish public expenditure, it is also necessary to include funds raised independently of the federations and the synagogues for either local, countrywide, or overseas organizations, institutions, or projects. Thus a city like Baltimore raised some $480,000 just for Israel-oriented projects in 1970–71 outside the Baltimore Federation framework, a figure that may in fact substantially exceed $500,000 if money collected by organizations not specifically oriented toward Israel but with projects in Israel is included. Some $175,000 was raised for the Reform and Conservative theological seminaries from Baltimore that same year, while the defense and service organizations raised a modest $175,000, a figure that is far larger in other large cities. All told, Baltimore Jewry raised another million dollars locally for organizations functioning outside the community and, because of the presence of the Ner Israel Rabbinical College and several day schools, almost tripled that sum for other institutions locally, most of which went to Orthodox bodies that are not usually federation beneficiaries. While Baltimore's particular exceptions may not be found in every other community, every major community has an exception of its own. (How does one figure Brandeis University's budget in the Boston area?)

Raising funds is a principal activity of American Jewry, indeed, the one activity that more than any other reaches out to the mass of Jews. It is only rivaled in that respect by synagogue attendence, and although the figures in both cases are hard to come by, it seems that the two activities run about neck and neck: as many Jews contribute to Jewish causes as attend synagogue during the year, while as many actively work on the campaign as attend synagogue regularly. The reasons for the

TABLE 31 RECEIPTS OF NATIONAL JEWISH AGENCIES FOR OVERSEAS PROGRAMS FROM FEDERATIONS, WELFARE FUNDS, AND OTHER DOMESTIC SOURCES, 1970, 1971*

	Federations and Welfare Funds[a]		Other Contributions		Other Income		Total	
	1971	1970	1971	1970	1971	1970	1971	1970
UJA and Beneficiary Agencies								
United Jewish Appeal[b] —Regular	$ 85,133,664	$ 80,591,573	$	$	$	$	$ 85,133,664	$ 80,591,573
—Emergency	127,455,540	97,957,492					127,455,540	97,957,492
Israel Education Fund			3,245,834	3,251,779			3,245,834	3,251,779
American Jewish JDC					868,900	614,200	868,900	614,200
United Israel Appeal					550,000[f]	451,350	550,000[j]	451,350
Jewish National Fund[c]			3,564,334	2,942,155	1,138,988	572,214	4,703,322	3,514,369
New York Association for New Americans[d]					91,482	85,911	91,482	85,911
ORT—Women's American ORT[d]			3,608,774	3,137,172	35,849	46,798	3,644,623	3,183,970
—American ORT Federation[d]					791,628	777,152	791,628	777,152
TOTAL UJA AND BENEFICIARIES	$212,589,204	$178,549,065	$10,418,942	$ 9,331,106	$ 3,476,847	$ 2,547,625	$226,484,993	$190,427,796
Other Overseas Agencies								
American Committee for Weizmann Institute of Science[e]	$	$	$ 2,904,803	$ 3,057,321	$ 1,403,713	$ 1,471,056	$ 4,308,516	$ 4,528,377
American Red Magen David			1,221,066	1,097,242	27,098	7,512	1,248,164	1,104,754
University-Technion Joint Maintenance Appeal	805,000)	777,851)					805,000	777,851
American Friends of Hebrew University[f]			10,434,000	6,607,591	5,176,000	1,579,555	15,610,000	8,187,146
American Technion Society[g]			2,782,790	4,853,104	1,453,107	1,119,497	4,235,897	5,972,601
American-Israel Cultural Foundation	198,757	210,806	1,885,486	2,217,172	42,754	58,999	1,926,997	2,486,977
Ezras Torah Fund[h]	7,371	6,848	469,019	401,429	10,685	9,301	487,075	417,578
Federated Council of Israel Institutions	108,322	103,743	74,236	73,954			182,558	177,697
Hadassah[i]	565,000	565,000	4,372,911	11,635,642	4,316,524	4,418,325	19,254,435	16,618,967
Jewish Telegraphic Agency[j]	247,807	214,228	12,810	17,096	242,684	212,522	503,301	443,846
National Committee for Labor Israel[k]	227,914	229,947	2,552,982	2,822,752	27,246	24,285	2,808,142	3,076,984
National Council of Jewish Women	20,000[j]	20,000[f]	760,815	753,494	383,548	380,259	1,164,363	1,153,753
United HIAS Service[l,m]	1,411,871	1,360,539	245,539	248,383	472,062	770,890	2,129,472	2,379,812
TOTAL OTHER OVERSEAS AGENCIES	$ 3,592,042	$ 3,488,962	$37,516,457	$33,785,180	$13,555,421	$10,052,201	$ 54,663,920	$ 47,326,343
TOTAL OVERSEAS	$216,181,246	$182,038,027	$47,935,399	$43,116,286	$17,032,268	$12,599,826	$281,148,913	$237,754,139

[a]Including joint community appeals.
[b]Cash received in each calendar year.
[c]Collections in the U.S., exclusive of global income of JNF.
[d]Excludes income from UJA; also income from campaigns abroad, from intergovernmental agencies, and from reparations income.
[e]Excludes contributions and earnings of Investment Fund; other income includes research grants.
[f]Includes $4.3 million in 1971 bequest.
[g]Includes Swope Endowment Fund.
[h]Excludes grants from other organizations.
[i]Amounts raised for JNF are excluded. Hadassah "other income" includes membership dues, Shekels, and Zionist Youth Funds.
[j]Excludes income from UIA.
[k]Excludes overseas and Canadian income.
[l]CJF estimate.
[m]Excludes overseas income and income from Claims Conference, but includes UHS income from NYUJA.
*Source: *American Jewish Year Book,* vol. 73; prepared by S. P. Goldberg.

TABLE 32   RECEIPTS OF NATIONAL JEWISH AGENCIES FOR DOMESTIC PROGRAMS FROM FEDERATIONS, WELFARE FUNDS, AND OTHER DOMESTIC SOURCES, 1970, 1971*

	Federations and Welfare Funds[a]		Other Contributions		Other Income		Total	
	1971	1970	1971	1970	1971	1970	1971	1970
Community-Relations Agencies								
American Jewish Committee	$ 952,000	$ 1,039,221	$ 4,604,600[b]	$ 4,404,936[b]	$ 1,535,800	$ 1,592,863	$ 7,092,400	$ 7,037,020
Anti-Defamation League	1,149,200	1,122,451	4,211,352	3,639,065	626,854	649,550	5,987,406	5,411,066
American Jewish Congress	472,272	458,665	1,206,035[c]	883,779[c]	532,475	492,343	2,210,782	1,834,787
Jewish Labor Committee[d]	210,152	199,207	296,070	285,362	6,328	1,500	512,550	486,069
Jewish War Veterans	92,072	103,050	27,200	22,750	515,240	530,802	607,312	633,852
NJCRAC	288,528	254,103			119,038[e]	111,082[e]	434,766	387,935
SUBTOTAL	$ 3,164,224	$ 3,176,697	$ 10,345,257	$ 9,235,892	$ 3,335,735	$ 3,378,140	$ 16,845,216	$ 15,790,729
Health and Welfare Agencies								
City of Hope	$ 3,180	$ 3,275	$ 8,899,362	$ 8,304,022	$ 7,659,931	$ 7,132,735	$ 16,562,473	$ 15,440,032
Leo N. Levi Memorial Hospital	28,289	28,655	316,026	286,956	922,860	808,252	1,267,175	1,123,863
Children's Asthma Research Institute and Hospital			1,716,369	1,626,037	591,782	594,037	2,312,716	2,224,834
National Jewish Hospital	4,565	4,760	4,568,600	4,351,027	2,961,734	2,054,391	7,547,748	6,420,715
Yeshiva U.-Albert Einstein College of Medicine and Hospital[f]	17,414	15,297	5,187,899	4,701,222	62,723,856	51,940,173	67,911,755	56,641,395
SUBTOTAL	$ 53,448	$ 51,987	$ 20,688,256	$ 19,269,264	$ 74,860,163	$ 62,529,588	$ 95,601,867	$ 81,850,839
National Service Agencies								
American Assn. for Jewish Education	$ 211,349	$ 208,731	$ 220,990	$ 114,905	$ 85,020	$ 70,860	$ 517,359	$ 394,496
Jewish Occupational Council	45,803	43,098	20,700	18,585	5,931	26,256	72,434	87,939
National Conference of Jewish Communal Service	11,470	11,452	1,454	11,263	26,126	30,934	49,050	53,742
National Jewish Welfare Board[g]	1,841,975	1,732,200	160,645	157,339	197,780	193,140	2,200,400	2,082,679
Synagogue Council of America	32,350	23,107	162,995	154,377	14,872	12,883	210,217	190,367
SUBTOTAL	$ 2,142,947	$ 2,018,681	$ 576,784	$ 456,469	$ 329,729	$ 334,073	$ 3,049,460	$ 2,809,223
Religious Agencies								
Reform Jewish Appeal	$ 93,537 }	$ 94,801 }	800,750	849,719	3,601,584	3,136,580	4,495,881	4,081,100
HUC-JIR			1,966,527	3,520,532	1,757,549	1,615,944	3,724,076	5,136,478
Union of American Hebrew Congregations	}	76,727 }	488,601	466,973	505,476	521,844	994,077	988,817
Jewish Theological Seminary[h]			6,626,467	6,134,824	2,434,990	1,973,927	9,061,457	8,185,478
United Synagogue of America[i]					1,359,574	1,183,581	1,359,574	1,183,581
Rabbinical College of Telshe	10,440	9,485	497,766	491,689	231,261	237,560	739,467	738,734
Rabbinical Seminary of America	9,022	9,095	258,687	232,867	320,437	265,096	588,146	507,058
Torah Umesorah	6,923	5,955	199,759	209,110	87,007	82,249	293,689	297,314
Beth Madrash Govoha	5,205	5,791	543,374	571,567	216,516	182,461	765,095	759,819
Yeshiva U.-Religious Affiliates[j]	—		381,300	381,300	1,194,538	1,194,538	1,575,838	1,575,838
SUBTOTAL	$ 125,127	$ 201,854	$ 11,763,241	$ 12,858,583	$ 11,708,932	$ 10,393,780	$ 23,597,300	$ 23,454,217

	Federations and Welfare Funds[a]		Other Contributions		Other Income		Total	
	1971	1970	1971	1970	1971	1970	1971	1970
Cultural Agencies								
American Academy for Jewish Reserve	4,736	3,080	14,735	4,925	19,222	16,745	38,693	24,750
American Jewish Historical Society	17,032	9,163	6,544	2,239	150,681	140,688	174,257	152,090
Bitzaron	2,415	2,455	12,623	12,826	13,956	15,035	28,994	30,316
B'nai B'rith Youth Service Appeal	1,334,718	891,288	4,905,142	4,507,434	912,309	1,007,286	7,152,169	6,406,008
Brandeis University	—	—	12,993,030	12,018,967	20,003,862	18,725,198	32,996,892	30,744,165
Conference on Jewish Social Studies	2,665	2,145	28,293	6,595	10,306	11,952	41,264	20,692
Congress for Jewish Culture[i]	1,135	1,000	49,267	51,620	8,701	5,794	59,103	58,414
Dropsie University	70,987	58,705	303,187	257,183	99,396	114,877	473,570	430,765
Histadruth Ivrith	24,781	18,422	106,047	60,354	113,353	122,798	244,181	201,574
Jewish Braille Institute	21,467	21,714	275,498	222,055	76,730	27,428	373,695	271,197
Jewish Chautauqua Society	10,330	10,541	374,990	362,812	25,773	24,951	411,093	398,304
Jewish Publication Society	20,433	15,868	48,501	47,777	474,816	516,049	543,750	579,694
JISPU and Herzliah	6,826	6,303	298,944	152,421	89,360	85,912	395,130	244,636
Leo Baeck Institute	5,977	2,330	149,223	104,256	12,300	6,327	167,500	112,913
National Foundation for Jewish Culture	179,428	161,580	12,225	14,295	—	—	191,653	175,875
Yeshiva U. (Other than Medical, Religious)[k,f]	52,431[l]	52,431	3,743,645	2,718,893	9,555,149	8,974,769	13,351,225	11,746,093
YIVO[f]	44,566	41,136	287,339	217,553	81,885	62,789	413,790	321,478
Zionist Organization of America[d]	28,775	27,474	635,010	584,351	1,161,396	1,078,378	1,825,181	1,690,203
SUBTOTAL	$ 1,828,702	$ 1,325,635	$ 24,244,243	$ 21,346,556	$ 32,809,195	$ 30,936,976	$ 58,882,140	$ 53,609,167
TOTAL DOMESTIC	$ 7,314,448	$ 6,774,854	$ 67,617,781	$ 63,166,764	$123,043,754	$107,572,557	$197,975,983	$177,514,175
TOTAL OVERSEAS AND DOMESTIC	$223,495,694	$188,812,881	$115,553,180	$106,283,050	$140,076,022	$120,172,383	$479,124,896	$415,268,314

[a] Including joint community appeals.
[b] Including N.Y.C. and Chicago Campaigns.
[c] Includes tour income.
[d] Excludes overseas income.
[e] Includes payments from national agencies.
[f] Yeshiva University is reported in part under health and welfare agencies and in part under religious agencies. In the medical school "other income" includes substantial amounts in government funds and hospital service grants.
[g] Income from centers included in federation income.
[h] Including University of Judaism, California.
[i] Excludes grants by other national agencies to avoid double counting.
[j] In the absence of data for 1971, prior year data were utilized for 1971.
[k] Includes building and endowment funds.
[l] Excludes grants from Claims Conference from National Foundation for Jewish Culture, and Memorial Foundation for Jewish Culture.
**Source: *American Jewish Year Book*, vol. 73; prepared by S. P. Goldberg.

crucial importance of fund raising should be clear. The vast sums required by American Jewry for the operation of its own internal institutions and programs and to carry its share of the world Jewish burden are of a magnitude that is usually provided only by governments through taxation. While those responsible for raising funds have attempted to instill in potential donors a sense that their contributions are not a matter of philanthropy but rather the voluntary acceptance of a tax burden, the work is still done voluntarily and is not simply a matter of setting the tax level and then collecting the money. Needless to say, this requires real effort. If the figures we have projected above are correct, the per-capita burden on every Jew in America, man, woman, and child, approximates $350 a year, a figure that compares with the local per-capita tax burden of most Americans.

Every organization that raises money has its own means of doing so, usually involving some kind of campaign. Synagogues probably rely more on membership than do any of the other institutions in American Jewish life, yet even most of them require building-fund pledges to be paid out over a number of years as part of a family's membership initiation and have periodic campaigns for additional capital funds when actual building is undertaken, which has come to mean about every fifteen to twenty years. Moreover, most synagogues quietly raise additional funds through solicitation of their wealthier members and have an annual appeal, usually on Yom Kippur, directed toward the entire membership.

Membership organizations such as the American Jewish Committee and B'nai B'rith usually set dues at such a rate that the total paid in by the membership every year offers them a basis for operation; but they are also dependent on federation allocations for their respective programs and on their own local campaigns in many places. These campaigns tend to consist of dinners at so much per plate, a technique that meets with local federation approval. They must obtain that approval if they wish to be beneficiaries of the overall federation campaign. Women's organizations have perfected their own ways of fund raising, which represent a major portion of their activities year round, whether through donor luncheons, sales projects, or solicitations of contributions in honor or in memory of family and friends. Jewish community centers also raise substantial amounts through membership fees, while other Jewish social-service agencies charge user fees in addition to their campaigns. Schools fall in the latter category as well; almost all of them charge relatively stiff tuitions and must raise additional amounts to cover deficits that can rarely be met out of tuition income even with federation subsidies.

With all that, "the campaign" for American Jews means the annual federation campaign. This is an elaborate effort involving thousands of people in the major cities and hundreds in the smaller ones. Originally a short affair in the spring or fall, increasingly it is becoming a year-round activity.

The usual campaign calendar of today runs as follows: the campaign itself is scheduled for the spring (United Fund campaigns and Israel Bond drives are conducted in the fall), which means February through May. Since the key to a successful campaign lies in getting the biggest givers to make their pledges early, to set a good pace, the practice has grown up to solicit them before the regular campaign, so that their gifts may become known in time to influence others. At first it was the practice to solicit advance gifts quietly in the fall, so as not to interfere with the scheduled fall fund-raising activities. In connection with that solicitation, "missions" to Israel developed: groups of potentially large givers would be flown to Israel for a week of intensive activity that would lead them to make larger contributions than they might otherwise have planned. These missions became so successful that the solicitation on the last day in Israel itself became a major factor in determining the overall results of each community's campaign. As the number of potentially large donors began to increase, the missions were scaled to accommodate different categories, and it became desirable to conduct the missions for the largest givers even earlier so that they could set the pace for the coming rounds. Quick high-prestige missions in the summer were developed, to bring the very largest givers for three or four days of "updating" by the leading figures in Israel—followed by solicitations. These missions are now held late in August, and since they involve prior preparation—to make certain that the pacesetters will indeed be pacesetters—work on the solicitation of those invited actually begins in June. Thus in the normal course of things, the very largest givers have made their pledges by the end of August or early September. In October and November the second rank of big givers go on their missions and make their pledges. This means that by January when the advance gifts activity—another precampaign effort—begins, only the third rank of givers is involved. The campaign leaders utilize the moral effect of these prior gifts during the actual campaign period, when solicitation is conducted on a mass basis.

By and large, mass solicitation is conducted through "divisions" of groupings of people based upon compatible interests. In most communities each business or profession is organized into its own division, as are such exceptional groups as women and young leaders (usually defined as those men and, increasingly, women under forty who are capable of giving exceptionally large gifts, no matter what their lines of endeavor). Thus men and women in the same occupations solicit one another. This enables peers to properly assess each others' ability to contribute and also helps eliminate embarrassments based on misunderstanding of giving capabilities. People within a particular division are likely to know the giving potential of others in their line of work. While they will not estimate it too high, they are not likely to estimate it too low either.

It is almost universally agreed that the best form of fund solicitation is personal solicitation. Meeting a peer face to face and asking his or her contribution is the best way to obtain maximum results, so personal solicitation is used wherever possible, particularly with the large givers.

Since it is also recognized that those who are better educated about the needs are more likely to respond to personal solicitation, continuing efforts at education of a very practical character have become part and parcel of the campaign on a year-round basis. The Israel missions are major educational tools and very successful ones at that. Increasingly, the federations have also come to the conclusion that the better-educated Jewishly their people are, the more likely they are to be open to solicitation. Thus they have made particular efforts with young leadership groups to give them a more extensive Jewish background of the kind that will lead to greater Jewish commitment and thus greater concern for Jewish needs. Limitations of time and manpower have meant that most of these educational programs have been confined to the larger givers, where their success has been demonstrated by the extraordinary increases in the size of gifts over the past decade.

Where solicitation in person is impossible, telephone solicitation is used instead. It is agreed that such solicitations are less successful, but if undertaken by personal friends and acquaintances still do have meaning. Telephone squads—people who solicit others they do not know personally—are used as a third level of activity, primarily to cover the large numbers of Jews who do not fall within the friendship networks of those otherwise active in the campaign. Finally, mailings are used to reach into as many Jewish households as possible, with the expectation that they will rarely produce results unless followed up by some more personal kind of solicitation.

It is characteristic of the campaign that everyone within the local federation is expected to undertake solicitation, from the president of the federation on down. Indeed, the formal positions in the campaign are not devices by which leaders can delegate work to others, but rather involve greater responsibility on their part for personal solicitation, as well as for presiding over meetings and forums designed to stimulate others to solicit. This is part of the personalized leadership in the "follow-me" pattern characteristic of the federations, which has done so much to make them the central institutions of American Jewish life. It is still possible to be a synagogue president without attending services regularly (although this is being discouraged), but one cannot be the president of a federation without personally undertaking to solicit the potential big givers in one's own sphere. And so it goes with the other offices as well. Lesser offices in synagogues do not require much participation in religious activities at all, whereas there is no office of any significance in a federation that does not bring with it the requirement for active participation in the campaign.

MAINTAINING THE BELIEF SYSTEM

When it comes to the problem of maintaining the common belief system, the communal institutions play a minimal direct role while the communal leaders play substantial informal roles—in this case partly through the private institutions of the Jewish community. The fact that membership in Jewish country clubs in so many communities is contingent upon making an appropriate contribution to the local federation, primarily to support Israel, is one means of enforcing conformity to the belief system that must be reckoned within the orbit of communal decision making. So, too, are the social pressures that encourage synagogue membership in all but the largest communities function as ways to maintain what is now the secondary element in the communal belief system—again, by informal rather than formal means.

By and large, the institutions of the American Jewish community avoid direct intervention in matters regarding the belief system, the enforcement of Jewish law, or the regulation of commercial activities (even those of a particularly Jewish character, such as kashruth), all of which were prominent features of Jewish communal life in other times and climes. This is a strong reflection of the impact of American individualism and commitment to "free enterprise." Thus with rare exceptions the regulation of kashruth has been treated as the private preserve of a certain segment of the Orthodox rabbinate rather than as a matter of communal responsibility. It is far more likely that the state government will regulate kashruth than the Jewish community. The only attempt by an American Jewish community to assert serious communal control over kashruth was the one made by the New York Kehillah nearly sixty years ago. It failed not only because the Jewish butchers did not want to cooperate and because the great meat-processing companies already engaged in kosher slaughtering did not feel any necessity to do so, but because both opponents of communal regulation successfully justified their refusal to participate on the ground that such regulation would violate the antitrust laws by establishing a monopoly over the slaughtering, processing, and sale of kosher food products.

FACTORS IN DECISION MAKING

A number of factors influence decision making in the American Jewish community, of which six stand out: (1) the penchant for government by committee, (2) the desire to avoid conflict, (3) the legitimacy of tension between the "national office" and local affiliates, (4) patterns of interorganizational competition ("duplication"), (5) sources of innovation and the initiation of programs, and (6) the role of personalities in the decision-making process.

Government by Committee

The immediate organizational tool for decision making in the American Jewish community is the committee. Committees—in all shapes, sizes, and forms—carry out the variegated business of the community, from the smallest synagogue to the Presidents' Conference (itself simply a high-level committee). The multiplicity of committees within organizations and institutions provides for a certain degree of diffusion of power among many decision makers and something akin to an intrainstitutional "checks and balances" system. Traditional forms of Jewish self-government have long relied upon the committee system for just those purposes.[4]

It can fairly be said that within the institutional and organization framework described in the previous sections, the mode of government of the Jewish community is government by committee, and power and influence accrue to those who can control the committees and their work. Domination of committees involves control at several points: selection of committee members, tasks and agendas, intelligence (in the military sense) available to the committee for its work, committee deliberations, committee output, and so on. Personality and other conflicts may well be focused more sharply in committees. In every case, committees are natural arenas for negotiation, and the widespread utilization of them encourages decision making through bargaining to reach consensus, in itself a classical Jewish mode. In sum, the dynamics of committee behavior are at least a partial factor in any decisions made by the leadership of the American Jewish community.

Conflict Avoidance

Despite the existence of conflict as part of life's reality, the avoidance of conflict is a major principle in the American Jewish community. Conflict avoidance is not synonymous with consensus. The latter involves a deliberate effort to allow the expression of various points of view on a policy or program and then reconciling them in such a way that all participants in the decision-making process are reasonably satisfied with the results. Conflict avoidance, on the other hand, may or may not involve the pursuit of consensus; its main concern is sheer prevention of clashes, however defined, even at the expense of some participants. This is not to say that American Jewish organizations do not often seek consensus but that conflict avoidance holds an even higher priority. Thus an individual or group that can make a disturbance will either be excluded from the decision-making process or, failing that, will be accommodated in order to stop the disturbance, even at the expense of other concerns.

In the aftermath of the Holocaust and because of the continuing crisis affecting the Jewish world, no issue is allowed to emerge as a matter of public controversy in the American Jewish community if it is felt that this might threaten the unity of the community. Open community conflict therefore tends to be confined to marginal matters. Especially where voluntary leaders are involved, every effort is made to avoid overt dissension. When issues are likely to provoke conflict there is every tendency to avoid raising them in the first place. If an issue that is likely to provoke conflict must be raised, every effort is made to arrive at a decision in such a way that there is no chance for the conflict to be expressed.

Certainly the notion of using conflict productively to achieve wider consideration of particular issues or to develop more options for the decision makers to consider—a characteristic feature of American politics—is almost unheard of on the American Jewish scene. This is perhaps less true where professionals are involved, since they are in a somewhat better position to tolerate conflict. But even among professionals the pattern holds because they are rarely in a position to function without the involvement of the voluntary leadership.

One consequence of this approach is that those defined by the communal leadership as "extremists"—youthful militants or intellectuals who have challenged the survival consensus by raising "controversial" issues —are disliked and even feared by the great "respectable" center that dominates most, if not all, of organized Jewish community life in the United States. The label of "extremist" is easily acquired; all one has to do is simply question decisions arrived at through the established patterns of decision making. By and large, these patterns involve a quiet allocation of resources according to the hierarchy of interests of the various community leaders, with emphasis on establishing and preserving an acceptable status quo. Changes or innovations are introduced on an incremental basis only, so as to raise as little controversy as possible. People working together over a long time learn how to cater to each others' interests in this regard almost intuitively. Anyone who challenges this pattern and creates "controversy" by so doing is likely to experience rejection even at the hands of persons who agree with him in principle. In the end, serious conflicts that may occur within the community are likely to be personal rather than substantive in origin. Perhaps the major exception is the emerging conflict between the firmly Orthodox and the rest of the American Jewish community over matters of religious law and practice.

In part this avoidance of conflict reflects the traditional desire of a minority to avoid any weakening of the ties that bind its members together. But it also reflects the fact that the voluntary leaders in the American Jewish community are overwhelmingly recruited from the world of business and commerce, where open conflict is considered bad form and decisions are reached in such a way as to minimize the appearance, if not the reality, of conflict. It is likely that the situation would be quite different if Jewish politicians were involved in making communal decisions, since politicians are schooled in the management of conflict and are thus not only unafraid of conflict but may even provoke it as a means for arriving at the decisions they seek.

The desire to avoid open conflict clearly rules out some issues from consideration, no matter how important they might be. It also enhances the role of the professional leadership, since it enables them to *administer* the community rather than requiring the voluntary leaders to *govern* it. In such situations the tendency is to rely upon the men trusted with the administration to make what still are, in the end, political decisions. Thus the professionals continue to gain power simply because they can organize decision making in such a way as to minimize the emergence of conflict, thereby earning the appreciation of the voluntary leadership.

Local Affiliates versus the National Office

One perennial conflict that is considered legitimate, provided it is not allowed to spread beyond limited tactical skirmishes, is the tension between the national office of an organization—e.g., "New York"—and the local affiliates—the rest of the country. In part it reflects the simple difference in constituency and interest of the two sectors, and in part it reflects a difference in situation between Jews located in the New York metropolitan area, with its particular environment and set of problems, and those located in other, smaller communities that have a different scale of operations. Even within the ranks of the Jewish federation movement, where "New York" as such is not a particularly important factor and the CJF itself is less dependent upon New York leadership than any other countrywide Jewish body, some of this tension exists.

This tension, by its very nature, can never be fully resolved, but there are shifts in its structure that cause immediate changes in the community's decision-making patterns. What can be said about the present situation, in general terms, is that organizations which have traditionally been New York–centered are losing power in the community as a whole, while those whose locus of power is in the localities are gaining.

This shift is not simply enhancing the matrixlike framework of decision making in the community but is shifting the structure of the matrix from its earlier emphasis on an indefinite number of ideological-functional power centers to a fixed number of territorial ones. Since the latter are more firmly united locally than the former ever were or could be at the national-office level, this is contributing to far more clear-cut organizational decision-making patterns within the matrix. It is also creating a whole new set of decision-making arrangements that cannot be accommodated in "the view from New York" and that encourage a very different kind of political bargaining than was characteristic of the New York–centered organizations in their heyday.

Interorganizational Competition ("Duplication")

Interorganizational competition within the same sphere, often referred to as "duplication," is another perennial feature of the American Jewish scene arising from the voluntary and associational character of the community. The attack on duplication is part of the standard rhetoric of American Jewish community life, and, in fact, organizational competition that has led to the involvement of competing organizations in the same issues in such a way as to muddy the waters has been a consistent problem in some spheres of American Jewish life. At the same time, competition itself is not always negative. Recent organization theory has suggested that just as fail-safe mechanisms are part and parcel of modern cybernetic technology, so too are redundant institutions required in human society to allow for alternative means to approach the same goals.[5] Redundancy serves to enable society to recognize human differences in method and approach and to avoid putting all its eggs into one basket. Particularly on the local plane, organizations functioning within the same sphere often develop patterns of sharing that effectively divide tasks so as to minimize overlapping.

Duplication is not likely to disappear on the American Jewish scene or even to be substantially reduced in the ways in which reformers usually suggest, because there is no realistic way to curb the proliferation of organizations in the American setting. When organizational consolidation does take place, it usually reflects a tightening of the organizational belt to cope with decline, a retreat rather than a step forward. (The creation of the American Zionist Federation is a case in point. When the Zionist movement in the United States was a vital and significant force, every Zionist party had its own autonomous organization and there was no movement toward even the kind of minimal linkage that federation provides. Only now that it has become apparent even to the wishful thinkers on the matter that the Zionist movement is in retreat, at least organizationally, has federation become a reasonable option.)

This is not to say that all efforts to control duplication reflect weakness. Within the sphere of community relations, for example, coordination came at a time when all the organizations were flourishing (and was, as a result, limited in its effect). Still, the recent abortive effort to consolidate the American Jewish Committee and the American Jewish Congress was a product of the fiscal problems faced by both organizations in a period of rising costs and diversion of Jewish funds for other tasks, coupled with a decline in the Congress's membership that threatens its viability.

Recognition of the realities of interorganizational competition is not the same as condoning the semianarchy that prevails in some sectors of American Jewish life and is justified in the name of a specious "pluralism" that is simply a manifestation of organizational self-interest. Better means of promoting coordination and limiting harmful duplication in ways that are consonant with the American situation are needed. The federations have generally found such means through their use of federal arrangements and the introduction of community planning based on federal principles. In part, they have been able to do so because duplication among their constituent agencies usually involves agencies doing the same thing but serving different constituencies or different segments of the same constituency, rather than agencies not only doing the same thing but trying to do it with (or to) the same people. It is in the latter situations that the real difficulties of coordination and duplication develop. So, too, competition among synagogues for members is far more tolerable—it can even be salutary—than, say, competition among community-relations organizations regarding negotiations with the Catholic Church.

Innovation and Program Initiation

While decision making in connection with established programs is more or less shared by the professional and voluntary leadership, innovation and program initiation are usually dominated by the professionals, if only because they are involved on a day-to-day basis and are recognized as having the programmatic expertise. Their positions, then, make them the initiators of a very high proportion of new activities and programs and the prime generators of new ideas. This is not to say that they are the *only* innovators and initiators; on the contrary, there are some very important areas where professionals, instead of initiating, have done no

more than respond. But there is no question that they bear a disproportionate share of the responsibility in these areas.

The sources of innovation are also related to how welcome new ideas
and programs are in the community. That in turn varies from one
functional sphere to another. The entire subject of innovation demands
extensive analysis in its own right.

Personalities

The role of personalities in Jewish communal decision making is not to
be underestimated, even though there have been substantial changes in
this regard in recent years. Ironically, personality conflicts are particularly significant at the highest levels of the countrywide organizations.
Perhaps because they are so detached from operational responsibilities,
the countrywide leaders can indulge in the luxury of personality conflicts
(which have always represented a major share of the political conflict
within those organizations). In the local communities, operational necessities lead to greater efforts to control such conflicts.

SYSTEMS OF COMMUNITY POWER AND INFLUENCE[6]

The way in which power and influence are structured in the various local
communities of American Jewry or in the American Jewish community
as a whole is a matter of no little importance. Theoretically one could
discover any one of three major forms of political control: autocracy,
oligarchy, and polyarchy.

Under the autocratic form, a single individual (in other times and
places, an intercessor with the powers that be known as a shtadlan) or
organization functioning as a corporate person (such as a chief rabbinate)
monopolizes power by being decisively involved in every significant community decision. Since autocratic control of this nature usually requires
some kind of force compelling Jews to be members of the Jewish community, it is extremely unlikely that it could ever exist in the American
Jewish community as we know it; nor is there any case on record of such
autocratic control in the United States outside of small synagogues and
in the Hasidic enclaves, whose members submit to the authority of a
rebbe of their own free will.

The second major form of political control is oligarchy, whereby a substantially closed group of individuals enjoy a virtual monopoly of power by reserving control over all significant decision making. Oligarchy, far more prevalent in the American Jewish world than autocracy, comes in several varieties. The simplest involves rule by a single element in the community, a small group with the same fundamental interests, whose members are closely linked with one another through a network of interlocking relationships. To persons who stand outside, this form of control may seem no different from autocracy. However, inside the controlling group itself decision making is collegial, if only because no individual is in a position to exercise control on his own. This kind of oligarchy is to be found in certain small Jewish communities, whose entire organized life centers around a single congregation, which in turn is dominated by a small group of individuals. Here, too, the open character of American Jewish life limits the extent to which such an oligarchy can exercise its power. Moreover, when the community grows large enough for competing institutions to develop, this form of oligarchy usually ceases to be a viable means of leadership.

Another kind of oligarchy is the multiple-element variety, which brings together leaders of a number of different elements in the community within the decision-making group. The group itself is self-selected and stands in more or less autocratic relationship to the remainder of the community. Since each element in the coalition has its own sources of power, one element can decisively influence community decision making without the others. The more elements that are represented in the oligarchy, the more open it becomes to various points of view in the community.

Multiple-element oligarchies are reasonably common among local Jewish communities in the United States. Indeed, it is probable that before World War II they were the dominant form of organization of power and influence in the American Jewish setting. Moreover, such countrywide organization as exists in the United States might very well be classified as falling into that category. In recent years it has become increasingly difficult for groups to "go it alone" on issues deemed to be of universal importance to American Jewry. They must coordinate their efforts with others within the establishment circle. The determination of which groups "count" in deciding how the community as a whole will speak is devolving more and more upon the establishment circle, a coalition of the groups themselves. The Presidents' Conference, for example, is a structural device that has been developed to coordinate a weak multiple-element oligarchy, in those areas in which the constituent groups are willing to coordinate.

A multiple-element oligarchy can be broadly based; it can be quite responsive to at least the articulate segment of the community; and it can be representative of the great majority, if not all, of its significant elements. In this instance it can be considered a representative oligarchy, which, in exercising its decisive influence over community decision making, gives every legitimate interest a share (albeit a highly structured one) in the process. Most local Jewish communities in the United States seem to fall within this category, especially those generally deemed to be the best organized. Communities like Detroit, Cleveland, and Minneapolis have developed oligarchies that are broadly representative. In fact, one suspects that if more participants in Jewish life sought a role in the organized community there would be no oligarchies at all.

Polyarchy—the third major form of political control—is a system in which no single individual, group, or element (or any exclusive combination of these) is able to monopolize power or become decisively involved in every significant community decision. Polyarchies are characterized by their relative openness and fluidity. Power is not only widely diffused but different issues or situations are likely to alter the relative influence of different groups, giving them greater or lesser roles in the decision-making process, depending upon their salience to the issue at hand. Moreover, leadership within these groups is likely to change with some frequency.

Organized polyarchy can be said to exist where the elements, groups, and individuals active in the community are mobilized in routine ways and exercise their influence through recognized channels. Since their participation is expected, coordination among them is possible on a regular basis.

When power is more widely diffused and the participants are less easily coordinated, a fragmented polyarchy exists. In a fragmented polyarchy it is difficult for both participants and observers to determine who has the power potential to achieve their goals. If sufficiently fragmented a polyarchy may become chaotic, but since chaotic polyarchy would signify a community in dissolution, it is a rare and ephemeral phenomenon indeed.

While we do not have the requisite data to draw solid conclusions at this point, on the basis of what is known it seems reasonable to hypothesize that most of the large Jewish communities in the United States fall somewhere between multiple-element oligarchies and organized polyarchies, with the greater number being representative oligarchies. Most of the small communities are either multiple-element or single-element oligarchies, perhaps by default. The American Jewish community as a whole is frequently portrayed as a chaos of competing oligarchies. In fact, it may very well be that the countrywide community is moving from a fragmented polyarchy to a representative oligarchy, not nearly so well formed or structured as the multiple-element oligarchy it sometimes seems to be and not as open as polyarchy might imply, but nevertheless following patterns of organization and fragmentation that combine increasing openness and representativeness with a measure of oligarchic control.

Oligarchy has long been a common pattern for organizing power in Jewish communities, at least since the crystallization of the idea of the Jewish polity as an aristocratic republic during the Second Commonwealth. In their best premodern form oligarchies have been aristocratic in character, and in their finest modern form, trusteeships of leaders seeking the good of the community. Degenerated, they fit the original meaning of the term: rule by a few for their own benefit.[7]

Ideal aristocratic republics have a way of becoming oligarchies when they fall short of the ideal. At its best oligarchic control is in itself a decent approximation of the ideal republic within the limits imposed by human nature. Indeed, to the extent that the term "oligarchy" implies rule by a few for their own personal gain, another term must be found to describe Jewish self-government. Classically, the leaders of the Jewish community have been considered to be trustees responsible for the commonwealth, and the demands placed upon them have echoed this principle of trusteeship. It is not inappropriate, then, to refer to oligarchic forms of control in their best sense as a trusteeship.

In more down-to-earth terms oligarchies frequently arise because there are power vacuums to be filled and only a few people interested in filling them. This is particularly true in contemporary American Jewish life. Given the concentric circles of involvement, the number of people even available for leadership is severely limited. This situation should not be underestimated. Indeed, whenever groups that feel themselves excluded do make their appearance on the Jewish scene, chances are that they will be co-opted and given a seat at the table simply because they ask for it—witness the response of the community to its young "radicals" in recent years.

The response of the overall community to the demands of youth in the late 1960s is illustrative of the processes of community politics in the American Jewish polity. The youth demands were raised belligerently in an ostensibly revolutionary manner, principally because those making the demands believed that the Jewish establishment was so entrenched and so unconcerned with their needs that normal political means would be unavailing. To the extent that those making the demands were outside the decision-making processes they were correct. They received the hearing that they did primarily because they utilized confrontation politics. At the same time, the rapidity of the response demonstrated how open the establishment was—at least on matters affecting youth, who are perceived to hold the future of American Jewry in their hands.

The first major use of confrontation politics came at the CJF General Assembly, held in Boston in 1969. It led to the creation of the Institute for Jewish Life, albeit on a scale radically reduced from what was discussed at the Boston meeting, where a $100-million endowment was suggested. A similar confrontation involving a sit-in in the offices of the New York Jewish Federation led to the establishment of a Division of Campus Affairs, whose first annual appropriation was $75,000. Similar confrontations of greater or lesser intensity in other communities around the country had similar results. We have already discussed the Philadelphia Federation's Commission on Campus Affairs, which was created—without confrontation—in response to complaints of individual young people to their parents and grandparents serving in leadership capacities in the Federation.

After the first year's spontaneous confrontation, the CJF and the local federations moved rapidly to begin to organize the sending of youth to the General Assembly on the assumption that it was best to bring in young people to see the decision-making process and to eliminate what was obviously ignorance of how the Jewish community governed itself. Thus each federation was asked to send several young people and to support the costs of their participation. At the 1970 General Assembly, held in Kansas City, a special youth program was arranged; young people were encouraged to attend and participate in the deliberations and even given special orientation sessions. The youths who showed up in Kansas City looked around for an issue, feeling it incumbent upon them to replicate the 1969 confrontation. They were hard put to do so until they noted that the official meals of the General Assembly did not provide for the *birkat hamazon* nor was the Sabbath ended properly with a Havdalah service. This became their cause and they were once again convinced that the establishment would put them down. To their great surprise—as well as that of the leadership itself in many cases—the General Assembly acceded to their demands, going so far as to institute the public recitation of the *birkat hamazon* after every meal, a practice that has become a regular feature of the CJF meetings.

By 1971 the young people could not come up with an issue, and the CJF staffers assigned to work with them began to search around desperately for one, feeling that they needed a victory. Nothing much came of this effort, but the irony of the shift should be apparent. In the meantime the CJF stimulated the funding of the Jewish Student Press Service and the creation of the North American Jewish Student Appeal to help fund countrywide student projects that were not directly eligible for local federation funding.

The Jewish establishment moved in the direction that it did partly because they felt that the young people were right in their demands even if wrong in their tactics. They were, in certain respects, pleased to be called to account and to be told that they should provide more support for Jewish education and act in more traditionally Jewish ways. They also saw in these young people their own heirs and therefore were particularly concerned with wooing them. Unquestionably they sought to co-opt the young people, even as they attempted to meet some of their demands. Nor did their actions significantly transform the structure of the federation movement or its decision-making processes. Locally and countrywide, youth were given token representation on boards and committees and a few even tried to make themselves heard; for the most part, however, they were either so stunned or impressed by the decision-making process that they sat back quietly in deference to their elders, listening rather than demanding.

As the countrywide tide of youthful rebellion subsided, so too did it in the Jewish community, leaving behind a residue of new activities and a cadre of youth leaders who had virtually made careers out of their new roles. They were fast becoming as isolated and unrepresentative of the mass of Jewish youth as their elders were of the mass of Jewish adults, probably more so.

The special nature of the Jewish polity—its core of religious principles and behavior patterns that must be preserved if the community is to survive meaningfully, its lack of an all-embracing territorial base and the special problem that imposes, its dependence upon a particular kind of dedicated leadership willing to assume grave burdens voluntarily—makes trusteeship a very reasonable solution to its problem of governance. At the same time, the community's necessary reliance upon the consent of its members to survive, the voluntarism that informs that consent, and the religious tenets that make survival meaningful demand a degree of openness and democratic participation that have generally kept Jewish trusteeships reasonably representative.

Leadership and Representation

Once we understand the system of power and influence in the American Jewish community, we are in a better position to understand the nature of its leadership and the ways in which it is or is not representative. The representative character of a community's leadership can be measured in two ways. Leaders who are elected by a broad-based electorate in a competitive manner are deemed to be representative by virtue of their election. Leaders can also be considered representative, even if they are chosen in ways that do not insure representativeness, when they are culturally, ideologically, and socially in tune with the people they are leading.

By and large, the second kind of leadership prevails in the American Jewish community. Indeed, in the few instances where there have been contested elections, it appears that the leaders chosen were not particularly representative but were, rather, the choices of organized minorities that managed to win against unorganized majorities. Paradoxically, it is precisely where elections tend to be pro forma that the leaders often are most broadly representative of the varied Jewish interests in the communities they serve. In fact, judging from the record, it seems that when pro forma elections have been converted into contests, the very representativeness of the leadership in that sense of the word is what has discouraged people from seeking real elections. Modern Jewish communities that have experimented with communal elections (Australia, for example) have not found them to be any better a solution to the problem of representation, because the turnout in such elections tends to be extremely low. Indeed, the smallness of turnout appears to be directly related to the degree of true freedom of association available to the Jews of the community in question.

Communal elections do not guarantee that statesmen will be elected to communal leadership either, since the mass-based organizations that can get their members to turn out in an election frequently are those that involve the most localistic Jews, whose leadership has the most limited perception of the needs of the larger community. Elections do have one important consequence, however: they raise to the inner circles of leadership people whose qualifications are not simply financial. In most cases they are people who have become leaders of some important organizational bloc that is able to turn out the vote. As such, they are more likely to be attuned to straightforward political considerations than are big donors, who do not have to cater to constituencies in any way.

Only when there is a feeling by some substantial community group that the existing leaders are not fundamentally representative are they challenged; then elections are transformed into contests. Since community leadership by and large consists of filling vacuums, it is often more difficult to recruit leaders and to determine whether they are representative or not. It is not as if many people were clamoring for a few places —indeed, it is just the other way around.

There is no question but that the Jewish community—a voluntary polity dependent for its functioning on the free choice of individuals who are willing to do their share to make it function—is indeed ruled by a certain kind of governing class composed of people who choose to make its tasks theirs, either as professionals or volunteers. The character of that governing class both reflects the character of the population it serves and contributes significantly to the shaping of the character of the community itself.

Because the sheer range of communal functions today requires such a variety of talents to fill its many leadership roles, the kind of simplistic exercises in describing leadership patterns in the Jewish community that were frequent in the past have been rendered obsolete. In a basically complex leadership network that is further complicated by the division between professionals and volunteers, special questions arise as to the relationship between leadership and decision making, recruitment and training, and the selection, mobility, and replacement of leaders of both types. These are questions that can not be easily answered on the basis of "representativeness" or some similar catchword.

From Fragmentation to Reintegration
The Polity Enters the Postmodern Era

POSTMODERN TRENDS IN JEWISH ORGANIZATION

The modern era has come to an end, its demise following in the wake of the events and developments of the first half of the twentieth century —especially World War II, the Holocaust, and the creation of a radically new technology. The present generation—Jews included—is the first of the postmodern era, and as such it faces a new set of problems peculiar to its circumstances. These problems, to be sure, have their roots in the era just ended, but they stem most immediately from the needs and concerns of a generation that has grown up in a society strikingly different from its predecessors'.

The change of eras is just becoming apparent to American Jewry. In recent years American Jews have been exercised over a number of trends —internal ones like intermarriage and the attrition of Jewish identity and, most recently, external forces that seem to threaten the "era of good feeling" that has shielded Jews in the aftermath of World War II—all of which darken an ostensibly clear horizon. Though some American Jewish leaders have sought to reassure their constituents that Jewish life in the United States was never stronger and its future never brighter, their assurances are based on the assumption that the new generation of American Jews is simply a continuation of the previous generation, which adjusted, however imperfectly, to the modern world. A closer examination of the situation would reveal that this is not the case, that there are new social and cultural phenomena at work, and that the Jewish community will succeed in its future efforts only insofar as it comes to grips with new developments.

The trends of the postwar period reached their culmination in the early 1960s. These were the years that saw the end of the vaunted "religious revival," as membership in synagogues first stabilized and then, by the late sixties, began to decline. New challenges emerged to threaten the established organizations. By the end of the 1960s the trends toward sorting out the various elements in the organizational structure of the Jewish community and harmonizing them within a common communications network had taken another step forward—partly as a result of the recession of one segment of the structure and partly as a result of the redefinition of the other.

The synagogues represented the receding element. It was not that their loss of membership was decisive, for indeed the actual losses were still relatively moderate. However, a series of events had robbed the synagogues of much of their claim to primacy. First, the changed American attitude toward organized religion in general rendered the synagogue more vulnerable to outside criticism, especially from the youth. Second, the emergence of a disaffected segment among American youth, which drew disproportionately from Jewish ranks, led to direct challenges to the synagogue as an instrument of the establishment. Finally, the continuing Israeli-Arab crisis, punctuated by the wars of 1967 and 1973, has served to confirm the realization that it is not simply a common concern with religious affiliation that binds Jews together; it is also their sharing of a common fate as a people.

After 1967 it became apparent that the synagogue's claim that it could harmonize Judaism with Americanism, by redefining Judaism in predominantly religious terms, was not all it was cracked up to be. Indeed, synagogue-centered Judaism turned out to be less attractive to the majority of American Jews than the broader definition embodied in Jewish tradition, which assigned the land of Israel a central place in Jewish concern. The synagogue even proved a handicap with regard to a certain segment of Jewish youth, who were "turned off" by Judaism as a "churchly" phenomenon in a secular age. Those same young people often found meaning in the more ethnic aspects of Judaism, at a time when ethnic nationalism was on the upsurge in America and around the world.

While the synagogues were receding, the federations were busy redefining their role and broadening their scope. In the 1950s, as we have seen, the leadership of the federations began to concern themselves with the problem of Jewish survival as something more than an issue of welfare or overseas relief. This tendency became a trend after 1960, with federations developing a deeper concern for Jewish education and culture and a wider interest in community planning in a host of ways. All this served to strengthen the hand of the federations as the all-embracing agents of Jewish communal life. Moreover, the federations became more mindful of traditional Jewish practices. They began to embrace the public observance of Jewish religious practices in their own programs and to encourage traditional and observant Jews to become involved in their ranks, thereby building bridges to segments of the Jewish community that had previously been outside their normal purview. By the end of the decade the federations were taking the most effective action toward developing ways to reach out to disaffected Jewish youth.

New organizational and functional patterns have begun to emerge in response to the dissatisfactions that have surfaced since the mid-1960s. Perhaps the best way to describe those patterns and the trends in Jewish community organization they may have initiated is to reexamine the functions that the Jewish community is called upon to perform in light of recent trends.

Religious Rites and Worship

The organization of religious rites and worship, the central concern of the Jewish revival of the 1950s, is also the issue that has provoked the greatest dissatisfaction and generated the most portentous changes. In general, the ferment among the young has led to an assault upon the contemporary organization of Jewish religious life, particularly the large suburban congregation, which is faulted for the inauthentic modes of religious observance that have developed within its precincts, the essential impersonality of its operations, and the "privatism" that animates its members' participation—all of which is perceived as having replaced the more intimate and communally oriented goals and patterns of the traditional synagogues. Young Jews who are seeking an authentic religious experience are also searching for new ways to organize their religious life. The development of *havurot,* the increase in the number of small congregations devoted primarily to worship and fellowship, and the emergence of new seminaries dedicated to both are all features of Jewish religious organization and innovation of the last few years.

In most respects these innovations represent a return to traditional standards, though in a new format. Thus it is not surprising that the pioneers of this trend in American Judaism were traditional-minded Jewish academics and scientists who, in the late 1950s and early 1960s, began to create their own synagogues. Their synagogues were both Orthodox and traditional—that is, while committed to the meticulous observance of Jewish law, they also involved a revival of the congregational organization that was common before the day of the large synagogue, emphasizing small membership composed of families highly committed to one another and seeking a great deal of interpersonal interaction besides the worship experience proper.

Since the mid-1960s this pattern has been followed with considerably more fanfare by Jewish academics and intellectuals from Conservative, and to some extent Reform, backgrounds, primarily through fellowships and "underground" seminaries. Their efforts are still too new to be assessed, other than to say that they have infused a certain dynamism into Jewish religious life that has carried beyond the confines of their fellowships and seminaries. By the mid-1970s a number of mainstream congregations were experimenting with *havurot* within their established institutional frameworks. Though some of these fellowships were no more than study groups by another name, a few congregations actually reorganized themselves into a collection of small groups seeking satisfying Jewish experiences. The *havurah* movement has not stopped the decline in synagogue membership nor has it halted the widespread state of crisis that the American synagogue is in. But the *havurot* have offered some hope of new directions.

External Relations

Organization for external relations has always been closely tied to defense. In fact, at one time the two were essentially inseparable, with the fight against anti-Semitism at the center of both. After World War II the intensity of the fight against anti-Semitism diminished, primarily because overt anti-Semitism had declined as a result of the world's reaction to the Holocaust. Defense then became a matter of fighting social discrimination, seeking rapprochement with the churches, and resisting atavistic elements, rather than a full-fledged battle. Jewish concern with external relations in the United States now turned toward the struggle to extend human rights generally, with the organized Jewish community in the forefront of the civil-rights movement. The beginning of the postwar period witnessed some ordering of the organizational structure for external-relations matters; by the mid-1960s a serious, if limited, assault on the very existence of such organizations was being mounted by persons who felt that they were no longer needed.

The Six-Day War brought an abrupt end to that era of relative calm. Jewish human-relations professionals, as we have observed, found that they still had to do battle for Jews. In the aftermath of the war anti-Semitism became somewhat more respectable, particularly when the New Left took to attacking organized Jewry under the rubric of "anti-Zionism," thereby encouraging the reemergence of right-wing anti-Semites, who had previously remained silent for fear of public rejection. Moreover, the more militant blacks rejected Jewish assistance in their own struggle and, indeed, identified with anti-Jewish elements in the Middle East conflict. The Yom Kippur War intensified these trends. Today Jewish external relations are once again beginning to revolve around the defense of more traditional Jewish interests.

In other aspects of external relations, new organizations emerged to claim a role. The Synagogue Council of America began to develop relations with its Protestant and Catholic counterparts and to seek a role as the Jewish "religious" spokesman on the national scene. After a period of jockeying for position with regard to expressing American Jewry's interests in Israel and other international problems, the Presidents' Conference, as already noted, was formed, uniting all the major Jewish organizations in a common front expressly for external-relations purposes.

Education

The trends in educational organization are more problematic, since education, as we have seen, involves and exposes all the ambivalences of contemporary Jewish life; it is here that the desire for survival comes most directly into conflict with the desire for full integration into the general society. After World War II there was an increase in enrollment in Jewish schools, with a concomitant decline in the number of hours of instruction and the breadth of the curriculum. This trend was stimulated by the transfer of Jewish education to the synagogue, which, as we have noted, made the teaching of "synagogue skills" and loyalties primary over more substantive materials.

By and large, the institutional patterns established in the 1950s persist. On one hand, the continued diffusion of the Jewish population into the further reaches of suburbia and the increased demands of the public schools on their students have made supplementary Jewish schooling more difficult, encouraging further reductions in hours and content.

On the other hand, the drive for intensive Jewish education among a minority of Jews has led to the development of a substantial day-school movement, a sharp departure from the thrust of Jewish activity during the modern era, when Jews tried desperately to break down all barriers that might keep them out of general schools and were even willing to sacrifice the Jewish education of their children to achieve integration. No group in the United States has been more fervent in its support of the public schools than the Jews, who perceived that free nonsectarian public education was the ultimate fulfillment of the Jews' emancipationist and integrationist dreams. Today, however, perhaps 100,000 Jewish students attend all-day schools, and all but one Jewish community of over seventy-five hundred has at least one such school. Moreover, the Jewish federations, which for years avoided extending any assistance to day schools, in many cases have now made them significant beneficiaries, if not constituent agencies.

The day-school movement was clearly strengthened by the fact that many Jews were caught in changing neighborhoods, where the public schools deteriorated before the Jewish population was ready to move. Faced with the problem that this presented, they sent their children to private schools, choosing Jewish private schools over others. By 1974, however, even day-school enrollment had stabilized. The decline in the Jewish birthrate added its mite to the combination of factors that had turned Jewish education from a "growth industry" to one of retrenchment.

The 1960s also witnessed the development of programs of Jewish studies in secular institutions of higher learning. Originally concealed under such rubrics as "Near Eastern studies" or "Semitic languages and literatures," these programs were pushed into the limelight at the end of the decade as a result of the demand for black-studies programs in the universities. Young Jews countered by demanding more extensive Jewish-studies programs, under that explicit label. Whatever the format, this has led to an increase in the number of college-age Jews exposed to Jewish education, often for the first time in a systematic way, and has also created new opportunities for American-born and -trained scholars in the field of Jewish studies.

While the Jewish community placed great hopes on these programs, it was also evident that, for all their value, such programs could not meet requisite Jewish communal needs beyond a certain point. The neutrality of the academy, even if stretched, had to limit the degree to which Jewish-studies programs could be used to train the new Jewish civil service, prepare Jewish educators, and foster Jewish culture. Only Jewish institutions can undertake these tasks. The rejection of independent programs in higher Jewish education conducted under Jewish auspices, which characterized the 1960s, may well give way to a return to such programs alongside, or in conjunction with, programs in the secular universities in the 1970s, as Jews seek to sharpen their own sense of independent identity.

Welfare

Organizational trends in the field of welfare are likely to continue along lines initiated in the late 1940s and 1950s. As the welfare state becomes more deeply entrenched, functions formerly performed by private or public nongovernmental agencies will draw upon even more government support. This pattern is likely to continue. At the same time, certain Jewish social-service agencies are finding new roles within the Jewish community. Specifically Jewish welfare services are assuming two forms: increasing attention to the treatment of middle-class ailments, primarily those of a psychiatric nature, and the provision of services to the aged and to people in changing neighborhoods, who for one reason or another have been left behind. In both cases the Jewish component is being stressed anew.

Enforcement of Community Norms

Another area that has undergone great change is the enforcement of community norms. Conformity to traditional Jewish law, which was always voluntaristic to some extent, has now become entirely so, and the organized Jewish community is not really engaged in that activity today. At the same time, new norms have developed that are subtly enforced by the community's organizational network. These revolve around the support of Israel and fund raising. Israel has become the primary norm of an increasingly secularized Jewish community, with virtually all Jewish organizations sharing in the task of enforcing those norms which relate to Israel and which, in a sense, have replaced the old halakhic norms, even in many of the synagogues.

Since some common standard seems to be necessary for the maintenance of a voluntaristic community, it is expected that norm enforcement will continue to be a task of Jewish organizational life. Behavior toward Israel, however, will not necessarily be the only norm that the community will enforce. After three hundred years of secularization and assimilation there is strong evidence that a revived concern with Jewish tradition is leading to its restoration as a vital norm. While different groups will be entitled to define "Jewish tradition" in various ways, identification with that tradition and acceptance of the responsibility for maintaining, fostering, and extending it seem to be reemerging as central norms in Jewish life, embraced by all Jewish organizations and enforced by them.

Public Finance

The least change is to be expected in the realm of Jewish public finance. American Jews must rely upon voluntary giving to maintain their organizational structure and activities. In recent years all major Jewish organizations have increased their demands upon the members of their community to meet expanded needs at home and abroad. There is every reason to believe that these demands will continue at a very high level. Nor is the response to those demands diminishing. On the contrary, there has been a sharp acceleration in giving as a result of the recurrent Middle East crisis. Though present levels are not likely to be sustained for long, a new and higher "floor" has probably been established that will be maintained even under less tense circumstances.

Defense

Organization for defense also took on new forms in the post–World War II era. In most Jewish communities local action against anti-Semitism was replaced as the major defense function by efforts to assist oppressed Jews abroad and, overwhelmingly, by assistance to Israel. American Jewry, understanding that the threat of local anti-Semitism had substantially diminished, saw as its primary defense task the maintenance of

Israel—not only as a place of Jewish refuge or a haven for Jewish refugees, but also as the symbol of the new and improved Jewish status in the world. Defense efforts in behalf of the state of Israel will undoubtedly continue to dominate the concerns of American Jewry in the foreseeable future. Indeed, Israel's isolation in the aftermath of the Yom Kippur War has heightened American Jewry's sense of solidarity with the Jewish state and even their sense of "apartness" from non-Jews, thereby reversing the trend of the 1950s and 1960s, when there was an almost universal belief that differences between Jew and gentile had been erased.

In the aftermath of the October 1973 war, Jews the world over were once again faced with the prospect that, in order to defend their basic interests, they might have to stand together even against the governments of their own countries. Particularly in the United States, where Jewish integration into the larger fabric of the society seemed almost complete, this came as a shocking discovery. Nevertheless, not only did most Jews seem prepared to rise to the challenge, but they were better equipped institutionally to do so than ever before. The test of defense was becoming the best test of the new Jewish polity.

THE TRUSTEESHIP OF GIVERS AND DOERS

Despite the limitations of the data, it is not unfair to conclude that the American Jewish community is governed by what may be termed a "trusteeship of givers and doers," in which decision makers who are generally self-selected on the basis of their willingness to participate control communal life in all its facets. They perceive their function to be one of managing the community's affairs in trust for its members, the Jewish people as a whole, just as earlier generations of leaders did. We have said that this sense of trusteeship is what keeps the communal leadership from being an oligarchy in the classical meaning of the term: a small body that manages the community for its own benefit. Every significant Jewish interest has the right to claim a place in the trusteeship of givers and doers and is accorded its place once it brings its claim to the attention of the appropriate leadership.

Although it is not elected in any systemically competitive manner, the trusteeship of givers and doers is representative in another way. It seems to reflect the attitudes, values, and interests of American Jewry, probably with considerable accuracy except perhaps in one respect: the leaders are probably more positively Jewish than the community's rank and file. Nevertheless, to the extent that it is desirable to broaden the community's base, it may be necessary to provide support for potential voluntary leaders who cannot afford to work for the Jewish community under present conditions. Perhaps funds should be made available to reimburse officers of major Jewish bodies so that they may take a leave of absence from their normal occupations without suffering a financial loss. Such an arrangement would open the doors of leadership to many people who presently cannot entertain the notion of assuming positions in American Jewish life beyond the synagogue level. There is no doubt that this would lead some people to make their careers in the Jewish communal world, not as professional administrators but as communal politicians. This would bring into being a different set of problems and possibilities, but it might be worth the effort.

The fact that elections are not likely to accomplish the purposes for which they are instituted does not mean that better ways to involve a wider segment of the American Jewish community in its crucial decision-making bodies cannot be developed. Any efforts in that direction must be founded on the recognition that oligarchy is likely to be the persistent form of Jewish life (in some respects it is even the classic form of Jewish political organization). The trusteeship of givers and doers seems to be the system that is fated for American Jewry, and probably for any Jewish community living in a voluntaristic environment like the United States. What is called for, then, is to make the oligarchies properly representative.

This might come about by encouraging a whole host of tendencies already present on the American scene and by adding others. Strengthening the federation movement, for example, offers the best opportunities for creating a systematic decision-making structure. In this connection, it is absolutely vital that the synagogues cease to be considered the private property of their members and be recognized for what they are: public institutions bearing significant communal responsibilities. This is not an argument against congregationalism; indeed, there is every reason to foster true congregational spirit in synagogues of proper scale, provided that it is not a euphemism for communal anarchy.

If this could be accomplished, it might be possible to devise ways in which elections conducted through the congregations would form a major part of the basis of representation in the federations, so that the leadership-recruitment process would reach down into every segment of the community. Under such circumstances, federations would become more completely and thoroughly communal agencies. Moreover, it would be possible to make better determinations as to who should conduct and finance the different activities of the Jewish community. The advances suggested here should be made on a proper federal basis, in the spirit of Jewish institutions, not through a centralization of power (either locally or countrywide), as is often suggested. This is absolutely essential, because attempts at centralization are bound to fail for both American and Jewish reasons.

In this connection, the greatest organizational problem in American Jewish life is no longer the problem of organization on the local plane, but the linkage between the bodies that purport to speak for the Jewish community countrywide. With some notable exceptions, they are the ones that are least harnessed to any kind of community-wide constituency. Although they claim—inaccurately—to speak for Jews outside as well as within their membership, in reality they often do not even speak for their own members.

It is not enough to say that their roles should be reduced, because in fact they do, or at least can, play a necessary role in the community. Rather, efforts must be made to guide them toward the role they can play most profitably for all concerned, a role that will add to their own power just when they are losing power in so many cases.

To this end, the great community-relations and mass-based organizations must become the effective equivalents of political parties and interest groups on the American Jewish scene. That is, they should assume the task of raising the difficult questions, suggesting the important innovations, and then taking the appropriate action that will lead to change within bodies that, by their very nature, must be more conservative and conciliatory if they are to maintain the communal consensus necessary for the community to remain united. There has been a trend in that direction, although not a clear-cut one, in recent years. For the sake of the future of the American Jewish community as a whole, it is a trend that deserves to be encouraged.

NEW DIRECTIONS IN THE AMERICAN JEWISH POLITY

The postwar generation has been a crucial one in Jewish history. After a three-hundred-year thrust toward communal fragmentation, the Jewish people in the United States and worldwide has moved itself around toward some real measure of reintegration. The creation of the state of Israel, the reconstitution of Diaspora communities in the wake of World War II, and the institutionalization of the American Jewish community as a polity all reflect the new condition.

The thrust of the modern era, beginning in the mid-seventeenth century and accelerating thereafter, was to fragment world Jewry. The tight communal organization of the Middle Ages was the first to give way. It was followed by the abandonment of life according to Jewish law on the part of a growing number of Jews (a majority by the twentieth century). In the past two generations even traditional ties to the community were abandoned by a majority of Jews, as they sought full integration as individuals into the larger society, leading to what seemed to be the ultimate fragmentation of world Jewry. In all of this American Jewry was in the vanguard. Traditional communal organization never existed in America, since it never had any legal support. Life according to Jewish law (or even Jewish tradition) was never the style of the majority. Pursuit of individual goals was always far more possible in the New World than anywhere else.

Then in the present generation, when fragmentation reached new heights, a movement toward reintegration around new vehicles and norms began to gain momentum. The Holocaust opened the door to a reconsideration of the need for Jewish unity. This plus the simple passage of time contributed to the postmodern breakdown of the rigid ideologies that divided Jews in the last third of the modern era (mid-nineteenth to mid-twentieth centuries). Finally, and most important, the creation of the state of Israel has given Jews a new and compelling focus that continues to enhance the interest of many in being Jewish. Israel's crucial role as a generator of Jewish ties regardless of other differences was effectively demonstrated at the time of the Six-Day War.

Accompanying this rediscovery of polity among Jews is a reintegration of the organizational components of the Jewish community, leading to the emergence of a more clear-cut structure and communications network linking them. More important, there has been an increase in the commitment of different kinds of organizations to the essential wholeness of the Jewish way of life. The rediscovery itself is clearly rooted in the acceptance of a new pluralism in Jewish life, one that is reflected in the organizational structure of the Jewish community. Pluralism, organized in a more or less permanent structural arrangement, leads to federalism, and federalism has been the traditional way Jews have maintained their organizational structures in the face of the various internal and external pressures they have confronted. As we have seen, contemporary Jews are no exception.

All this may well represent a beginning in the efforts to overcome the fragmentation of Jewish life produced by revolutionary liberalism and socialism on one hand and American Protestantism on the other. Given a new growth in the will to be Jewish among some American Jews, the Jewish community of the coming generation is likely to pursue this reintegration, which also involves the reintegration of American Jewry with world Jewry, as its central political thrust.

Organizationally, the American Jewish community has never been in better condition. American Jewry may well have discovered a pattern for itself that can meet the challenges of communal governance within a free society. Organizational advances, however, will not solve the problem of the individual who must decide whether or not to be seriously Jewish. All institutions can do is to facilitate a positive decision in that direction.

Appendixes
Notes
Index

Appendix A

The American Jewish Community's Response to the Yom Kippur War
A Case Study in Organizational Dynamics*

There is no better way to get a sense of the American Jewish community in action as a polity than by examining its response to an event of magnitude, in this case, the Yom Kippur War of October 1973. The war both sharpened the political dimension of American Jewish life and the political links between American Jewry and Israel within the world Jewish polity. It did so even as it took the edge off the unqualified adoration of Israel of the post-1967 years. Indeed, there may well be a correlation between the two effects, since true *political* relations depend upon mutual understanding and are limited by unidirectional idealization and adulation.

When the Arabs attacked at 2 P.M., Middle East time, October 6, most of the Jews of Israel were completing the Musaf service of Yom Kippur.

*The original version of this study was prepared for the President's Study Circle on World Jewry Seminar on the Response of World Jewry to the Yom Kippur War, held at the residence of the president of Israel in Jerusalem on December 24–26, 1973. The seminar was sponsored by the Institute of Contemporary Jewry of the Hebrew University in Jerusalem, under the direction of Professor Moshe Davis. The author acknowledges with gratitude the assistance of Alex Grobman, whose diligent efforts made it possible for this project to be completed in a very short time. The study itself was conducted during the two months from the outbreak of the war to mid-December 1973. Primary data sources used included the daily news dispatches of the Jewish Telegraphic Agency and selected American newspapers, reports in the Anglo-Jewish press, memoranda, press releases, and information bulletins from the major American Jewish organizations, and extensive interviews with leading figures of American Jewry. A full set of documentary materials and interviews is now on deposit in the Shazar Documentation Center of the Institute of Contemporary Jewry. Selected materials are also held in the Center for Jewish Community Studies.

Six thousand miles to the west (where it was six hours earlier), the services were just beginning for the great centers of American Jewry from the Atlantic coast to the Great Lakes. In the Middle West, where it was 7 A.M., only the most pious were on their way to synagogue, while on the West Coast, at 5 A.M. the community had not yet begun to stir. Thus the great bulk of American Jewry confronted the Yom Kippur War at the beginning of their sojourn in the synagogues of the land. In the course of the day few Jews who identified themselves as such were to be out of touch with their fellows. As a consequence, the mobilization of the Jewish community for this latest crisis in Jewish history was to take on a unique dimension in the United States as in the rest of the Jewish world.

The sources of mobilization were primarily those of the organized Jewish community, and in the end even the individual and spontaneous responses that did not begin as organized efforts were made effective through the organized community. All in all, the crisis reaffirmed recent patterns of development in American (and world) Jewry and strengthened tendencies catalyzed by the Six-Day War in June 1967, which, in turn, sharpened the polity aspects of organized Jewish life in America.

Tens—even hundreds—of thousands of Jews came forward in one way or another to do something for Israel through organized channels, and it is in light of their actions that we can speak of "American Jewry" in the following pages. At the same time there is evidence—equally incomplete—that a not-inconsiderable segment of the Jewish population in the United States did not respond in any visible way. While many of these "Jews of silence" did identify with the struggle of their people in their hearts and minds, others simply did not care and at least some supported the other side. While nobody knows how many absented themselves from the community or who they were, perhaps as many as one-third of American Jewry fell into that category.

Four forms of mobilization were in evidence: (1) fund raising, including the United Jewish Appeal, Israel Bonds, and miscellaneous other fund-raising efforts; (2) volunteering, including volunteering for service in Israel, voluntary efforts to mobilize the community in the United States, especially in connection with fund raising, and efforts to donate blood for the Israeli wounded; (3) political action, namely, direct efforts to influence American policy toward Israel and the war; (4) public identification, including activities designed to enable people—primarily as individuals—to identify with Israel and Jewry at the time of crisis, with or without a direct political motivation or purpose (e.g., advertisements in newspapers, rallies, marches, demonstrations, and the like).

FUND RAISING

As could have been predicted, the most obvious way in which American Jews responded to the crisis was through fund raising. The outpouring of funds was far greater than any given by the American Jewish community before, paralleling that by the rest of the Jewish world—but even more significant, because the Jews in the United States started from a higher base. There were four immediate reasons for this. In the first place, the big givers had already been accustomed to contributing large sums and to expanding already-generous gifts in times of crisis.

Moreover, the sense of crisis deepened as the first few days passed. The initial shock was followed almost immediately by a feeling of confidence that Israel would easily beat the Arab armies. This feeling was reinforced to some extent by early reports from Israel, which were very sketchy and tended to emphasize the positive comments of Defense Minister Moshe Dayan, and Army Chief of Staff David Elazar, both of whom predicted a smashing Israeli victory within the first couple of days. But by Monday, October 8, or at the latest Tuesday, general press and television reports from the area, most of which came from Arab sources—and at the worst moment in the fighting from Israel's point of view—gave a picture of potential disaster for Israel. That stimulated a renewed sense of shock and in some places a fear of almost panic proportions, because it went against the patterns of thought that had become entrenched since the apparently easy Israeli victory of the Six-Day War. If there was any potential for hysteria, American Jews acted it out along lines that had become customary in the past half century or more: by rushing to give money.

In addition, the community was better organized than ever before to mobilize funds and to extract the largest possible amounts from most big donors. By nightfall of October 6 an experienced, multifaceted organization went into operation and has continued to operate ever since. Built upon patterns established during the Six-Day War and strengthened through several intervening emergencies of lesser magnitude (for example, the American Jewish community's mobilization to help the Jewish victims of the Pennsylvania floods of June 1972), this organizational instrument also took on some new dimensions as part of the wartime experience.

Finally, the fact that the war broke out on Yom Kippur not only gave it a symbolic meaning for American Jews, as it did for the rest of world Jewry, but the fact that Jews were in their synagogues, where many rabbis already schooled to know what would be needed took immediate steps to raise money, probably led to some wider coverage of potential donors at the very beginning.

The Varieties of Fund Raising

Fund raising fell into four categories. First and central were contributions to UJA. The American Jewish leadership pledged itself to raise $900 million, of which $750 million was to go to Israel as part of an emergency drive that would encompass the 1974 regular campaign. These funds were to be raised through the usual channels, namely, the local Jewish federations coordinated by the CJF, assisted by UJA. The first step in that effort was the commitment taken within the first twenty-four hours of the war to raise $100 million in cash immediately. By the end of the first week, $107 million had been raised, an unprecedented figure.

The second major form of fund raising was the drive to sell Israel Bonds. The American Jewish leadership committed itself to raise $600 million for the purchase of Israel Bonds through 1974, utilizing the regular mechanisms of the Israel Bond Organization in the United States.

Third, on a much lower level from the perspective of the sums involved, were the continuing fund-raising activities for the usual Israeli institutions, including Histadrut, Hadassah, the universities, and the various Zionist and religious institutions.

Finally, there were the special crisis-oriented drives, e.g., for ambulances for Magen David Adom. In this latter connection many spontaneous fund-raising efforts were initiated, mostly by people with the best of intentions, in the heat of the crisis. The organized Jewish community made every effort to restrict and even stop them, viewing them as potentially diversionary from the two main campaigns and likely to produce smaller gifts than could be extracted by the larger organizations.

While every effort was made to keep this latter type of drive to a minimum, there was a drastic change this time in connection with the third. Although the major organizations that regularly conduct campaigns for funds in the United States agreed to suspend or curtail their efforts for at least several months, it was quickly decided that for many of them full suspension would not be demanded. On the contrary, organizations ranging from the Labor Zionist Alliance to B'nai B'rith informed their members that fund raising for their special purposes would go on as usual over and above the major drives. This was partly because of the timing of the war. Unlike the Six-Day War, which came at the end of the campaign year and did not directly impinge upon ongoing efforts the Yom Kippur War broke out the height of many of the important special-purpose drives held annually in the fall. Powerful groups within Israel and the American Jewish community were not willing to forgo the funds that were due to be collected to maintain their programs. Indeed, the Histadrut issued a special call for cash as soon as the war broke out on the grounds that its Kupat Holim hospitals would bear the brunt of caring for the wounded, and an initial $500,000 was transmitted in response to the call on October 8.

The organizations raising funds for Israel were all screened by the National Committee on Control and Authorization of Campaigns for Israel, which functions under the aegis of the American Section of the World Zionist Organization (WZO). This committee, which was originally created in 1950, had just been reorganized in September. Its twenty-two members include representatives of the UJA, CJF, United Israel Appeal, JDC, New York UJA, the Jewish Agency, and the World Zionist Organization. The American Section of the WZO serves as its secretariat, and the National Committee itself is linked with a parallel body in Israel composed of Israeli government and Jewish Agency officials at the highest level. In connection with the latter body, the National Committee arranged for the Israeli universities (which have less clout in such matters) to suspend their independent efforts to raise funds until April 1, 1974, the beginning of the new fiscal year in Israel. The authorized women's organizations had the least restrictions placed on them because it was felt that their fund sources were minimally competitive with the big gifts being sought.

In the other cases fund raising was authorized on a limited basis, subject to local federation veto, until January 1, after which restrictions would be lifted. The major problem came in connection with the American Red Magen David, which refused to accept the directives regarding coordination from its Israeli parent. As a result the National Committee was authorized to place public sanctions on it. This led to a meeting between the National Committee and the ARMD in which the latter agreed to come into line and even turn over to UJA the money it had raised in excess of its normal campaign income.

New Steps in Organization

The third element, which ultimately became the most important, was the formal initiation of the 1974 campaign three months early, in place of the emergency drive that would necessarily run into the 1974 campaign scheduled for the first several months of the new year. There were several reasons for that decision, not the least of which was that the 1974 campaign had begun informally in June 1973 when the biggest donors —the UJA executive committee—made their pledges. It was expanded in August when the rest of the major contributors were flown to Israel on a special mission to make their pledges. Thus many if not most of the country's biggest donors had already made pledges by October 6. They were approached to increase their pledges, but it was considered only reasonable to ask them to do so within the regular framework.

Beyond these immediate reasons, the decision to conduct the emergency fund as a regular annual campaign represented another major step forward in the organization of American Jewish life and reflected the ever-increasing sophistication of the organized Jewish community in the United States. It clearly reflected the degree to which the annual campaign has now become a year-round affair. Today it is hard to hold a separate emergency campaign at any time. Rather, emergencies lead to what is in effect the imposition of an emergency tax on top of the regular effort.

Another reason for dealing with the emergency as part of the annual campaign was the realization that, while Israel's extraordinary needs had to be met, other Jewish needs should not be neglected. This led to the negotiation of an unprecedented agreement between the CJF and UJA, on one hand, and the Israeli government and the Jewish Agency, on the other, whereby it was agreed that the American Jewish community would undertake to raise $900 million in contributions for 1974, $750 million of which would go to Israel and the other $150 million would stay in the United States to be used for domestic purposes—an increase of $25 million over the amount raised for domestic purposes the year before. It was agreed on both sides that a strong American Jewish community was essential in the Jewish world, and that the local communities' needs in a time of inflation and expanding efforts on the Jewish educational front deserved to be met as part of the overall emergency effort. This was the first time that Israel and UJA formally acknowledged the interdependence of Israeli and Diaspora needs, the first time that a major emergency in Israel did not mean an abandonment or a pullback on the domestic scene in the United States. Thus the agreement marked the emergence of a new stage in the history of Israel-Diaspora relations and of the organized life of contemporary Jewry.

Another organizational advance came when an agreement to coordinate their campaigns was signed between UJA and the CJF on one side, and the Israel Bonds Organization on behalf of the Israeli government on the other. Heretofore it had tacitly been understood that the Israel Bonds Organization would negotiate some arrangement with each local federation (at least in the major communities) so that its major solicitation would not overlap the federation campaign. In fact, the synagogues, which do not play an institutional role in the federation campaigns, became the major vehicles of the Israel Bonds Organization for general solicitation. Despite the fact that many of the same people are involved in both, over the years there has been friction between Bonds and the federations in competition for the same dollars. Thus a countrywide agreement represented a major new departure. The effective result of this was that October and November became Federation-UJA months in 1974, while Bonds launched its general campaign in December under the rubric "Maccabee Month."

A third major area of organizational advance took place in the relationship between the federations and the synagogues. In September the CJF had established a committee on federation-synagogue relations. But before it could even begin to function, events gave the entire effort an unexpected push.

Partly because the war broke out on Yom Kippur and the critical days of fund raising continued through Sukkot and partly because of the way in which American Jews have come to turn to their synagogues in times of crisis, the synagogues had access to far more Jews on an immediate basis than any other body in the United States. Recognizing this, the federations utilized this opportunity for fund raising, and in an hour of crisis the rabbis and synagogue leadership responded in a cooperative spirit. While no formal agreements were reached, it was reasonably clear that a new page had been turned in federation-synagogue relations.

The fourth major achievement brought about by the war was the unification of the two major Jewish fund-raising campaigns in New York City, the UJA campaign and the federation philanthropies drive. New York City was the last Jewish community in the U.S. of any consequence to have resisted the unified fund-raising approach that has become characteristic of the American Jewish community, whereby the local Jewish welfare federations serve as the central fund-raising bodies for UJA and other Jewish needs. There, the Federation of Jewish Philanthropies continues to be primarily oriented toward health and social-welfare institutions, and UJA has remained separate to raise funds for overseas and some countrywide agencies, such as the Jewish Welfare Board and the United HIAS Service.

In the last several years there have been quiet moves made toward greater coordination between the two campaigns with the ultimate hope that they would be joined. Progress was slowly being made on that front when overtaken by events. By the outbreak of the war the two groups had reached an agreement to set up a joint endowment fund, to share one computer, and to combine certain administrative operations. In September they had agreed to establish a standing committee through which representatives of both bodies would meet to discuss common problems on a regular basis.

The war broke out during the period when the Federation conducts its campaign; its opening fund-raising meeting had already been held and the first contributions were coming in. The UJA campaign was not scheduled to begin until February 1, 1974. Leaders of both organizations realized that this timetable would have to be suspended, so they met together to consider the options. Rather than postpone the Federation program or limit the UJA Emergency Campaign to big gifts (leaving the mass solicitation till the regular time), they agreed that the two campaigns would be merged for at least that year. So together they launched a drive for $280 million: $250 million for UJA and $30 million for the Federation. This represented a great increase over the $72 million raised by UJA in the spring of 1973 and a significant increase over the $20 million raised in the fall of 1972 by the Federation.

The voluntary leadership and the staffs of the two organizations were combined to undertake the campaign. The major effort was to be focused not only on raising the additional funds, but in getting people who gave to one campaign but not the other to contribute to the combined campaign and thus be available for both in the future. At the meeting where the agreement was announced and the campaign began, the president of UJA spoke in behalf of local needs and the president of the Federation spoke in behalf of UJA. The results were so successful in every respect that in 1974 it was agreed that the merger would be made permanent.

The Pace of Fund Raising

So fund raising began immediately. In many synagogues the appeal on Yom Kippur day has regularly been devoted to Israel bonds. But on October 6, 1973, appeals were made for both bonds and contributions. In synagogues where such appeals are not normally made and the time is used for an appeal for the congregations, appeals were made in behalf of Israel instead.

The night of October 6, after Yom Kippur, a meeting was held in New York City at the home of Israel's economic minister to the United States. It included as many people as could be gathered quickly from the national leadership of UJA, the UJA of Greater New York, the Israel Bonds Organization, and the CJF, to get information from Israel regarding the situation and to plan for the initiation of an immediate countrywide fund-raising campaign. That night they scheduled a meeting for the next day that would bring together members of the executive committee of UJA, all of whom were contacted by telephone. (It should be noted that the various boards and committees of UJA are not really operating entities but rather are composed of members chosen for the size and relative importance of their contributions in their various communities.) The Israel Bonds Organization also called a meeting of its leaders to be held in New York City on Sunday morning.

On Sunday some seventy-five leaders of UJA and the CJF met. It had been arranged for them to talk by telephone with Israel's finance minister at that time, Pinchas Sapir, who was still in Israel, plus others in Israel and Washington. Minister Sapir requested that American Jews immediately mobilize $100 million in cash within the week. The movement to do so began on Monday as groups in each of the Jewish communities were called by UJA and the CJF working in cooperation. Meetings of leaders (meaning major contributors) were held in many communities simultaneously, where they listened in unison to piped-in telephone messages from Israeli and American Jewish leaders requesting funds.

These gatherings represented the more formal aspects of the initial drive; informally there were continuous contacts between communities and major contributors from Saturday evening on. In general, people were requested to pay any outstanding pledges, make or revise upward their 1974 pledges in line with the new needs, and make the largest possible cash advances on future gifts. People were asked to borrow funds from banks to produce the required cash. The major banks in each community (non-Jewish of course) were contacted and lines of credit were arranged so that money would be available. The response was everything anyone expected and more. The $107 million raised was accompanied by stories of men borrowing money at high rates of interest to provide cash, people mortgaging their houses, women giving jewels, and the like.

In the meantime, less affluent donors began to make their contributions, either through their synagogues or by simply mailing them to their local federations. In some cases congregations called special congregational meetings to pray for Israel's victory and to raise funds to make that victory possible. Synagogues and their rabbis even offered their own manpower to the federations as part of the mobilization effort—a response as unprecedented as the acceptance of funds on the Sabbath and holidays. By mid-November, the Conservative movement claimed to have raised $82 million through its congregations. Young Israel broke all precedent by setting up bicycle brigades to collect pledges on Saturdays and Sundays.

On Tuesday night, October 9, communities across the country held open rallies to raise funds from their general contributors. The rallies met with varying degrees of success. In New York City, where mass meetings to raise money were not feasible, WPIX-TV was used for an Israel Emergency Fund telethon on Sunday night, October 21. The many celebrities who appeared raised approximately $3.5 million from tens of thousands of contributors.

People also began raising funds literally in the streets of the major cities. In New York, Los Angeles, Detroit, Cleveland, Saint Louis, and Hartford sound trucks were driven through the streets of Jewish neighborhoods and suburbs asking for contributions. Hats and coin boxes were passed, particularly at rallies. This presented something of a problem since there was no way to determine whether the money was being properly collected and honestly turned over to the appropriate authorities in all cases. While people were putting $100 bills into these street-corner boxes, it was nevertheless felt that this was not the most productive way to collect the largest amounts from the individuals involved.

Hence the organized Jewish community sought to quash this kind of spontaneous giving. Here the National Committee on Control and Authorization of Campaigns for Israel took the lead in requesting that that style of campaigning be abandoned. At least in communities outside New York City, ways for small givers to respond in at least a semispontaneous manner were better institutionalized once the regular campaign apparatus was mobilized. In some cities merchants in predominantly Jewish shopping districts staged sale days in which either the gross receipts or the profits from their sales were contributed to the local federation drive for Israel.

By and large, however, the major funds came from the relatively small number of very big donors, and generally from those who had already been identified as big contributors. There were three gifts to UJA of $5 million, several of $2 million or more, and some forty gifts of $1 million or more. The largest previous gift had been $3 million, and the $1 million barrier had been broken only a few years before, so it is apparent that virtually all the individuals and firms making such gifts increased their previous levels of giving. On the other hand, relatively few new people came forward. Apparently those who had not let themselves be "discovered" in 1967 did not do so in 1973 either.

If the fund-raising drive had any major weakness, it was in its failure to reach down properly to middle-level and small givers. This is the result of a calculated policy pursued by UJA and the federations for many years, designed to maximize the efforts of campaigners by concentrating on the biggest donors, where limited resources will produce the most substantial results. The fruits of that policy are that the biggest givers are very much cultivated, have been well educated regarding Israel's needs, and can be mobilized to do great things in times of an emergency. Either because it is very difficult or too costly to do so, or simply because of neglect, middle-range givers have not been subjected to the same kind of educational effort over the years. Thus many potential $10,000 and $20,000 donors still gave only $500 and $1,000. It seems that the mass of small givers cannot be properly cultivated, given the limited manpower available to work with them.

Thus the size of middle-level and small gifts tended to be determined spontaneously even when their solicitation was organized. This, of course, varied from community to community. In smaller communities, where it was possible to organize parlor meetings for almost everyone, most Jews were approached in such a way as to extract more from them than they might otherwise have given. In the larger cities it is always difficult to reach down to the larger numbers, and this time was no exception. The technique adopted wherever possible was to call people together for group meetings in homes and ask them to make their pledges at those meetings. When a pledge was considered inadequate, among the big givers at least, the pressure of the meeting was used to obtain a more appropriate amount. This technique was probably used less in meetings of middle-level givers because it is less accepted there, and probably not at all among small givers, most of whom seem not to have been exposed to meetings in any case. The use of this device reached unprecedented proportions. Moreover, the meetings often cut across the usual campaign divisions, combining donors from different levels and breaking down the divisions of trade, business, and profession that are usually carefully observed in the campaign organization.

The meetings themselves were often called by using Jewish youth as volunteer messengers to deliver meeting invitations by hand and thus obviate reliance on the mails. Of course the proverbial telephone squads manned by both men and women in the local federation headquarters played an important role in both invitation and solicitation.

The Advantages of Organization

In the last analysis even the most "spontaneous" forms of giving were at best only semispontaneous—that is, they had organized efforts behind them. The campus is a good example. Student gifts for UJA far exceeded any previous campus effort, with $700,000 reported in the first month alone. On one hand, this represented a spontaneous outpouring. On the other, it was clearly the presence of some Jewish campus instrumentality, either a Hillel Foundation or a functioning student organization, that provided the organizational framework for mobilizing the funds. As a general rule, the better organized the campus, the greater the amount of money that was raised. The same held true for faculty giving. Where faculties had been organized for campaign purposes in the years following the Six-Day War (which had given a tremendous impetus to the organization of faculty for campaign and other purposes in many cities), relatively substantial funds were collected. Where there was no organization the response was sporadic.

No doubt because the war continued for as long as it did, the campaign this time took on another phase. After the first week of initial cash gifts, the big givers were approached again and asked to increase their contributions. The formal framework for this was the visit of Pinchas Sapir, Arye Dulzin, acting chairman of the Jewish Agency, and Chaim Laskov, a former chief of staff of the Israeli army, to the United States at the invitation of UJA. Five meetings were convened around them, one a countrywide meeting of Jewish communal leaders in New York sponsored by UJA and the CJF and then four regional meetings in New York, Miami, Los Angeles, and Chicago under the same sponsorship, to make certain that leading contributors from every organized Jewish community had an opportunity to meet personally with the three Israeli representatives. It was at those meetings that the decision was formally made to launch the 1974 campaign immediately. While such a decision is formally made by each of the 225 separate local Jewish federations— there is no national body that could make such a decision in their stead —their response was unanimous because it seemed the most practical thing to do. Under this rubric of transforming an emergency gift into a 1974 pledge under emergency conditions, a basis was provided for requesting increases of gifts already made. The first three weeks of the crisis saw a mobilization of over $300 million, or approximately the total amount raised in the regular 1973 campaign. Of course the precise increase in response varied considerably from community to community.

Improvements in the organizational framework introduced since 1967 made a great difference, particularly at the big-gift level. When the figure of $900 million was agreed on, the leaders of the countrywide campaign were able to develop a profile of what kind of gifts they would need from what kinds of people, in order to achieve that sum (for example, how many gifts of over $1 million they would need, how many gifts of over $500,000, how many gifts over $100,000 and so on). Since 80 percent of the funds come from about 5 percent of the donors, over the years enough information has been gathered about this 5 percent to make such a profile possible. In addition, in each local community it was possible to make decisions as to what was expected from different individuals, so, for example, if a person who gave $100,000 in past years announced that he was going to give $500,000 it was possible to go to him, if warranted, to tell him that he was expected to give $2 million.

All this fund-raising activity required a tremendous amount of staff work. In the local communities the regular staffs were put on an emergency basis, and volunteers were used at a pace that massively exceeded their usual great efforts in normal campaigns. The structure of the campaign in each community is such that a great deal of the work is done by volunteers in any case, with the professionals providing support, technical services, planning assistance, and the like. Because it has long been an accepted proposition in the United States that only a giver can extract funds from another potential giver, volunteers have consistently played a major role in this dimension of Jewish communal life. They picked up their usual mantle in the emergency, in many cases dropping everything else to spend full time at it for the initial days or weeks of the drive.

On a countrywide basis the work is done primarily by professionals, because here it is not so much a matter of personal solicitation as of providing the information and the organized effort necessary to enable the local communities to do the soliciting. In this case the regular staffs were augmented by the staffs of other fund-raising bodies, which suspended normal operations during the emergency. For example, each Israeli university has an office in the United States with its own fund-raising staff; several Israeli hospitals have similar fund-raising structures. These people were, by and large, taken off their special campaigns (which were suspended or reduced for the duration) and put to work on the overall UJA campaign, providing additional trained manpower to get the job done.

Two important factors stand out in connection with the fund-raising responses: the effect of education and the effect of organization on the overall effort.

The best response came from people who had been educated to appreciate Israel's situation and her needs. The young men who mortgaged their homes to contribute additional funds to Israel were almost invariably persons who had been through the various young leadership programs, specifically those of the CJF, its local affiliates, and UJA over the past few years, who had been to Israel to get an intensive view of the situation, who had been educated through seminars and conferences in the United States and whose general Jewish consciousness had been raised by these efforts of the federation movement and UJA. These people were open to be moved by the crisis and to respond accordingly. Similar results were produced up and down the line. Faculty members, who are notably bad contributors, gave more generously in those cases where campaigns had been conducted in the past and had involved an educational effort. College students came forward because concerted efforts had been made from within their own ranks and by the organized

Jewish community to educate them Jewishly over the past several years.

The educational achievement itself would not have come about without the availability of the organizational framework to stimulate and manage it. That framework has become increasingly better articulated in recent years. Its various pieces have been linked more closely with one another while at the same time undergoing internal improvement within each element. By now there exists in the American Jewish community a reservoir of personnel who can be mobilized in times of emergency, a framework within which they can be activated, and a set of procedures for their mobilization that enables the work to be done on a mass basis with considerable dispatch.

There was another, hidden organizational dimension as well: so many people mailed in their checks spontaneously to their local federations that a month later the federation workers had not yet been able to open all the envelopes. This means that the continued federation campaigns have left their impact—Jews know where to send their money at a time of crisis, and an announcement of need in the synagogue or simple television coverage is sufficient to trigger a response in an entirely voluntary manner. In sum, the combination of a desire to help and mechanisms through which to help made the difference.

VOLUNTEERING

A New Sophistication

The handling of volunteering in the 1973 situation also reflected certain organizational improvements over 1967. First it should be noted that, relatively speaking, there was a tremendous outpouring of volunteers offering their services to Israel. Some 30,000–40,000 people actually made their names known to the proper authorities.

The volunteers fell into two categories: the skilled, especially doctors, and the unskilled, particularly young people who wanted to lend a hand in a general way. Many doctors were willing to leave their practices or university positions to go to Israel to offer their specialized skills. In some cases whole groups of doctors volunteered, and in one or two cases it was reported that a doctor was able to volunteer his whole staff.

The principal characteristic of this volunteering effort was its relative sophistication. Volunteering was especially heavy among the kind of doctors likely to be needed in Israel—orthopedists, plastic surgeons, and burn specialists, for example. Many doctors who had served in Vietnam came forward to share their expertise in dealing with the kinds of wounds created by modern weaponry. This greater sophistication in volunteering was also evident among the unskilled volunteers in a different way. In both cases it reflected a greater knowledge of Israeli conditions and needs abroad in the American Jewish public than ever before.

Medical volunteers were screened by Hadassah, whose staff called Jerusalem every day to ascertain current needs before certifying them for passage. As it turned out, relatively few medical volunteers were accepted because the need was not that great. The Israelis themselves were generally able to provide the medical manpower needed. In some cases, particularly among doctors who had been to Israel, individual enterprise got them into the country; then they made their appearance at the hospitals or even close to the battlefields, where they were used if there was any need for them. In most cases, men and women who registered as volunteers and waited to be called never moved past that stage. In at least a few cases doctors arrived in Israel but found nothing to do and returned home unsatisfied. It seems clear that by and large it took connections for doctors to find ways to be of service and that the best connections were personal ones that individual doctors had forged with Israeli counterparts, as is usually the case in the highly personalized Israeli society. If a doctor knew somebody in the right position, a place was usually found for him; if someone equally qualified came without knowing somebody and without having been placed beforehand, only luck enabled him to find a way to be useful.

Unskilled volunteers faced the same situation in exaggerated form. Some of the volunteering was spontaneous, but much of it was stimulated by organized American Jewry, particularly Zionist and quasi-Zionist groups who sent out a call for volunteers at the very beginning of the war, on the assumption that Israel would need huge quantities of people to fill in for those mobilized. In many cases this call was not designed simply to promote volunteering. It has been a central principle of Israeli policy that volunteering should be considered a step toward immigration, and that volunteering is good because it creates a pool of potential immigrants. Part of the call for volunteers reflected that long-range goal as much as or more than short-term needs. The personal testimony of some of the volunteers indicates that people who were working at jobs in the United States were called and told that Israel needed volunteers, that they should drop everything and go. Being strongly committed to Israel, they did so—only to find when they arrived that the need was not nearly so great. In general, these were people who had already spent time in Israel as students or frequent visitors and had a continuing relationship with the country and its people that made them especially concerned about Israel's security and a special understanding of the situation that they would find as volunteers there. In fact, this was a strong characteristic common to many of the volunteers, skilled and especially unskilled. As a consequence, they were only moderately disillusioned when they arrived to find less need for them than had been proclaimed. In general, the quality of the volunteers seems to have been very high.

On the other hand, sophistication operated in the selection and screening of potential volunteers as well. In general, the management of volunteers was the one major task that fell to organized Zionism in the United States. In matters of fund raising and political action Zionists played a role as individuals or as parts of larger groupings, but organized Zionism had no special role to play. This was not the case with volunteering, which because of its connection with immigration remains one of the major tasks left to organized Zionism in the United States.

The organization of the bulk of the volunteer effort fell to the American Zionist Youth Foundation, which has become the strongest Zionist instrumentality on the American scene and the one that has had the most success in the American Jewish community in the past decade. The AZYF managed its volunteer recruitment and screening program through its Sherut La'Am division. Apparently the Sherut La'Am program, which has been declining in the last few years, was eager for the opportunity to reactivate itself. The AZYF sought volunteers through publicity in the media, but set out the conditions of volunteering imposed by the Israeli government. The first was that only people between the ages of eighteen and twenty-four willing to give a minimum of six months' service in Israel and to pay their own transportation (at a reduced rate) were eligible for consideration. (There was some talk of accepting volunteers for a minimum of three months, and perhaps in some cases this was done. The evidence is not clear on the subject.) These two conditions in themselves disposed of a goodly share of the original applicants. (It should be noted that some Jewish organizations in the United States undertook to provide the money for individual volunteers' fares, and the AZYF itself provided some "scholarships." In at least one case, that of the American Sephardi Federation, this was announced as a major element in their supplementary fund-raising activities.)

Screening and Placement

The entire effort reflected part of the Zionists' ambivalence toward the volunteers. On one hand they wanted to stimulate immigration to Israel, but on the other they wanted to avoid a repetition of the 1967 experience, when masses of unorganized volunteers, many with personal problems, descended upon Israel. Moreover most of the volunteers were totally unskilled in those areas that were crucial to the Israeli economy. They could only do the most menial kinds of labor—yet their expectations were not those of menial laborers. If American Jewry had had a reservoir of young electricians, plumbers, mechanics, and truck drivers, they would have been able to render a great service to Israel. As it was, most of the volunteers could only help in baking bread, cleaning chicken coops, or picking crops, because they did not have the skills to do more than that. This invariably led to a certain amount of disappointment on the part of volunteers who were unaware of the Israeli situation and who came expecting to be allowed to drive tractors and do exciting work on a kibbutz or elsewhere.

To cope with this the American Zionist Youth Foundation in 1973 established a fairly elaborate screening program in New York City and worked with its contacts in other major cities to do the same. In at least some cases the organizations that had been activated during the Six-Day War and had continued to exist in some tenuous way, perhaps as screeners for the Sherut La'Am program, sprang into action again. In Philadelphia, the Philadelphia Volunteers for Israel, a body of Zionists of the new style that had come into existence in late May 1967 and had continued to play a number of roles in screening people for various kinds of Israeli programs, was able to reactivate itself on a full-scale basis and to undertake the screening tasks as they had before. In many cities the Jewish community centers served as screening facilities.

Placement was the second cardinal rule of the AZYF program. It was determined that no volunteer group would be sent unless there was some reasonable indication in advance there would be places to serve in Israel. As a result, in the first month only 772 prospective volunteers were actually accepted in New York out of the tens of thousands who offered their services, even though most of those who came forward at this time otherwise passed the screening. (Approximately one-third of the volunteers accepted came from the Greater New York area and another two-thirds from the rest of the country, a ratio not disproportionate to the general distribution of Jewish population in the United States.)

By the end of the first month Israel had offered 1,155 places for American volunteers, 150 of which were for religiously observant ones; 812 volunteers had actually been sent, with another 293 being readied to be sent (100 to religious settlements). As a result, even of the persons accepted, relatively few had arrived in Israel in the first month following the war, although other groups were scheduled to go.

Unorganized Volunteers

In addition to the organized volunteers, a certain number of unorganized volunteers managed to get to Israel on their own. Almost without exception, they were people who had been in Israel for extended periods before and knew the ropes in dealing with Israelis. Through friends and connections, they managed to wangle space on aircraft bound for Israel (a difficult problem even for the AZYF) and then found themselves assignments in the country. Some of them were very helpful in filling in, doing even the most menial tasks such as collecting garbage. To no little extent this was because they knew that they were not going to be given fancy jobs to do but, indeed, had to make themselves available to do the work necessary to keep society moving. It is to the credit of the American Jewish community that a number of young people, many of whom were candidates for advanced degrees in American universities, were so committed to Israel that they were willing to drop everything and go do that kind of work, precisely because they knew the situation.

Overall it must be concluded that, unlike fund raising, which was of great importance to Israel, the volunteer effort was primarily of importance to American Jewry as a means of participating more actively in the war effort. Its impact on Israel was peripheral since relatively few volunteers went and even fewer took special skills with them. This is in no small measure because the kind of replacement manpower that Israel needed was not available among American Jewry, and probably not among Diaspora Jewry in general.

POLITICAL ACTION

The Presidents' Conference

If, from the Israeli point of view, fund raising was the most vital activity undertaken by American Jewry in support of Israel and volunteering the least, political action fell somewhere in between. In the years between 1967 and 1973 the organization of American Jewry for political action had also undergone some improvement. The Conference of Presidents of Major Jewish Organizations, formed in an effort to coordinate the "external relations" of the American Jewish community so that the community could at least speak with one voice (or close to it) in dealing with the outside world, had acquired a certain institutionalized character and some real recognition as the channel for Jewish representations to the American authorities. In part this was because of structural developments in the American Jewish community already noted; in part it was because communication between the Israeli government and American Jewry on matters affecting Israel was centralized through the Presidents' Conference (as the body is generally called).

This is not to say that the Conference has become an independent entity with operating powers of its own. It is not the umbrella organization of the American Jewish community, as it is frequently advertised to be in the Israeli mass media. It is a coordinating body, able to pull together the various groupings in American Jewish society on many, if not most, foreign-affairs issues, particularly those affecting Israel, and to urge local groups into action when the need arises. If anything, the 1973 war confirmed the position of the Presidents' Conference as the coordinating body in its sphere and strengthened its role. (Curiously enough, this occurred even while the body's actual activities were drastically restricted at the request of the Israeli government.)

As in the case of the fund-raising bodies, the Presidents' Conference sprang into action on the night of October 6. Its policy committee met that evening and moved immediately to call together the leadership of American Jewry to indicate the community's support for Israel, to communicate with the Israeli government, and to mobilize for political action. Telegrams went out that evening to all the member organizations of the Conference, inviting them to meet with Abba Eban on October 7 at the Plaza Hotel in New York City, for a report on the situation. Eban's report was, to the five hundred Jewish organizational leaders at least, a confusing one, partly because the situation in Israel was at that time extremely unclear. Since no specific requests for action were forthcoming, the Conference proceeded on the assumption that the first task was to support a UN-established cease-fire and to request unspecified "supportive assistance" for Israel on the part of the American government. The most specific action to come out of the meeting was a strong endorsement of the fund-raising efforts of the American Jewish community. At the same time the policy committee of the Presidents' Conference decided to call a national leadership convocation in Washington, for October 9, which would bring together ten delegates from each of its affiliated organizations around the country and other Jewish leaders, to express their solidarity with Israel publicly and privately in the nation's capital. It was assumed that by that time they would know better what kind of political action was required.

The convocation was a great public success, attended by one thousand people from all parts of the country. By the time it was held it had become apparent that the fighting was going to continue for longer than had initially been expected. Thus the highest-priority item on the agenda was not a cease-fire but American replenishment of the Israeli arsenal. The key demand of the emergency convocation was that the American government immediately undertake to supply Israel with military equipment. Beyond that, the meeting generally reaffirmed the Israeli position regarding peace in the Middle East. The Arabs were termed aggressors. The nations of the world were criticized for their indifference to Arab terrorism and their contribution to aggression through their indifference (at that point it was not fully clear how much Israel would be isolated by world reaction). Reliance on the UN as a peace-keeping mechanism was rejected, and a call was made for direct negotiations among the parties concerned.

The mood of the conference was one of great anxiety and eagerness to act. By October 9 it had become apparent to American Jewry that the Arabs had won initial successes. Indeed, the news reports were such that the Arab successes were magnified even beyond their reality. Moreover, American Jewry had witnessed the spectacle of the United Nations Security Council's absolutely refusing to label the Arabs aggressors (much less bring about a cease-fire) because of the adamant position of a majority of its members, and most especially the Soviet Union, in support of the Arab states. American Jews were deeply shocked and impressed by the picture of Yoseph Tekoah, Israel's ambassador to the

UN—alone, isolated from his fellows, subjected to verbal attacks—that was broadcast on American television.

Other than expressing the sentiments of American Jewry through resolutions and serving as a forum whereby prominent American politicians could identify themselves with Israel's struggle, the Conference was, in effect, told to do nothing. The Israeli government took into its own hands the entire responsibility for negotiating with the American government regarding other aspects of the war. While Jacob Stein, president of the Presidents' Conference, did see President Nixon and Secretary of State Kissinger (the latter with some frequency) and no doubt individual Jewish leaders and influentials contacted their respective congressional delegations (and perhaps even people in the administration) to solicit general support for Israel and also specific support for arms shipments, the Jewish community did not make any further moves as a body. By the weekend the U.S. government announced that it was indeed launching an airlift of supplies to Israel, so that the apparent necessity for action passed.

A number of the key figures in the Presidents' Conference were not happy with being relegated to the sidelines, but in accordance with the past policy of the American Jewish community generally they accepted without serious challenge the decision by the Israeli government that they were to stand by and wait. In the meantime they busied themselves with efforts to mobilize American public opinion in behalf of Israel and with acknowledging the help of those political leaders who had spoken out in favor of Israel. They met periodically to receive briefings from Israeli diplomatic figures so as to be able to keep their members informed, and sent out news bulletins passing on that information (to the extent that it could be made public).

When the cease-fire went into effect the Conference turned its efforts toward mobilizing tourism to Israel and some peripheral attempts to make known which countries had responded negatively to Israel's needs as a result of the Arab oil boycott. Immediately following the cease-fire they were asked by the Israeli government to assist in developing a modest amount of public pressure in behalf of the Israeli prisoners in Egypt and, most particularly, in Syria. On November 2 they had a second Presidents' Conference meeting, attended by up to five delegates from each organization, to meet with Prime Minister Golda Meir and to receive a report from her. These major meetings all received substantial press coverage, especially in Israel, and were used primarily as a sign of American Jewry's public identification with Israel rather than as direct tools of political action. Obviously it is not possible to make a sharp distinction between the public identification of a major voting group and political action, but to the extent that public identification is a more passive form of political action, that is what was involved in those meetings.

The Presidents' Conference first real opportunity for action was in connection with the Arab pressure on Japan to change its Middle East policy and even to break off diplomatic relations with Israel. The Conference went to work in its usual manner, requesting local Jewish communities to make their views known to the Japanese authorities and moving on a countrywide basis to meet with the Japanese ambassador to convey to him formally the sentiments of American Jewry. Besides those overt moves, informal steps were taken to make clear that American Jewry was willing to consider appropriate countermeasures to any unfavorable Japanese actions. For example, it was made known that some 40 percent of Japanese exports to the United States passed through the hands of American Jews. Informal talk of a counterboycott was encouraged, or at least allowed to spread. It seems that in these efforts the Presidents' Conference had at least the tacit support of the American government, which made its own views on Japan's actions public. This undoubtedly enhanced the impact of the American Jewish effort, which may indeed have had some real effect on the Japanese refusal to break off relations with Israel, even as they announced a shift in their policy from neutrality to a pro-Arab stance.

Local Response, Contradictions, and Conflicts

In addition to the Presidents' Conference itself, every one of its constituent organizations undertook to mobilize its own membership in behalf of Israel—generally, but not entirely, within the limits passed on to them by that body. Of these organizations the American Jewish Congress probably took the most independent stance, in connection with the so-called Jackson amendment, of which more below. One of the salient characteristics of the American Jewish community is the lack of centralized control over the actions of its individual groups and organizations. Another is American Jewry's knowledge of the techniques of political influence, like other American groups. Together these two characteristics create a spontaneous combustion of their own on the political front.

Without waiting for "marching orders" from Jerusalem or New York, most organizations asked their members to make their views known to the president, the secretary of state, and the Congress as soon as the war broke out. Thus the war of the telegrams began immediately.

After word filtered down to the grass-roots level that the effort was not necessary there was a slackening off, but that in turn led to reports of a shift in the "balance of mail" being received on Capitol Hill. Arab and pro-Arab forces were reported to have launched their own counteroffensive against further American involvement in the Middle East (i.e., assistance to Israel), ostensibly basing their case on purely American grounds. This led to an immediate revival of organized Jewish efforts to influence their representatives in Washington, with or without instructions to do so.

Thus the Jewish community took steps to mobilize support for President Nixon's request for a congressional appropriation of $2.2 billion to support Israel's purchases of American war matériel. The mere suggestion of the request was enough to trigger bulletins from the appropriate countrywide Jewish organizations to their local affiliates, providing the names of the relevant senators and congressmen to be contacted. There was a corresponding response locally, limited only by the confusion created by the Israeli government's silence regarding the need for American Jewish support.

In terms of this kind of intra-American foreign policy effort the National Jewish Community Relations Advisory Council also played a role. It moved to mobilize the local community-relations advisory councils, all of which were standing by of their own accord, and served primarily to provide them with up-to-date information on the situation in the Middle East, as that information was released to them by the Israelis, and on the activities of the Presidents' Conference and other American Jewish bodies. They, too, sent telegrams to the appropriate political figures and sought to mobilize their local affiliates to secure statements of support from local political, labor, and religious leaders. One of the major functions of the NJCRAC was to distribute information on responses obtained in different communities so as to encourage other communities to move in the same direction. Several of the local community-relations councils and various other organizations established "hot lines" that people could call to get the latest news about the war.

Aside from the tacit disagreement between the American Jewish leadership and the Israeli government over whether the American Jewish community should take active steps in support of the Israeli position, there was one area of overt conflict within the Jewish community during the crisis. The supporters of the struggle to secure emigration rights for Soviet Jewry insisted upon continuing their work even during the war. The Presidents' Conference and the rest of the American Jewish establishment wanted a moratorium on that effort so as to concentrate on the problem at hand. But the groups active in behalf of Soviet Jewry claimed that they were receiving encouragement from official Israeli sources to continue their efforts, thus giving them a certain legitimacy. This conflict has not been resolved. To the extent that it surfaced publicly—and every effort was made to prevent that—it did so in connection with the then still pending Jackson-Vanik amendment to the administration-backed trade bill, which forbade granting most-favored-nation status to Russia as long as the Soviets interfered with Jewish emigration.

In general, the American Jewish establishment had supported the Jackson-Vanik amendment but without much active effort, since the Israeli government had previously conveyed the impression that it did not want the matter pushed too hard. Among the major Jewish organizations only the American Jewish Congress had openly opposed the amendment, on the grounds that American-Soviet détente was more important in the long run than the likely effect the amendment would have on the immediate problems of Jewish emigration from the Soviet Union. The administration opposed the amendment all along.

Here the American Jewish community was caught in a cross fire. On one hand, high administration officials used the opportunity presented by the war to urge the American Jewish leadership to play down its support for the amendment as detrimental to Secretary of State Kissinger's efforts to enlist Russia's cooperation in the interest of a just peace. The American Jewish leadership accepted this position. When the various leaders conveyed to the appropriate members of Congress their temporary wish to soft-pedal the issue, Senator Jackson's response was highly critical of them. He indicated that he would not suspend his efforts even if it meant exposing their opposition. As a result of those discussions, the American Jewish leadership reconsidered its stance and agreed not to suspend their efforts in behalf of the amendment, even for the duration. As it happened, the administration itself withdrew its request for most-favored-nation status for Russia, at least temporarily.

If this was in any respect a "victory" for American Jewish political action, it was really a greater victory for the non-Jewish senators and congressmen who favored the amendment and refused to allow the Jews to stop supporting it.

Mobilizing Non-Jewish Support

One thing the American Jewish community did start out to do on its own, was to arouse the sentiment of the American public in behalf of Israel and to secure the public support of church, ethnic, labor, and veterans' groups, as well as the media.

The American Jewish Committee, the American Jewish Congress, and the Anti-Defamation League of B'nai B'rith took the lead in appealing to their contacts in the Christian community for support. There is every reason to believe that the American Jewish leadership looked upon the Christian community's response to the 1973 crisis as a test of the changed dialogue that came about as a result of the Six-Day War.

In 1967 American Jews were truly shocked at the lack of Christian response to their concern for Israel. That lack was widely discussed in the aftermath of the war. It was concluded that one of the main problems was that in the effort to create some kind of dialogue, Jews had failed to make clear to their Christian counterparts exactly what place Israel holds in the Jewish scheme of things, not only politically but theologically. It was discovered soon enough that it was extremely difficult for Christians to grasp the principle that a land could be so important to a religious group. Moreover, many Christians were not really prepared to accept that idea even after they began to understand it.

Between 1967 and 1973 the Christian-Jewish dialogue underwent a very real change. Instead of being a dialogue between brothers seeking to reestablish a familial relationship, it became almost an exercise in foreign relations, at least from the Jewish point of view. The Jews, recognizing that they had to live in a predominantly Christian world, felt that it was better to be able to talk with their Christian counterparts, to know them and to have relationships with them, than to be isolated from them, even though they did not expect much sense of brotherhood to result from the talks. This was a major retreat from the earlier optimism of the dialogues, but it reflected a realistic assessment of the realities of the Jewish-Christian relations.

Even that assessment may have been too optimistic. The Christian response to the Yom Kippur War was stronger than in 1967, but was still quite limited. The few recognized Christian leaders who have consistently demonstrated their pro-Jewish feelings or their interest in maintaining a close alliance with the Jewish people did speak out, although most of them had to be asked to do so by their Jewish contacts.

A new element on the scene this time were the ethnic groups that are newly emergent as forces on the American scene. Here the American Jewish Committee played a prominent role. Some years ago the Committee launched a program to reach out to white ethnic Americans on the grounds that they had been a substantially neglected element in American society and that their legitimate interests deserved more attention, both for reasons of justice and in light of Jewish interests. These efforts brought some return in terms of support for Israel in 1973, although in the main it too was limited to individuals who had personally become very involved in the Committee effort or to groups that had a stake in Israel's anti-Soviet stance.

As in the past, the Jews' greatest support came from the leadership of organized labor. In general, labor, still dominated by its old guard, remains as friendly to Israel as it did twenty-five years ago. Both the Jewish Labor Committee and the Labor Zionist Alliance played some role in working with the labor leadership.

Similarly, the Jewish War Veterans worked among the general veterans' organizations in the United States and obtained their support for Israel. By and large, they also received a sympathetic ear because of a convergence of interests. The American veterans' organizations tend to be highly suspicious of the Soviet Union and détente, and strongly supportive of forces that oppose Soviet expansionism.

Despite many disappointments nationally with regard to obtaining support from non-Jews, as is invariably the case in the United States there was a great diversity in local reactions. In some communities a broad spectrum of non-Jewish leaders spoke out strongly for Israel; in others there was little or no response. In almost every case the crucial factor was the relationship between the local Jewish leadership and their non-Jewish counterparts.

Public Demonstrations

The line between political action and public identification is obviously a thin one. Fifty or sixty thousand Jews gathered in a square in New York City in support of Israel is not exactly an apolitical phenomenon. No sensible observer would doubt that political figures noted the demonstrations that did occur. Nevertheless, regardless of who organized the demonstrations, the people who attended them undoubtedly did so to express personal solidarity with Israel in the most public kind of manner.

One of the most significant aspects of the 1973 war is that American Jews, like those in other countries, took to the streets to express their solidarity with Israel. In some respects the public manifestations of Jewish solidarity in 1973 were extensions of a mood that began at the time of the Six-Day War. In 1967 Jews did not go out in the streets as readily. Just as they were summoning the initiative, the war ended. In 1973 the rallies erupted in as nearly a spontaneous manner as possible. In the last analysis it was not spontaneity that produced rallies, only spontaneous responses that produced crowded rallies. The organized Jewish community was there, ready to call the rallies into being, set up the sound amplification systems and the podiums, invite the appropriate figures and Jewish leaders to attend, organize programs, and notify the media.

In New York, the American Zionist Youth Foundation took the lead in organizing the largest of the American Jewish rallies, which brought fifty to sixty thousand people together on October 7 in the plaza outside the United Nations, simultaneously with the first meeting of the Presidents' Conference. In the various Jewish communities outside New York, the local community-relations councils are generally responsible for organizing rallies, and as a general rule they assumed the responsibility this time as well. The Jews who came to these rallies were highly committed to Israel's cause, anxious to proclaim their commitment publicly, and, among the young, willing to fight with anyone who came to oppose them; in the first few days scuffles broke out between Jewish demonstrators and Arab counterdemonstrators.

The rallies that were held after the cease-fire reflected organized efforts to apply pressure more than spontaneous feeling, although they continued to capitalize on the spontaneous response of American Jewry. On

November 5 a rally was held in New York's garment district in behalf of the Israeli prisoners of war, officially sponsored by the Presidents' Conference. For maximum impact it was held the day before the New York City elections, and all the mayorality candidates and other political leaders attended. Similarly, an emergency demonstration and prayer service was held before the Syrian mission to the United Nations in behalf of the POWs held by Syria. Another rally was held in front of the Red Cross Building in Washington.

Perhaps a more useful way of examining public identification is by looking at the responses of various groupings within the American Jewish community. First, and not unexpectedly, youth were the most visible element in the demonstrations. What is significant is that this time adult Jewish leaders also participated in the marches, something that would not have occurred so readily a few years ago. As for the participating youth, they consisted of persons who were preponderantly already highly involved in Jewish life: youth groups and particularly the students of Jewish schools were major sources of rally participants.

The Jewish schools were also natural points for organized activity in identification with Israel, primarily for their own students. For most schools the pattern of activity was the same: religious services, an emergency-fund drive, perhaps some kind of special money-raising activity such as a cake sale, correspondence with Israeli soldiers, a letter-writing campaign to congressmen or to the president of the United States, asking for American support for Israel. After the casualty figures were announced, many schools held memorial services for the Israeli fallen. The fund-raising drives in the schools alone collected some $1 million. In New York, the Board of Jewish Education held a demonstration of Jewish school children on October 25, with a turnout of approximately fifteen thousand students. In general it seems that the Yom Kippur War continued the process, begun during the Six-Day War, of making the American Jewish schools more cognizant of Israel and making their curriculums, if not Israel-centered, then at least more closely linked with Israeli issues.

The Response on the Campus

Perhaps the sharpest change in reaction between 1967 and 1973 was that found among college students. Jewish college students were stirred in 1967, but then a whole host of issues impinged upon their response: the

Vietnam War was at its peak, campus unrest was great, the New Left was riding high. By 1973 the American involvement in the Vietnam War had effectively ended, the campuses had subsided and indeed had sunk into an apathy that discouraged public displays of commitment of any sort, and the New Left had dwindled to modest proportions. Jewish student activity on the campuses in support of Israel was the exception rather than the rule.

All the foregoing reasons created a much greater campus response than in 1967, but none of them are sufficient as explanations. Although it is unlikely that the situation would have allowed for serious Jewish campus response without the shift that had taken place, there had to be certain positive factors present to stimulate that response as well. First and foremost among those positive factors was the existence of a separate Jewish student movement that had emerged over the years and had survived after the general student movement went into decline. In the late 1960s a certain percentage of the activist Jewish students of all persuasions discovered their Jewish interests and realized how those interests separated them from their non-Jewish peers; a Jewish students' movement developed. In some cases it was as radical in orientation as the general student New Left; in others it was far more moderate. But in any case it was Jewish.

The Jewish student movement was not a very large one, any more than was the general student movement even at its peak; only a small percentage of the American student population was involved at any time. But the Jewish students showed a very real staying power that was not generally characteristic of the others. Today it survives almost alone on campus after campus. As a result there was a Jewish student press when the war broke out, and the various campus newspapers were connected through the North American Jewish Student Network. There was even a countrywide Jewish Student Appeal, which had been set up by the students in cooperation with the CJF and certain key faculty and young leadership figures associated with the CJF to raise funds for student activities.

Second, the sense of Jewish isolation from Third-World politics had grown among sensitive Jewish students on the campus, so that they were increasingly prepared to function separately from the main student groupings. This sense of isolation began with the Arab-Israel confrontation: as student radicals began to support the Arab position, Jewishly committed radicals felt more isolated from their fellows.

Third, the Jewish student movement had successfully rallied around the cause for Soviet Jewry and had retained its vitality even as other youth movements were breaking apart.

Finally and very importantly, the existence of organized vehicles for Jewish student response made a great difference. On the campuses, as everywhere else, organization seemed to be the key to effective response, to the channeling of spontaneous activity not only in useful directions, but in the directions that made what activity there was count for more than sheer numbers would suggest.

It should be noted that the campus response, while very visible in one sense, was mixed to a certain degree, perhaps somewhat more so than in the general Jewish community. While thousands of students went to rallies, given the total number of Jewish students it is hard to say how many actually showed any signs of support for Israel. It was on the campus that the first visible signs of polarization in the Jewish community became apparent, albeit in a modest way. There were Jews on the campus who spoke out against Israel (although they were fewer in number and spoke more quietly than they might have a few years before, when the New Left was stronger). This marks the campus off to some extent from the general Jewish community, where even the apathetic Jews were not opposed to Israel, but simply uncaring.

The Yom Kippur War bridged whatever was left of the generation gap among committed Jews. Perhaps the best example of this was the reaction of the youth at the 1973 CJF General Assembly.

One major aspect of the General Assembly has been its role as a vehicle to stimulate involvement of college youth and faculty in the affairs of the American Jewish community. Beginning in 1969, when a group of young Jewish radicals, assisted by some Jewish professors, virtually stormed the General Assembly in Boston, the CJF and its constituent federations have to a greater or lesser degree made serious efforts to bring youth to the meeting and to prepare programs for them. It has generally been assumed that even though many of them are relatively moderate because they are chosen by their local federations, the young people who come will be searching for issues through which to confront the adult community. As they had been in the past several years, the initial plans made by the youth for the 1973 General Assembly were oriented toward such a search for issues of confrontations.

All this went overboard with the coming of the war. The young people came to the General Assembly seeking advice from the adults as to how to better mobilize their efforts and the efforts of their peers in behalf of Israel, rather than seeking any confrontation. The community was knit together in a way that it had not been in the past.

If the reaction among Jewish college students seemed on the whole to be on the plus side, the reaction among the Jewish faculty was more mixed. On one hand, the successful construction of organizational and institutional links between faculties and communities in many different localities since the Six-Day War seems to have paid off with more campus activity, particularly in the fund-raising sphere, than ever before. Concrete identification with Israel was made possible in specific ways, rather than simply through signing petitions and statements.

On the other hand, the polarization among the Jewish faculty may have been even greater than in 1967. That year there was a division between the involved and the apathetic, with many of the latter virtually apologizing for their apathy after the war had reached its successful conclusion. The evidence seems to indicate that in 1973 there were fewer apathetic faculty members, but there was a larger group who were either overtly or covertly hostile to Israel. Still, the fact that very few Jewish professors were willing to criticize Israel openly, and that many who disagreed with Israel's policies, for whatever reason, were still willing to support Israel in her hour of need, is of great significance.

The key organization in the faculty effort continued to be the American Professors for Peace in the Middle East, a group born out of the Six-Day War and kept alive in the intervening years through a number of academically orientated programs designed to bring Israel and its problems to the campus in an intellectually respectable way. It was immediately available as an instrumentality when a crisis came again. APPME's own stand was, for the first time, openly pro-Israel. While the organization's sympathies had always been clear, until the Yom Kippur War some kind of balance was attempted, at least formally. The war essentially ended that.

To summarize, public identification was closely linked to political action but separated from it to the extent that it involved the spontaneous desire of Jews to express their solidarity with Israel, even more than it involved the mobilization of those same Jews to make an impact on the political scene. It is difficult to estimate the number of Jews who actually participated in public identification actions, but the figure is probably between 5 and 10 percent. Since that would involve some 300,000 to

600,000 people, the impression that it made was extremely vivid. Moreover, it is true that for every person who actually made himself visible in this way, there were an undeterminate number of others who identified with this action passively, for a whole host of legitimate reasons that do not reflect any lower level of identification with Israel. Still, it would be a mistake to assume that 300,000 or even 600,000 Jews identifying strongly, plus all those passively associated with that identification, meant that the Jewish community was united in its positive concern for Israel as a special ingredient in their lives. By the very nature of things, we do not know how many American Jews were apathetic in the real sense of not caring—how many had assimilated so far that the problem of Israel simply did not interest them. There is some reason to believe that the signs of polarization that were most visible on the campus also existed to some extent within the general Jewish community; that is, Jews who cared at all cared even more than they did in 1967, while those who did not cared even less than six and a half years earlier.

SOURCES OF THE RESPONSE

The Organized Community

The Yom Kippur War offers a classic case of how organization makes the whole greater than the sum of its parts. Five to 10 percent of American Jewry could make its weight felt because that response was organized. Moreover, the existence of institutionalized channels through which the spontaneous desire to respond could be directed were of crucial importance to the translation of spontaneous feeling into action.

Take the pattern in one community of twenty thousand Jews in the Middle West. The first word of the war spread as individuals came to synagogues on Yom Kippur morning after having heard the radio. After a certain point, radios were set up in the synagogues themselves (a phenomenon repeated even in some very Orthodox synagogues in the United States), and news bulletins were announced from the pulpit as the services proceeded. Following Yom Kippur, the leaders of the local federation called a meeting of the community's influentials to begin organizing fund raising. As word was received from New York, they moved step by step toward calling mass meetings, at which spontaneous energy could be channeled into fund-raising activities. On the campus

Jewish students flocked to the Hillel Foundation, where they went about creating their own rallies and fund-raising campaigns. None of this would have been possible had not a structure existed before the war and had not institutionalized channels of organizational activity existed.

Several institutionalized channels within the organized Jewish community made the response possible. The prime channel was the UJA-CJF local federations. They not only raised funds, but almost dominated the channels for communication of news within the Jewish community, because the diffusion of information was tied so closely to the generation of contributions. As it turned out, even the major link between the Jewish communities of America and Israel was provided by the CJF and UJA. As in 1967, the two groups set up a Telex system linking eighty-five Jewish communities across the country. Bulletins were sent out twice a day to the federation offices in those cities giving news of campaign progress.

The capstone of the fund raisers' effort was the CJF General Assembly, where some twenty-five hundred American Jewish leaders from 150 communities, spanning several generations, came together—not to raise money and not even to do the usual civic business of the Jewish community, but simply because that was the place for Jews to be in an hour in which the Jewish people was beleaguered.

A second institutionalized channel was that of the public and community-relations organizations, topped by the Presidents' Conference. The latter body really came into its own as a result of the Yom Kippur War, which, because of its lightening impact, required concerted action and did not allow time for the individual organizations that constitute the Conference to do very much on their own. By and large, the internal memorandums of the individual organizations consist of instructions to their officers, chapters, and affiliates to follow the lead of the Presidents' Conference. Thus this channel, which has been under development for the expression of the external-relations concerns of American Jewry was made more solid. No doubt much of the new strength in this channel is due to the fact that American Jewry takes its cues from the Israeli government in all matters that affect Israel in the area of external relations. This in itself has encouraged the development of a single voice for American Jewry in that field, something which Israel wants in any case.

The real question is whether that voice is in any respect an independent one, or is simply a conduit either from the internal American side (namely, its member organizations) or from the Israeli side. The evidence from the Yom Kippur War is that the Conference is primarily a conduit when it comes to Israeli matters. It seems that the disjointed situations created by seeming to be the spokesman for the largest Jewry in the world, on one hand, and being unable to speak except when told to, on the other, led to a degree of confusion, nervousness, and even resentment within the Presidents' Conference that by the very nature of things was not easily dispelled.

A third conduit was that of organized Zionism. By and large, organized Zionism does not play an important independent role in American Jewish life, despite some resurgence of Zionist organizational activity in recent years with the creation of the American Zionist Federation (one of the results of the Six-Day War). The long-time location of fund-raising activities in the federations and the more recent transfer of representation activities to the Presidents' Conference has left organized Zionism with immigration-oriented responsibilities within the larger community. In the 1973 crisis these took the form of organizing the volunteers for Israel. The Zionist bodies were also clearly visible on this occasion within the framework of the Presidents' Conference. They were far less visible even as individuals among the fund raisers. Relatively few of the major figures in the fund-raising arena are considered Zionists; rather, they are today's "non-Zionists," at least for representation purposes on the reconstituted Jewish Agency.

Finally, there were the synagogues. Partly by the accident of Arab timing and partly as the result of the cumulative experiences of American Jewry, the synagogues occupied an important place in the initial stages of the American Jewish response. The fact that most Jews heard the news in their synagogues and many were first solicited for contributions there was in many respects an accident of timing. Nevertheless, over the past decade American Jews have shown that, at least for those among them who care, the synagogue is the first place Jews turn to in times of trouble, when they want to be with their fellows.

This phenomenon has clearly strengthened the synagogue in the American Jewish scheme of things, but it has also forced the synagogues into closer cooperation with the rest of the community. The synagogues can serve as gathering places for large numbers of Jews, but by their very nature they are not capable of mobilizing the Jewish community as such for a major national effort. That requires more cosmopolitan organization. In the 1973 crisis the desire of Jews generally to do something led the synagogue leadership, which is usually reluctant to engage in joint action, to enter into alliances with federations in order to achieve desired common goals.

TOWARD GREATER ORGANIZATIONAL INTEGRATION

In looking back at the Yom Kippur War, what is most noticeable is its impact on the continuing organizational integration of American Jewry, and the growing centralization of organized American Jewish life. We have already noted that little more than a generation ago the five spheres of American Jewish activity—religious-congregational, educational-cultural, community relations, communal-welfare, and Israel-overseas— functioned substantially separated from one another.* In the 1950s the first and last two spheres developed integrating ties with one another. After the Six-Day War the community-relations sphere began to be pulled into the communal-welfare/Israel-overseas orbit, and tentative links were forged between the latter and the educational-cultural sphere as well.

The Yom Kippur War seems to have strengthened the links between all of the spheres and even initiated, at least on a temporary basis, greater links between the religious-congregational and the communal-welfare spheres for the first time. This pattern parallels governmental and organizational developments throughout the Western world: the thrust of the twentieth century has been to integrate what was once separate, but in such a way as to increase the complexity of the entire system because of the greater complexity involved in the interaction of its various parts. The American Jewish community is still in the relatively early stages of this process. It was moving in that direction in any case, but two Israeli wars in six years have hastened developments.

Similarly, the Yom Kippur War, like the Six-Day War before it, has led to increased centralization of power and authority within the American Jewish community. The process of centralization within the communal-welfare and Israel-overseas spheres has been going on for a long time. The Yom Kippur War increased it to the extent that the needs of Israel became the basis for establishing a new level of support for local functions, with the decision as to what that level should be, at least in general terms, made through an agreement between UJA, the CJF and the government of Israel. The implications of this are enormous. It is true

*See pages 206–26.

that in the past raising money for Israel's needs has been the key to increasing the amounts of money available locally, because Israel has offered the drama and excitement needed to generate larger sums than might otherwise have come forward; but heretofore the division of funds has been a matter to be negotiated between the local committees and UJA. Now for the first time negotiations must be conducted within established countrywide limits, namely, a $25 million increase, a limit based upon a written agreement negotiated by representatives of the most powerful elements in the Jewish people as a whole.

In addition to centralization at that level, the war has probably contributed to centralization on another level as well. The great need for funds for Israel caused independent institutions not connected with Israel to suspend or abandon their own campaigns. Even though most of those campaigns were resumed after the crisis, they were severely handicapped by the diversion of the resources to meet Israel's needs. In the coming years the federations will be the only bodies able to increase or even maintain their revenues. Thus there will be every incentive for other Jewish institutions and organizations to come to the federations in search of more money, even for the support of established programs.

This trend is already very visible. As the federations have taken on greater planning and programing responsibilities, they have cautiously extended their funding to agencies in the other spheres, except the religious-congregational one. In doing so, they have generally aided in the upgrading of communal services, as well as in the fostering of greater unity in the Jewish community. Thus the results have been overwhelmingly positive. But even with their general commitment to self-restraint in imposing their policies on constituent and recipient agencies, their extension of funding privileges has been accompanied, quite properly, by a demand on their part for some say in the programs of those agencies.

This process is not only likely to continue, but has probably been accelerated as a result of the war and the funding agreement that emerged from it. Synagogues are already beginning to turn to federations in search of support for their schools. This trend is likely to expand, and it may even be that federation funding will find its way into other activities previously the preserve of the religious-congregational or any of the other activity spheres of American Jewry.

Appendix B

Communities with Jewish Populations of 100 or More, 1978 (Estimated)

Source: *The American Jewish Year Book,* 1979

State and City	Jewish Population	State and City	Jewish Population	State and City	Jewish Population
ALABAMA		**CALIFORNIA**		Metropolitan	
*Anniston	100	*Alameda & Contra		Area)	2,000
*Birmingham	4,000	Costa counties	28,000	Petaluma	320
Dothan	265	*Antelope Valley	350	*Pomona Valley[c]	3,500
*Gadsden	180	Bakersfield (incl. in		*Riverside	1,200
Huntsville	650	Kern County)		*Sacramento	5,700
*Mobile	1,200	El Centro	125	Salinas	240
*Montgomery	1,625	Elsinore	250	San Bernardino	1,900
Selma	210	Fontana	165	*San Diego	23,000
Tri-Cities[a]	120	*Fresno	2,200	*San Francisco	75,000
Tuscaloosa	315	Kern County	850	*San Jose	14,500
		Lancaster (incl. in		*San Pedro	300
		Antelope Valley)		*Santa Barbara	3,800
ALASKA		*Long Beach	12,500	*Santa Cruz	1,000
Anchorage	420	*Los Angeles		*Santa Maria	200
Fairbanks	210	Metropolitan		Santa Monica	8,000
		Area	455,000	*Santa Rosa	750
ARIZONA		Merced	100	Stockton	1,050
*Phoenix	25,000	Modesto	260	*Sun City	800
*Tucson	8,000	*Monterey	1,500	Tulare and Kings	
		*Oakland (incl. in		County	155
		Alameda & Contra		Vallejo	400
ARKANSAS		Costa counties)		*Ventura County	5,000
*Ft. Smith	160	Ontario (incl. in			
Hot Springs	600	Pomona Valley)		**COLORADO**	
*Little Rock	1,740	*Orange County	35,000	*Colorado Springs	1,000
*Pine Bluff	175	*Palm Springs	4,500	*Denver	30,000
Southeast Arkansas[b]	140	*Pasadena (also incl.		Pueblo	375
Wynne-Forest City	110	in Los Angeles			

State and City	Jewish Population	State and City	Jewish Population	State and City	Jewish Population
CONNECTICUT		*Lakeland	800	*Quad Cities[g]	3,000
*Bridgeport	14,500	Lehigh Acres	125	Quincy	200
Bristol	250	*Miami	225,000	Rock Island (incl. in	
Colchester	525	*Orlando	10,000	Quad Cities)	
*Danbury (incl. New		*Palm Beach		*Rockford	1,025
Milford)	3,000	County	40,000	*Southern Illinois[h]	2,000
*Greenwich	2,200	*Pensacola	725	*Springfield	1,150
*Hartford (incl. New		Port Charlotte	150	Sterling-Dixon	110
Britain)	23,500	*Sarasota	5,400	*Waukegan	1,200
Lebanon	175	St. Augustine	100		
Lower Middlesex		*St. Petersburg (incl.			
County[d]	125	Clearwater)	10,000	**INDIANA**	
*Manchester	1,200	*Tallahassee	1,000	Anderson	105
*Meriden	1,400	*Tampa	7,000	Bloomington	300
*Middletown	1,300			*Elkhart	160
*Milford	500	**GEORGIA**		*Evansville	1,200
*Moodus	150	Albany	525	*Ft. Wayne	1,350
*New Haven	20,000	*Athens	250	*Gary (incl. in	
*New London	4,500	*Atlanta	22,000	Northwest Indiana -	
*Newtown	375	*Augusta	1,500	Calumet Region)	
*Norwalk	4,000	Brunswick	120	*Indianapolis	11,000
*Norwich	2,500	*Columbus	1,000	Lafayette	600
Putnam	110	Dalton	235	Marion	170
Rockville	525	Fitzgerald-Cordele	125	Michigan City	400
*Stamford	11,000	Macon	785	Muncie	175
Torrington	400	*Savannah	2,600	*Northwest	
*Valley Area[e]	700	*Valdosta	145	Indiana-Calumet	
Wallingford	440			Region[i]	5,000
*Waterbury	2,800	**HAWAII**		Richmond	110
Westport	2,800	Honolulu	1,500	Shelbyville	140
*Willimantic	400			*South Bend	2,600
Winsted	110	**IDAHO**		*Terre Haute	450
		Boise	120		
DELAWARE				**IOWA**	
*Wilmington (incl.				Cedar Rapids	330
rest of state)	9,500	**ILLINOIS**		Council Bluffs	245
		Aurora	400	Davenport (incl. in	
		*Bloomington	125	Quad Cities, Ill.)	
DISTRICT OF COLUMBIA		*Champaign-		*Des Moines	3,300
*Greater Washing-		Urbana	1,000	Dubuque	105
ton[f]	160,000	*Chicago		Fort Dodge	115
		Metropolitan		Mason City	110
FLORIDA		Area	253,000	Muscatine	120
*Brevard County	2,250	Danville	240	Ottumwa	150
Daytona Beach	1,200	Decatur	450	*Sioux City	1,090
*Fort Lauderdale	50,000	East St. Louis (incl. in		Waterloo	435
Fort Myers	300	So. Ill.)			
Fort Pierce	270	*Elgin	700		
Gainesville	700	*Galesburg	130	**KANSAS**	
*Hollywood	30,000	*Joliet	800	Topeka	500
*Jacksonville	6,000	*Kankakee	260	*Wichita	1,200
Key West	170	*Peoria	2,000		

State and City	Jewish Population	State and City	Jewish Population	State and City	Jewish Population
KENTUCKY		Greenfield	250	*Rochester	240
*Lexington	1,400	*Haverhill	1,600	*St. Paul	9,750
*Louisville	9,200	Holyoke	1,100	*Virginia	100
Paducah	175	*Hyannis	245		
		*Lawrence	2,550	**MISSISSIPPI**	
LOUISIANA		Leominster	1,525	*Clarksdale	160
*Alexandria	760	Lowell	2,000	*Cleveland	180
*Baton Rouge	1,100	*Lynn (incl.		*Greenville	500
Lafayette	600	Peabody)	19,000	*Greenwood	100
*Lake Charles	250	Medway	140	*Hattiesburg	180
*Monroe	300	Milford	245	*Jackson	750
*New Orleans	10,600	Mills	105	*Meridian	135
*Shreveport	1,600	*New Bedford	3,100	Natchez	140
		Newburyport	280	Vicksburg	260
MAINE		North Berkshire	675		
Augusta	215	Northampton	350	**MISSOURI**	
*Bangor	1,500	*Peabody	2,600	*Columbia	350
Biddeford-Saco	375	*Pittsfield	1,685	*Joplin	115
Calais	135	*Plymouth	500	*Kansas City	19,000
*Lewiston-Auburn	1,000	*Salem	1,150	Kennett	110
*Portland	3,500	Southbridge	105	Springfield	230
*Waterville	300	*Springfield	11,000	*St. Joseph	490
		Taunton	1,200	*St. Louis	60,000
MARYLAND		Webster	125		
*Annapolis	2,000	*Worcester	10,000	**MONTANA**	
*Baltimore	92,000			*Billings	160
Cumberland	250	**MICHIGAN**			
Easton Park		*Ann Arbor (incl. all		**NEBRASKA**	
Area[j]	100	Washtenaw		*Lincoln	1,050
Frederick	400	County)	3,000	*Omaha	6,500
*Hagerstown	275	Battle Creek	245		
Hartford County	420	*Bay City	650	**NEVADA**	
*Montgomery		*Benton Harbor	650	*Las Vegas	13,500
County[f]	70,000	*Detroit	80,000	Reno	380
*Prince Georges		*Flint	2,395		
County[f]	20,000	Grand Rapids	1,500	**NEW HAMPSHIRE**	
*Salisbury	300	Iron County	160	*Claremont	130
		Iron Mountain	105	*Concord	350
MASSACHUSETTS		*Jackson	375	*Dover	425
*Amherst	750	*Kalamazoo	650	Keene	105
*Athol	110	*Lansing	1,800	Laconia	160
*Attleboro	200	Marquette County	175	*Manchester	2,000
*Beverly	1,000	Mt. Clemens	420	*Nashua	450
*Boston (incl.		Muskegon	525	*Portsmouth	700
Brockton)	170,000	*Saginaw	550		
*Brockton	5,200	*South Haven	100	**NEW JERSEY**	
*Fall River	3,000			*Atlantic City (incl.	
*Fitchburg	300	**MINNESOTA**		Atlantic County)	11,800
*Framingham	16,000	Austin	125	Bayonne	8,500
*Gardner	100	*Duluth	1,000	*Bergen County[k]	100,000
*Gloucester	400	Hibbing	155	*Bridgeton	375
Great Barrington	105	*Minneapolis	22,090		

State and City	Jewish Population	State and City	Jewish Population	State and City	Jewish Population
*Camden[l]	26,000	*Vineland[u]	3,335	Queens	379,000
*Carteret	300	*Wildwood	425	Staten Island	21,000
Elizabeth (incl. in Union County)		Willingboro (incl. in Camden)		Nassau-Suffolk	605,000
*Englewood (also incl. in Bergen County)	10,000			Westchester	165,000
				New Paltz	150
		NEW MEXICO		Newark	220
*Essex County[m]	95,000	*Albuquerque	4,500	*Newburgh-Middletown	4,900
Flemington	875	Las Cruces	100	*Niagara Falls	1,000
Gloucester County[n]	165	Santa Fe	300	Norwich	120
Hoboken	500			*Olean	140
*Jersey City	8,000			*Oneonta	175
Metuchen (incl. in North Middlesex County)		NEW YORK		Oswego	100
		*Albany	13,500	Parksville	140
		Amenia	140	Pawling	105
Millville	240	Amsterdam	595	*Plattsburg	275
*Monmouth County	30,000	*Auburn	315	Port Jervis	560
		*Batavia	165	*Potsdam	175
*Morris-Sussex Counties[o]	15,000	Beacon	315	*Poughkeepsie	4,900
		*Binghamton (incl. all Broome County)	4,000	*Rochester	21,500
Morristown (incl. in Morris County)		Brewster	175	Rockland County	25,000
*Mt. Holly	300	*Buffalo	22,000	*Rome	205
Newark (incl. in Essex County)		Canandaigua	135	*Saratoga Springs	500
		*Catskill	200	*Schenectady	5,400
New Brunswick (incl. in Raritan Valley)		Corning	425	Sharon Springs	165
		Cortland	440	South Fallsburg	1,100
North Hudson County[p]	7,000	Dunkirk	200	*Syracuse	11,000
		*Ellenville	1,450	*Troy	1,200
*North Jersey[q]	33,500	*Elmira	1,400	*Utica	2,500
*Northern Middlesex County[r]	17,500	*Geneva	300	Walden	200
		*Glens Falls	360	Warwick	100
*Ocean County	12,000	*Gloversville	535	Watertown	250
*Passaic-Clifton	7,800	Herkimer	185	White Lake	425
Paterson (incl. in North Jersey)		*Highland Falls	105	Woodbourne	200
		Hudson	470	Woodridge	300
Paulsboro	165	*Ithaca	1,000		
Perth Amboy (incl. in North Middlesex County)		Jamestown	185	NORTH CAROLINA	
		*Kingston	2,400	*Asheville	1,000
Plainfield (incl. in Union County)		Liberty	2,100	*Chapel Hill-Durham	1,650
		Loch Sheldrake-Hurleyville	750		
*Princeton	2,600	Monroe	400	*Charlotte	3,000
*Raritan Valley[s]	18,000	*Monticello	2,400	*Fayetteville (incl. all Cumberland County)	500
Salem	230	Mountaindale	150		
*Somerset County[t]	6,000	Greater New York	1,998,000	*Gastonia	220
Somerville (incl. in Somerset County)		New York City	1,228,000	Goldsboro	120
Toms River (incl. in Ocean County)		Manhattan	171,000	Greensboro (incl. in N.C. Triad)	
*Trenton	7,200	Brooklyn	514,000	High Point (incl. in N.C. Triad)	
*Union County	39,500	Bronx	143,000		

State and City	Jewish Population	State and City	Jewish Population	State and City	Jewish Population
*North Carolina		OREGON		*Oil City	165
Triad[v]	2,700	Corvallis	140	Oxford-Kennett	
*Raleigh	1,375	*Eugene	1,500	Square	180
Rocky Mount	110	*Portland	8,700	*Philadelphia	
Whiteville Zone[w]	330	Salem	200	Metropolitan	
*Wilmington	500			Area	295,000
Winston-Salem (incl.		PENNSYLVANIA		Phoenixville	300
in N.C. Triad)		Aliquippa	400	*Pittsburgh	51,000
		*Allentown	4,980	*Pottstown	700
		*Altoona	1,200	Pottsville	500
NORTH DAKOTA		Ambridge	250	*Reading	2,800
*Fargo	500	Beaver	115	Sayre	100
Grand Forks	100	*Beaver Falls	350	*Scranton	4,190
		Berwick	120	Sharon	470
		*Bethlehem	960	Shenandoah	230
OHIO		Braddock	250	*State College	450
*Akron	6,500	*Bradford	150	Stroudsburg	410
Ashtabula	160	Brownville	150	Sunbury	160
*Canton	2,710	*Butler	340	*Uniontown	290
*Cincinnati	30,000	Carbon County	125	Upper Beaver	500
*Cleveland	80,000	*Carnegie	100	*Washington	325
*Columbus	13,000	Central Bucks		Wayne County	210
*Dayton	6,000	County	400	West Chester	300
East Liverpool	290	*Chambersburg	340	*Wilkes-Barre	4,300
*Elyria	275	Chester	2,100	Williamsport	770
Hamilton	560	Coatesville	305	*York	1,600
*Lima	290	Connellsville	110		
Lorain	1,000	Donora	100	RHODE ISLAND	
*Mansfield	600	*Easton	1,300	*Providence (incl. rest	
*Marion	150	Ellwood City	110	of state)	22,000
*Middletown	140	*Erie	940		
New Philadelphia	140	Farrell	150		
Newark	105	Greensburg	300	SOUTH CAROLINA	
Piqua	120	*Harrisburg	4,750	*Charleston	3,200
Portsmouth	120	*Hazleton	800	*Columbia	2,150
*Sandusky	150	Homestead	300	Florence	370
*Springfield	340	*Indiana	135	Greenville	600
*Steubenville	405	*Johnstown	600	Orangeburg County	105
*Toledo	7,500	Kittanning	175	*Spartanburg	295
*Warren	500	*Lancaster	1,900	Sumter	190
*Wooster	200	*Lebanon	425		
Youngstown	5,400	Lock Haven	140	SOUTH DAKOTA	
Zanesville	350	*Lower Bucks		*Sioux Falls	135
		County[y]	18,000		
		McKeesport	2,100	TENNESSEE	
OKLAHOMA		Monessen	100	*Chattanooga	2,250
Muskogee	120	Mt. Carmel	100	Johnson City[z]	210
*Oklahoma City	2,000	Mt. Pleasant	120	*Knoxville	1,350
Oklahoma City		New Castle	400	*Memphis	9,000
Zone[x]	190	New Kensington	475	*Nashville	3,700
*Tulsa	2,600	Norristown	2,000	Oak Ridge	240
		North Penn	200		

State and City	Jewish Population	State and City	Jewish Population	State and City	Jewish Population
		*Rutland	350	*Seattle	13,000
		*St. Johnsbury	100	*Spokane	800
TEXAS				*Tacoma	750
*Amarillo	300				
*Austin	2,000	**VIRGINIA**			
Baytown	300	*Alexandria (incl.		**WEST VIRGINIA**	
*Beaumont	385	Falls Church,		*Bluefield-Princeton	190
Brownsville	160	Arlington County		*Charleston	1,150
*Corpus Christi	1,020	and urbanized		*Clarksburg	205
*Dallas	20,000	Fairfax County)f	30,000	Huntington	350
De Witt Countyaa	150	Arlington (incl. in		*Morgantown	200
*El Paso	4,500	Alexandria)		*Parkersburg	155
*Ft. Worth	2,800	*Danville	180	Weirton	150
*Galveston	645	Fredericksburg	140	*Wheeling	650
*Houston	27,000	Hampton (incl. in			
Kilgore	110	Newport News)			
*Laredo	420	*Harrisonburg	115	**WISCONSIN**	
*Longview	185	Hopewell	140	*Appleton	325
*Lubbock	350	*Lynchburg	275	*Beloit	120
*McAllen	295	Martinsville	135	*Eau Claire	120
*North Texas		*Newport News (incl.		*Fond du Lac	100
Zonebb	100	Hampton)	3,000	Green Bay	440
Odessa	150	*Norfolk (incl.		*Kenosha	250
Port Arthur	260	Virginia Beach)	11,000	*Madison	3,000
*San Antonio	6,500	*Petersburg	600	Manitowoc	175
Texarkana	100	*Portsmouth (incl.		*Milwaukee	23,900
*Tyler	500	Suffolk)	1,150	Oshkosh	120
*Waco	700	*Richmond	10,000	*Racine	405
*Wharton	170	*Roanoke	800	*Sheboygan	200
		Williamsburg	120	*Superior	165
UTAH		*Winchester	110	Waukesha	135
Ogden	100			*Wausau	155
*Salt Lake City	2,200	**WASHINGTON**			
		Bellingham	120	**WYOMING**	
VERMONT		Bremerton (incl. in		*Cheyenne	255
Bennington	120	Seattle)			
*Burlington	1,800				

*Denotes estimate submitted within two-year period.

aFlorence, Sheffield, Tuscumbia.

bTowns in Chicot, Desha, Drew counties.

cIncludes Alta Loma, Chino, Claremont, Cucamonga, La Verne, Montclair, Ontario, Pomona, San Dimas, Upland.

dCenterbrook, Chester, Clinton, Deep River, Essex, Killingworth, Old Lyme, Old Saybrook, Seabrook, Westbrook.

eAnsonia, Derby-Shelton, Oxford, Seymour.

fGreater Washington includes urbanized portions of Montgomery and Prince Georges counties, Maryland, Arlington County, Fairfax County (organized portion); Falls Church, Alexandria, Virginia.

gRock Island, Moline (Illinois); Davenport, Bettendorf (Iowa).

hTowns in Alexander, Bond, Clay, Clinton, Crawford, Edwards, Effingham, Fayette, Franklin, Gallatin, Hamilton, Hardin, Jackson, Jasper, Jefferson, Jersey, Johnson, Lawrence, Mascoupin, Madison, Marion, Massac, Montgomery, Perry, Pope, Pulaski, Randolph, Richland, St. Clair, Saline, Union, Wabash, Washington, Wayne, White, Williamson counties.

[i]Includes Crown Point, East Chicago, Gary, Hammond, Munster, Valparaiso, Whiting, and the Greater Calumet region.

[j]Towns in Caroline, Kent, Queen Annes, Talbot counties.

[k]Allendale, Elmwood Park, Fair Lawn, Franklin Lakes, Oakland, Midland Park, Rochelle Park, Saddle Brook, Wykoff also included in North Jersey estimate.

[l]Includes Camden and Burlington Counties.

[m]Includes contiguous areas in Hudson, Morris, Somerset, and Union counties.

[n]Includes Clayton, Paulsboro, Woodbury. Excludes Newfield; see Vincland.

[o]See footnote (m).

[p]Includes Guttenberg, Hudson Heights, North Bergen, North Hudson, Secaucus, Union City, Weehawken, West New York, Woodcliff.

[q]Includes Paterson, Wayne, Hawthorne in Passaic County, and nine towns in Bergen County. See footnote (k).

[r]Includes Perth Amboy, Metuchen, Edison Township (part), Woodbridge.

[s]Includes in Middlesex County, Cranbury, Dunellen, East Brunswick, Edison Township (part), Jamesburg, Matawan, Middlesex, Monmouth Junction, Old Bridge, Parlin, Piscataway, South River, Spottswood; in Somerset County, Kendall Park, Somerset; in Mercer County, Hightstown.

[t]Excludes Kendall Park and Somerset, which are included in Raritan Valley.

[u]Includes in Cumberland County, Norma, Rosenheim, Vineland; in Salem County, Elmer; in Gloucester County, Clayton, Newfield; in Cape May County, Woodbine.

[v]Greensboro, High Point, Winston-Salem.

[w]Burgaw, Clinton, Dunn, Elizabethtown, Fairmont, Jacksonville, Lumberton, Tabor City, Wallace, Warsaw; and Dillon, Loris, Marion, Mullins, S.C.

[x]Towns in Alfalfa, Beckham, Cadelo, Canadian, Cleveland, Custer, Jackson, Kingfisher, Kiowa, Lincoln, Logan, Oklahoma, Payne, Roger Mills, Tillman, Washita counties.

[y]Bensalem Township, Bristol, Langhorne, Levittown, New Hope, Newtown, Penndel, Warington, Yardley.

[z]Includes Kingsport and Bristol (including the portion of Bristol in Virginia).

[aa]Includes communities also in Colorado, Fayette, Gonzales, and La Vaca counties.

[bb]Denison, Gainesville, Greenville, Paris, Sherman, and Durant (Oklahoma).

Appendix C

Jewish Federations, Welfare Funds, Community Councils

Source: *The American Jewish Yearbook,* 1974–75

This directory is one of a series compiled annually by the Council of Jewish Federations and Welfare Funds. Virtually all of these community organizations are affiliated with the Council as their national association for sharing of common services, interchange of experience, and joint consultation and action.

These communities comprise at least 95 per cent of the Jewish population of the United States and about 90 per cent of the Jewish population of Canada. Listed for each community is the local central agency—federation, welfare fund, or community council—with its address and the names of the president and executive officer.

The names "federation," "welfare fund," and "Jewish community council" are not definitive and their structures and functions vary from city to city. What is called a federation in one city, for example, may be called a community council in another. In the main these central agencies have responsibility for some or all of the following functions: (a) raising of funds for local, national, and overseas services; (b) allocation and distribution of funds for these purposes; (c) coordination and central planning of local services, such as family welfare, child care, health, recreation, community relations within the Jewish community and with the general community, Jewish education, care of the aged and vocational guidance; to strengthen these services, eliminate duplication, and fill gaps; (d) in small and some intermediate cities, direct administration of local social services.

In the directory, the following symbols are used:

(*) Member agency of the Council of Jewish Federations and Welfare Funds.

(†) Receives support from Community Chest.

CONTINENTAL UNITED STATES

ALABAMA

Birmingham

*†Birmingham Jewish Federation (1935; reorg. 1971).

Jewish Community Council (1962).

Mobile

* Mobile Jewish Welfare Fund, Inc. (Inc. 1966).

Montgomery

* Jewish Federation of Montgomery, Inc. (1930).

Tri-Cities
Tri-Cities Jewish Federation Charities, Inc. (1933; Inc. 1956).

ARIZONA
Phoenix
* Greater Phoenix Jewish Federation (including surrounding communities) (1940).
Tucson
* † Jewish Community Council (1942).

ARKANSAS
Little Rock
* Jewish Welfare Agency, Inc. (1911).

CALIFORNIA
Kern County
* Jewish Welfare Fund & Council of Kern County, Calif. (1967).
Long Beach
* Jewish Community Federation (1937); (sponsors the United Jewish Welfare Fund).
Los Angeles
* † Jewish Federation-Council of Greater Los Angeles (1912; reorg. 1959) (sponsors United Jewish Welfare Fund).
Oakland
* † Jewish Welfare Federation of Alameda and Contra Costa Counties (1918).
Orange County
* Jewish Federation-Council of Orange County (1964; Inc. 1965); (sponsors United Jewish Welfare Fund).
Palm Springs
* Jewish Welfare Federation of Palm Springs-Desert Area (1971).
Sacramento
* † Jewish Federation of Sacramento (1948).
San Bernardino
* San Bernardino United Jewish Welfare Fund, Inc. (1963; Inc. 1957).
San Diego
* United Jewish Federation (including San Diego County) (1935).
San Francisco
* † Jewish Welfare Federation of San Francisco, Marin County and the Peninsula (1910; reorg. 1955).
San Jose
* † Jewish Federation of Greater San Jose (including Santa Clara County ex-cept Palo Alto and Los Altos) (1930; reorg. 1950).
Stockton
Stockton Jewish Welfare Fund (1948).
Ventura
Ventura County Jewish Council—Temple Beth Torah (1938).

COLORADO
Denver
* Allied Jewish Community Council (1936); (sponsors Allied Jewish Campaign).

CONNECTICUT
Bridgeport
* United Jewish Council of Greater Bridgeport, Inc. (1936); (sponsors United Jewish Campaign).
Danbury
* Jewish Federation of Danbury (1945).
Hartford
* Hartford Jewish Federation (1945).
Meriden
Meriden Jewish Welfare Fund, Inc. (1944).
New Britain
* New Britain Jewish Federation (1946).
New Haven
* New Haven Jewish Community Council, Inc. (1928); (sponsors Combined Jewish Appeal) (1969).
New London
* Jewish Community Council of Greater New London, Inc. (1950; Inc. 1970).
Norwalk
* Jewish Community Council of Norwalk (1946; reorg. 1964).
Stamford
* United Jewish Federation (Reincorp. 1973).
Waterbury
* † Jewish Federation of Waterbury, Inc. (1938).

DELAWARE
Wilmington
* † Jewish Federation of Delaware, Inc. (1935).

DISTRICT OF COLUMBIA
Washington
* United Jewish Appeal of Greater Washington, Inc. (1935).

FLORIDA
Clearwater
* Jewish Welfare Fund of Clearwater, Inc. (1963).
Hollywood
* † Jewish Welfare Federation of Greater Hollywood (1943).
Jacksonville
* Jacksonville Jewish Community Council (1935).
Miami
* † Greater Miami Jewish Federation, Inc. (1938).
North Broward
*Jewish Federation of North Broward, Inc. (1967).
Orlando
* Central Florida Jewish Community Council, Inc. (1949).
Palm Beach
* † Jewish Federation of Palm Beach County, Inc. (1938).
Pensacola
Pensacola Federated Jewish Charities (1942).
St. Petersburg
* Jewish Community Council, Inc. (1950).
Sarasota
* Sarasota Jewish Community Council, Inc. (1959).
Tampa
* Jewish Community Council of Tampa, Inc. (1941).

GEORGIA
Atlanta
* † Atlanta Jewish Welfare Federation, Inc. (1905; reorg. 1967).
Augusta
* Federation of Jewish Charities (1937).
Columbus
* Jewish Welfare Federation of Columbus, Inc. (1941).
Savannah
* Savannah Jewish Council (1943); (sponsors UJA-Federation Campaign).

IDAHO
Boise
Southern Idaho Jewish Welfare Fund (1947).

ILLINOIS
Champaign-Urbana
* Federated Jewish Charities (1929);

(member Central Illinois Jewish Federation).
Chicago
* † Jewish Federation of Metropolitan Chicago (1900).
* Jewish Welfare Fund of Metropolitan Chicago (1936).
Jewish United Fund of Metropolitan Chicago (1968); (Fund raising and planning arm of Federation and Welfare Fund).
Decatur
* Jewish Federation (member Central Illinois Jewish Federation) (1942).
Elgin
* Elgin Area Jewish Welfare Chest (1938).
Joliet
* Joliet Jewish Welfare Chest (1938).
Peoria
Central Illinois Jewish Federation (1969).
* Jewish Community Council & Welfare Fund of Peoria (member Central Illinois Jewish Federation) (1933; Inc. 1947).
Rock Island—Moline—Davenport—Bettendorf
*United Jewish Charities of Quad Cities (1938; comb. 1973).
Rockford
* † Rockford Jewish Community Council (1937).
Southern Illinois
* Jewish Federation of Southern Illinois †including all of Illinois south of Carlinville and Cape Girardeau, Missouri) (1941).
Springfield
* † Springfield Jewish Federation (member Central Illinois Jewish Federation) (1941).

INDIANA
Evansville
* Evansville Jewish Community Council, Inc. (1936; Inc. 1964).
Fort Wayne
* † Fort Wayne Jewish Federation (1921).
Indianapolis
* Jewish Welfare Federation, Inc. (1905).
Lafayette
* Federated Jewish Charities (1924).
Michigan City
* United Jewish Welfare Fund.

Muncie
Muncie Jewish Welfare Fund (1945).
Northwest Indiana
* † Northwest Indiana Jewish Welfare Federation (1941; reorg. 1959).
South Bend
* Jewish Community Council of St. Joseph County (1946).
Jewish Welfare Fund (1937).

IOWA
Cedar Rapids
Jewish Welfare Fund of Linn County (1941).
Davenport
*Davenport Jewish Welfare Fund (1921).
Des Moines
* Jewish Welfare Federation of Des Moines (1914).
Sioux City
* † Jewish Federation (1921).
Waterloo
* Waterloo Jewish Federation (1941).

KANSAS
Topeka
Topeka-Lawrence Jewish Federation (1939).
Wichita
* Mid-Kansas Jewish Welfare Federation, Inc. (1935).

KENTUCKY
Louisville
* Jewish Community Federation of Louisville, Inc. (1934); (sponsors of United Jewish Campaign).

LOUISIANA
Alexandria
* The Jewish Welfare Federation and Community Council of Central Louisiana (1938).
Baton Rouge
* Greater Baton Rouge Jewish Welfare Federation (1971).
Monroe
* United Jewish Charities of Northeast Louisiana (1938).
New Orleans
* † Jewish Welfare Federation of New Orleans (1913; reorg. 1962).
Shreveport
* Shreveport Jewish Federation (1941; Inc. 1967).

MAINE
Bangor
† Jewish Community Council (1949).
Lewiston—Auburn
* Jewish Federation (1947) (sponsors the United Jewish Appeal).
Portland
* Jewish Federation Community Council of Southern Maine (1942); (sponsors United Jewish Appeal).

MARYLAND
Annapolis
Annapolis ·Jewish Welfare Fund (1946).
Baltimore
* Associated Jewish Charities & Welfare Fund, Inc. (a merger of the Associated Jewish Charities & Jewish Welfare Fund) (1920; reorg. 1969).

MASSACHUSETTS
Boston
* † Combined Jewish Philanthropies of Greater Boston, Inc. (1895; reorg. 1961).
Brockton
* Combined Jewish Philanthropies of the Brockton Area, Inc. (1939).
Fall River
* Fall River Jewish Community Council (1949).
* Fall River United Jewish Appeal, Inc. (1949).
Fitchburg
Jewish Federation of Fitchburg (1939).
Framingham
* Greater Framingham Jewish Federation (1968; Inc. 1969).
Haverhill
Haverhill United Jewish Appeal, Inc.
Holyoke
* Combined Jewish Appeal of Holyoke (1939).
Lawrence
Jewish Community Council of Greater Lawrence (1906).
Leominster
* Leominster Jewish Community Council, Inc. (1939).
Marblehead
* Jewish Federation of the North Shore, Inc. (1938).
New Bedford
* Jewish Welfare Federation of Greater New Bedford, Inc. (1938; Inc. 1954).

Pittsfield
† Jewish Community Council (1940).
Springfield
* Springfield Jewish Federation, Inc. (1938); (sponsors United Jewish Welfare Fund).
Worcester
* Worcester Jewish Federation, Inc. (1947; inc. 1957); (sponsors Jewish Welfare Fund, 1939).

MICHIGAN
Bay City
Northeastern Michigan Jewish Welfare Federation (1940).
Detroit
* † Jewish Welfare Federation of Detroit (1899); (sponsors Allied Jewish Campaign).
Flint
* Jewish Community Council (1936).
Grand Rapids
* Jewish Community Fund of Grand Rapids (1930).
Kalamazoo
* Kalamazoo Jewish Federation (1949).
Lansing
* Jewish Welfare Federation of Lansing (1939).
Saginaw
* Saginaw Jewish Welfare Federation (1939).

MINNESOTA
Duluth
* Jewish Federation & Community Council (1937).
Minneapolis
* Minneapolis Federation for Jewish Service (1929; Inc. 1930).
St. Paul
* United Jewish Fund and Council (1935).

MISSISSIPPI
Jackson
Jewish Welfare Fund (1945).
Vicksburg
Jewish Welfare Federation (1936).

MISSOURI
Kansas City
* † Jewish Federation & Council of Greater Kansas City (1933).
St. Joseph
* United Jewish Fund of St. Joseph (1915).

St. Louis
* † Jewish Federation of St. Louis (incl. St. Louis County) (1901).

NEBRASKA
Lincoln
* † Lincoln Jewish Welfare Federation, Inc. (1931; Inc. 1961).
Omaha
* † Jewish Federation of Omaha (1903).

NEVADA
Las Vegas
* Las Vegas Combined Jewish Appeal (1973).

NEW HAMPSHIRE
Manchester
* † Jewish Community Center (1913).

NEW JERSEY
Atlantic City
* Federation of Jewish Agencies of Atlantic County (1924).
Bergen County
* † Jewish Federation of Community Services, Bergen County, N.J. (including most of Bergen County [1953]).
Camden County
* † Jewish Federation of Camden County (1922); (sponsors Allied Jewish Appeal).
Central New Jersey
* Jewish Federation of Central Jersey (sponsors United Jewish Campaign); (1940; expanded 1973 to include Westfield and Plainfield).
Englewood
* United Jewish Fund of Englewood and Surrounding Communities (1952).
Jersey City
* United Jewish Appeal (1939).
Metropolitan New Jersey
* † Jewish Community Federation (sponsors United Jewish Appeal) (1923).
Morris County
United Jewish Fund of Morris and Sussex Counties.
North Jersey
* Jewish Federation of North Jersey (formerly Jewish Community Council) (1933); (sponsors United Jewish Appeal).
Passaic
* Jewish Community Council of Passaic-Clifton and Vicinity (1933); (sponsors United Jewish Campaign).

Perth Amboy
* Jewish Community Council (1938); (sponsors United Jewish Appeal).
Raritan Valley
* Jewish Federation of Raritan Valley (1948).
Shore Area
* Jewish Federation of the Shore Area (1971).
Somerset County
* Jewish Federation of Somerset County (1960).
Trenton
* Jewish Federation of Trenton (1929).
Vineland
*Jewish Community Council of Greater Vineland, Inc. (1971); (sponsors Allied Jewish Appeal).

NEW MEXICO
Albuquerque
* Jewish Community Council of Albuquerque, Inc. (1938).

NEW YORK
Albany
* Albany Jewish Community Council, Inc. (1938); (sponsors Jewish Welfare Fund).
Broome County
* The Jewish Federation of Broome County (1937; Inc. 1958).
Buffalo
* † United Jewish Federation of Buffalo, Inc. (1903); (sponsors United Jewish Fund Campaign).
Elmira
* Elmira Jewish Welfare Fund, Inc. (1942).
Glens Falls
Glen Falls Jewish Welfare Fund (1939).
Hudson
Jewish Welfare Fund of Hudson, N.Y., Inc. (1947).
Kingston
* † Jewish Community Council, Inc. (1951).
Middletown
* United Jewish Appeal of Middletown, N.Y. (1939).
New York City
* † Federation of Jewish Philanthropies of New York (including Greater New York, Nassau, Queens, Suffolk, and Westchester counties) (1917).
* United Jewish Appeal of Greater New York, Inc. (New York City and Metropolitan areas including Nassau, Suffolk and Westchester counties) (1939).
Newburgh
* † United Jewish Charities, Inc. (1925).
Niagara Falls
* Jewish Federation of Niagara Falls, N.Y., Inc. (1935).
Port Chester
* Jewish Community Council (1941); (sponsors United Jewish Campaign).
Poughkeepsie
Jewish Welfare Fund-United Jewish Appeal (1941).
Rochester
* Jewish Community Federation of Rochester, N. Y., Inc. (1937).
* United Jewish Welfare Fund of Rochester, N. Y., Inc. (1937).
Schenectady
* Jewish Community Council (including surrounding communities) (1938); (sponsors Schenectady UJA and Federated Welfare Fund).
Syracuse
* Jewish Welfare Federation, Inc. (1918); (sponsors Jewish Welfare Fund [1933]).
Troy
*† Troy Jewish Community Council, Inc. (1936).
Utica
* Jewish Community Council of Utica, N.Y., Inc. (1933, Inc. 1950); (sponsors United Jewish Appeal of Utica).

NORTH CAROLINA
Asheville
Jewish Community Center.
Charlotte
* Charlotte Federation of Jewish Charities (1940).
Greensboro
* North Carolina Triad Jewish Federations (1940).

OHIO
Akron
* Akron Jewish Community Federation (1935).
Canton
* Jewish Community Federation of Canton (1935; reorg. 1955).
Cincinnati
*† Jewish Federation of Cincinnati and Vicinity (merger of the Associated Jew-

ish Agencies and Jewish Welfare Fund)
(1896; reorg. 1967).
Cleveland
*† Jewish Community Federation of
Cleveland (1903).
Columbus
* Columbus Jewish Federation (1925;
merged 1959).
Dayton
*† Jewish Community Council of Dayton (1943).
Lima
* Federated Jewish Charities of Lima
District (1935).
Steubenville
* Jewish Community Council (1938).
Toledo
* Jewish Welfare Federation of Toledo,
Inc. (1907; reorg. 1960).
Warren
* Jewish Federation (1938).
Youngstown
*† Jewish Federation of Youngstown,
Ohio, Inc. (1935).

OKLAHOMA
Ardmore
Jewish Federation (1934).
Oklahoma City
* Jewish Community Council (1941).
Tulsa
* Tulsa Jewish Community Council
(1938); (sponsors Tulsa United Jewish
Campaign).

OREGON
Portland
*† Jewish Welfare Federation of Portland (including state of Oregon and adjacent Washington communities) (1920;
reorg. 1956).

PENNSYLVANIA
Allentown
* Jewish Federation of Allentown, Inc.
(1938; inc. 1948).
Altoona
*† Federation of Jewish Philanthropies
(1920; reorg. 1940).
Butler
* Butler Jewish Welfare Fund (incl. Butler County) (1938).
Easton
*† Jewish Community Council of Easton, Pa. and Vicinity (1939); (sponsors
Allied Welfare Appeal).

Erie
*† Jewish Community Welfare Council
of Erie (1946).
Harrisburg
* United Jewish Community (1933).
Hazleton
* Jewish Community Council (1960).
Johnstown
* Jewish Community Council (1938).
Lancaster
* United Jewish Community Council of
Lancaster, Pa. (including Lancaster
County excepting Ephrata) (1928).
Levittown
* Jewish Community Council of Lower
Bucks County (1956, inc. 1957).
New Castle
* United Jewish Appeal of New Castle,
Pa.
Norristown
*† Jewish Community Center (serving
Central Montgomery County) (1936)
Philadelphia
* † Federation of Jewish Agencies of
Greater Philadelphia (1901; reorg. 1956).
Pittsburgh
* † United Jewish Federation of Pittsburgh (1912; reorg. 1955).
Pottsville
* United Jewish Charities (1935).
Reading
* Jewish Community Council (1935);
(sponsors United Jewish Campaign).
Scranton
* Scranton-Lackawanna Jewish Council
(including Lackawanna County) (1945).
Sharon
* Shenango Valley Jewish Federation
(1940).
Uniontown
* United Jewish Federation (1939).
Wilkes-Barre
* The Wyoming Valley Jewish Committee (1935); (sponsors United Jewish Appeal).
York
* United Jewish Appeal.

RHODE ISLAND
Providence
* Jewish Federation of Rhode Island
(1945).

SOUTH CAROLINA
Charleston
* Jewish Welfare Fund (1949).

Columbia
* Jewish Welfare Federation of Columbia (1960).

SOUTH DAKOTA
Sioux Falls
* Jewish Welfare Fund (1938).

TENNESSEE
Chattanooga
* Chattanooga Jewish Welfare Federation (1931).
Knoxville
* Jewish Welfare Fund, Inc. (1939).
Memphis
*† Jewish Service Agency (including Shelby County) (1864, inc. 1906).
* Jewish Welfare Fund (including Shelby County) (1934).
Nashville
*† Jewish Federation of Nashville & Middle Tennessee (1936).

TEXAS
Austin
* Jewish Community Council of Austin (1939; reorg. 1956).
Beaumont
* Beaumont Jewish Federation of Texas, Inc. (org. and inc. 1967).
Corpus Christi
*† Corpus Christi Jewish Community Council (1953).
Combined Jewish Appeal of Corpus Christi (1962).
Dallas
*† Jewish Welfare Federation (1911).
El Paso
*† Jewish Community Council of El Paso, Inc. (including surrounding communities) (1939).
Fort Worth
* Jewish Federation of Fort Worth (1936).
Galveston
* Galveston County Jewish Community Council & Welfare Association (1936).
Houston
* Jewish Community Council of Metropolitan Houston, Inc. (including neighboring communities) (1937); (sponsors United Jewish Campaign).
San Antonio
*† Jewish Social Service Federation (including Bexar County) (1922).

Tyler
Federation of Jewish Welfare Fund (1938).
Waco
Jewish Welfare Council of Waco (1949).

UTAH
Salt Lake City
* United Jewish Council and Salt Lake Jewish Welfare Fund (1936).

VIRGINIA
Hampton
Jewish Community Council (1944).
Newport News
* Jewish Federation of Newport News, Inc. (1942).
Norfolk
* United Jewish Federation, Inc. of Norfolk and Virginia Beach, Va. (1937).
Portsmouth
* Portsmouth Jewish Community Council (1919).
Richmond
* Jewish Community Council (1935).
Roanoke
* Jewish Community Council.

WASHINGTON
Seattle
* Jewish Federation & Council of Greater Seattle (including King County, Everett and Bremerton) (1926).
Spokane
Jewish Community Council of Spokane (including Spokane County) (1927); (sponsors United Jewish Fund) (1936).

WEST VIRGINIA
Charleston
* Federatied Jewish Charities of Charleston, Inc. (1937).
Huntington
* Federated Jewish Charities (1939).
Wheeling
* United Jewish Federation of Ohio Valley, Inc. (1933).

WISCONSIN
Appleton
* United Jewish Charities of Appleton.
Green Bay
* Green Bay Jewish Welfare Fund.

Kenosha
  * Kenosha Jewish Welfare Fund (1938).
Madison
  * Madison Jewish Welfare Council, Inc. (1940).
Milwaukee
  * Milwaukee Jewish Federation, Inc. (sponsoring Milwaukee Jewish Welfare Fund Campaign) (1938).
Racine
  * Racine Jewish Welfare Board (1946).
Sheboygan
  * Jewish Welfare Council of Sheboygan (1927).

Appendix D

Jewish Community Studies: A Selected Bibliography

Much of the empirical research on the American Jewish community has been conducted on the local plane, as befits a community so locally-centered. The principal components of that research have been local histories and demographic surveys—the former often filiopietistic in tone and emphasizing the piquant rather than the development of the mainstream of Jewish life locally, and the latter primarily designed as applied studies to aid Jewish institutions in their local planning. The occasional comprehensive academic study has begun to give some shape to the other materials.

The following list is selective, not exhaustive, and is designed to give every reader some sense of the literature presently available and the specialist some sense of the lacunae to be filled. The principal sources of historical articles are *American Jewish Archives,* published by the American Jewish Archives of the Hebrew Union College–Jewish Institute of Religion (cited below as *AJA*); *The American Jewish Historical Quarterly,* previously the *Publications of the American Jewish Historical Society,* published by the American Jewish Historical Society (cited below as *AJHQ*); and the various state and regional historical journals, listed below under their respective states. The *American Jewish Year Book* (cited below as *AJYB*), published since 1899, remains an invaluable resource. The *Encyclopaedia Judaica* has comprehensive articles on most American Jewish communities which, while varied in quality, often provide the best available introductions to the chronological and institutional development of those communities. A very useful, if more popular, community-by-community survey is available in Bernard Postal and Lionel Koppman, *A Jewish Tourist's Guide to the U.S.* (Philadelphia: Jewish Publication Society, 1954).

ALASKA

Bloom, Jessie S., "The Jews of Alaska," in *AJA* 15 (1963), pp. 97–116.

Glanz, Rudolph, *Jews in American Alaska: 1867–1880* (New York, 1953).

Postal, Bernard, "The Jews of Alaska," *Jewish Heritage* 11, no. 1 (Summer 1968): 48–53.

———, "Alaska," *AJYB* 61 (1960): 165–69.

CALIFORNIA

Western Jewish Historical Quarterly

Meyer, M. A., *Western Jewry* (Los Angeles, 1916).

Stern, Norton B., *California Jewish History: A Descriptive Bibliography* (Glendale, Cal. 1967).

Los Angeles

Glanz, Rudolph, *The Jews of Southern California from the Discovery of Gold Until 1880* (New York, 1960).

Massarik, Fred, "A Report on the Jewish Population of San Francisco, Marin County and the Peninsula," Jewish Welfare Federation of San Francisco, Marin County and the Peninsula, 1959.

Newmark, Harris, *Sixty Years in Southern California* (Boston and New York, 1930).

Soref, Irwin, "The Jewish Community of Los Angeles in Retrospect," *Reconstructionist* 18, no. 15, Los Angeles issue (1952/53): 8–12.

Vorspan, Max and Gartner, Lloyd C., *History of the Jews of Los Angeles* (Philadelphia, 1965).

COLORADO

Breck, A. D., *Centennial History of the Jews of Colorado, 1859–1959* (Denver, 1960).

Uchill, Ida Libert, *Pioneers, Peddlars and Tzadikim* (Denver, 1957).

DELAWARE

Weiss, Adina and Aron, Joseph, *The Jewish Community of Delaware* (Philadelphia, 1961).

DISTRICT OF COLUMBIA

Bigman, Stanley K., *The Jewish Population of Greater Washington in 1956* (Washington, D.C., 1957).

Greenberg, Evelyn Levov, "Isaac Pollock: Early Settlers in Washington, D.C.," in *AJHQ* 48 (1958/59): 1–18.

Jewish Historical Society of Greater Washington, *The Record* (1967–).

FLORIDA

Liebman, Seymour B., "The Cuban Jewish Community in South Florida," *AJYB* 70 (1969): 238–46.

GEORGIA

Heuhner, Leon, "The Jews of Georgia in Colonial Times," *Publication of the American Jewish Historical Society* 10 (1902): 65–95.

Lebeau, James, "Profile of a Southern Jewish Community: Waycross, Georgia," *AJHQ* 57, no. 4 (June 1966): 429–45.

Plaut, W. G., "Two Notes on the History of the Jews in America," *Hebrew Union College Annual* 14 (1939): 575–82.

Stern, M. H., "Some Additions and Corrections to Rosenswaike's 'An Estimate and Analysis of the Jewish Population in the United States in 1790,' " *AJHQ* 53 (1963/64): 285–92.

Sufker, Solomon, "The Jewish Organizational Elite of Atlanta, Georgia," and "The Role of Social Clubs in the Atlanta Jewish Community," in *The Jews: Social Patterns of an American Group,* Marshall Sklare, ed. (Glencoe, Ill., 1958), pp. 249–70.

HAWAII

Levinson, Bernard H., "Hawaii," *AJYB* 61 (1960): 170–71.

ILLINOIS

Champaign-Urbana

Mancelbaum, David G., "A Study of the Jews in Urbana," *Jewish Social Service Quarterly* 12 (1935): 230ff.

Chicago

American Jewish Congress, *A Guide to Jewish Chicago* (New York, 1972).

Bregstone, P. P., *Chicago and Its Jews* (Chicago, 1933).

Felsenthal, Bernard, "On the History of the Jews of Chicago," *Publication of the American Jewish Historical Society* 2 (1894).

Gutstein, Morris A., *A Priceless Heritage* (New York, 1953).

Guysenir, Maurice G., "The Jewish Vote

in Chicago," *Jewish Social Studies* 20, no. 1 (June 1968): 121–37.

Rawidowicz, Simon, ed., *The Chicago Pinkas* (Chicago, 1952).

The Sentinel's History of Chicago Jewry: 1911–1961 (Chicago, 1961).

Highland Park

Sklare, Marshall and Greenblum, Joseph, *Jewish Identity on the Suburban Frontier* (New York, 1967).

Park Forest

Gans, Herbert J., "The Origin and Growth of a Jewish Community in the Suburbs: A Study of the Jews of Park Forest," in *The Jews: Social Patterns of an American Group,* Marshall Sklare, ed. (Glencoe, Ill., 1958), pp. 205–48.

INDIANA

Muncie

Gordon, Whitney H., *A Community in Stress* (New York, 1964).

———, "Jews and Gentiles in Middletown," *AJA* 18 (1966): 41–70.

IOWA

Glazer, Simon, *Jews of Iowa* (Des Moines, 1904).

Des Moines

Rosenthal, Frank, *The Jews of Des Moines: The First Century* (Des Moines, 1957).

Wolfe, Jack Seymour, *A Century with Iowa Jewry* (Des Moines, 1941).

LOUISIANA

Kaplan, Benjamin, *Eternal Stranger* (New York, 1957), pp. 39–43.

Lemann, Bernard, *The Lemann Family of Louisiana* (Donaldsville, La., 1965).

Louisiana Church and Synagogue Archives, *Inventory of Jewish Congregations and Organizations* (New Orleans, 1941).

Nasatir, A. P. and Shpall, Leo, "The Texel Affair," *AJHQ,* 53, no. 1 (1963): 3–43.

Shpall, Leo, *Jews in Louisiana* (New Orleans, 1936).

New Orleans

Feibelman, Julian B., *Social and Economic Study of the New Orleans Jewish Community* (Philadelphia, 1941).

Korn, Bertram W., *The Early Jews of New Orleans* (Waltham, Mass., 1969).

Reissman, Leonard, "The New Orleans

Jewish Community," *Jewish Journal of Sociology* 4, no. 1 (June 1962): 110–23.

Shreveport

Hewitt, Louise Matthews, *Days of Building: History of the Jewish Community of Shreveport, La.* (Shreveport, 1965).

MARYLAND

Baltimore

Isaac M. Fein, *The Making of an American Jewish Community* (Philadelphia, 1971).

Litt, Edgar, "Status, Ethnicity and Patterns of Jewish Voting Behavior in Baltimore," *Jewish Social Studies* 22, no. 3 (July 1960).

MASSACHUSETTS

Boston

Axelrod, Morris; Fowler, Floyd J.; and Gunn, Arnold, *A Study of The Jewish Population of Greater Boston* (Boston, 1967).

Jewish Boston: A Guide for Students and Newcomers, 5730, 1969–70 (Waltham, Mass., 1969).

Wieder, Arnold A., *The Early Jewish Community of Boston's North End* (Waltham, Mass., 1962).

Newburyport

Warner, W. Lloyd and Srole, Leo, "Assimilation or Survival: A Crisis in the Jewish Community of Yankee City," reprinted in *The Jews: Social Patterns of An American Group,* Marshall Sklare, ed. (Glencoe, Ill., 1958), pp. 347–56.

Springfield

Goldstein, Sidney I., *A Population Survey of the Greater Springfield Jewish Community* (Springfield, Mass., 1968).

MICHIGAN

Katz, Irving I., *The Beth El Story, with a History of the Jews in Michigan before 1850* (Detroit, 1955).

United States, Work Projects Administration, Michigan Historical Records Survey Project, "Inventory of the Church and Synagogue Archives of Michigan: Jewish Bodies," mimeographed, 1940.

Detroit

Gurin, Arnold, *The Functions of a Sectarian Welfare Program in a Multi-Group Society: A Case Study of the Jewish Welfare Federation of Detroit* (Ann Arbor, 1965).

Mayer, Albert J., *The Detroit Jewish Community: Geographic Mobility, 1963–1965 and Fertility* (Detroit, 1966).

Meyer, Henry J., "The Economic Structure of the Jewish Community in Detroit," *Jewish Social Studies* 2, no. 2 (April 1940).

Michigan Jewish History

MINNESOTA

Gordon, Albert I., *Jews in Transition* (Minneapolis, 1949).

Plaut, W. Gunther, *The Jews in Minnesota: The First Seventy-Five Years* (New York, 1959).

———, *Mount Zion, 1856–1956: The First Hundred Years* (Saint Paul, 1956).

MISSOURI

Kansas City

Sacks, Howard T., "The Development of the Jewish Community of Kansas City, 1864–1908," *Missouri Historical Review* 60, no. 3 (April 1966): 350–60.

Saint Louis

Bowman, S., "Tribute to Isidore Busch" (1920).

Gorwitz, Kurt, "Jewish Mortality in St. Louis and St. Louis County, 1955–1957," *Jewish Social Studies* 24, no. 4 (1962): 248–54.

Makovsky, D. I., *The Philipsons, the First Jewish Settlers in St. Louis, 1807–1958* (Saint Louis, 1958).

NEW JERSEY

Camden

Weiss, Adina and Aron, Joseph, *The Jewish Community of Greater Camden, N.J.* (Philadelphia, 1961).

Westoff, Charles T., *Population and Social Characteristics of the Jewish Community of the Camden Area, 1964* (Cherry Hill, N.J., 1965).

Vineland area

Brandes, Joseph, *Immigrants to Freedom* (Philadelphia, 1971).

Goldstein, P. R., *Social Aspects of the Jewish Colonies of South Jersey* (New York, 1921).

NEW MEXICO

Fierman, Floyd S., "The Spiegelbergs: Pioneer Merchants and Bankers in the Southwest," *AJHQ* 56 (1967): 371–451.

Parrish, W. J., *Charles Ilfeld Company: A Study in the Rise and Decline in Mercantile Capitalism in New Mexico* (n. p., 1960).

———, *The German Jew and the Commercial Revolution in Territorial New Mexico, 1800–1900* (n. p., 1960).

NEW YORK

Buffalo

Adler, Selig, and Connolly, Thomas E., *From Ararat to Suburbia: The History of the Jewish Community of Buffalo* (Philadelphia, 1960).

New York City

Frieder, Steven E., "Intergroup Relations and Tensions in New York City," *AJYB* 71 (1970): 217–28.

Glanz, Rudolf, "The History of the Jewish Community in New York," *YIVO Annual of Jewish Social Science* 4 (1949): 34–50.

———, "German Jews in New York City in the Nineteenth Century," *YIVO Annual of Jewish Social Science* (1956/57): 9–38.

Glazer, Nathan and Moynihan, Daniel P., *Beyond the Melting Pot* (Cambridge, Mass., 1963).

Goren, Arthur A., *New York Jews and the Quest for Community: The Kehilla Experiment, 1908–1922* (New York, 1970).

Gorenstein, Arthur, "The Commissioner and the Community: The Beginnings of the New York City Kehilla (1908–1909)," *YIVO Annual of Jewish Social Science* 13 (1965): 187–212.

Grinstein, Hyman, *The Rise of the Jewish Community of New York, 1856–1860* (Philadelphia, 1945).

Hapgood, Hutchins, *The Spirit of the Ghetto: Studies of the Jewish Quarter of New York* (New York, 1965).

Kaganoff, Nathan M., "Organized Jewish Welfare Activity in New York City (1848–1860)," *AJHQ* 16, no. 1 (September 1966): 27–62.

Kranzler, George, *Williamsburg: A Jewish Community in Transition* (New York, 1961).

Landesman, Allen F., *Brownsville: The Birth, Development and Passing of a Jewish Community in New York* (New York, 1967).

McGill, Nettie Pauline, "Some Characteristics of Jewish Youth in New York City," *Jewish Social Science Quarterly* 14 (1937): 267ff.

Rischin, Moses, *The Promised City: New York's Jews, 1870–1914* (New York, 1964).

Yass, Irving, "The Jewish Community of New York," *AJYB* 5760 (1959/1960), pp. 44–54.

Rochester

Rosenberg, Stuart E., *The Jewish Community in Rochester, 1843–1925* (New York, 1954).

Syracuse

Rudolph, B. G., *From a Minyan to a Community: A History of the Jews of Syracuse* (Syracuse, N.Y., 1970).

OHIO

Cleveland

Janowsky, Oscar I., "The Cleveland Bureau of Jewish Education: A Case Study (1924–1953)," *AJHQ* 14, no. 3 (March 1956): 323–57.

Wisenfeld, Leo, *Jewish Life in Cleveland in the 1920's and 1930's* (Cleveland, 1965).

OREGON

Nodel, Julius J., *The Ties Between: A Century of Judaism on America's Last Frontier* (Portland, Ore., 1959).

Suwol, Samuel M., *Jewish History of Oregon* (Portland, Ore., 1958).

PENNSYLVANIA

Norristown

Weiss, Adina and Aron, Joseph, *The Jewish Community of Norristown, Pennsylvania* (Philadelphia, 1961).

Philadelphia

Baltzell, E. Digby, "The Development of a Jewish Upper Class in Philadelphia," reprinted in *The Jews: Social Patterns of an American Group,* Marshall Sklare, ed., (Glencoe, Ill., 1958), pp. 271–88.

Belsh, Jerry, *Jewish Philadelphia: A Guide for College Students* (Philadelphia, 1972).

Federation of Jewish Agencies of Greater Philadelphia, *A Study of the Jewish Population of Center City Philadelphia* (Philadelphia, 1966).

Klein, Esther M., *A Guidebook to Jewish Philadelphia* (Philadelphia, 1965).

Wolf, Edwin and Whiteman, Maxwell, *The History of the Jews in Philadelphia* (Philadelphia, 1975).

Pittsburgh

Pittsburgh Section National Council of Jewish Women, *By Myself I'm a Book: An Oral History of the Immigrant Jewish Experience in Pittsburgh* (Waltham, Mass., 1972).

RHODE ISLAND

Rhode Island Jewish Historical Notes

Newport

Chyet, Stanley F., *Lopez of Newport* (Detroit, 1970).

Gutstein, M. A., *The Story of the Jews of Newport* (New York, 1936).

Providence

Goldstein, Sidney and Goldscheider, Calvin, *Jewish Americans: Three Generations in a Jewish Community* (Englewood Cliffs, N.J., 1968).

SOUTH CAROLINA

Elzas, Barnett A., *Various Jewish Cemeteries of South Carolina* (Charleston, 1910).

———, *The Jews of South Carolina* (Charleston, 1903).

Golden, Harry L., *Jewish Roots in the Carolinas* (Charlotte, N.C., 1955).

Charleston

Reznikoff, Charles and Engelman, Uriah Z., *The Jews of Charleston* (Philadelphia, 1950).

Tobias, Thomas J., *The Hebrew Orphan Society of Charleston, S.C., Founded 1801: An Historical Sketch* (Charleston, 1957).

Columbia

Hennig, Helen, *The Tree of Life: Fifty Years of Congregational Life at the Tree of Life Synagogue, Columbia S.C.,* (Columbia, 1945).

UTAH

Watters, Leon J., *The Pioneer Jews of Utah* (New York, 1952).

VERMONT

Feuer, Louis S. and Perrine, Merwyn W., "Religion in a Northern Vermont Town: A Cross-Century Comparative Study," *Journal for the Scientific Study of Religion* 5, no. 3 (Fall 1966): 367–82.

WEST VIRGINIA

Shinedling, A. I., *West Virginia Jewry: Origins and History, 1850–1859,* 3 vols. (Philadelphia, 1963).

WISCONSIN
Milwaukee

Mayer, Albert J., *Milwaukee Jewish Population 1964–1965* (Milwaukee, 1967).

Polsky, Howard W., "A Study of Orthodoxy in Milwaukee: Social Characteristics, Beliefs and Observances," in *The Jews: Social Patterns of an American Group,* Marshall Sklare, ed. (Glencoe, Ill., 1958) pp. 325–36.

Swichkow, Louis J., "The Jewish Community of Milwaukee, Wisconsin, 1860–1870," *AJHQ* 47, no. 1 (September 1957): 34–59.

Swichkow, Louis J. and Gartner, Lloyd L., *The History of the Jews of Milwaukee* (Philadelphia, 1963).

Notes

CHAPTER 1

1. Marshall Sklare documents this in depth in *Jewish Identity on the Suburban Frontier: A Study of Group Survival in the Open Society,* volume 1 of the Lakeville Studies (New York: Basic Books, 1967).
2. For a discussion of the modern era as a three-century phenomenon, see Daniel J. Elazar, *Cities of the Prairie* (New York: Basic Books, 1970), introduction and appendix.
3. Jacob Katz discusses the initial impact of this change in *Tradition and Crisis* (New York: Free Press, 1961), while Milton Himmelfarb assesses the consequence of modernity for contemporary American Jews in *The Jews of Modernity* (New York: Basic Books, 1973).
4. There is no proper history of American Jewry. Two general works include Anita Libman Lebeson, *Pilgrim People* (New York: Harper, 1950) and Oscar Handlin, *Adventure in Freedom: Three Hundred Years of Jewish Life in America* (New York: McGraw-Hill, 1954), both prepared before the 1954 tercentenary of the original settlement. In the intervening years no new comprehensive history has been written, although Abraham Karp has edited the five-volume *The Jewish Experience in America* (New York: Ktav, 1969), a collection of articles originally published in the *American Jewish Historical Quarterly* that covers the range of American Jewish history.

    For a study of Jewish acquisition of full civil rights in the United States, see Jacob Rader Marcus, *Early American Jewry* (Philadelphia: Jewish Publication Society, 1953). Ben Halpern evaluates the meaning of this openness in *American Jewry: A Zionist Analysis* (New York: Herzl Press, 1956).
5. Charles Liebman analyzes this in *The Ambivalent American Jew* (Philadelphia: Jewish Publication Society, 1973). See also Daniel J. Elazar, "The Kenites of America," *Tradition* (fall 1967).
6. For a comprehensive and penetrating analysis of mythic versus nonmythic world views, see Henri Frankfort, *Before Philosophy* (Baltimore: Penguin Books, 1967). Yehezkel Kaufmann treats the problem from the perspective of Israel's monotheistic revolution in *The Religion of Israel* (Chicago: University of Chicago Press, 1960), a one-volume abridgment of his great eight-volume Hebrew work, *Toldot HaEmunah HaYisraelit,* selected and translated by Moshe Greenberg.

7. Alexis de Tocqueville, *Democracy in America,* (1835), introduction.
8. Halpern, *American Jewry.*
9. See, for example, Lloyd Warner, *American Life—Dream and Reality* (Chicago: University of Chicago, 1953).
10. Moshe Davis, "Centres of Jewry in the Western Hemisphere—A Comparative Approach," *Jewish Journal of Sociology,* 5, no. 1 (June 1963): 4–26.
11. The liberal tradition in America is analyzed by Louis Hartz, *The Liberal Tradition in America* (New York: Harcourt, Brace and Jovanovich, 1955). Liebman traces contradictory Jewish trends in *The Ambivalent American Jew.* See also Himmelfarb, *The Jews of Modernity.*
12. The classic statement is that of Horace M. Kallen in "Cultural Pluralism versus the Melting Pot," *The Nation* 100, no. 190–94 (February 18–25, 1915): 217–20.
13. See Will Herberg, *Protestant, Catholic, Jew* (Garden City, N.Y.: Anchor Books, 1960).
14. See Gerhard Lenski, *The Religious Factor* (Garden City, N.Y.: Doubleday, 1963).
15. See Sklare, *Jewish Identity.*
16. Patterns of Jewish religious observance in the postwar generation are profiled in the following sources, among others: Abraham G. Duker, "Religious Trends in American Jewish Life," *YIVO Annual of Jewish Social Science* 4, 1949. Sidney Goldstein and Calvin Goldscheider, *Jewish Americans: Three Generations in a Jewish Community,* (Englewood Cliffs, N.J.: Prentice-Hall, 1968); *National Jewish Population Study* (New York: Council of Jewish Federations and Welfare Funds, 1974). See also the various demographic studies of local communities cited in Appendix D.
17. Louis A. Berman has provided a comprehensive study of this problem set in the context of American Jewish life as a whole in *Jews and Intermarriage* (South Brunswick, N. J.: Thomas Yoseloff, 1968). See in particular his bibliography for other sources on American Jewish life. See also Milton M. Barron, "Jewish Intermarriage in Europe and America," *American Sociology Review* 11 (1946):7–13; Sidney Goldstein and Calvin Goldscheider, "Social and Demographic Aspects of Jewish Intermarriages," *Social Problems* 13, no. 4 (1966):386–99; Albert Isaac Gordon, *Intermarriage: Interfaith, Interracial, Interethnic* (Boston: Beacon Press, 1964); Ruby Jo Reeves Kennedy, "Single or Triple Melting Pot? Intermarriage Trends in New Haven, 1870–1940," *American Journal of Sociology* 49 (1944):331–39; David Kirshenbaum, *Mixed Marriage and the Jewish Future* (New York: Bloch, 1958); Erich Rosenthal, "Jewish Intermarriage in Indiana," *American Jewish Year Book,* 68 (1967):243–72; idem, "Studies of Jewish Intermarriage in the United States," *American Jewish Year Book,* 64 (1963):3–53; *National Jewish Population Study Preliminary Report on Intermarriage* (New York: Council of Jewish Federations and Welfare Funds, 1974); Reuben R. Resnick, "Some Sociological Aspects of Intermarriage of Jew and Non-Jew," *Social Forces* 12 (1933): 94–102; Charles E. Shulman, "Mixed Marriage, Conversion and Reality," *CCAR Journal* 11, no. 4 (1964): 27–32; Marshall Sklare, "Intermarriage and the Jewish Future," *Commentary* 37, no. 4 (1964):46–52; Werner J. Cahnman, ed., *Intermarriage and Jewish Life: A Symposium* (New York: Herzl Press and the Reconstructionist Press, 1963), pp. 143–57.
18. The present state of the American Jewish family is discussed in Jack Balswick, "Are American Jewish Families Closely Knit?," *Jewish Social Studies* 28, no. 3 (July 1966):159–67. The rising Jewish divorce rate is discussed in Idalynn Hertzberg, Rose Nemiroff, and Morton R. Startz, "Survey of Divorces (Jewish and Mixed) in Hamilton County, by the Jewish Family Service Bureau, Cincinnati, Ohio, February 1957 through November 1960," in *Jews and Divorce,* Jacob Fried, ed. (New York: Ktav, 1968); J. D. Rayner, "Divorce—Jewish Style" (con't), *Jewish Digest* 15 (May 1970):-29–32; Jacob Fried, ed., *Jews and Divorce* (New York: Ktav, 1968).

The drug problem is symptomatic of recent trends toward the disintegration of traditional Jewish values among American Jews. See, for example, B. R. Anderson, "Drugs and Jewish Youth," *Hadassah Magazine* 53, March 1972; J. Boeko, S. L. Brail, G. Greenblatt, D. Scher, "The Drug Problem—A Community Center Experience," *Journal of Jewish Community Service* 47 (winter 1970):123–26; W. J. Leffler, "Drugs and Jewish Youth" (con't), *Jewish Digest* 19 (April 1974):15–18.

19. Mordecai M. Kaplan, *Judaism as a Civilization* (New York: Reconstructionist Press, 1957). See also his *The Future of the American Jew* (New York: Macmillan and Company, 1948).

CHAPTER 2

1. This follows the general opinion of the historians. See, for example, Oscar Handlin, *Adventure in Freedom: Three Hundred Years of Jewish Life in America* (New York: McGraw-Hill, 1954) and Charles Liebman, *The Ambivalent American Jew* (Philadelphia: Jewish Publication Society, 1973). Before the Russian revolution European rabbinical authorities were of two opinions about emigration to the New World: some forbade it altogether and some, such as the Hafetz Haim, suggested that it would be permissible for Jews to come to America temporarily to become wealthy and then return to a "proper" Jewish environment. Eli Ginzberg brings personal evidence of this in his biography of his father, the late Louis Ginzberg, *Keeper of the Law: Louis Ginzberg* (Philadelphia: Jewish Publication Society, 1966).

2. On Jewish economic activities and occupations in the New World, see "Economic History—U.S. Jewry," *Encyclopaedia Judaica,* 16:321, and Nathan Reich, "The Economic Structure of Modern Jewry," in *The Jews: Their History, Culture, and Religion,* Louis Finkelstein, ed. (Philadelphia: Jewish Publication Society, 1949).

3. E. A. Speiser suggests this role for Abraham and the other patriarchs in *Genesis,* volume 1 of the Anchor Bible (Garden City, N. Y.: Doubleday and Company, 1964).

4. See Seymour Martin Lipset and Everett C. Ladd, Jr., "Jewish Academicians in the United States: Their Achievements, Culture, and Politics," *American Jewish Year Book,* 72 (1971):89–128.

5. See Sidney Goldstein, "American Jewry, 1970: A Demographic Profile," *American Jewish Year Book,* 72 (1971).

6. See Ray Allan Billington, *America's Frontier Heritage* (New York: Holt, Rinehart, and Winston, 1967) and Daniel J. Elazar, *The Metropolitan Frontier: A Perspective on Urbanization in America* (New York: General Learning Press, 1973).

7. Frederick Jackson Turner has provided us with the classic discussion of the impact of geography on American life in *The Significance of Sections in American History* (Gloucester, Mass.: Peter Smith, 1950). For an application of the Turner thesis to American Jewish life, see Daniel J. Elazar, "The Impact of Sectionalism on American Jewry," paper presented at the meeting of the American Jewish Historical Society, Philadelphia, 1962.

8. This section is based upon my unpublished paper cited above. A full set of references is provided in that paper. See also Appendix D of this volume.

9. Ibid.

10. For recent examinations of small-town Jewry, see *Jewish Heritage* 15, no. 2 (Winter 1974) and *Sh'ma* 5, no. 87 (February 7, 1975).

11. In addition to the author's previously-cited paper, the bulk of the data for this section is taken from John Higham, "Social Discrimination against Jews in America, 1830–1930," *Publication of the American Jewish Historical Society* 47 (September 1957):1; John P. Roche, *The Quest for the Dream* (New York: Macmillan, 1963); Morris U. Schappes, ed., *A Documentary History of the Jews in the United States* (New York: Schocken, 1971); and Charles H. Stember et al., *Jews in the Mind of America* (New York: Basic Books, 1966).

CHAPTER 3

1. Yehoshua Arieli examines this individualism and its sociopolitical ramifications with 'the eyes of an Israeli with a European Jewish background in *Individualism and Nationalism in American Ideology* (Cambridge, Mass.: Harvard University Press, 1967).

2. This estimate is based on Charles Liebman's calculation of the number of actually Orthodox Jews in the United States in 1955, in "Orthodoxy in American Jewish Life," *American Jewish Year Book,* 66 (1965). Liebman suggests that there are 200,000 Sabbath-observers in the Orthodox manner in the United States, out of 700,000 members of Orthodox synagogues and another 300,000 unaffiliated Orthodox. This writer's projection of the number of non-Orthodox Jews who would fit into the same category is in part an extension of Liebman's calculations of the Jewish involvement of members of selected Conservative congregations, evidence regarding the behavior of graduates of selected non-Orthodox day schools and products of Hebrew-speaking camps, and assessments of the personal involvement of members of the Jewish civil scene. The 5 percent also corresponds to the figure of 5.1 percent of Jewish academics who define themselves as "deeply religious" in Seymour M. Lipset and Everett C. Ladd, Jr., "Jewish Academicians in the United States; Their Achievements, Culture, and Politics," *American Jewish Year Book* 72 (1971):110, a category that includes Orthodox and observant Conservative Jews, who are considered the key groups in the inner circle.

3. Polls on church attendance in the United States show that some 15 percent of American Jews attend services at least once a week. Considering that the overwhelming majority of those in the innermost circle attend at least weekly and that perhaps 2 percent have attended during the week in which they were polled (the question is "Have you attended religious services during the past week?") because of some special occasion (e.g., a bar mitzvah), that leaves some 10 percent, virtually all of whom fall into the second category, to which can be added the relatively small number of nonsynagogue-goers (for secularist or other reasons) who fall into this category nonetheless. For annual data on synagogue attendance, see *The Gallup Opinion Index* (Princeton, N.J.: American Institute of Public Opinion, 1965).

4. This category can be calculated by subtracting the 15 to 20 percent in the first two categories from the 47 to 50 percent of American Jews who, the studies estimate, belong to synagogues, plus the small additional percentage that belong to other Jewish organizations but not synagogues. See Lipset and Ladd, "Jewish Academicians," pp. 89–128, which indicates that 27.37 percent of all Jewish academics consider themselves moderately religious; this probably embraces both the second and third circles. Since perhaps a quarter of the 50.3 percent which they classify as largely indifferent to religion are members of Jewish organizations or congregations "for the children" or some similar reason, and academics are somewhat more estranged than other Jews, their figures can be interpreted as confirming this estimate.

5. The calculation is based upon the approximately 20 percent beyond the first three circles who have been synagogue members at one time or another, plus those whose only contact with the Jewish community seems to be contributions to UJA.

6. This tends to be a category dominated by intellectuals. Lipset and Ladd indicate that 10.3 percent of the Jewish academics are opposed to religion, but as many as half may maintain an *ethnic* identification with the Jewish people.

7. Calculations based on the intermarriage data tend to bear out these estimates. In particular, the *National Jewish Population Study Preliminary Report on Intermarriage* (New York: Council of Jewish Federations and Welfare Funds, 1974).

8. See "Federalism" in *International Encyclopedia of the Social Sciences* (New York: Collier-Macmillan, 1970) and Delbert R. Hillers, *Covenant: The History of a Biblical Idea* (Baltimore: Johns Hopkins Press, 1969).

9. See, for example, Jose Faur, "Understanding the Covenant," *Tradition* 9, no. 33–55

(April 1968), and Daniel J. Elazar, "Kinship and Consent in the Jewish Community," *Tradition* 14, no. 4 (fall 1974).

10. The primary source in English that provides an overview of the history of Jewish communal organization is Salo W. Baron, *The Jewish Community, Its History and Structure to the American Revolution* (Philadelphia: Jewish Publication Society, 1942).

11. See "Community" in *Encyclopaedia Judaica,* 5:807–53.

12. See Charles S. Liebman, "Dimensions of Authority in Contemporary Jewish Life," *Jewish Journal of Sociology,* June 1970, and Arthur Hertzberg, "The Changing American Rabbinate," *Midstream* 12, no. 1 (January 1966):16–29.

CHAPTER 4

1. For a good introduction to the American synagogue, its antecedents, role, and problems, see the two-volume anthology edited by Jacob Neusner, *Understanding American Judaism* (New York: Ktav, 1975) particularly the articles by Wolfe Kelman, Marshall Sklare, and Abraham J. Feldman. Marshall Sklare is the principal student of the American synagogue. His conclusions are principally available in *The Jews* (New York: Free Press, 1958); *Conservative Judaism: An American Religious Movement* (Glencoe, Ill.: Free Press, 1955); and *Jewish Identity on the Suburban Frontier: A Study of Group Survival in the Open Society,* volume 1 of the Lakeville Studies (New York: Basic Books, 1967).

2. The Reform movement in America has been well studied, relatively speaking. Among the standard works on the subject are Sefton D. Temkin, "A Century of Reform Judaism in America," *American Jewish Year Book,* 74 (1973):3–75; W. Gunther Plaut, Theodore I. Lenn et al., *Rabbi and Synagogue in Reform* Judaism (New York: Central Conference of American Rabbis, 1972); and Leonard J. Fein et al., *Reform Is a Verb* (New York: Union of American Hebrew Congregations, 1972). See also the selections of Neusner, ed., *Understanding American Judaism,* particularly part 5.

3. The Central European Jews are commonly referred to as "Germans" because they tended to speak German regardless of what part of Europe they came from. Only a portion actually came from the confines of the German Confederation, but almost all came from German-speaking homes or aspired to assimilate into German culture, as did most of the cultured elements of Central Europe during the nineteenth century.

4. See *American Jewish Archives,* special issue on the one hundredth anniversary of the founding of the Union of American Hebrew Congregations.

5. See *National Jewish Population Study* (New York: Council of Jewish Federations and Welfare Funds, 1974) for data on synagogue membership.

6. For a history of the Conservative movement, see Moshe Davis, *The Emergence of Conservative Judaism* (Philadelphia: Jewish Publication Society, 1963). See also Sklare, *Conservative Judaism.*

7. See Edwin Wolf, 2nd, and Maxwell Whitemen, *The History of the Jews of Philadelphia: From Colonial Times to the Age of Jackson* (Philadelphia: Jewish Publication Society, 1975). Leeser is deserving of full-length biographical treatment, a project that could also throw considerable light on the dynamics of Jewish community life in the nineteenth-century United States.

8. Useful materials on the Conservative movement include Davis, *The Emergence of Conservative Judaism;* Simon Greenberg, *The Conservative Movement in Judaism: An Introduction* (New York: National Academy for Adult Jewish Studies, United Synagogue, 1955); Abraham J. Karp, *A History of the United Synagogue of America, 1913–1963* (New York: United Synagogue, 1964); Jacob Neusner, "Conservative Judaism in a Divided Community," *Conservative Judaism* (summer 1966); Sklare, *Conservative Judaism;* and Mordecai Wauman, ed., *Tradition and Change: The Development of Conservative Judaism* (New York: Burning Bush Press, 1958). See also Neusner, ed., *Understanding American Judaism,* particularly part 7.

9. The principal study of Reconstructionism is Charles S. Liebman, "Reconstructionism in American Life," *American Jewish Year Book,* 71 (1970):3–99. See also Neusner, ed., *Understanding American Judaism.*

10. The definitive work on American Orthodoxy has been done by Charles S. Liebman. See his "Orthodoxy in American Jewish Life," *American Jewish Year Book,* 66 (1965) and "Left and Right in American Orthodoxy," *Tradition* 15, no. 1 (winter 1966). See also Jerry Hochbaum, "The Changing Socio-Religious Profile of American Orthodoxy," *Tradition* 9, no. 1–2 (spring-summer 1967):138–46; Nancy J. Schmidt, "An Orthodox Jewish Community in the United States: A Minority within a Minority," *Jewish Journal of Sociology* 7, no. 2 (December 1965):176–206); and Neusner, ed., *Understanding American Judaism,* particularly part 6.

11. See Solomon Poll, *The Hassidic Community of Williamsburg* (New York: Free Press of Glencoe, 1962).

12. See Israel Rubin, *Satmar: An Island in the City* (Chicago: Quadrangle Books, 1972).

13. Neusner brings together a number of the most important articles on the American rabbi and rabbinate in *Understanding American Judaism,* including the important work by Charles Liebman. See in particular parts 3 and 4. See also Sklare, *The Jews.*

14. This section is based upon my "The Impact of Sectionalism on American Jewry," paper presented at the meeting of the American Jewish Historical Society, Philadelphia, 1962, as updated.

CHAPTER 5

1. The sources of the discussion in this chapter include the community studies listed in Appendix D but rely most heavily on the systematic research done by the author and others at the Center for Jewish Community Studies over the past two decades. The author has additionally benefited from extensive participation in the activities of the American Jewish community, locally and countrywide, during a similar period of time.

2. For an elaboration of the principle of noncentralization as it applies to the United States, see Daniel J. Elazar, *American Federalism: A View from the States* (New York: Thomas Y. Crowell, 1972).

3. Ernest Stock describes this phenomenon in "The Absence of Hierarchy: Notes on the Organization of the American Jewish Community," *Jewish Journal of Sociology 21,* no. 2 (December 1970).

4. The Center for Jewish Community Studies has conducted such studies in several smaller communities, including Camden County, New Jersey, Delaware (Wilmington), and Norristown, Pennsylvania. In the course of its work, its researchers have also systematically explored the decision-making process in Atlanta, Boston, Cleveland, Columbus, Denver, Detroit, Los Angeles, Minneapolis, Oakland, Philadelphia, Phoenix, and San Francisco.

5. See *National Jewish Population Study* (New York: Council of Jewish Federations and Welfare Funds, 1974) for data on synagogue membership by community size.

6. Sidney Goldstein, "American Jewry, 1970: A Demographic Profile," *American Jewish Year Book,* 72 (1971):34–38.

7. See, for example, Salo W. Baron, *The Jewish Community, Its History and Structure to the American Revolution* (Philadelphia: Jewish Publication Society, 1942).

8. The Jewish population in the territory of the Vaad Arba Artzot (Council of the Four Lands) of greater Poland numbered 92,000 households at its maximum. See Hayim Hillel Ben Sasson, "Council of the Four Lands," *Encyclopaedia Judaica,* 5:993.

9. See Moshe Davis, *The Emergence of Conservative Judaism* (Philadelphia: Jewish Publication Society, 1963), pp. 101ff., 197–99, 378–85, and passim.

10. See Abraham Karp, "New York Chooses a Chief Rabbi," *Publication of the American Jewish Historical Society* 44, no. 3 (March 1955):129–98.

11. Arthur A. Goren has written the definitive work on the New York Kehillah, *New York*

Jews' Quest of Community (New York: Columbia University Press, 1970).
12. For a history of the federation movement from its inception to 1960 written by an insider see Harry L. Lurie, *A Heritage Affirmed* (Philadelphia: Jewish Publication Society, 1961). Lurie was the long-time executive director of the CJF through its formative years.

CHAPTER 6

1. In almost every locality where a comprehensive organization exists, it is known as the Jewish Federation—informally if not formally. The precise title differs from situation to situation. For example, in Philadelphia it is known as the Federation of Jewish Agencies, in Atlanta as the Jewish Welfare Federation and with increasing frequency simply the Jewish Federation. Of the 229 communities with comprehensive-representative organizations listed in the 1974–75 *American Jewish Year Book,* 125 use the term "federation" in their names and 54 use "community council" (or "community center" in a few cases). Twenty-eight more use some version of "welfare fund" or "agency" and 21, the term "united." Some combine two or all three in their names.
2. The "cosmopolitan"-"local" dichotomy occupies an important place in sociological thought. Its roots lie in the work of Ferdinand Toennies, *Community and Society: Gemeindschaft und Gesellschaft* (East Lansing: Michigan State University Press, 1957), and it has received its finest American expression in Robert Merton, *Social Thinking and Social Structure* (Glencoe, Ill.: The Free Press, 1957). See also Carle F. Zimmerman, *The Changing Community* (New York: Harper and Brothers, 1938) and Alvin W. Gouldner, "Cosmopolitans and Locals: Towards an Analysis of Latent Social Rules," *Administrative Science Quarterly,* 1958. I have applied it in "Cosmopolitans and Locals in Contemporary Community Politics" (with Douglas St. Angelo), in *Proceedings of the Minnesota Academy of Science* (May 1974).
3. For a discussion of the implications of this combination, see Daniel J. Elazar, *A Case Study of Failure in Attempted Metropolitan Integration: Nashville and Davidson County, Tennessee* (Chicago: National Opinion Research Center, 1961).
4. The organizations comprising the American Zionist Federation claimed to have registered some 700,000 *shekalim* (roughly equivalent to memberships) in a major drive prior to the elections to the 1972 Zionist Congress and, on that basis, can claim to be the largest mass-based organization in the country; but in fact each of its constituent bodies registered its own members to make up that total, so that half that number consisted of Hadassah members; at least 100,000 involved duplications, and the remaining 250,000 were divided among the other adult bodies plus a number of youth groups. All told, only some 113,000 actually voted in the elections, although in the context of American Jewish life that must be considered a substantial figure.
5. Lloyd W. Gartner, ed., *Jewish Education in the United States,* (New York: Teachers College Press, 1970). Zvi Adar, *Jewish Education in Israel and in the United States* (Tel Aviv: KNIE, 1969) (in Hebrew); Daniel J. Elazar, "Jewish Education and American Jewry: What the Community Studies Tell Us," *Pedagogic Reporter,* March 1970. Oscar I. Janowsky, "The Cleveland Bureau of Jewish Education: A Case Study (1924–1953)," *American Jewish Historical Quarterly* 54, no. 3 (March 1965):323–57; "The Jewish Community School" (symposium), *Jewish Education* 35, no. 2 (Winter 1965):67–95; Louis J. Kaplan, "Jewish Education and the Community," *Journal of Jewish Communal Service* 42, no. 4 (summer 1966):303–12; Judah Pilch, ed., *A History of Jewish Education in America* (New York: American Association for Jewish Education, 1969); Alvin Schiff, *The Jewish Day School Movement in America* (New York: Jewish Education Committee Press, 1966); Oscar I. Janowsky, ed., *The Education of American Jewish Teachers* (Boston: Beacon Press, 1967).
6. Research efforts of the CJF, certain local federations, the Center for Jewish Community Studies, and even the national offices of the countrywide synagogue federations have

not succeeded in developing more than partial, incomplete data that can be used, at best, to make rough estimates of the expense involved.

7. Arnold J. Band, "Jewish Studies in American Liberal Arts Colleges and Universities," *American Jewish Year Book,* 67 (1966):3–30.

8. For histories of the American Jewish Committee and the Anti-Defamation League, see Naomi W. Cohen, *Not Free to Desist: The American Jewish Committee, 1906–1966* (Philadelphia: Jewish Publication Society, 1972); John P. Roche, *The Quest for the Dream* (New York: Macmillan, 1963); and Nathan C. Belth, ed., *Not the Work of a Day* (New York: Anti-Defamation League of B'nai B'rith, 1965).

9. See Harry L. Lurie, *A Heritage Affirmed* (Philadelphia: Jewish Publication Society, 1961).

10. For material on the social service agencies, see Graenum Berger, *The Jewish Community Center: A Fourth Force in American Jewish Life* (New York: Jewish Education Committee Press, 1966).

11. For a history of the JDC, see Herbert Agar, *The Saving Remnant: An Account of Jewish Survival* (New York: Viking Press, 1960) and Yehuda Bauer, *My Brother's Keeper: A History of the American Jewish Joint Distribution Committee, 1929–1939* (Philadelphia: Jewish Publication Society, 1974).

CHAPTER 8

1. For a history of Jewish education, see Lloyd W. Gartner, ed., *Jewish Education in the United States* (New York: Teachers College Press, 1970). See also Daniel J. Elazar, "Jewish Education and American Jewry: What the Community Studies Tell Us," *Pedagogic Reporter,* March 1970.

2. Marshall Sklare, *Jewish Identity on the Suburban Frontier: A Study of Group Survival in the Open Society,* volume 1 of the Lakeville Studies (New York: Basic Books, 1967); Arthur Hertzberg, "The Changing American Rabbinate," *Midstream* 12, no. 1 (January 1966):16–29; Charles Liebman, *The Ambivalent American Jew* (Philadelphia: Jewish Publication Society, 1973).

3. Charles Liebman, "The Training of American Rabbis," *American Jewish Year Book,* 69 (1968).

4. Hertzberg, "The Changing American Rabbinate."

5. See S.P. Goldberg's "Jewish Communal Services: Programs and Finances," which appeared in the annual summary of the *American Jewish Year Book* between 1956 and 1972. Other sources of data include Philip Bernstein's unpublished report on local community financing, prepared for the American Jewish Committee Task Force on the Future of the Jewish Community in America. Ezekiel Pearlman, at author's request, prepared a similar set of estimates for the Jewish community of Philadelphia.

6. See Charles S. Liebman, *American Jews and Israel* (Philadelphia: Center for Jewish Community Studies, Research Paper IC3) and Leonard J. Fein et al., *Reform Is a Verb,* (New York: Union of American Hebrew Congregations, 1972).

7. See Daniel J. Elazar, "Involving Intellectuals," *Jewish Heritage,* (fall 1967); reprinted in *Jewish Affairs,* February 1968.

8. See Jacob Neusner, *Contemporary Judaic Fellowship in Theory and in Practice* (New York: Ktav Publishing House, 1973).

9. This is consistent with the pattern in other masculine-dominated societies—for example, in the Afro-Asian world today, where the mass of women are rather strictly excluded but women born into the leading families can often achieve greater heights than women in open societies.

10. The decline of the *Congress Monthly* from weekly to biweekly to its present monthly status is a sad commentary on the current state of Jewish journalism.

11. See in particular Liebman, *The Ambivalent American Jew.*

12. Milton Himmelfarb *The Jews of Modernity* (New York: Basic Books, 1973) and Murray Friedman, *Overcoming Middle Class Rage,* (Philadelphia: Westminster Press, 1971).

CHAPTER 9

1. See Naomi Cohen, *Not Free to Desist: The American Jewish Committee, 1906–1966* (Philadelphia: Jewish Publication Society, 1972) and John P. Roche, *The Quest for the Dream* (New York: Macmillan, 1963). See also the annual articles on intergroup relations in the *American Jewish Year Book*.

2. The best source of current material on social services and welfare is to be found in the papers prepared annually for the General Assembly of the CJF.

3. This section is based on the sources cited in chapter 8, note 5.

4. See, for example, Salo W. Baron, *The Jewish Community, Its History and Structure to the American Revolution* (Philadelphia: Jewish Publication Society, 1942).

5. See, for example, Martin Landau, "Federalism, Redundancy, and System Reliability," in *Publius* 3, no. 2 (fall 1973).

6. This typology is adopted from Daniel J. Elazar, "The Reconstitution of the Jewish Community in the Postwar Period," *Jewish Journal of Sociology,* December 1969. I have also applied it to American cities in my *Cities of the Prairie* (New York: Basic Books, 1970).

7. I elaborate on this theme in "Kinship and Consent in the Jewish Community," *Tradition* 14, no. 4 (fall 1974).

Index